HERMANN BECKH (1875-1937) studied Law and later Sanskrit, becoming Professor of Oriental Studies at the University of Berlin. A master of ancient and modern languages, he wrote extensively on religious and philosophical subjects, including Buddhism, Indology, Christianity, Alchemy and Music. In 1911, he heard a lecture by Rudolf Steiner and was inspired to join the Anthroposophical Society, where he soon became a valued co-worker. In 1922, he helped found The Christian Community, a movement for religious renewal. His many books are gradually being translated from the original German and published in English.

Hermann Beckh

MARK'S GOSPEL
THE COSMIC RHYTHM

Hermann Beckh

With Forewords by Rudolf Frieling
and Neil Franklin

Translated by Alan and Maren Stott

TEMPLE LODGE

Temple Lodge Publishing Ltd.
Hillside House, The Square
Forest Row, RH18 5ES

www.templelodge.com

This new edition of the complete text, with corrections and an additional Foreword by Neil Franklin, is published by Temple Lodge in 2021

First published in English by Anastasi Ltd., Herefordshire, in 2015

Originally published in German under the title *Der kosmische Rhythmus im Markus-Evangelium* by Rudolf Geering Verlag, Basel, in 1928; 2nd edition, with Foreword by Rudolf Frieling, published by Verlag Freies Geistesleben, Stuttgart, in 1960

A CIP catalogue record for this book is available from the British Library

ISBN 978 1 912230 73 0

Cover by Morgan Creative
Typeset by Symbiosys Technologies, Visakhapatnam, India
Printed and bound by 4Edge Ltd., Essex

Isis-Sophia
Des Gottes Weisheit
Sie hat Lucifer getötet
Und auf der Weltenkräfte Schwingen
In Raumesweiten fortgetragen.

Christus-Wollen
In Menschen wirkend
Es wird Lucifer entreißen
Und auf des Geisteswissen Booten
In Menschenseelen auferwecken
Isis-Sophia
Des Gottes Weisheit.

Rudolf Steiner

[concluding words summarizing the lecture 'Search for the New Isis, the Divine Sophia: The quest for the Isis-Sophia', Dornach, 24 Dec. 1920. GA 202]

Es leuchtet gleich Sternen
Am Himmel des ewigen Seins
Die gottgesandten Geister.

Gelingen möge es allen Menschenseelen
Im Reich des Erdenwesens
Zu schauen ihrer Flammen Licht.

Rudolf Steiner

Isis-Sophia
Wisdom of God:
she has been slain by Lucifer,
and on the rhythm of cosmic forces
he has carried her into the widths of space.
The will of Christ
at work in human beings
shall wrestle from Lucifer
and on the boats of spirit-knowledge
awaken in human souls
Isis-Sophia
Wisdom of God.

Rudolf Steiner

Like stars there shine
in the sky of eternal being
Spirits sent by God.

May all human souls
in the kingdom of earthly existence
be able to behold their flaming light.

Rudolf Steiner

Contents

Table of Signs of the Zodiac

♈ The RAM (Aries) 

♉ The BULL (Taurus) 

♊ The TWINS (Gemini) 

♋ The CRAB (Cancer) 

♌ The LION (Leo) 

♍ The VIRGIN (Virgo) 

♎ The SCALES (Libra) 

♏ The SCORPION/EAGLE (Scorpio)  

♐ The ARCHER (Sagittarius) 

♑ The GOAT (Capricorn) 

♒ The WATERMAN (Aquarius) 

♓ The FISHES (Pisces) 

Foreword to the English-language edition by the General Editor of the *Collected Works* of *Rev. Prof. Hermann Beckh*

It is not unusual to find a book considered to be 'weighty'. This might mean long sentences, abstruse references, unexpected probings of the status quo, serious topics ... The opposite is probably 'glib': author and reader are hand in glove, we read what we like to read, we are comforted in that the author pleasantly confirms our shared world-view. The glib might be useful, even justifiable to those involved either in essential community-building or in selling to a ready market. But, on the other hand, what is really meant by 'weighty'? Is this a positive or negative adjective? Does it simply mean a depth of scholarship or difficult thinking? Recondite references?

'Weighty' by itself is already a metaphor, but one that can be expanded into an analogy. My intuition suggests the adjective is primarily related to earthly depths. In some locations, geology reveals that the ground is a superficial deposit of the last millennia. Elsewhere we are walking upon perhaps tens or hundreds of millions of years of consolidation and metamorphosis unappreciated by the casual observer. The idea of *depth* when applied to gospel studies has at least two applications. On the one hand it is quite insufficient to restrict an enquiry to the early years of Christianity, even when O.T. traditions are duly considered. Equally fragile is the notion that everyday waking consciousness is sufficient to take in what God has spoken to humanity. A truly serious book on Mark's Gospel will attempt to plummet not only the sacred texts of the last five or six thousand years but also the profounder levels of consciousness described, for example, by Gautama Buddha and Rudolf Steiner. How deeply can one go?

In 1928 there was only one person in Europe who, apart from fluency in Hebrew, Greek and Latin from his schooldays onwards, had a professorial knowledge of Tibetan, Sanskrit, Pali and Avestan which could be applied to Mark, facilitated by advanced meditational realizations. Today we are extremely fortunate—to say the least—that when The Christian Community establishment declined the publication of the commissioned *Mark's Gospel: The Cosmic Rhythm*, Rudolf Geering in Basel accepted the task and brought out the weighty study and its sequel (1930) that was not only the pinnacle of anthroposophical gospel studies at the time but also texts that would challenge and inspire readers after a century had passed and the issues intensified: can technology *save* us?

One did not need to be much of a theologian in the 1920s, whether in London, Paris, Berlin or Stuttgart, to realize that the Gospel of Mark was being assaulted—'critically examined'—from many quarters. One of the first things to go was its integrity: the gospel became a scissors-and-paste assemblage of distantly remembered oral stories or of readings for preaching (pericopes). Instead of an organic or artistic whole there was an arrangement, similar to the popular musical arrangements of earlier melodies that were increasingly welcome in the ballroom. If the whole was made up of constituent parts, then a great number had to be rejected on the grounds of being more than natural or contrary to everyday sense perception. The demythologizing red pencil scored out vast swathes of the text. That the gospel could possibly be anything more than an uncertain scribal copy of a copy of an unknown source was blatantly in error—textual transmission became the more reputable area of study. On the other hand, if the gospel could not be any kind of reliable historical record then it had to be an imaginative solar myth wherein the three years' ministry resembled the course of Hercules' twelve labours—with no hint of an actual incarnation.

Today it is sometimes very difficult to appreciate in a heart-felt way the extent of materialism and the intellectual mind-set of the 1920s, although Kathleen Raine's *Autobiographies* go a long way to paint a true picture of Cambridge and London at the time. When Hermann Beckh was composing *Mark's Gospel: The Cosmic Rhythm* in the middle of the decade, it was as if contemporary critical readers, say, of *Macbeth* would be dwelling on fabrication, adaptation, Holinshed's and other's chronicles and the nature of a paying audience, to the total exclusion of the Bard's driving, comprehensive exploration of the tragic equation.

Although The Christian Community and the Stuttgart Seminary, where Beckh was at home, had perforce to come to terms with hyper-inflation in the first seven years of its life, there was a genuine youthful optimism as congregations grew and relations with both the Goetheanum and the local branches of the Anthroposophical Society were generally warm and supportive. Yet by 1928 there must have been some unease in the face of the generally amoral artistic world as well as of scientific advance. In 1924 Edwin Hubble announced that Andromeda , previously believed to be a nebula, is actually another galaxy; 1925 saw P.M.S. Blackett conducting experiments with colliding atoms with the first photographs of nuclear reactions and A.P. Weiss' *A Theoretical Basis of Human Behavior* reduced psychology to a physical science; then the speed of light was measured with high accuracy by A. Michelson in the following year. In 1927 P.W. Bridgman's *The Logic of Modern Physics* put the capstone on the scientific study of matter: all propositions that were not based on verifiable sense-perceptible evidence were to be utterly excluded.

With regard to the study of Mark's Gospel, it is worth pausing to note what was being lost as Stalin took control of the U.S.S.R. and Hitler had developed a power base that included the Brownshirts, then the paramilitary *Schutzstaffel* (S.S.). Within the Christian world as a whole, few people could doubt the *goodness* of the gospel, but its *veracity* as a historical record was largely dismissed by Reformed theologians; its *beauty* in overall structure was unperceived. Even in the Orthodox Churches the beauty of liturgical readings remained tied to seasonal extracts. Thomas Aquinas, quoted by James Joyce in *A Portrait of the Artist as a Young Man* (1916), had analyzed the essential qualities of beauty as wholeness (*integritas*), harmony of parts (*consonantia*) and radiant clarity (*claritas*). Broadly speaking, by 1928 Reformed Germany had lost all grasp of the wholeness, harmony and overall radiance of Mark's Gospel. Perhaps in Berlin, Marburg and Tübingen where a good deal of new theology was written, modern city life also had very little that could be called beautiful in the face of screeching trams and heaving railway stations.

When Beckh was asked to write on the gospel around 1926 he was initially reluctant, but in fact exceptionally well prepared. With hindsight, now that the *Collected Works* are also available to English readers, it seems a justifiable claim that Beckh's earlier life and studies were pathways not only to each individual publication and growing insights but at the time an unrecognized *training*, both in scholarship, musiciality and meditation, when the call to write on Mark came. The young man and student in Munich was immersed in the entire musical repertoire, but especially Wagner in piano reduction and in performance. As he later explained, 'The cosmic rhythm in tonality. This really lives in me; this is my theme.' In his early 20s as a Doctor of Jurisprudence, an expert in civil law and a circuit judge in Bavaria, Beckh knew what was acceptable as evidence and argument. With such an astute, analytical mind and a highly sensitive ear, Beckh was already in a unique position in the early 1920s when he became an authorized lecturer for anthroposophy and astounded large audiences at the Goetheanum with lectures on the source of speech.

If Mark's Gospel were to be rescued as a whole, true, good and beautiful, this was not to be achieved by anything glib or superficial. Nor was it enough to call solely upon enormous scholarly erudition or a prayerful, mature heart and soul.

Today, when anyone wishes to plant a new orchard bearing rich fruit, it is unavailing simply to plough and fertilize: this is but to scratch the surface, something that Beckh's colleagues Rittelmeyer, Bock and Frieling could do with facility during those early years. What is actually needed is a true specialist, a professional with equipment beyond the reach of local farmers. It is necessary to bring in the heavy sub-soiling machinery, a massive device that plunges deep into the ground to break up the compacted strata beneath the field. Only then will the fruits become plentiful.

N.V.P. Franklin, 2021

Translator's Introduction

Practically, Beckh's lecturing style has been preserved here, despite more recent changes in academic procedures and habits. On the one hand, an almost 90-year-old text need not pretend to be something else. On the other hand, the content is not subject to a sell-by date. As in the sequel on John's Gospel, Beckh's essentially descriptive, slightly repetitive style of exposition so musical in its form, has been retained with all the cross references. To repeat, the subject is less the imparting of knowledge than in recognizing (*erkennen*) 'what is'.

To help the reader, the author's sentences—perfectly clear, but frequently overlong and involved by any standard—have been arranged into reasonable lengths; his sometimes page-long paragraphs arranged into manageable units; most of his notes included in the text—they frequently contain essential points. Dr. Frieling's informative Foreword is included, also Beckh's useful Appendix (missing from the second German edition, 1960), that summarizes much and even contains Leading Thoughts, plus new Appendices on aspects mentioned in the main text. Some subtitles and even bullet-points have been added to help the eye. I have updated bibliographical details and some details of biblical passages in English translation; my short notes and those of the editor, intending to be helpful, are enclosed in editorial square brackets [ ].

Because they are technical terms of spiritual science (anthroposophy)—which at the same time is an artistic and moral pathway—for the stages of higher consciousness (that is, our thinking consciousness), Imagination, Inspiration and Intuition begin with a capital letter. (The traditional three stages on the practical mystic path are also known, for example, as 'Probation; Purification, or Enlightenment; and Initiation'.) For *das Ich*, the 'I' is given inverted commas, simply because this word in English is not usually used as a noun. The experience to which the expression points, however, is the cardinal experience itself, to which the term used above for Elijah's strange experience, 'the inner voice' or 'voice of thin silence' [LXX], points. 'Mystery', too, is a technical term; the 'Mysteries' or 'Mystery-centres' were the only educational centres in the ancient world. And capitals for our Earth as a being; she is that just as much as is Jupiter, or the Sun. These are not silent worlds.

Such comprehensive concepts are at the same time artistic; here Beckh's musical studies can enrich the account as possibly the best travelling companion—as Beckh himself suggests more than once. Two attempts to introduce Beckh's approach to 'what is' appeared in *The Language of Tonality* (Introduction and Appendix 2). Without star-charts, without notated musical examples, the author nevertheless makes the zodiacal system accessible. *Beckh explores the source of inspiration anterior—prior in more than a temporal sense—to both language and music.* Through and in recognizing, or reflecting, this 'unity of twelve', the inner voice—'*musikē*', understood by Plato as a mus-ish educational force, and sometimes (Hauer, Steiner, and others) also called 'melos' ('tune', or musical line)—is once again *heard.*

Addition, 2021: In reviewing the situation of Beckh's present standing, alongside the widespread ignorance of his contributions, we have met only two seriously meant criticisms:

(i) In an endnote Chr. Rau,[1] a scrupulous theologian whose inspiring work repays study, writes concerning Beckh's fundamental approach:

> Thus incorrectly Hermann Beckh, *Mark's Gospel—The Cosmic Rhythm,* who with ♒, ♉, ♌, ♏, distinguishes an astral cross from a physical and etheric cross, whereas according to Rudolf Hauschka (*The Nature of Substance,* RSP 2002) and Rudolf Steiner (2 July 1922 in GA 213, *Human Questions and Cosmic Answers*) two of the four signs stand as polar opposites.

In this brief note, it is implied that the wrong zodiac was chosen. However, Beckh always insisted that he was concerned with the imprint of permanent *signs,* not the variable *constellations*; the lecture in GA 213 gives indications regarding substances in Earth and Cosmos, but not signs or constellations. Beckh's work on the 'cosmic rhythm' in music and the gospels researches the classical *tropical zodiac*—not the *sidereal zodiac* (the stars in the sky), but the permanent imprint (*signs*) on the soul of the Earth, or 'aura of the Earth'—a phrase used by Kepler and frequently quoted with approval by Steiner, i.e. the time when sign and constellation coincided, when Christ walked the Earth—as *spiritually* active today, for the blessing is permanent. In the sequel Beckh defends his use of the traditional, or tropical zodiac that he apparently took for granted as understood by readers of *Mark's Gospel: The Cosmic Rhythm.* The matter is further complicated: horticulture is also mentioned by Chr. Rau in an article, yet, as he himself points out, it pertains to the lunar, rather than a solar, zodiac.[2]

(ii) Kurt von Wistinghausen (*Der Unbekannte Evangelist,* Stuttgart 1983; Eng. tr. 'The Unknown Evangelist', in MS, forthcoming), like

H. Beckh, E. Bock, J. Hemleben and others, is intent to differentiate the apostle John, son of Zebedee, from the 'beloved disciple', Lazarus-John. The latter, as Rudolf Steiner claimed long ago (GA 8, 1902) is the author of the Fourth Gospel. The Johannine Mystery is a major one in the present exposition of Mark's Gospel. In his concise yet well-researched account, Wistinghausen, while retaining all due respect, states the issue: both Beckh and Bock are not quite free (he claims) from the confusion of centuries regarding the author of the Fourth Gospel. In short, Beckh, and after him Emil Bock, suggest the 'beloved disciple', Lazarus-John, was present at events in the gospel story *before* the raising of Lazarus, when John the brother of James is mentioned as present (notably, the raising of the youth of Nain and of Jairus' daughter where the legends speak of the presence of Lazarus, and again the Transfiguration).

On the face of it, Wistinghausen and others appear right on their own terms. Yet there also seems to be a serious misreading. The attempt to trace our spiritual origins back to the New Testament and to this very issue of resurrection necessarily involves learning what the initiation of the disciples, particularly of 'the one', actually entails. Here we can but point to the issues.

We may consider a recorded conversation of Werner Klein and Emil Bock, priests of The Christian Community, with Rudolf Steiner (Feb. 1924):[3]

> Do the sons of Zebedee belong anyway to the intimate circle of the Twelve? To the starry circle where Christ saw Himself mirrored?
>
> *Rudolf Steiner*: It must be a mistake if it is written thus in the gospels. We must not be surprised if mistakes do occur, because the apostles were able to exchange their physical bodies with one another under the prevailing, very different soul-conditions of that time. The three disciples in the Garden of Gethsemane belonged at any rate to the most intimate circle of the Twelve and Lazarus, too, belonged to it.

The 'different soul-conditions' may help to place in context the issue under review, prompting the initial question, how much of the gospel story is a shared spiritual experience, for example, of the *evangelist* himself? John Mark himself, we know, although not one of the Twelve who actually witnessed the whole ministry, was nevertheless intimately involved in the events of rebirth enabling him to write his gospel. Beckh assumes the evangelists wrote from exact spiritual vision. He writes, for example, of Mark, as 'probably the greatest, and at the same time most humble, of all initiates of all time' (p. 53). And Beckh follows in detail Steiner's explanation that the first half of John's Gospel was inspired by the spiritual presence of the Baptist John. The term 'eye-witness' requires to be redefined. 'For what the one, who actually became the bearer of the initiation process, works through, he gains for the others', is how Beckh puts it (p. 232 below). John the apostle is 'inwardly united with Elijah-John', the Baptist (p. 201), whose disciple he no doubt was before following Jesus. Elijah-John is disembodied but in close contact to John the apostle, son of Zebedee, and the other disciples. Elijah-John eventually meets 'over the "grave of Lazarus"' the sacrifice of the one who later writes of himself as the 'disciple whom Jesus loved'. (Beckh takes him to be one of the Twelve; this assumption is questioned.) This has to summarize the tremendous Mystery of the 'two Johns' who become one, mentioned in Steiner's remarkable 'Last Address'. Cf. Beckh below, p. 274:

> The invalid (Lazarus) and 'son of the widow' dies; he who is overshadowed by the Elijah-John power, penetrated by the Elijah-John being, experiences the resurrection. Here too we recognize the revelation of the meaning of the sign of the Crab ♋; 'He must increase, but I must decrease.'

Beckh, in his whole attempt to describe the spiritual, Mystery events, brings Cain and Abel into the discussion and the two paradisal Trees, and he mentions Hiram, builder of Solomon's temple, and Christ's resurrection-body as the new temple. The initiation process assumes: Lazarus-John was *spiritually* present at the tremendous spiritual event of the Transfiguration, although there is no direct account in the Fourth Gospel; he was *physically* present at the Last Supper if we can read between the lines.[4] Indeed, the evangelist and all subsequent listeners and readers of the gospel are also present at all the events, inasmuch as Johannine initiation is calling, that is, Johannine synthesis, 'that they may be one' (John 17:21).

The Professor, too, attempts to lead *his* readers to see for themselves, and so, to add to the concept of 'soul-conditions', our own experience has to guide us, that is, our experience of the social unities of family, of educational, national and 'Western' contexts at least gives us cause to ponder. If the purely *spiritual level* is the region we seek, we progress in what the poet Keats called 'the veil of soul-making' where experiences are 'felt along the pulses', which inform the on-going search for clarity, for eventual Initiation into 'what is'. We may all agree in hoping one day to catch up with those going before who have left beacons for us[5]—with an important proviso, bearing in mind Mark 13:37. Thus, the wider issue is the challenge to learn to read the gospel not in the manner of a modern biography, or a reporter's account—'scissors and paste' techniques, with a hypothetical 'Q', et al—but as a distinct genre of its own. To this end, alongside the remarkable contributions of his critics, it is now high time to reassess Beckh as an exact, pioneer guide of authentic vision.[6]

My enormous thanks go to Neil Franklin, Ph.D., for many valuable editorial suggestions—and much more. My busy wife managed to check the first draft translation. Dr. Katrin Binder helped with the revision for this edition. As always, all remaining blemishes derive from my negligence and ignorance.

Alan Stott
Stourbridge, Michaelmas 2014, rev. Epiphany 2021

Foreword to the 2nd German edition (1960)

During the nineteenth century, when history became a subject of study, progressive researchers attempted without dogmatic restrictions to construct the life of Jesus 'as it really was' out of the gospels. The original picture of the simple man of Nazareth was seen as over-painted and estranged through the pious glorifications of Church theology. The concern was to free it through removing those accretions that had grown into a mythology.

In contrast to this, at the beginning of the twentieth century, a different view came to the fore. The 'mythological' element in particular increasingly drew attention to itself. It was asked, Can one really abstract the God-redeeming mythology from the gospel? Is it indeed only a removable over-painting, or perhaps the thing itself? The essential thing that cannot be removed without making the whole thing meaningless? The conclusion was reached that not only John's Gospel—already suspected at the end of the eighteenth century as unhistorical—tells the myth of a god. With the Synoptic Gospels, it was found to be basically not different. This includes Mark, who from the mythological view was hitherto thought the least demanding and consequently amongst the evangelists the most sober historian.

As a book title, William B. Smith throws *Ecce Deus* as a *parole* at the researchers of the 'simple man of Nazareth'. 'Behold a god!'—the content of the gospels is about a god. Such narration is not built on biographical dates and notes. It is 'cosmically' orientated. It takes its scenes from the starry heavens; the moving, dramatic element it takes from the Sun moving through the zodiac. Jesus of the gospels—does He not resemble more a Sun-god than the reforming rabbi of those researching the life of Jesus? The key to the gospels has been found in astral mythology!

Around 1910 a culmination of this direction of research can be observed. The two volumes of the *Christusmythe* by Arthur Drews appeared in 1909 and 1911. In Germany in 1910 the following books inclining to 'astral mythology' were published: *Hat der Christus der Evangelien wirklich gelebt?* by Peter Jensen; from the Polish of A. Niemojewski *Gott Jesus*; by John MacKinnon Robertson *Die Evangelienmythen* from a bigger work in English, *Christianity and Mythology* (London: Watts & Co 1900/10); by S. Lublinski *Das werdende Dogma vom Leben Jesu*. Moreover, it belongs to the physiognomy of these years that a book appeared in German, that of the 'citoyen français' Ch. Fr. Dupuis 'in the third year of the Republic': *Origine de tous les cultes*. Throughout the nineteenth century people referred to this bold, revolutionary book of 1796, throwing it into the exciting debate under the title *Ursprung der Gottes-Verehrung*. (Likewise, at the time of the French Revolution, C. Fr. Volney in 1791 had presented the Christian drama of history as the progression of the Sun through the zodiac.) In this connection it should be mentioned that in 1910 the *Monistenbund* ('Fellowship of Monists') in Berlin organized a public discussion on the theme 'Did Jesus really live?' There followed in 1911 *Ecce Deus* by W.B. Smith, in 1911 *Der Astralmythos von Christus* by Chr. P. Fuhrmann.

The researchers mentioned proceeded from the supposition, to them obvious, that the myth is free-roaming fantasy. They would not dream of posing the question of truth, whether something like a Sun-god really exists. With the proof of astral-mythological content and structure, the view of the gospels taken as reports of an historically lived life was dismissed. This can be already gleaned from some of the above-mentioned book titles. Especially Arthur Drews went with a fierce missionary eagerness against the historicity of the figure of Jesus.

But in this Christologically interested time, something else took place. Rudolf Steiner brought out his book *Christianity as Mystical Fact* in a second edition (GA 8, 1910). In his lecture-cycles he presented the stellar aspect of the work of Christ. In his lecture-cycles, *The Spiritual Guidance of Mankind* (GA 15, 1911) and *The Gospel of Matthew* (GA 123, September 1910) he presents the stellar aspect of Christ's work. In the context of a lecture-course *Excursus on the Gospel of Mark* (GA 124, Berlin 1910-11), he spoke in Berlin, on 6 Dec. 1910 (GA 124. Lecture 2) especially on the cosmic, starry ordering principle in the composition of Mark's Gospel. But he did so in a way that is fundamentally distinguished from the approach of the above-mentioned researchers of astral mythology. Spiritual science, anthroposophically orientated, founded by Rudolf Steiner, with the methods of modern scientific consciousness goes on to recognize supersensory realities. Through this the stellar cosmos appears in a new light. Myth can be honoured again as the expression of metaphysical facts in the language of visionary pictures. Anthroposophy also leads to the decisive insight for understanding Christianity. In the case of Christ Jesus, the myth of death and resurrection of the redeeming, heavenly God in the earthly events has taken on an historical actuality. The *Ecce Deus* ['Behold the God'] connects harmoniously with Ecce Homo ['Behold the Man'].

In the Berlin lecture of 6 December 1910 [GA 124], Rudolf Steiner said, amongst other things, 'the writer of Mark's Gospel read in the heavens the corresponding events for what happened in Palestine'. As an example, over the opening narration of Mark, which tells of John the Baptist, the Baptism in the Jordan and the first disciples, he allows the starry script 'Waterman–Fishes' to shine. With this he gave the key for the arrangement of the events presented in Mark.

Steiner's words on the theme 'Christ and astral-mythology' were truly contemporary. They were spoken at the right hour. But the astral mythologists did not acknowledge it. In those days there was no pupil of Steiner who, taking up the indication for the stellar composition of Mark's Gospel, could have related it to the textual details.

Instead Arthur Drews (1865-1935) stepped into this vacuum in 1921 with his book *Das Markus-Evangelium als Zeugnis gegen die Geschichtlichkeit Jesu* (Ulan Press 2012), ['Mark's Gospel as the Testament against the Historicity of Jesus', with twelve illustrations and twelve star-maps]. Here he truly follows the text and attempts to marshal evidence that the Sun progresses three times through the zodiac, beginning with Waterman–Fishes. Drews had arrived in his own way to this fact. It is tragic in his research that he encountered phenomena which, with his materialistically narrow methods of research, he was unable to meet.

Into this spiritual and historical situation, in 1928 Hermann Beckh's book appeared—*Der kosmische Rhythmus im Markus-Evangelium*, translated as *Mark's Gospel: The Cosmic Rhythm.*

Professor Beckh (1875-1937) made a name for himself with his important book *Buddha und seine Lehre*, first pub. in 1916, new edition by Freies Geistesleben, Stuttgart 1958 [Eng. tr. *Buddha's Life and Teaching*, Temple Lodge 2019]. In 1911 Beckh met Rudolf Steiner's anthroposophy, into which he entered ever more deeply. In 1922 he became a founder priest of the Movement for Religious Renewal, 'The Christian Community'. Its leading personalities, Dr. Friedrich Rittelmeyer and Lic. Emil Bock with whom Beckh worked in Stuttgart, drew his attention to Drews' book on Mark. Bock wrote about this.

> One day we decided that we had to put from our side something positive towards the negative theology of Arthur Drews ... Beckh at first didn't want to take it up. But because, during the last part of his life, he was

> increasingly involved with the stars and the relationship of the constellations to earthly destiny, this finally sparked the flame. Thus in 1928 the classic text *Der kosmische Rhythmus* ... came about ... which, far more consistently than Drews could manage, worked out the laws of the stars in the second gospel [Emil Bock. *Zeitgenossen, Weggenossen, Wegbereiter.* Stuttgart: Urachhaus 1959. 132].

Beckh first spoke publicly on this theme during a conference in Freiburg in the summer of 1926. Towards the end of 1928 the book appeared.

This study, carried out by Beckh with his own lovable enthusiasm of the discoverer, would probably have been made clearer and supplemented in a second edition. That is to be taken into consideration when the text essentially reproduces his first edition unchanged. The Appendix from that edition is omitted here [German ed. 1960]. The diagram that appeared at the end of the first edition is inserted here [1960] on p. 33.

Compared to 1928, the book today meets a vastly changed world-conception. 'Space probes' initially stimulate a materialistic view of the cosmos. Satellites and rockets contribute what they do to 'demythologize' what for earlier generations was still 'the heavens'. All the more important is it, then, also to learn to see cosmic phenomena with other eyes. Beckh's book on Mark is a contribution in this direction. It helps to give Christianity again its cosmic dimensions. The significance of this book does not diminish what a reading of it emphasizes—how much work is still to be achieved if bridges are to be made between Rudolf Steiner's spiritual view of the cosmos and the notions our contemporaries generally bring towards the stars.

Dr. Rudolf Frieling (1960)

Foreword to the 1st German edition (1928)

Theological research has already felt the narration of Mark's Gospel in the context of heavenly facts, though not yet recognized and presented in all its details. In this context, the revealed 'cosmic rhythm' throws a new light on the whole construction of the gospel. Through a way of studying the gospel, thanks to Rudolf Steiner and his comprehensive works on spiritual themes, the facts of this rhythm receive a spiritual meaning that was still looked for in these theological studies. Mark's Gospel, today still regarded by many as a 'simple devotional writing' becomes a unique panorama of a tremendous spiritual event, whose scenes, rising to ever-greater climaxes, reach us as an astonishing aspirational drama. In these scenes, facts are revealed of a spiritual path leading into the depths of the Christian mystery.

'But is not all this pure fantasy?' the modern thinker and sceptic, trained in the exact natural sciences, will object. 'Am I to believe all this?' questions the 'simple reader of the gospels' and the harmless 'believer', brought up in church tradition, astonished by the greatness of the scenes.

The author has tried to show a way through, between presuppositions and 'beliefs'—that can so easily become superstition. A third way exists that leaves the soul free, leading to an inner beholding. This, free from presuppositions and free from dogma, compares with the experience of any other great drama. The scenes are allowed simply to speak, by *bringing them alive through our thinking*.

Then of themselves, through inner devotion, earlier for the one person, later for the other, inner organs of perception are developed. Through their stimulus, they will say whether and how far a spiritual reality stands behind these scenes, and of what kind and nature this reality is.

Hermann Beckh
Stuttgart, 11 Nov. 1928

Introduction

The Character of Mark's Gospel

In the narration of Mark's Gospel a cosmic rhythm can be found somewhat related to the path of the Sun through the twelve zodiacal signs. Initially, this has been seen by a theologically directed research far removed from all spiritual research, anthroposophy and theosophy. This research is associated above all to the names Erbt, Stucken, Drews, Henson and Njemojewaki. It is thought that stellar facts, heavenly events and heavenly constellations are written into the gospel. It was found that the evangelist does not tell of an earthly life, but a solar life. The essential thing for such an 'astral-mythological' research is that the facts, researched with all diligence, devotion and acumen, cannot actually be taken seriously in the sense of finding Christ at work in them. For such a research can only imagine heavenly events according to earthly-material ideas. An assumed connection between heavenly events and earthly happenings consequently cannot be made. So, basically it is obvious that in the gospel these listed stellar facts and solar rhythms can only be taken as 'astral mythology', as some sort of stellar superstition of past ages, a mystical amusement for an old-fashioned generation. Individual representatives of this research, because they believe they have found only heavenly facts in the gospel, come to the conclusion that the life of Christ is not historical at all. The decisive results for the whole research pursued with such diligence conclude that this life is not an earthly fact.

A spiritual manner of observation as understood here finds it moves on another level, perceiving in all reality spiritual beings in heavenly as well as earthly events. It can ascribe a meaning to the idea that Christ, a heavenly, spiritual being, lived in the human vessel of Jesus of Nazareth. In this sense anthroposophy, as always intended and presented by Rudolf Steiner, finds the *earthly fact* of Christ. This as such is only to be found through spiritual research, not in historical research based on the reliability of external documents. And this spiritual research shows it is not necessary to deny the actuality of Christ's earthly life from these cosmic contexts, discovered in the gospel from a whole differently constituted theological, astral and mythological direction of research. For precisely this influence of stellar facts and solar rhythms in the gospel narrative rests on the fact that in Christ a heavenly being, the spiritual Being of the Sun, united Itself with the Earth.

(The question of Christology addressed here has its parallel in Buddhist studies. People also look for a solar mythology in the accounts of Buddha's life. And a cosmic rhythm can really be shown, similar—though not identical—to the cosmic rhythm of the gospel. Émile Senart's researches (*Essai sur la Légende du Buddha*. Paris 1882; BiblioLife/Bibliobazaar 2008; www.archive.org) are the most well known in this direction. No scholar of insight *for these reasons* has questioned the historical existence of Buddha. Even for someone who cannot accept these things seriously in a spiritual sense, will have to say: certain followers of a religious founder label him as a Sun-hero and consequently narrate the story of his life in solar-mythological pictures; from this it does not follow that the person himself did not exist, even if all the details of the narration were simply mythological, wanting historical actuality.)

Precisely in these gospel contents, which for another direction of research must appear as a proof of the untruth and unhistorical nature of the gospel, the method of observation meant here is able to find truth. From the beginning, however, the misunderstanding is to be excluded, as if by 'truth of the gospel' is meant only what today is taken as historical truth, the actuality of merely external, physical events. That this cannot be the case is already clearly obvious from the sufficiently known, easily discovered 'contradictions in the gospel'. We only need to point to the completely different narration of the finding of the first disciples in John's Gospel and in the other gospels. For example, the completely different chronological moment for the Cleansing of the Temple—this is placed by John at the beginning (John 2), by the others at the end, before Golgotha (in Mark 11)—and many other things. The solution, for instance, to relinquish the historicity of John's Gospel, in order to be able to save it for the other gospels, does not work, for yet more 'contradictions' remain among these others, called the Synoptic Gospels. Even apparently insignificant differences—for example, with the entrance into Jerusalem two donkeys are mentioned in Matthew, only one donkey in the other gospels—remain precisely 'contradictions'. And whoever wants at any price to retain the character of a gospel-revelation in the sense of outer physical facts, will have to give up if, other things being equal, he is to remain consistent. Even the way out sought by a direction of research associated with the name of Pfleiderer—today long superseded—to give up the historicity of the other three gospels, in order to claim it within certain limits at least for Mark, does not succeed. Just the results of the present account, through which the content of Mark's Gospel is transposed into a completely different, a spiritual-cosmic sphere, speak more than all the others for the weakness of this once favoured hypothesis.

The tragedy of theology today is that it has to destroy the credibility of those documents which it researches with such diligence, devotion and exactitude. In the face of this, Rudolf Steiner always emphasized that in order to find the truth of the gospel accounts, one first has to learn to read the documents. We have first to understand their language. It has to be recognized that they are not at all, and not at all intended as, historical documents in the ordinary sense. They originate from higher experiences in consciousness. They also present such experiences for the most part as their contents. They are, as expressed in a specific spiritually directed research, *initiation accounts*. To show this for Mark's Gospel is the task of the present work.

It will be shown that specific experiences of a Christian Johannine initiation are presented. These experiences are linked with those of Christ's earthly life itself and woven in an intimate, deeply spiritual sense. Even where these experiences are narrated as outer earthly events, in the telling many things point to quite other realms than that of the earthly event—think of the 'Transfiguration of Christ' on the Mount. Not everything in this narration relates only to the actuality of outer earthly events. Many things appear as the *picture for a spiritual event, whose reality is experienced in a higher consciousness*. Whether such a higher consciousness exists, and what the reality of such experiences comprises, can only be decided through the experience itself. Only those who have found the way to this consciousness can know something about it. The gospel will reveal in a new light the most significant disclosures to whoever seriously seeks the way and has the moral strength inwardly to rethink, to overcome assimilated prejudices and old thought-patterns, and inwardly to relax. Especially John's Gospel and Mark's inwardly closely related gospel disclose *how* they can search and find the way to such a higher consciousness. It is no coincidence that precisely the narration of Mark's Gospel shows how the details of this 'way' stand in the context of the facts of Christ's earthly life and the overarching, cosmic solar rhythm.

When it is discovered how in the gospel a specific pictorial language prevails, how extensive sections of the gospel at least bear this pictorial character—those who have an idea of what is meant here by 'higher consciousness', will no longer confuse these pictures with those of mere allegory or fable. They will recognize how they express a beholding of higher reality. Such a beholding in pictures through which a spiritual reality is revealed, will be named here as *Imagination*. An even higher stage of knowledge, in which something like a direct dialogue is found with the spiritual contents revealed in these pictures, will be named *Inspiration*. These expressions will be used not in a general sense, but in the specific technical meaning in which Rudolf Steiner uses them in anthroposophical texts. In these texts *Intuition* is spoken of as a third, highest stage of knowledge lying beyond Imagination and Inspiration, understood as that inner becoming-one with the objects of knowledge, comprehended in the essential depths.

The whole question concerning the truth of the gospel moves forthwith into a new light when it is recognized how the contents of the gospel, especially those of Mark's Gospel, are conceived not as fantastic but, resting on the reality of a higher consciousness, as real Imagination in the above-characterized sense. This is not to suggest the simple presentation of outer events, of a purely external physical actuality, plays no role at all. Even from such a presentation of external, sensory reality we may take it that, though in individual cases difficult to prove, and to a different extent in the different gospels—least of all perhaps in Mark—it forms an element of the gospel contents. And we will distinguish this element—whose firm confirmation belongs to the greatest difficulties of all explanations on the gospels, not at all solved with external methods of research—from another more Imaginative element.

But even with such Imaginations it is not as though it has nothing to do with the outer actuality. As already with the normal dream—which indeed is also a form, a specific decadent kind of picture-consciousness it takes pictures from the day-consciousness, so it is also in a certain sense the case with the higher Imagination meant here.

Now, an outer experience really experienced in day-consciousness is so often woven into the picture-world of our dreams. So too this can be the case with the picture-world of the higher, beholding consciousness. It is possible that one takes the gospel contents extensively only for a narration of outer events. In a certain sense it is indeed absolutely so that all outer earthly events, all the outer events of the story, can be understood as the picture of a spiritual event lying behind it and in it. We are able to raise ourselves to a mental picture (*Vorstellung*) or

Imagination that in Christ a spiritual being of a high kind, a heavenly being, has united itself with the earthly world. We will also be able to conceive how the individual facts of the life of Christ, the whole events in Palestine at the Turning Point of Time, in a special sense and to a higher degree, can pictorially express a spiritual, heavenly event.

We shall come to discuss how in the narration of Mark's Gospel the heavenly aspect is more strongly emphasized than the earthly side of the events. What really were the external events around the Turning Point of Time in Palestine cannot be learnt directly from the gospel narrative, including that of Mark's Gospel. It can only be brought to light through spiritual research of the highest order. In lectures held in Christiania (near Oslo), 1913 (*The Fifth Gospel.* Lecture-course. Christiania, 1-6 Oct. 1911. GA 148), Rudolf Steiner gave the beginning of such an undertaking. It is not possible for the present account to want somehow to go beyond the beginnings given there. It has to be content with presenting the cosmic rhythm in Mark's Gospel—certainly demonstrably already partly known by others—without actually being able to enter into the question how this cosmic rhythm relates to the purely outer facts of the earthly life of Christ, how the outer events in Palestine actually took place.

In his publication *The Spiritual Guidance of Man and Humanity* (GA 15, Lecture 3; 8 June 1911), Steiner touches on this question, not directly connected to the problems of Mark's Gospel. He speaks of a connection of real outer facts of the life of Christ with the stellar constellations, emphasizing how in the three years of the actual earthly life of Christ, from the thirtieth to thirty-third year of the life of Jesus in Palestine, Christ always stood under the influence of the whole cosmos. He took no step without the cosmic forces working into him. That which as horoscope at the birth of a human being works in from the heavenly forces of the cosmic hierarchies as the essence of the stars, this, Steiner emphasizes, worked here in every moment. He points out how for this reason often the stellar constellation for the deeds of Christ is gently indicated. For example, when with a healing it mentions, 'and when the sun was set, they brought the sick to him, and he healed them' [Mark 1:32], this indicates the corresponding healing forces that could work precisely after sunset. Those who were ill were attended to with the forces of the cosmos, working as *Christ* in Jesus.

> Thus, we see when Christ Jesus walked the earth as the earthly expression of a specific relationship of the cosmos to the human forces ... That

> which otherwise with other people flows into earthly existence at birth, flowed into Christ Jesus *at every moment*. And when the Mystery of Golgotha was happening, that which rayed out of the cosmos entered into the spiritual substance of the earth and since then is united with the spirit of the Earth.

Anyone who knows about spiritual healing, will sense something of the forces working in an especially strong manner in Palestine around the Turning Point of Time. He will not doubt the fact that Christ Jesus healed the ill and possessed, the blind and deaf-mute, that healings as related in the gospel did take place and even in large numbers. Precisely in such stories of healings he will doubtless find an element of the outer event, of the external facts.

Nevertheless, with such stories he will agree that the point of view of outer actuality is not the only possibility, that here alongside it the Imaginative point of view can play a role. A healing of a blind person can stand as a *picture* how Christ takes from the disciples their spiritual blindness, how he wakes spiritual vision in them; a healing of a deaf-mute can be the picture how Christ, as it were, loosens the spiritually tongue-tied disciples, conveying the gift of the spiritual word; healing the possessed can be a picture for how He overcomes certain soul-hindrances that are hindering the right placing of oneself into the forces and context of the Earth.

This point of view gains in significance precisely when we recognize in the gospels, especially in Mark, what role is played by the initiation of the disciples through Christ. Through such an Imaginative interpretation of such a healing story—and also with other stories this interpretation comes into question—we need not dismiss the outer actuality of the event under all circumstances. It may well be that as an outer event it did take place at some time (even if admitting such a possibility is still no proof for the real fact) and that the point of view how and why the story is told in a specific gospel, nevertheless is not the historical but the Imaginative event. Let us consider the Healing of the Blind Man (Mark 8: 22-26), which is clearly inwardly related to John 9. Already the relatively short tale in Mark points out some features (vv. 23-25), in which the living element of the outer event speaks to us. But to a much higher degree it is the case with the more detailed narration in John's Gospel (note especially John 9:6, 8-11, 18-23 and 27).

When we recall that we are probably dealing here with a spiritual seeing, not an experienced outer event, we will feel the living, eloquent manner of John 9, as something unique in all literature. And it will lie far from us to place this Healing of the Blind Man somehow *only* as the picture for some initiation-event accomplished by Christ in initiating the disciples. And yet this point of view *does* play a role. And if from here we compare once again the narration in Mark with that of John, taking into account the whole character of Mark's Gospel as an initiation document—the details of which will be increasingly worked out in the present work—we will perhaps feel that the essential point of view of Mark's account is that of the Imagination.

However, in fact it is precisely John's Gospel, taken by many as the one-sided spiritual gospel, which may not infrequently and in a much stronger measure be recognized as representing the purely outer side of an event. John's Gospel, like all the gospels, contains many Imaginative components. More than the other gospels, it contains in addition both Inspiration and Intuition, and to that extent is the spiritual gospel. And yet this most spiritual of all gospels—hitherto in theology so little observed—is, at the same time, the one in which the outer sensory reality is to be acknowledged, sometimes more than in the other gospels, along with the elements of Imagination, Inspiration and Intuition.

Corresponding to the predominantly Imaginative character especially of Mark's Gospel, the object of the following account picturing a 'cosmic rhythm' is not to be understood as if we are adding something to the outer events—which the external, literally understood narration of Mark's Gospel is supposed to describe. We are not *adding* the horoscope or even the respective zodiacal sign (the relevant position of the Sun), even in those individual cases where a meeting of points of view appears possible. (For example, in Mark 6 the 'Feeding of the Five Thousand' is narrated, which as we shall show stands in the Fishes. John's narration of the event contains the statement [John 6:4]: 'Now the Passover, the feast of the Jews, was at hand.' This really does indicate the time when the Sun approaches its transition to the Ram, that is, still standing in the Fishes.) Then the events would have to be embraced by one or another of the twelve heavenly, zodiacal signs, and at any one time the events of one month. The account in detail will show in all clarity that the 'cosmic rhythm' of Mark's Gospel cannot be understood in this sense.

Like the adherents of a certain astral-mythological direction of research, the present account also puts aside all outer actualities of Christ's earthly life, for the sake of the heavenly facts (still to be shown) in the gospel narrative. However, it does have to admit to these adherents, that it cannot take this narration as a mere historical account in the customary sense as the mere description of outer events. The present account has to take the viewpoint that what it will present in Mark's Gospel, the cosmic rhythm standing in harmony with heavenly events, is evidence that *spiritual events* form the actual content of Mark's Gospel. What is related as an outer event is initially present as the picture for a spiritual event, even when these pictures in a variety of ways—sometimes more, sometimes less—touch, or could touch, on what outwardly happened in Palestine.

Early Church representations of the four evangelists link them with the four beings ['beasts', 'living creatures'] of the Apocalypse (4:7) embracing the enigma of the human being. *Matthew* appears as the human being or angel, *Mark* as the Lion, *Luke* as the Bull, and *John* as the Eagle. We can find relationships with the anthroposophical fourfold human being—physical body, etheric body, astral body, and 'I', or ego.

- *Matthew* relates to the physical, the human member carrying the earthly forces.
- *Mark* relates to the human life-organism ordered to the cosmos, related to the cosmic forces, to the 'etheric body' as it is named in anthroposophy. (Already the process of plant growth revealing the nature of the etheric world of life, cannot be understood out of the merely physical but out of the cosmic contexts.)
- *Luke* would in this sense express more the feeling soul, the 'astral' body.
- *John* with his eagle's wings of thinking directly expresses the spiritual nature of the human being, the 'I'. The differences between the four evangelists now appear in a new light.

It can be immediately understood how Mark as the cosmic gospel, presenting the cosmic point of view, makes visible the cosmic solar rhythm. In plant growth, too, throughout the course of the year the laws of the etheric world which the life-body bears in itself are revealed. To a vigorous observation of the external, through an external clarification of that which is outward, not just with the aim of establishing 'contradictions', the four evangelists then declare themselves from their different approaches, and on this basis are changed into a higher harmony.

The contradictions only remain 'in place' for those who cannot release themselves from the notion that the evangelists only present the outer side of events, that they wanted only to tell of outer events according to external points of view. The contradictions disappear when it is recognized how the different evangelists, with their different intentions and different spiritual viewpoints, illuminate the spiritual side of the events.

The Essence of the Cosmic Rhythm

In order to understand the essence of the cosmic rhythm, shown in detail in the following presentation, it is not necessary immediately to look up to the starry heavens and in a one-sided manner to think only of stellar facts and starry constellations. Precisely for this reason this presentation cannot participate in the theological, astral-mythological school of thought, which by studying the separate sections of the gospel continuously pays attention to all possible details of the star-map. This presentation cannot participate in the often very external manner which in certain books—of which Arthur Drews' *Markus-Evangelium* has become the most well-known—so to speak, dividing out over the star-map all the possible points of the gospel narration. In no way should it be disputed from the beginning whether in the future a really spiritual approach could be possible which would discover such far reaching 'stellar facts' in the gospel narratives. Until today, however, a really spiritual presentation of uncertain facts has been neither found nor given. And the present presentation will initially and in essentials limit itself to the gospel-rhythm related to the course of the Sun through all twelve zodiacal signs. This will be shown not in the external manner of certain astral-mythological writings, but in a more spiritual sense.

The 'cosmic rhythm' meant here contained in the narration of Mark's Gospel is a spiritual fact, which in the annual course of the Sun through the twelve zodiacal signs is externally reflected in the 'heavenly writing'. (Concerning the essence of such a 'great coded writing' contained in the facts of nature and the heavens, beautiful sentences can be found at the beginning of the poetic prose of Novalis, *Die Lehrlinge zu Sais.*) We can become immediately aware of the spiritual fact of the cosmic rhythm:

in our own lives,
in participating in the course of the year,
in considering the human form,
the spiritual essence of the human being,
the essence of musical sound and the musical keys.

This also can be felt (as attempted in the essay *The Essence of Tonality*) as a parallel to what is revealed in the course of the year and its rhythm.

And this rhythm again is like a small reflection of that of the course of the day, as also in the 'Platonic cosmic year', in the backwards displacement of the first day of spring through all twelve zodiacal signs in the course of 25,920 years we find its greater cosmic counter-picture. Only when we come to study the variety of domains of revelation of what is held in common, do we penetrate to the spiritual essence of what is meant here by the cosmic rhythm.

Let us begin from the rhythm of the year. Here again without initial recourse to stellar constellations and zodiacal signs, we clearly experience the summer and winter solstices, the spring and autumn/ fall equinoxes as the four great turning points. And this not only externally, but by spiritually recognizing an experience of the course of the year and the natural year, we can participate very strongly and clearly in it. The religious rite[7] is splendidly suited to re-awaken feelings sunken in the subconscious through the progress of materialism today in human consciousness. Our whole feeling for the world and the inner life, when we are able to attend to it, is very different at Christmas, Easter, St John's-tide and Michaelmas.

Right into physiological phenomena, this shows how our life is not only inwardly linked with the solar rhythm, but also with the lunar rhythm. Sensitive natures are able directly to feel this. So, thanks to the monthly rhythm, there arises of itself the three periods lying between the four turning points of solstice and equinox. (Proceeding from this given rhythm, the actual transition takes place not on the first of the month but around the twentieth or twenty-first day of the month.) The feeling is different at Eastertide, in the full blossoming of May, and in June up to midsummer; it is another in November, in the time before Christmas (Advent), during winter and Epiphany.

We do not always need to glance at specific stellar constellations and the zodiac—which are not meaningless names lacking a context—in order to make sense when it is said, the Sun (or even, our earthly yearly rhythm) during the time after midsummer, when on the progression of the point of sunrise and sunset in a northerly direction is followed again by the retreat in a southerly direction, stands in the sign of the Crab (because the Sun makes a reverse, crab-like movement in its course, as does a certain sense for life). Or when the discussion is how in May, during the time of most abundant blooming and blossoming in nature, the Sun stands in the sign of the Bull, we do not need to think of a specific stellar constellation. Yet we may also think on the Bull revealing and witnessing to the strength of life.

And we can feel with the dying of natural life during November, the linked sign of the Scorpion simply as the power that now places the sting of death into the life of nature. Without beholding the starry heavens, too, we can understand Scorpio in this sense as the *sign of death*. And we can simply feel at the autumn equinox and Michaelmas lying under the 'sign of the Scales', without looking for the stellar constellation, indeed a certain displacement of time has taken place following the precession of the equinoxes. We can feel this when entering the Scales as the expression that days and nights temporarily acquire once again the same duration.

In this way, we can think of the rhythm of the course of the year in twelve monthly divisions, inwardly participate in this, and in this sense speak of the twelve signs of the Ram, Bull, Twins, Crab, Lion, Virgin, Scales, Scorpion, Archer, Goat, Waterman and Fishes, without initially bothering about the stellar constellations of the same name. For specific astronomical reasons, they no longer coincide at all today with the 'sign', as meant here. Then we simply experience:

♈ the Ram (Aries) as the 'lighting up of the year' at Eastertide,
♉ the Bull (Taurus) as the month of May with its fullness of blooms,
♊ the Twins (Gemini) as the time of moving towards Midsummer,
♋ the Crab (Cancer) as the first period following this,
♌ the Lion (Leo) as the warm climax of the summer (August),
♍ the Virgin (Virgo) as the end of the summer, the calming of the light during the September days,
♎ the Scales (Libra) as the season of Michaelmas (whose beginning, seen astronomically, falls during the Virgin),
♏ the Scorpion (Scorpio) as the death of natural life in November,
♐ the Archer (Sagittarius) as the season of Advent,
♑ the Goat (Capricorn) as the Christmas and post-Christmas time,
♒ the Waterman (Aquarius) as the first delicate feeling of spring in February,
♓ the Fishes (Pisces) as the actual spring.

This rhythm initially found in the course of the year, correspondingly applied to the course of the day, is simple and obvious.

- During the course of the year the increase of the light belongs to the Ram, to Eastertide. (The beginning of spring itself, the spring equinox, lies today, seen astronomically, in the Fishes, and the Ram is only reached somewhat later after Easter.) During the course of the day, we have the sunrise and the hour (more exactly, the double-hour) after sunrise.

- The summer solstice arriving during the course of the year corresponds in the course of the day to the hour of midday (for this reason, one can see the Twins as the sign of the 'great midday').
- The annual retrograde motion in the Crab, the first reduction of the light after the turning of midsummer corresponds in the course of the day to the beginning of the afternoon.
- The autumnal equinox in the sign of the Scales corresponds in the course of the day to the evening hour, sunset.
- The summer corresponds to the day, and winter to the night; the time of Advent (in the sign of the Archer) corresponds in the course of the day to the evening hour, sunset.
- Advent, leading to the winter solstice (the Archer) corresponds to arriving at midnight.
- Christmas as the time following the winter solstice (the sign of the turning of the mountain Goat) corresponds in the course of the day to the hour after midnight.
- The pre-spring sign of the Fishes corresponds in the course of the day to the early morning hour, the hour before sunrise.

As in the yearly and daily rhythm, we can also speak of a day and night-side in the circle of twelve keys—rendered in the 'tempered system [of tuning]'. The bright keys with sharps as the 'upper' keys face the darker keys with flats as the 'lower' keys.

- The 'ascent of the light' in 'the Ram' (♈) musically corresponds to the transition from the lower to the upper keys with C-major (cf. the expressive C-major transition at 'Let there be light' in Haydn's *Creation*).
- The arrival in the heights of light and the height of midday in 'the Twins' (♊) musically corresponds to D-major.
- The first reduction [of light] in the Crab (♋) corresponds to A-major.
- The transition that takes place in the Scales (♎) from the day to the night side (autumn equinox, sunset) would musically lie opposite C-major with the keys of F#-major/G♭-major.
- The favourite and expressive keys of Chopin's *Nocturnes*, D♭-major and A♭-major, lead—as in the zodiac the 'death sign', the Scorpion (♏) and the Archer (♐)—ever deeper into the 'night'. Their darkness comes out especially through the corresponding dusky minor keys—expressed most strongly in B♭-minor and F-minor.
- The turning point in the sign of the mountain Goat (♑), the increase of light after the winter solstice and midnight would musically correspond to E♭-major. In B♭-major, corresponding to the time when the Sun stands in Waterman (♒), we see the brightness increases.

- In F-major preparing for the day-side (♓, sign of the Fishes) there lies the actual arrival of light, as the course of the day brings the hour before sunrise, the course of the year the initial spring days, the time before Easter.

The day-bright world of Wagner's *The Mastersingers* lies chiefly in the upper keys; the 'dark nocturnal land' of *Tristan and Isolde* lies in the lower keys (A♭-major). The knowledge of the spiritual nature of what is always meant here as 'cosmic rhythm' is very much promoted, if it succeeds, initially in the experienced time-rhythms in the outer happenings of nature and also in music, in the world of musical sounds. These indeed are somewhat super-spatial, to do rather with what is ordered in time. Yet what is here meant is anticipated beyond general musical feeling in a certain 'feeling for the musical keys'. Anyone unable to follow this can readily accept that the theme encroaches on what is essential. Those seeking ways to understand will find further details in the writer's essay *The Essence of Tonality* [Anastasi Ltd. 2001, 2008[2] and *The Language of Tonality.* Anastasi Ltd. 2015].

Incarnation and the Zodiac

Let us turn from the world of time and of music to the spatial and spatially formed world. Here for a deeper spiritual enquiry the creative rhythm of world-becoming is revealed, especially in that form which stands before us as a summary of the whole world-creation and its secrets as the 'crown of creation'. It stands in the form that appears to the way of thinking meant here as the 'small world' in the greater world, as 'microcosm' in the macrocosm—in the *human form.* (For details, see Rudolf Steiner, *The Human Being in the Light of Occultism, Theosophy and Philosophy,* lecture-course Christiania, June 1912 [GA 137]).

A spiritual way of thinking finds the creative beings living in the 'great world', in the macrocosm. In their round dance of the great cosmic rhythm, mutually alternating, through aeons of world-events they allow their forces to radiate into the earthly realm. Out of these forces as out of twelve regions of space, forces ray in; through many metamorphoses these have formed the present human form. These forces that have been involved especially in forming the human head are called those of the Ram (♈). This does not mean they created some kind of supersensory 'ram' upon the human head, but those spiritual beings especially active on the configuration of the human head, allow their forces to ray in through the stellar constellation of the Ram, from that sphere of the cosmos that today is astronomically fixed. In the 'Ram', we could also say, the human form raises itself into the upright; it turns with its *forehead* to the *stars*; here it develops the light of the eyes and the power of thinking. It is the same sign where during the course of the year and the course of the day we see the light arise, the same where we find in the 'circle of keys' the key of C-major, of clear thought.

During the course of the year Easter and Michaelmas, during the course of the day sunrise and sunset, in the circle of keys C-major and F#-major/G♭-major (respectively, the ascent to the keys with sharps, and the descent to the keys with flats) stand in a certain reciprocal relationship. We find this relationship of sign and counter-sign, Ram (♈) and Scales (♎), also on the human form—in the head, in the Ram, the human being raises himself to the heavens; in the hips—which indeed correspond to the zodiacal sign of the Scales—he holds the balance, as do the balancing pans of the scales. Even on the human form one can see the essence of the 'Scales', without initially bringing into view some kind of stellar sign of the zodiac. In the 'Ram' and the 'Scales', we could also say, the human being places himself in the right balance into the earthly forces; this constellation relates above all to the human being's earthly incarnation.

Once found, this point of view offers a key to understand the gospel, for the cosmic rhythm in Mark's Gospel, when we find as in the Ram, or in the constellation of Ram-Scales, Christ actively placing himself into the earthly forces or affirming himself in these forces, or—as is the case with the healings of the possessed—He helps others to place themselves aright into the forces of the earth. Without initially looking up to the starry heavens, we can form for ourselves with the gospel the clearest and most distinct idea of the essence of the constellation of Ram–Scales. On the human form standing before us we can become aware of the spiritual being of the constellation Ram-Scales. We find it in the rhythm of the gospel narration, then again in the picture of the Representative of Humanity who places Himself into the earthly forces, Christ-Jesus.

In the book *Knowledge of the Higher Worlds—How is it Attained?* [GA 10] Rudolf Steiner describes how the organ of 'the two-petalled lotus-flower' can be found in the region of the Ram, on eye-level (in the 'area between the brows') in the human 'supersensory organism'.

From here the rays proceed through which the human being as 'I' experiences himself and as 'I' communicates with the beings of the spiritual world. The human senses in general are related to the zodiacal forces governing the human form. However, the usual 'five senses' are exceeded. Rudolf Steiner develops the twelve senses of man in the Appendix to the book *Riddles of the Soul* [GA 21] and in *Cosmic Being and Egohood* (Lecture 3, Berlin 20 June 1916. GA 169). In this ordering, the human 'sense of the ego' (under which Steiner understands the perception of the 'I' in another human being) belongs to the region of the Ram, the forces of the head working in the region of the eyes and forehead.

The forces of speech, the forces of the larynx, are fashioned out of the region of the Bull (♉). To the zodiacal sign of the Bull, we can say, belongs the *word*, the word in the creative-Johannine sense, the Logos (of the twelve senses, the 'sense of thinking' belongs here). The creative cosmic Word is revealed in the rhythm of the natural year when we experience lush blooming and sprouting, growth and becoming. In the sections of the gospel where this sign comes into consideration, it is found, of course, when simply the 'word' forms the decisive content. These sections are those especially where the living word of Christ meet with the dying words, with the dead human statutes of the Pharisees and scribes, or where the healings of the sick take place out of the living power of the divine Word. In this sign, too, stands the most significant section where in the initiation of John the power of the word passes over to the greatest disciple of Christ. (To show why and how far all this is the case requires the later consideration of the gospel narrative in all its details.)

The counter-sign of the Bull—that is, opposite on the circular arrangement of the twelve signs—the Scorpion (♏) has today become the sign of death. The visible context in the life of nature between the time of abundant blossoming and sprouting, the climax of the love-life in nature in May and its dying down in November, is also revealed in the human form. The forces of speech in the Bull at work in the region of the larynx face the forces of sexuality in the Scorpion. The connection between the forces of speech and of sexuality is also known to mainstream physiology—recall the change of voice in lads at puberty—and for a spiritual view that looks on the creative and developmental future significance of the forces of the word shows still deeper sides of this connection. In this region, which once as the 'Eagle' was the origin of the solar life (Rudolf Steiner, *Occult/Esoteric*

Science, GA 13; and *The Spiritual Hierarchies.* Lectures, Düsseldorf. 12-18 April 1909. GA 110), are those Powers involved in the Fall of man who approached the essence of the human being. The Eagle became the Scorpion carrying the sting of death. The Egyptian Isis saga told by Plutarch, too, shows how the Sun-bright Osiris was killed by his dark brother during the time when the Sun stands in the Scorpion. Primeval memories of humanity live in these sagas. The highest Mysteries of life and death are enclosed in this region.

Precisely at this point lies a principle Mystery of the Johannine Christian initiation as presented in Mark's Gospel. In the sign of the Scorpion where others enter their crisis, succumbing to the powers of death and of the consciousness-robbing sting of death, John becomes the victor over the powers of death. He becomes the one who re-acquires and re-enlivens the lost creative Word, who changes the Scorpion again into the Sun-Eagle. As the account will show, this is shown still more clearly in detail at an essential, decisive point in the narrative of Mark's Gospel.

In the human form, the shoulders in their duality are assigned to the 'Twins' (♊), the place where the upper arm begins. In the arrangement of the twelve senses we find here the 'sense of the word'. The counter-sign, the Archer (♐), stands at the point where this dual arrangement in the lower human being is given to the thigh. In the order of twelve senses, the 'sense of balance' is found here. In the gospel there stands in the Twins the places where Christ assembles the Twelve around Himself. Here the initiation of the disciples begins; the experience of the Word of Inspiration is prepared in them. It is shown how at these places the 'sons of Zebedee', James and John, appear especially as the 'heavenly Twins'. Moreover, further profound contexts for precisely this sign will be discussed, when—as will happen in the next section—we glance at the stellar constellation itself, at the revelation of the twelve cosmic forces in the 'heavenly script'. The Twins and the Archer, which in the rhythm of the year and of the day represent the 'great midday' and the 'deep midnight', have in the gospel a corresponding significance. In the sign of the Archer—in which we find, for example, the Transfiguration, as well as the death on Golgotha—the experience of death appears in the foreground in its special significance for Christian initiation.

Following the exalted sign of the Twins there follows the sign of descent and change of the Crab (♋), as in the rhythm of the year the summer solstice is followed by the descent of the year, when the Sun enters a retrograde motion, its crab movement. On the human form we are led here to the ribs, to the chest. In the Old-Testament narration, the biblical account in Genesis of the creation of Eve out of Adam's rib points to a descent of consciousness of prelapsarian, or paradisal humanity. We can for the first time sense the historical, developmental meaning of these signs, that then play such a significant role, especially in the initiation accomplished in the disciple John. The rich and various details have to remain for the presentation of the gospel that follows.

We recall how in the lecture-cycle *Human and Cosmic Thought* (Berlin, 20-23 Jan. 1924. GA 151) Steiner rediscovers the twelve heavenly signs in twelve world-conceptions. Combined with other points of view, the whole, rich variety of possible world-views, or perspectives, is spiritually channelled. With the sign of the Crab is linked the mental world-view of materialism, of sense-bound thinking. Forces that lead the human being into [a spiritual attitude of] sensuality, of a thinking bound to the earth, govern in the 'maternal' sign of the Crab, even governing breast-feeding—note the connection of the word *mater*, *'Mutter'*, 'mother' and *'Materie'*, 'matter'. These forces are changed in the Johannine 'metamorphosis of the Earth' into higher forces of resurrection. In the gospel, the sign of the Crab is specially related to the disciple John, who is initiated by Christ, as the counter-sign is related to John the Baptist. On the human form, the mountain Goat (♑) corresponds to the knee, and in the twelve senses to the 'sense of movement'. In the rhythm of the year the Crab and the Goat are assigned to the summer and winter solstices respectively, showing a mutual inversion, and it is similar in the gospel.

In the Lion (♌) the forces of the human heart beats. In his *Occult/ Esoteric Science,* Rudolf Steiner shows how the world-heart (that is, the heart of the Earth planet during its 'Saturn' stage) also begins to beat in the Lion, and in the same region will cease to beat. The physiology of the Middle Ages speaks of the heart as the *primum vivens, ultimum moriens* ('what was first to live is the last to die'). And in the gospel, the Lion is the sign that governs and regulates the rhythm of the others from within, and consequently in Mark is treated in a more esoteric manner, differently from the rest. We shall adduce finer details in the account that follows.

The counter-sign to the Lion is the Waterman (♒), corresponding in the human form to the lower leg. In the gospel, the contrast of Waterman and Lion stand in an important relationship of baptism by water and baptism by fire and the spirit. And in John's Gospel, in the story of the change of 'the water of the etheric' into 'the wine of the "I"' at the wedding in Cana, we recognize the contrast of these two signs. With the twelve senses the Lion corresponds to the 'sense of warmth', the Waterman to the 'sense of life'.

In the deeper regions lying below the heart we are led after the Lion to the sign of the Virgin (♍), corresponding within the human form to the pit of the stomach and the solar plexus, that area governed by the delicate, intimate forces of the unconscious and subconscious, which we find developed as a kind of sense of sight with specially talented personalities (see Justinus Kerner. *Die Seherin von Prevorst.* Stuttgart: Steinkopf 1999). In the context of Steiner's conceptions regarding the 'twelve senses', we find the 'sense of sight' in this Virgin-etheric sign; we find with the Ram at eye-level the 'sense of "I"'. These significant aspects, perhaps not obvious at the first glimpse, can become ever more understandable with deeper contemplation. Where the 'Virgin' is initially apparent in the gospel, it has to do with Christ's wanting to awaken in the disciples the forces of spiritual vision. Virgin-etheric forces of the 'bread of life' are what are always dispensed in the sign of the Virgin. In the gospel this sign with the counter-sign of the Fishes belongs to the especially significant 'Last Supper constellation'. In both great miracles of Feeding [of the Four Thousand and of the Five Thousand] the Mystery of 'bread and fishes' is gently indicated from this region.

The Fishes (♓) appear on the human figure as the feet, through which the human being connects to the Earth and especially the earthly-forces. In the arrangement of the twelve senses, the feeling of the 'sense of touch' is allocated to the Fishes. As with the Virgin, forces live here of a delicate unconscious and subconscious nature. However, they are changed to forces of a higher kind in Christian initiation beginning with the 'Washing of the Feet'. Esoteric insights concerned with the Mystery of human-becoming in the context of world-becoming (see, in addition to *Occult/Esoteric Science*, both Rudolf Steiner's lecture-courses on *The Gospel of St John*: Hamburg, 18-31 May 1908 [GA 103], and Cassel, 23 June–7 July 1909 [GA 112]) find, how in the Fishes—during a time in the past when in the rhythm of the whole cosmic year the Sun had its spring point in the Fishes, where today it finds itself again—the human form still rayed through by solar forces first touched the physical earthly forces. Sun and Earth, until then united, began to draw apart. The feet aligned to the Fishes are, as it were, that part which still retains a memory of the first touching of Earth with the Sun, and with the solar forces that remained united with the Sun. These Christ-forces, which at that time were in the sign of the Fishes, separated from the Earth, united with it again in the same sign in the Baptism in the Jordan. This leads to the beginning of Mark's Gospel and to the cosmic rhythm it reveals.

Already in early Christian times the secret of Christ was always connected to that of the Fishes. The Greek word for fish, *ἰχθύς—ichthys* (in a remarkable way, this word contains the German word *'Ich'*, the 'I'), is an acrostic [in Greek] for 'Jesus Christ God's Son Saviour'. Behind this lies hidden the indicated deeper context of spiritual science.

In the Virgin live the more natural forces of the etheric world, of the bread of life; in the Fishes those forces live that through the spirit, the 'I', that is to say, the etheric metamorphosed by Christ. We recall the gospel narration of bread and fishes. In his book *Theosophy* [GA9], Steiner coined the phrase 'Life-spirit' for these metamorphosed etheric forces of an ennobled kind. In Indian theosophy, 'buddhi' is the term.

The Supersensory Human Members and the Zodiac

This leads us to another standpoint, also important for a contemplation of the gospel. This explains that the 'twelve signs' are not only arranged to the twelve parts of the human form, but also to the 'spiritual members of the total human being', as found in anthroposophy. It should be remembered from the beginning, that such an approach cannot in the usual meaning be a 'proof'; it is also not to be taken dogmatically but without prejudice to prove how far it offers a useful key to open up the Mysteries of life and of the cosmos. We find the rhythm meant here when we follow not the usual sequence of signs but in steps of five—that is, from the first to the sixth, then from the eleventh, from there to the fourth, the ninth, and so on. Then, the physical body is allocated to the Ram, the etheric body to the Virgin, the astral body to the Waterman; the Crab, Archer, Bull are allocated respectively to the forces of the sentient soul, mind-soul and consciousness-soul (or spiritual soul).[8]

It can easily be surmised, how, for example, the Crab, as the sign for the sensuality and enclosure in sensory existence, corresponds to the 'sentient soul' directed to the sensory side of existence; the logos-sign of the Bull more to the spiritual 'consciousness-soul'. In the Scales—another important viewpoint for illuminating the gospel—the higher development of the human being begins, his education to 'Spirit-self' (Steiner's term for the soul and astral nature, illuminated and transformed by the 'I', termed in Indian theosophy *'manas'*). *Manas*, Spirit-self, belongs to the sign of the Scales; *buddhi*, 'Life-spirit' to the Fishes lying five signs further. In the Lion is revealed *atman*, the 'Spirit-man': the earthly-physical nature changed and spiritualized right into the blood, the place where baptism in fire and blood takes the place of baptism by water. This, too, is important to illuminate the gospel and the understanding of the initiation of John. The remaining three signs reaching beyond—the mountain Goat, Twins and Scorpion-Eagle—lead beyond the immediate human nature into still higher degrees of Christian initiation. They indicate the realm of the Holy Trinity, of the Spirit, of the Son and of the Father. These topics may at first be simply stated. In the course of the studies on the gospel they will achieve more significance and importance.

The Three Crosses

The relationship of sign and counter-sign, where the arrangement of the human form to the zodiac comes into view, is also important for an explanation of the gospel. We see throughout in the rhythm of the gospel arriving at a specific sign, how the counter-sign is involved and chimes in. In the story of the Feedings and the Last Supper, the constellation Fishes–Virgin is evident—with different emphases, first the one then the other; in the climaxes of the initiation the constellations Twins–Archer are closely linked. Similarly a relationship is found between the Ram–Scales and the Crab–Goat. With the former sign the etheric life-forces in some manner enter in, and with the latter sign the physical earthly forces. In a similar manner, the partnerships of Scorpion–Bull, and Waterman–Lion can be recognized. One is able to find that what is revealed there is related to the astral, soul-element.

Furthermore, it can be recognized how in this viewpoint an arrangement of the twelve signs forms three crosses. These can be called the etheric, the physical and the astral crosses. The *physical cross* corresponds in a certain sense to the forces of the Father, the *astral cross* to the Spirit and the *etheric cross* to the Son. The Last-Supper constellations carrying the 'etheric cross' we are able to address as Christ's cross in this specific sense. In its one axis it carries the Last-Supper constellation (Fishes–Virgin), in its other axis the constellation of Golgotha (Twins–Archer).

The cross of the Father corresponds in its four points to the four main stations of the *rhythm of the year*: Easter—Michaelmas—St John's-tide–Christmas. We find the four points of the 'astral cross' in the well-known early Christian presentations of the *four evangelists*:

- Waterman/Matthew, 
- Bull/Luke, 
- Lion/Mark, 
- Scorpion-Eagle/John.  

In the reversion of the Scorpion to the Eagle the Mystery of John's initiation is expressed.

These four points are also related to the four *elements* water, air, fire and earth, and the *temperaments* (phlegmatic, sanguine, choleric and melancholic). John, the melancholic, is related to the element of earth; Matthew, the phlegmatic, to water; Luke, the sanguine to air; Mark, the choleric, to the element of fire (Lion). In this way, each of the three crosses has its points with the four different elements and temperaments.

Likewise, with the circular arrangement of the twelve signs, it is possible to link each of the three points to a respective element and temperament. One can speak of an 'earthly triangle of the melancholic temperament' (the 'Johannine triangle'), of a fire-triangle of the choleric temperament, and so on. Each of these triangle points touches another point of the three crosses. One will be able to say, for example, that the Johannine triangle has its apex with the Crab in the physical, its other two corners (the base) with the Fishes in the etheric, the Scorpion in the astral element. Moreover, as one can speak of 'the cross of Christ', that it is in the Fishes of the earthly forces and the 'melancholic triangle', in the Virgin the forces of the air of the 'sanguine triangle', in the Twins the water-forces of the 'phlegmatic triangle', in the Archer the fire-forces of the 'choleric triangle'.

The gospel speaks to us of the heavenly signs perhaps most clearly and directly in the story of the two Feedings, the 'Feeding of the Five Thousand' (Mark 6) and in the 'Feeding of the Four Thousand' (Mark 8).

It is not coincidence that with the one Feeding seven, with the other five loaves are shared, that with the one seven, with the other twelve baskets of full fragments remain over. In the 'twelve baskets' we see the whole 'twelve heavenly powers' of the 'whole human being' (as described above). In the full Johannine Christian initiation, the twelve heavenly powers lay hold of the *lower* human being of will. Around the human being the twelve signs arrange themselves into an above and below, a day-side and a night-side. The former begins with the forces of the head in the Ram, the latter with Scorpion. Between the Ram and the Scales lies the upper more conscious part of the human make-up (the 'system of the senses and the nerves' and of the 'rhythmic system'). Between the Scorpion and the Fishes lies the darkest, the most deeply unconscious, the will part of the human make-up ('the system of digestion and of the limbs'), which only finds its full illumination in the Christian-Johannine initiation that begins with the Washing of the Feet.

Rudolf Steiner points out that with the Feeding of Five Thousand, the secret is expressed of the 'fifth post-Atlantean epoch', that is our present age. The number four thousand relates to the other Feeding to the fourth epoch, the then contemporary epoch. The five lower dark forces, and therewith those in the 'twelve baskets' picturing the whole human being, will be fulfilled in future ages through initiation. The 'five loaves' relate to these five powers of the lower human being of will, whereas the 'seven loaves' correspond to the seven powers of the higher human being. The one Feeding embraces, so to speak, only the day side, the human day-consciousness, whereas the other also works down into the sub-conscious, the night-side of the human make-up. For this reason, there remain over with the one Feeding only seven, with the other twelve baskets. Outwardly it is not intellectually conceivable why from seven loaves only seven baskets remain over, and from five loaves twelve. For an explanation of the gospel both are significant. When only the day-side of the human make-up is taken hold of, which (as will be seen) is a 'daytime experience', the 'day-sign' of the Virgin is primarily emphasized. With the other Feeding the night-side of the human make-up is also laid hold of, which (as will be seen), is a night-experience, the 'nocturnal' sign of the Fishes is in the first place emphasized.

Everything here about the twelve zodiac signs and their revelation:

> in the rhythm of the year,
> in the course of the day,
> in the circle of keys,
> in the human form,
> in the human senses and
> in the spiritual make-up of the human being

is understandable—even without looking up to the starry heavens or consulting the star charts. All this can gain important perspectives for explaining the gospel, without our initially concerning ourselves with astronomical facts. The explanation of the gospel meant here has really nothing to do with a new kind of 'star superstition'.

But the other approach is certainly possible. We imagine for ourselves the spiritual nature of the twelve heavenly powers and their reflection in the 'cosmic rhythm' of Mark's Gospel—at first independent of the starry heavens and star-maps. What is first found purely spiritually we now seek in the 'great coded script' (to use Novalis' phrase) of the starry heavens. We now set our gaze in the night sky to the twelve shining starry signs of the zodiac, in order to read what we have found also in the heavenly starry script, perhaps ourselves approaching a step towards understanding the 'spiritual script of the universe'. Our feelings facing the heavens will be deeply spiritualized, our reverence for the gospel itself immeasurably increased, when we now see the narrated facts also, as it were, light up before us in the heavenly starry script. This will be discussed in the following chapter.

The Stellar Constellations of the Zodiac

From the point we have reached in the discussion, let us turn our gaze to the starry constellations of the zodiac, in order also to read in the starry script that which is found and revealed purely on the Earth during the course of the year and of the day, in the circle of keys, on the human form and in the spiritual nature of the human being. As we are led through the course of the year, through the rhythmical change of seasons and natural life, the Sun travels through all twelve starry constellations of the zodiac. Their names we have partly already related to the earthly experiences of the rhythm of the year. We could, for example, recall the 'Scales' simply as the transitional regaining of the balance of day and night at the beginning of autumn/fall. But then it will not fail with its impression to awaken a feeling of the 'starry script', when the starry constellation that the Sun enters at that time of year draws attention to three bright stars to be observed standing together in a triangle. One can imagine the picture of a pair of scales from above downwards with two weighing pans. We experience the scales in the earthly rhythm of the year when the Sun really does stand in the starry constellation of the Scales. More accurately put, it stood at that time in the Scales when those events related by the evangelist took place.

Meanwhile, the precession of the equinox has moved everything by some days. The Spring Equinox no longer falls in the Ram but in the Fishes. Only in its further course will the Sun reach the constellation of the Ram as the month in which the spring commences. The 'precession of the equinox' concerns the Sun's retreat over about 25,920 years [the 'Platonic year'] through the whole zodiac. (Seen astronomically this phenomenon is ascribed to the turning of the Earth's axis. This results in the Earth always pointing to different regions of space.) The precession of the equinox results in the fact that the earthly signs corresponding with the rhythm of the year no longer quite coincide with the heavenly signs, or constellations. Both coincided when Christ Jesus walked on the earth. At that time, when in Christ Himself the heavenly and earthly rhythms met, the starry script completely corresponded with the experience of the earthly year. And with the whole present studies it should be noted that they relate to the context of that time and not that of today.[9] So here we may take the Ram simply as the spring sign, the Scales as the autumn sign, and so on.

If we search for the starry constellations of the zodiac in the sky at night, we must be clear that we won't find that constellation in which the Sun stands at present. Always that constellation of the zodiac will be visible in the sky at night from which the Sun is really furthest removed. Imagine ourselves standing on a winter night at a point where we are able to survey the whole horizon. We shall survey perhaps seven constellations of the zodiac, where the first and the seventh at least are partly visible. We will see, for example, when in the east the Virgin is rising, in the west the Fishes is setting, at least in part. In the south, high in the sky, stand the Twins, between them and the Fishes, stand the Ram and the Bull, between the Twins and the Virgin, stand the Crab and the Lion. This, for instance, would be the image of the midnight heavens in the time after Christmas (the bright star Spica, though, will appear in the Virgin somewhat towards morning; visible in the evening sky towards spring). The Ram borders in the east; in the west a part of the Scales is still visible. In this way seven constellations of the zodiac are visible; the five others not visible, under the horizon, are, as it were, under the Earth. Already in this sense one can speak of seven upper, light and five lower, dark constellations of the zodiac.

Glancing at music, we recall seven upper, high, keys with sharps, including C-major, and five lower, dark keys with flats. This we can do by differentiating the Ram, Bull, Twins, Crab, Lion, Virgin and Scales as the seven bright, 'summer constellations' from the five dark, 'winter constellations': Scorpion, Archer, Goat, Waterman and Fishes. (In the night sky, we still count the Fishes with the 'night constellations', even though today, towards the end of its period, the first day of spring is reached in the Fishes).

From what has already been said, we can conclude that especially the darkest winter nights can present in a most beautiful way the view of these shining 'summer constellations'. The view of the stars of the winter sky is much more beautiful and brighter than of the summer sky. Not only does the darkness of the winter nights allow the stars to shine brighter, for in the summer the longer lasting daylight influences the brightness of the stars. It is really also because, when the zodiac comes into consideration, the clearer, radiant constellations are seen during the winter, the darker, more dusky ones in the summer. In the winter skies the Bull, Twins and Lion are the especially clear zodiacal constellations. The Bull is a whole starry region with many bright stars and characteristic starry groups forming smaller constellations. The most well-known are the small group of seven stars, the Pleiades, and the one open circle or triangle, the Hyades.

The abundant growth and blossoming of the plant world, the radiant climax in the revelation of the creative word in nature, falls in the time when the Sun stands in this large and brightest zodiacal constellation, the Bull. Alongside it the Twins with the characteristic pair of stars Castor and Pollux, the two equally bright in magnitude, and next the Lion, whose four brightest stars form a trapezium, among which is the bright star, Regulus.

The differentiation of seven bright summer constellations, which are then visible in a winter sky, from five winter constellations, which are visible in the summer sky, is also expressed through another fact. In summer the course of the Sun rises higher in the sky than in winter. In winter the path of the zodiac, and with it the course of the Moon and the planets, spans higher in the sky than in summer when it lies flatter over the horizon. The high point of the zodiac is formed by the constellation of the Twins in a midwinter night, and then towards spring at an ever earlier nocturnal hour.

High in the zenith above the asterism of Sirius and Orion (not part of the zodiac), which are the most beautiful and brightest of the whole starry heavens (Sirius is the brightest of all the fixed stars; Orion the brightest of all the constellations). In the ancient Mysteries these constellations were regarded as especially sacred, and felt as a revelation of the highest divinity. Sirius, the star of Zarathustra [see the author's monograph *Zarathustra*, Eng. tr. in *From the Mysteries*, p. 88ff.], for the Egyptians was the star of Isis, and Orion the constellation of Osiris. Proceeding today from the gospel, we find in these constellations Sirius and Orion, over which the zodiac arches, the *sacred mount of the heavens*. Sirius and Orion appear in the starry script, as it were, as the mount, *on which Christ prayed*, and where He assembled the Twelve around him (Mark 3:13), as Drews points out in his book on Mark's Gospel (p. 157). In the discussion, it has already been pointed out how in these moments two of the disciples, the twin 'sons of Zebedee' (James and John) play a special role. Proceeding from the picture offered, when, let's say on a February night, high over the 'sacred mount of the heavens', over Sirius-Orion, the 'heavenly Twins' shine. It forms, as it were, the tip of the 'Sacred Mount', or stands over it. The most impressive moment is when Sirius with the three inner stars of Orion's belt, stand over the horizon approaching the level, presenting the base of the triangle whose apex is high above in the Twins. Towards the end of February this can be observed in the early hours of the night. The form of the 'Sacred Mount' offers comparison with that of a resting chalice, open towards the bottom.

Much paler and dusky is the aspect of the starry heavens, especially of the zodiac, in a midsummer night. On a July night about 10 o'clock, if we look up to the heavens, we shall still see in the west—and even if impaired through the summer brightness—the bright star Spica shining in the Virgin. With the neighbouring constellation the Scales, it still belongs to the upper, higher part of the zodiac. We see how the Scales, as it were, keeps the two halves of the zodiac separate. It divides the Virgin from the Scorpion as the first and main constellation belonging to the 'night side' of the zodiac. One cannot actually name this constellation 'dark'. More than any other constellation it is characteristic for the summer night sky with its dusky and threateningly sparkling stars recalling a dragon's tail. This star that today appears demonic-looking, symbolizing and bearing in itself the 'sting of death', is, however, in its own way uniquely beautiful. Sublime Mysteries of solar life, already touched on in this study, permits us to guess that from another viewpoint, in his children's book, *Mein Sternenpathe, oder Sternkunde für Kinder und andere liebe Leute* [Chemnitz: Verlag Max Muller, 1923], Karl Josef Friedrich [a Lutheran pastor] called it the 'flowering twig'. In the winter heavens with the 'heavenly Twins' shining bright over Sirius-Orion the 'Sacred Mount', we could attempt inwardly and meaningfully to link the ciphers of the great heavenly script with the pictures and facts of the gospel. We could also take our beginning in summer from this threatening, sparkling 'constellation of death' in the southern heavens, whose significance in the gospel story (as we shall show in detail) is so serious and critical.

Observing the summer picture of the zodiac—it embraces, as we have seen, precisely those constellations in which the Sun stands not in the summer half but in the winter half of the year—there are links, still in the south, between the Archer and the Scorpion, whose numerous stars become indistinct in the navel of the Milky Way. The Archer was felt in the ancient Mysteries as bound to the Scorpion, forming with it the 'constellation of death'. The Twins are seen as the constellation of the 'great midday'; the Archer as that of the 'deep midnight'. The one corresponds to music in the key of D-major, the other the nocturnally dark A♭-major. The constellation is particularly impressive as it rises above the horizon, when we see streaming from it the constellation of death, as it were the heavenly stream of the Milky Way, which the Indians call the 'heavenly Ganga'. When we begin to decode the 'heavenly script', it can show us in a most significant way how inwardly to link this sight with the most significant facts of the gospel. Above all, the death on Golgotha itself stands in the Archer.

To the Archer are joined further to the east (or south-east) towards the nocturnal dark region of the mountain Goat, the most dusky of the zodiacal signs, near the two not very bright stars standing characteristically slanting, sticking out as the 'horns'. In the ancient Mysteries this area of the sky at night was called the 'heavenly wilderness'. The Baptist John was found in the 'wilderness' or the 'heavenly wilderness', the heavenly counter-picture of 'loneliness of soul'. This heavenly constellation adjoins a likewise dusky constellation, the Waterman, showing no characteristic grouping of stars. It likewise is related to John and his baptism by water, as we shall see in detail. In the external aspect one can already strongly feel the *darkness* that has not reached the moment when the light shines. It is the constellation of the 'forerunner' that announces the beginning of the light but itself still stands in the heavenly darkness.

Adjoining the Waterman is the region lacking stars, the Fishes. For the outer view the Fishes forms the 'zero point' in the zodiac. Spiritually seen, the rising of the light ensues, the light of the year and the light of Christ. This sign forms again the transition to the bright summer constellations, that is, those constellations through which the Sun passes in the summer half of the year. Next comes the Ram, not yet mentioned in this section. In its grouping this sign, too, like the Crab between the Twins and the Lion, is less characteristic than the other summer constellations.

When toward spring and Easter, Sirius-Orion, the radiant starry asterism, the illuminating ornament to the winter heavens, turns to its setting in the west, gradually setting in the shimmer of daylight, another star becomes visible towards Easter ever earlier and clearer. Similar to Sirius in the ancient Mysteries, it was an 'Isis star'. This bright star with a uniquely mild, almost white light is Spica, in the Virgin. Spica means head, or sheaf, of corn [more exactly, 'ear of wheat, barley']; the constellation is thus called the 'Virgin with the sheaf'. Two stars of the Virgin, we could also say, always shine in the heavens, the winter one sets in the spring, the summer one consequently rises. The one, Spica in the Virgin, belongs to the zodiac itself, the other, Sirius, is overarched by the zodiac in the central region of the heaven of fixed stars. It is called the 'Sacred Mount of the Heavens'.

Both stars are deeply connected with that which in the ancient Mysteries was experienced as the 'heavenly provision for the way'. It transfers us to times when people did not see the stars as today, as shining points in the sky. People really beheld in pictures. In ancient Egypt the image linked to Sirius-Orion was of the Queen of the World adorned with a starry diadem. She brings to birth the son of the Sun. She was beheld again by John, the writer of the Apocalypse. People saw not only the pictures, but also life-giving forces, forces of the heavenly life-ether that were absorbed.

An unspecified, general feeling regarding the stars did not exist, but they were gathered in a differentiated manner into specific individual regions of the starry heavens. One such region of the experienced great cosmic chalice was in particular that of Sirius-Orion (to the Egyptians linked with Isis and Osiris), another was the constellation of the 'Virgin with the sheaf', the bread of life. Especially from these constellations, the ancients felt the 'draught of life' of the stars—the ancient Indians spoke of the soma drink—the cosmic provisions for the way, the heavenly life-ether, the bread of life. The story of Joseph and his brethren in the Old Testament takes us to the time when the stellar bread of humanity began to become scarce, when the forces of ancient vision and the experience of cosmic communion of humanity became exhausted. But in Egypt, in the centres of early sacred Mysteries, they could still be sought. When this experience of humanity began to disappear, they could still be renewed from the initiates in the Mysteries, until even there they disappeared.

Increasingly, the connection between the earthly and the heavenly became lost, until they found their renewal in Christ. In Him were renewed the great cosmic chalice experience and communion experience—of which the visible chalice of the physical communion is the cultic reflection. It was once there in the early prehistoric humanity and in the early Mysteries. What at that time was drawn out of the more dreamy, unconscious or subconscious forces of the soul (out of the 'sentient soul', in Steiner's terminology), can now be found out of the 'I', in freedom and full consciousness, when the Christ-force has become strong enough in human beings. With the 'bread of life' (Spica in the Virgin) is linked in this sense the Christ-'I'-power in the Fishes. The life-ether is engendered anew through the 'power of the Son' in the 'I'. In this sense Christ speaks, 'I am the bread of life'.

Christ, Who in his inner being (*κοιλια, koilia*, 'belly': John 7:38)[10] in the 'I' and in the heart, allowed the source of life to spring afresh, becomes at the same time the new revealer of the starry script (see R. Steiner, *Christ and the Spiritual World.* Lectures, Leipzig 28 Dec. 1913–2 Jan. 1914 [GA 149]). Spica in the Virgin, the 'heavenly sheaf', belongs above all to those stars which we are again able to experience spiritually when re-enlivening the forces in ourselves, when in an especially profound sense we are able to form a link with the narrated facts in the gospel. With the 'experience of cosmic communion' we are able to link to a sensitive, opened Heart inwardly felt still today as the enlivening, constructive, consoling forces of this mildly shining star with its white light. And it will be especially significant for us to see it bordered by the heavenly zodiac from the Virgin and the Fishes. Then we are seeing the bread of life in the sign of the 'Virgin with the sheaf'; in the sign of the Fishes also in the sky, we see that constellation already discussed in this study in another connection. What has been presented has already shown that earthly bread and fishes is not meant. We behold in the heavens the loaves and the fishes in both stories of the Feedings in the gospel—to which a third Feeding belongs, narrated in the last chapter of John's Gospel.

The great Christ-communion constellation governing the whole gospel shines in the heavens before our eyes. When the Last Supper (Mark 14) is read, we find ourselves in reality in that same constellation as it was already announced in the parables of the sower and of the seed, and in the Baptism in the Jordan. When the gospel speaks of 'loaves and fishes', in the first instance the most significant fulcrum is given where we are able to link the content of the gospel narration with the starry script. The meaning and the essence of this starry script begins to unveil itself.

The expression *'starry script'* is at the same time a reminder not to remain with the mere script, with the mere viewpoint of the stars and constellations to which we have raised ourselves from the merely earthly viewpoint of the great rhythm. But through the script we are to penetrate to the contents, to the deeds of spiritual beings. From the stars we raise ourselves to the heavenly hierarchies as the spiritual beings of the world (see especially R. Steiner. *The Spiritual Hierarchies*. Düsseldorf. 12-18 April 1909. GA 110; Lecture 7, 16 April 1909).

The Cosmic Sun-Rhythm in Mark's Gospel in its Relationship to the Mystery of John and the Johannine Initiation

When we follow the 'cosmic rhythm' of Mark's Gospel in its narration of Christ's life on Earth from the Baptism in the Jordan to the death on Golgotha, there results three rounds of the Christ-Sun through the twelve heavenly signs. To show this in detail is the task of the whole following study. The three rounds of the cosmic solar rhythm in Mark's Gospel are not simply repetitions. It will be shown how the meaning of each individual sign is realized on an ever-higher level. We are led to ever-higher cosmic heights, in ever-deeper solar depths of Christ's being. The picture of three ascending spirals, arching ever higher, offers itself. We could take an ever more beautiful and expressive concept from music by speaking of 'three octaves' in reference to this cosmic solar rhythm, or solar harmony.

Mark has secretly included these three rounds, spirals, or octaves of the cosmic, solar rhythm into the 'three years' of the earthly life of Christ. Though not directly referred to, they can be found in the narration of John's Gospel from the three references to the Jewish Easter festival of Passover. Like John's Gospel, Mark's is also a Christ-gospel in which Christ's being is bound to the bodily vessel of Jesus of Nazareth. The stories of his childhood are not given, as they are in Matthew and Luke, but like John Mark begins with the incarnation of Christ in the Baptism in the Jordan. In this event the heavenly and the earthly, which were separated in primordial times, mutually meet. This contact occurs in that sign in which the transition from the night-side to the day-side, from the heavenly to the earthly, so also it is found in the zodiac, in the sign of the Fishes. This sign is above all a sign of Christ and the Christ-Initiation, as in the cosmic rhythm of Mark's Gospel.

Like a significant 'prelude'—if we may use this normal musical expression with this cosmic 'rhythm'—the sign of the Fishes is anticipated by the two signs that somehow always relate to John the Baptist (♑ ♒). John the Baptist gives his name to the great prelude to the Christ-revelation in Mark's Gospel. In the most significant manner, as Rudolf Steiner has already indicated, Mark's Gospel begins with the Mystery of John's baptism. With each return of the respective sign, in each round or octave of the solar rhythm, this secret of John is also revealed on an ever fresh and higher level.

The cosmic solar rhythm lying as the veiled basis of Mark's Gospel and its three octaves lies in the name 'Ioannes', Germ. Johannes, Eng. John (as in Heb. Jonah, dove); the secret can be found in the three vowels of this name (I–O–A, I–A–O). I-A-O and I-O-A are two different forms of an ancient, primordial word that is known to contain the 'divine name' also in the Hebrew Yahveh and [the Medieval form] Jehovah, which ultimately leads to the 'Mystery of the "I"' (the name that everyone can give only to themselves). I-A-O can be seen as the vowel-form of the name Yahveh (originally only the consonants Y-H-V-H), whereas I-O-A shows the proper vowel sequence of the Jehovah form of the name. With the concluding O, embracing the depths of being, the 'ring of eternity', we look more at *becoming*, with the form that the O has in the middle (I-O-A) at the *being* of the divine. Since the rhythm of Mark's Gospel, in the becoming of John (which first leads to being), presents the becoming of the divine, it is based on the sequence I-A-O, which also appears in the Greek *ἰάομαι* 'to heal' (meaningful for those who see how healing powers lie in rhythm). The one who sees all this realized in being (I-A-O) is then a *Ιωάννη* Ioannes, Johannes, John.

John is in no way a name in the normal sense, as usually given to a human being. *Whoever in understanding, appropriating the great cosmic rhythm, has approached the revelation of the Christ Sun-Being, and has taken into Himself the revelation of the Christ Sun-Being in the great rhythm of cosmic becoming, is a John.* We can't actually say of such a person that 'he is called John', but 'he *is* it' or 'he will *become* it'. Deep secrets of being or becoming a John are revealed in Mark's Gospel and in its 'cosmic rhythm'. Thereby it is not without significance that the writer of Mark's Gospel—as we read in the Acts of the Apostles 12:12, 12:25 and 15:37—himself bore the name of John [John Mark], that is, was a John, had undergone the Johannine initiation. From the three cited passages we see that 'Mark' was only a second name, a nickname. Even the reference that his mother was called Mary (Acts 12:12), points to most significant Mystery contexts. Mark, the writer of the cosmic gospel, would not have been able to present the earthly life of Christ borne by the cosmic solar rhythm, and the initiation resting on this rhythm, unless he himself had taken part in this initiation—had he not been penetrated as John himself into the Mysteries of Christ.

When we understand the secret of the name John in the indicated sense, then it is clear that between the two bearers of the name John in the gospel there has to be some kind of relationship. This relationship is between the Baptist John in the 'prelude' of Mark's Gospel, and the disciple John, whose story of initiation, or becoming, is described emerging ever more clearly and mightily towards the end of the gospel. This leads once again into specific deeper contexts of Mark's Gospel. We see ourselves shown two sides of the secret of John, the one especially revealed at the beginning of Mark's Gospel, the other at the end, when we connect the end of Mark's Gospel with John's Gospel with which it is inwardly closely related.

We can see one side of this secret when we take into account what is indicated in Mark's Gospel itself (Mark 6:15, 9:13, 1:2), known as the Elijah-John Mystery. Rudolf Steiner has shown how Elijah was not physically incorporated in the Old-Testament events but worked more as a spiritual being, overshadowing and inspiring specific individualities. In this manner Elijah also worked through the Baptist as the 'angel' of John the Baptist (Mark 1:2).

This Elijah-angel already active in pre-Christian Old-Testament times and then finally with power in John the Baptist, is the great forerunner of Christ in world-development. The Baptist, the last and greatest of the pre-Christian initiates, was overshadowed by him. He became the one who recognized the Turning Point of Time, the Christ Sun-Mystery of the great rhythm of time and of the cosmos. He recognizes in the One who stood before him by the Jordan, the bearer of this Mystery—the Christ [the 'anointed one']. Of all the great pre-Christian initiates, John the Baptist stands before us as the one who came into the greatest proximity, directly near to Christ. His being is completely sacrifice and devotion.

Through the baptism of John the cosmic Christ was, as it were, called down into the vessel of Jesus of Nazareth, bereft of its earlier 'I'. In this decisive meeting for his life and work with Christ—but which was also his ending—he, as it were, sacrifices into this meeting his own being and essence, his own angel. From this moment on we see him dwindling, dying, even before he meets his destiny of death instigated by Herodias. But even his death is a sacrificial death, a sublime spiritual, sacrificial deed preparing the path for the sacrificial death on Golgotha. A glance at the cosmic rhythm, the zodiacal signs, clearly reveals the inner relationship between John's sacrifice and that on Golgotha.

The realm of the angels (*εὐαγελιον*, 'gospel'), of whose beginning is announced in the preparatory activity of the Baptist at the beginning of Mark's Gospel, increasingly spreads out under the influence of

John's sacrifice. It pours forth its rays into the whole activity of Christ and His disciples, into the whole initiation of the disciples led by Christ. The description of this forms an essential part of the narration of Mark's Gospel. Through this, the Grail event—as we could call it—takes place in the Mystery of the two great miracles of Feeding. In this event the same angelic being is revealed who already in the Elijah story and the Elisha story in the Old Testament had accomplished the miracle of the increase of bread. Not only Christ, but also the disciples themselves are decisively involved in what takes place. In a deeply affecting way, Mark's Gospel shows us how the disciples can never remain at this height. At that sign, which we have met from various viewpoints as bearing the sting of death, their initiation vacillates and reaches a point of crisis. The flight of the disciples in Gethsemane with the betrayal of Judas and Peter's ensuing denial, standing again in the death-sign of the Scorpion, is but the deeply affecting climax of a crisis. With careful attention, its gradual development and effect can be traced through the whole of Mark's Gospel. This abandonment of Christ by the disciples, their scattering into isolation, named by a Greek word *σκορπισθητε*, 'you will be scattered' [John 16:32], sounds like an indication of the basic zodiacal secret, pointing to the sting of death of the Scorpion.

Out of this crisis, the other disciples are not able to find the aim of initiation during the lifetime of the Master. Their consciousness still succumbed to the sting of death. But this brings into increasingly stronger relief the initiation of the one, the only one, who really did become the great Christ-initiate and disciple of Christ, the disciple of love. He is the 'disciple whom the Lord loved', as he is called in John's Gospel. This 'love' is to be understood in a sublime, the highest meaning of the Mysteries. Upon this one human being increasingly descends the realm of the angels, who earlier worked through the Baptist. In this influence the becoming of the new, the 'Christened' John, was accomplished. A Mystery is indicated here, for which a significant stimulus for its solution is given in Rudolf Steiner's 'Last Address' (Michaelmas Eve 1924; in GA 238) that can be felt as a testament. *Without the inner work on what was then received, the whole present work would not have been possible* (see Appendix 4).

The saying, 'He must increase, I must decrease', not only means the relationship of John the Baptist and Christ, but also the relationship of the old and of the new, the pre-Christian and the Christian John. And without our wanting dogmatically to press anything, or with outer theories and notions in some kind of crude manner to enclose the depths and delicate Mysteries governing here, we can nevertheless feel something more when we find the viewpoint sufficiently deeply in the spirit-sphere. Precisely out of the essence of Christ as the world's turning point, all the great differences of the pre-Christian and the Christian Johannine revelation become clear. Regardless of all the differences of outer personalities, the *uniqueness of John's being* is apparent. In the 'Mystery of both Johns' the duality is somehow resolved into a unity.

Let us look once again at the personality of the great Christ-initiate, the disciple John, who plays such a decisive role in Mark's Gospel. We saw over the portal to Mark's Gospel, the *Mystery of Elijah-John*. How should we name the other side, where the *becoming of the great disciple of Christ* is increasingly worked out towards the end of Mark's Gospel? Which outer personality do we behold, when we look for the human form of the great disciple of Christ?

At this point the whole understanding of Mark's Gospel stands or falls. So, too, does the whole reception, itself serving the appreciation of Mark's Gospel, of the full study of what Rudolf Steiner presented first in the book *Christianity as Mystical Fact* [GA 8] and what he said in his lectures on John's Gospel concerning the waking, or 'raising of Lazarus' (John 11). In a significant manner we are allowed to feel a connection of this person with the 'disciple whom the Lord loved' (John 11:5). Early legends relate how Lazarus, who at that time was still a rich man, with treasures of ancient wisdom, was a sanctified priest of the temple in Jerusalem. The waking, or 'raising of the young man of Nain' through Christ (Luke 7), which Lazarus was able to experience, made such a deep impression that he decided to give away all his earthly riches and treasures of wisdom and, like the young man of Nain to whom his being was linked, to seek the way which, through the situations of deepest need, death and the grave, lead to re-awakening.

From there, so the legends relate, he fell into a deep taciturnity and into a kind of long illness, which increased to that infirmity which preceded that 'waking, or raising of Lazarus' through Christ Jesus, narrated in John 11. This awakening, convincingly explained by Rudolf Steiner, is an initiation-event like that of the 'young man of Nain'. The expression 'son of the widow' (Luke 7:12), used of the young man of Nain, belongs to the language of the Mysteries. It relates to specific Mystery processes and initiation-experiences.[11] It is found in the Old

Testament with personalities who, as we shall show, also relate to the Mystery of Lazarus-John.

The raising of Lazarus, Steiner helps us to recognize, concludes the one 'becoming John' of the great disciple of Christ. He is the same as the one who, in reference to the one 'becoming John' in Mark's Gospel, is called 'John' from the beginning. In John's Gospel itself the disciple's name 'John' is never used. He is only called the 'disciple whom the Lord loved', whereas the singular invalid, also the first to arise from the grave (John 12:1), is called 'Lazarus'. On this invalid, this Lazarus, the writer of John's Gospel looks back as on a stranger, or a person who has become a stranger. The being who now filled him, the being called John, could only fully move in, in order to live in him, who was that 'other', the invalid—because Lazarus, still burdened with Cain's curse on humanity, had sacrificed himself. The name 'John', the name of the disciple, is not to be found in John's Gospel; the name 'Lazarus' is not to be found in Mark's Gospel. And yet it can be seen how the events which lead to the 're-awakening' narrated in John 11, the whole process of the one becoming John for this person, the Johannine initiation—which out of the failed initiation of the other disciples comes increasingly into relief—is narrated in full detail precisely in Mark's Gospel. In Mark's Gospel we are led precisely to the point of imagining that event which as such is not narrated in that gospel but in John 11.

The *Elijah-John Mystery* stands over the entrance to Mark's Gospel, and the *Lazarus-John Mystery* stands over the exit. Firstly, by recognizing how the two meet and penetrate, we gradually appreciate the depths of the Johannine initiation. And we increasingly recognize how Mark's Gospel in its presentation of the becoming of John, the initiation of John has its own content. Mark, who himself bore the name of John, and who had gone through the Johannine intuition, felt himself called to develop in his gospel the secrets of the primordial Johannine initiation, effected through Christ Himself. He did this not in an insistent way—already the situation with the church of that day required much consideration—but with the most delicate reticence. Only someone could find it who really from the depth of his heart can search for the key to understand the gospel and its pictorial script. Having found it, we shall increasingly recognize that the gospel appeared at the first glance to speak of Christ and Christ events, but it actually far rather shows us events of the Johannine consciousness. It lets us see, as it were, right through the Johannine consciousness to Christ and the Christ-events. Studies of this sort cannot in the usual sense 'prove', at the very least in a roundabout way, for instance, prove something with three sentences. Only by patiently letting the whole consideration make its effect can one approach its meaning. The procedure—and this more or less with everything that is discussed in this exposition—is neither to take it in some kind of dogmatic manner, nor hastily to rely on it. Rather check whether and how far it is suited to offer a key to understand the gospel.

When the latter is the case, then from here at once a new and significant light is shed on the context of the two gospels which, in the narrower sense indicated at in the beginning of the section, are the Christ-gospels: Mark's Gospel and John's Gospel, that means, only a presentation of the three years of Christ's earthly life forms their content. Then it can be felt that Mark's Gospel is a direct prelude to John's Gospel. The connection of Mark's Gospel to John's Gospel was first indicated by Rudolf Steiner in his lecture-cycle *The Gospel of St Mark.* In his gospel studies, Emil Bock has presented important motifs in a clear light. The present work focuses on how the 'cosmic rhythm' is inwardly connected to the gospel and illuminates it.

One will be able to say, not outwardly as proof but only as inwardly experienced sentences: actually there has only been *one* person, or being, in the whole history of the Earth, who could directly speak of Christ and His Mysteries, and was qualified to do so. This was the *disciple John*. In this sense there is only *one* pure gospel of Christ—John's. Both Matthew and Luke, in their introductions also relate the childhood stories of Jesus of Nazareth. They are more like gospels of Jesus, though, of course, the Mystery of Christ perpetually shines through the figure of Jesus. Matthew's Gospel, in the way it allows us to see Peter, the 'rock of the Church', in a certain narrow sense is the *gospel of Peter*. Luke's Gospel, in the way it not only narrates the stories of the birth, but also in another more hidden context, presents the Virgin and Mother, is the *gospel of Mary*.[12]

Even Mark's Gospel that so deeply leads into the solar secrets and solar rhythm of Christ, speaks in the sense meant here not directly of Christ Himself, but of him who became the one who truly *knows Christ.* He is the one who can speak, and may speak directly, of Christ. *Mark's Gospel is in this sense a John-gospel, as John's Gospel is the actual gospel of Christ*.

In reviewing the significant theme of Mark's Gospel picturing the initiation of Lazarus-John, let us look once more at the picture of the silent invalid, who is awoken by Christ out of the sleep of the grave, who overcame Cain's curse on mankind, and who became the re-awakener and re-enlivener of the creative solar Word lost as a result of the Fall of man. Out of the experience of deepest silence, the outcome of most deeply moving metamorphosis of soul, we see in John the re-birth of the lost creative, solar Word.

John is the only one of the Twelve disciples[13] who in the earthly life of Christ Jesus, in his initiation through Christ, in full consciousness re-found the 'lost creative Word'. All the other disciples, failing in the initiation, failed to re-find this Word, until in the talking in tongues of the experience of Pentecost, the substitute for what had not been found, yet not a full substitute, was distributed amongst them. The fully conscious experience of the Johannine Word out of the 'I' is something different from the experience of the Word at Pentecost, which for the other disciples, Peter at their head, was something arriving from outside that overcame and overwhelmed.

The one who kept silence for so long, stands facing the other, who, gifted with old powers of the word, spoke too soon. Peter, the 'rock of the Church', who was given the illumination, the premature confession of Christ at Caesarea Philippi (Mark 8), was immediately lost to the power of darkness that increasingly darkened his consciousness, his '*I*'. The denial following Gethsemane is the climax of this extinction and loss. Soon after Peter lost the prematurely grasped word to the power of darkness, the impressive narration in Mark's Gospel relates how the 'lost word' of humanity was laid hold of with inner full power by the one becoming John. Soon after the Transfiguration, in which there dawned for him the meaning of Christ's sacrifice of death—yet for Peter still remaining not understood—we see the hitherto silent one become the leader who speaks. When we look at the 'cosmic rhythm', we find how this takes place in that zodiacal sign of the twelve, which is always the 'sign of the word'. The whole event of the gospel standing in this sign reveals how the one becoming John penetrates ever deeper into the Mysteries of the divine creative word. Peter's denial 'I am not' (*οὐκ εἰμι*) stands facing the Johannine 'I am'. Out of Christ's I-AM, John finds again the lost creative word.

Consequently, the beginning of John's Gospel, 'In the beginning was the word', affects us so strongly with primordial power. Seen purely intellectually, similar sentences can be found in some gnostic, Alexandrian writers. What lends them the unique effect at the beginning of John's Gospel is the inner full power, with which, as we can feel, it is written there. An inner full power as only the one possesses who, by overcoming the power of death to which the others succumbed, could really find again the 'word in the primordial beginning'. The re-found creative Word itself, we feel, speaks through the writer of John's Gospel. And it shows in the Gospel of John, out of the I-AM of Christ, how the way to this lost word of humanity can be re-found. How John himself found it, forms the content of Mark's Gospel.

Here we touch again the secret of the 'cosmic rhythm'. Let us look yet again at all that can be found of the Johannine secret and the Johannine initiation in Mark's Gospel. We recognize the greatest rhythm—in the course of the year, in the realm of musical sounds, in the human form and the nature of the total human being, the self-revealing creative rhythm as the rhythm of the solar Word re-found by John. And we recognize in the way we were led in Mark's Gospel from stage to stage of this rhythm, in the picture of the solar life and solar rhythm of Christ at the same time the gait and rhythm of the one becoming John, the Johannine initiation. Directly with the secrets of the Johannine initiation, this threefold progress of the Christ-Sun through the twelve heavenly signs, as it is to be seen in Mark's Gospel, can be followed. And the sentence at the beginning of this chapter, claiming how in the name of John and in the vowels of this name (I–A–O), the secret of this rhythm is contained, will make the claim clearer.

We have spoken of the three rounds, or octaves, of the great solar rhythm. In the first of these rounds, on the first degree, we see still in the light, in the scenes and parables, there appears (I); on the second degree, in the second octave as in an inner listening (A); on the third and highest degree, as it were, brought right into the depths of the corporeality, laid hold of and understood in the innermost being (O). John himself becomes one with the cosmic word. We can also name these three degrees as those of Imagination (I), Inspiration (A) and Intuition (O), using anthroposophical technical terms of higher cognition. Through these three stages of Imagination, Inspiration and Intuition, the Johannine initiation is accomplished, the re-finding through John of the lost creative word. The secret of the name John itself, in a deeply meaningful way becomes revealed through the cosmic rhythm of Mark's Gospel. As something completely natural to him, the writer of Mark's Gospel carried this rhythm in himself, as he himself walked the path through a Johannine initiation. We are permitted to behold him as one, probably the greatest, and at the same time most humble, of all 'initiates' of all time.

PART I

The First Round of the Sun-Rhythm

The Goat and Waterman in their Relationship to John the Baptist (Mark 1:1-8)

In the sign of the Fishes, the transition from the lower dark to the upper bright part of the zodiac takes place, from the nocturnal side to the diurnal side, from the heavenly to the earthly. This transition can be found within this sign of the Fishes itself. In the same sign, in which at one time the Sun and the Earth, Heaven and Earth separated, the return of the Sun-Being Christ into the Earth took place.

As far as the earthly life of Christ is concerned, a study of the cosmic rhythm has to begin with the Fishes. It has already been pointed out that this appearance of Christ in the sign of the Fishes in Mark's Gospel like a prelude anticipates John and his baptism in the signs of the mountain Goat and the Waterman, both belonging to the night side of the zodiac. In both these signs there takes place what we can always call the *sacrifice of John the Baptist*. The angelic being who lived in, or overshadowed John, is *Elijah-John.* (Cf. Matt. 11:14, 17:12f.; Mark 9:13; Luke 1:17, 7:27. John 1:21 is no proof of the contrary, because here the Jordan-baptism and with it the sacrifice of the Elijah-angel into the sphere of Christ has already taken place.) This being sacrificed himself into the earthly incarnation of Christ and into the initiation of the disciples closely bound with the earthly deeds of Christ. The initiation of the greatest of Christ's disciples climaxes in Lazarus-John, in the one who becomes John.

The *Elijah*-John motif, as we saw, governs the beginning of Mark's Gospel, the *Lazarus*-John motif the end—though the name Lazarus is not used by Mark. It is significant that this becoming-John always returns with John's sign of Goat-Waterman. It is woven into all three degrees of the cosmic rhythm. Where it appears at the beginning of the gospel, as the prelude to the first

octave of the solar rhythm, it relates to the appearance of the Baptist by the Jordan and to the first degree of the sacrifice of John that takes place in the Jordan-baptism.

The motif of one 'calling in the loneliness' (*βοωντος εν τη ερημω*), 'crying in the wilderness' as the AV/KJV has it, is linked to the sign of the mountain Goat. The spiritual station of soul-loneliness is meant, before the appearance of the 'I' lights up. John the Baptist stands at this unique place of the human soul. He is still waiting for the descent of the 'I' during the time of the final descent of humanity and the most extreme human darkness. The earthly wilderness or desert pictures this loneliness of soul. In ancient times the zodiacal sign of the Goat was called the 'heavenly desert', and still today whoever observes this constellation can receive the impression of darkness and duskiness, of loneliness in the heavens. In this more heavenly than earthly loneliness, we spiritually find John the Baptist.

The 'wild honey' with which John nourishes himself would be something like 'honey of the heavenly wilderness', the life-ether of the stars, that which the Indians called the 'heavenly soma'. We recall in the Buddha legends, how the Buddha-child still waiting in his mother's body, was nourished with 'cosmic honey drops' from a bowl of beryl. The Baptist had a strong and living connection with the etheric element of the cosmos, as the picture of the 'honey of the heavenly wilderness' indicates. With the physical side of the Earth—as the somewhat obscure picture of the locust food appears to suggest—he had only a phantom-like, shadowy connection, not yet penetrated by the 'I'. From these four signs of the physical or earthly cross (♈ ♎ ♋ ♑) (see p. 34), the Ram is the darkest, the most unearthly. It is the only one of the four signs belonging here lying on the nightly side of the zodiac. Whatever is physical and earthly about John the Baptist appears as the still mostly dark-filled part of his being. It belongs to that part of the Earth where the earthly character is still the least emphasized.

In the pictorial language of fairy tales, the 'coat of all kinds of fur' relates to the physical side of human beings—think of the Grimms'

fairy tale *'Allerleirauh'* ('All-kinds-of-fur'). The picture of camel hair, with which John is clothed, can also express how his earthly-physical side was woven through in a special manner by the cosmic etheric forces. In its gait and nature the camel, as the 'ship of the desert', is aligned to the etheric element.

On the human form, in knee and elbow, the Goat is initially the sign of willfulness, of obstinate natures and self-seeking convictions. If you bow the knee in prayer, it expresses reverence for the divine. Then self-will undergoes a change of thinking to a soul-searching and repentance. In this sense we find with John the Baptist in the sign of the Ram preaching to people to change their thinking (*μετανοειτε*, from which the noun *μετανοια*, v. 4; usually translated 'repentance'). In Christ, the consummated turning of the divine towards the human meets in John the Baptist a turning of the human towards the divine.

And we will have to notice how this sermon to 'change your thinking' always returns when the sacrifice of John appears on some new level. Initially this being sacrifices himself into Christ Himself, and we then see, as it were, this being delivering a Baptist-sermon (Mark 1:15). Later the sacrifice is increasingly distributed to the whole circle of disciples. The force of Elijah-John flows ever more into the initiation of the group of disciples. The Twelve now preach the sermon to 'change your thinking' (Mark 6:12). Later we shall be able to observe how this happens precisely at the moment when the cosmic rhythm—then on the second degree of the second octave—again enters the sign of the Ram.

To the motif of 'crying in the wilderness', the loneliness of the 'heavenly wilderness', to the motif of the sermon to change your thinking, is then added that of the baptism by water for those who repent, who change their [habits of] thinking, for that is the prerequisite. This motive of preaching linked with the zodiacal sign of the Goat; that of the baptism by water links with the sign of the Waterman. Rudolf Steiner has indicated how with this opportunity those who were baptized were immersed into the water of the Jordan in such a way that their etheric body was released or loosened. They already experienced

the life-panorama, the review of the earthly life lying behind them in a comparable way to the many experiences of sudden disaster, or cases of near-death by drowning, falls in the mountains, and so on. People understood their former life with everything that it contained as if it were an account of debts, a failure in relation to the divine. Recognition of their sins brought them to confession. With this event the 'water of the Jordan' appeared, on the one side present in all physical reality, and on the other side as a picture for the 'water of the etheric'. For the etheric element, earthly water is a symbol and reflection. And this etheric is seen again in the heavenly picture, in the sign of the Waterman.

To this activity of John out of the etheric element of the cosmos, there arrives in addition with Christ the activity out of the 'I'. We can also speak of the 'forces of Elijah', he who received and distributed the cosmic life-ether as heavenly provisions, a bread of life. To the sheer heavenly-etheric of the sign of the Waterman, there belongs what Christ adds as a solar 'I'-power, the sign of the Fishes. In his lecture-cycle *Excursus on the Gospel According to St Mark* (GA 124. Lecture 4, Berlin, 16 Jan. 1911), Rudolf Steiner describes how John had received the 'Waterman initiation'. He indicates that He who comes after him would receive the initiation of the Fishes. One can find this indication about the sign of the Fishes in Mark. John the Baptist speaks of how after him comes one mightier, 'the latchet of whose shoes' he is 'not worthy to stoop down and unloose' (Mark 1:7).

John recognizes he doesn't reach to the feet of Christ—in the zodiac, the feet belong to the 'Fishes'—that he is not worthy to stoop to the feet of Christ. With these feet to stand on, in the sign of the Fishes—allocated in the 'twelve senses' to the sense of touch—the human being touches the Earth. Coming from the kingdom of the heavenly hierarchies, Christ is the One who is strong enough to come into contact with the Earth, really to unite in a human incarnation with the Earth and the forces of the Earth. Christ, the God, carries precisely the possibility of becoming a total human being out of the 'I'.

John is a human being, but in his being he is completely turned to the heavenly element. Something similar is conveyed in the pictures of the deeply meaningful Old-Testament myth of Abel, the 'heavenly brother' of the earthly Cain. Abel, unlike Cain, is not strong enough to master the earthly forces. Consequently, overcome on Earth by his earthly brother, he turns to the heavenly and divine as his element. Christ as God lives in the earthly sphere; John as a human being lives in the divine sphere.

Where upper and lower, heavenly and earthly meet, in the zodiacal sign of the Fishes, both the Baptist and Christ have to find each other. John is the great being of humanity who stands so close to the divine that he can recognize the Person standing before him by the Jordan as the chosen bearer of Christ—recognizing Christ, as it were, raising Himself out of the Baptism, beholding the descent of the Christ. And the same being in which this unbelievable, surpassing initiated great one refers to himself, speaks the humble words of unloosing the latchet of shoes, that he, of no value, can only stoop to the feet of the Other. He speaks the words which we also feel can reveal that which passes over from the sign of the Waterman to that of the Fishes.

A similar significant relationship lies also in the following verse (v. 8), where John's baptism with water is placed facing Christ's baptism with the spirit, the baptism with the Holy Spirit—Matthew and Luke have, 'with the Holy Spirit and with fire'. This placing opposite each other can be viewed in the zodiac, too, by looking at the generally significant relationship of sign and counter-sign. The counter-sign of the Waterman is the Lion. We shall see how the Lion as the 'house', the esoteric sign of the Sun, unlike the other zodiac signs is not given its externally arranged section in the narration of Mark's Gospel. It has to be experienced in a more inner manner, standing in and over the others. Such a passage, where out of the words of Mark's Gospel we are able to recognize the 'cosmic Lion', is the saying concerning the baptism in the spirit, the baptism of fire and of blood by Christ. It is placed facing and replacing John's baptism of water and of the ether.

In the blood the 'I' is revealed, which Christ now brings afresh into the process of becoming human and into human initiation. Water is thereby changed into blood, or if we look at the pictorial language of the constellation carrying John 2 (the marriage in Cana), indicated indeed in Mark 1:8—the water of the etheric human being into the wine of the 'I', of the 'I'-borne earthly human being. Where the physical is changed out of the 'I' right into the blood, the 'Spirit-man' [in Steiner's terminology], or *atman* [in Indian terminology], is revealed. This is aligned to the Lion, whereas the Waterman is the sign of the sheer astral connection to the etheric. In this way, rising in a kind of 'circle of fifths', we can find the individual supersensory human members in the heavenly zodiac (see above, p. 33f.).

All ancient initiations had essentially to do with that which was experienced between the astral and the etheric—it was called the revelation of the 'maternal' principle—whereas the paternal-principle, that which lies between the 'I' and the physical of the human being, comes anew in Christ. The whole John 2 concerning the marriage in Cana illuminates this significant motif in the evolution of mankind.

In researching the gospels, it becomes increasingly apparent how specific heavenly signs are aligned in many ways to specific stereotype words and phrases in the gospels. In this sense there belongs to the sign of the Waterman the words of John, 'I baptize you with water', to the Lion the words of Christ's baptism of the spirit, the baptism with 'the Holy Spirit and of fire', through which in the change of the physical (right into the blood) the seed of 'Spirit-man' is sown.

In a similar manner as the words of the baptism by water align to the Waterman, and to the Lion those of the baptism by fire and of the spirit, we can align to the Goat the other words attributed to John—'change your thinking'. If we then seek for the saying to the counter-sign of the Goat as a sign of a turning point, in the upper, bright part of the zodiac which we would have thought written in that sign of a turning point, the Crab, then we would not find the actual words in Mark—where its meaning is really to be found everywhere—but in

John 3:30: 'He must increase but I must decrease.' Not only in these words is a Mystery expressed between John and Christ, but also one between the 'two Johns', the Baptist and the disciple.

The days grow shorter from the summer solstice onwards, which up to then grew ever longer. We feel how from now on again the winter solstice, the Mystery of Christmas, grows in a counter direction. So stands John the Baptist as the last great pre-Christian initiate at that point where earthly evolution has unfolded mostly towards the Sun-side, the day-side of consciousness. In the descent of Christ, the Earth received into itself the seed through which it can evolve again towards the spiritual, towards 'becoming a spiritual Sun' (cf. the poem '*Daß auch sie einst Sonne werde*' [That it (the Earth) will one day become a Sun] by Christian Morgenstern in *Wir fanden eine Pfad*, München: Piper 1920/ Basel: Zbinden 2014).

In the decaying and dying of the Earth the spiritual [planet] can now grow again. John the Baptist knew the meaning of this world-turning-point. He pointed to the great announcer and preparer of the way of the future Christ-Earth in this meaning (*Sinn*), and the 'change of meaning, of thinking' (*Sinnesänderung*) necessary for human beings. And John the disciple is then the one who, like the other John on the decrease, is then in this way bound with the increase of the Earth and humanity towards the spirit, to the one who carries in himself as a living being Christ and the Christ-future of the Earth and of humanity. John the Baptist's being, still bound to the past of humanity, offers itself, as it were, into the becoming of the Christ-future—and to him who carries the becoming of this Christ-future in the first instance, the disciple John.

The Christ-Sun-Sign of the Fishes:

The Baptism in the Jordan and the Calling of the first Disciples (Mark 1:9–20)

In the far past of earthly becoming, when the Earth and the Sun separated, the Sun stood in the sign of the Fishes, in the same sign in which today again the first day of spring occurs. In this sign, then, there lives the memory of the one-time primordial harmony of earthly existence and solar existence. In the same sign, in which at one time with the splitting-off of the Sun, the solar-being Christ *left* the earthly scene, He re-joined Himself anew to the Earth. This connection—or the beginning of this connection—took place in the Baptism in the Jordan. It stands in the 'cosmic rhythm' of Mark's Gospel in the Sun-sign of the Fishes. The same sign was again reached in the 'Transfiguration', when a higher stage of this harmony of Christ's solar being with the Earth was realized. Not without meaning and inner connection we find in both places (Mark 1:11, 9:7) the words of the Son of the Sun: 'You are (or 'that is') my beloved Son …' (cf. this cosmic context of the Fishes, p. 32 above).

The Fishes is where the transition takes place from the lower dark to the upper bright part of the zodiac—and likewise in the Scales the transition from the bright to the dark part. The Fishes is the sign in which also in the earthly events the light is kindled in the darkness. Heavenly being, from which everything earthly originates in the first place, links itself again with earthly being.

In this sign of the meeting of the upper with the lower, the heavenly with the earthly, in the sign of the Fishes by the Jordan, two beings meet. These two are the God, Who takes on earthly existence, Who descends into the earthly element, and the human being who actually cannot carry the earthly element—consequently the saying about 'loosing the latchet' of the shoes—who in his consciousness actually remains in the heavenly, divine world. There he finds his living element, and out of this life in the divine—we recall the story of Enoch

in the Old Testament—he finds the possibility to meet the Christ, or rather him who now receives the cosmic Christ into himself. As closely as possible, right into external appearance, the two have to meet at the Jordan. The God who becomes human, and the human being who inwardly is still so close to the divine, stood side by side.

We can divine a relationship of both personalities, or beings, rooted in the primordial beginnings. The narration in Luke's Gospel (Luke 1:41) expresses how, with the meeting of both mothers, the relationship between the Jesus-being and the John-being was revealed. In his paintings of the meeting of the mothers, Raphael has meaningfully and clearly pictured the Jordan-baptism in the background. Already in the study of the beginning of the chapter, it was seen how the words about a garment of camel hair, the food of locusts[14] and wild honey are to be understood spiritually. The picture of the rude ascetic that has so often been painted does not correspond to the reality. Not in the picture of the raw, filthy ascetic are we to imagine John the Baptist, but in a fine, transparent spirituality and a similarity to Christ.

Out of this whole relationship of John the Baptist and Jesus of Nazareth, the bearer of Christ, anchored in the depths of the primordial history of the Earth revealed in the Jordan-Baptism, it will be understood how that event was not something external, moving him personally no more deeply. On the contrary, a significant sacrifice is expressed in this Baptism. The one being in fact completely sacrificed himself into the other. The being of the last and greatest of the pre-Christian initiates offered himself to the one greater coming after him, who himself was to be the bearer of the cosmic Christ Himself.

In the Mystery of such a sacrifice, the transition of highest strength, the highest fullness of being into earthly history has always taken place. He who hitherto was the greatest, offers his being in order that another can now be the greater. And the event that took place in the Baptism is something unique in world-history, for not only a new initiate arose out of the waters of the Jordan but a being of the cosmic hierarchies, the cosmic Christ Himself, had united Himself to the

earthly vessel of a man who had sacrificed his human 'I' to the divine. And the sacrifice of John-Baptist took part directly in this sacrifice of Christ-Jesus; the one sacrifice united with the other, flowed over into the other. The intimate sharing that John-Baptist's being hitherto experienced with the personality of Jesus of Nazareth, is also expressed in this sacrifice, in this crossing over. The Elijah-angel of the Baptist—significantly indicated in Luke 1:17 and Mark 1:2—is received in this sacrifice, as it were, into Christ's being. He becomes, as it were, the lowest rung of the hierarchical heavenly ladder that at the Jordan sinks down into the human vessel of Jesus of Nazareth, abandoned by its human 'I'. John 1:51 contains a clear allusion to this secret.

With Emil Bock (*Studies in the Gospels*), we can imagine that the picture of the descent of the dove connected with the event of the Baptism also contains in this sense a Mystery of the sacrifice of John's being. Dove is 'Jonah' in Hebrew, containing a clear echo of the name John [Ioannes]. At the Jordan the important offering of himself and dying into [the Other] begins, so important for the whole event of the gospel; we find in Luke 7 a certain climax. The deed of Herod only concluded what was already predisposed.

The fact that something of the being of John Baptist had sacrificed itself into Christ is also expressed in Mark's Gospel. John's sermon, delivered in the sign of the Ram, 'change your thinking', after the Baptism is now delivered by Christ (1:15). Likewise later in the further effects of John's sacrifice, the same words form the content of the disciples' preaching (6:12).

In order to apprehend the comprehensive zodiac signs, we have always to look at the opposite sign (the diagram in this book clearly shows the arrangement). In this sense, the Crab belongs to the Goat, the Lion to the Waterman, and the Virgin to the Fishes. In both Feedings—as indicated above in the Introduction—we meet both signs as 'loaves and fishes' in a clear and eloquent manner. They form in the gospel the great 'communion constellation'—in the Last Supper of Christ (Mark 14), itself the consummate, central constellation. This is

not merely something cultic but the sacrifice of divine love and divine being into the evolution of the Earth. Here the sign of the Virgin signifies more the etheric; that of the Fishes signifies more the 'I'-side of the constellation meant here.

In the star-sign of the Virgin—which we know as the 'Virgin with the sheaf', Spica (see above, p. 42f.)—people felt the bearer of the bread of life, the cosmic provisions for the way, or nourishment of the Grail. In the early pre-Christian Mysteries the cosmic life-ether was received and experienced. Through Christ uniting with the 'I' and received into the 'I', this now springs as the new source of life *from within* the human being (cf. John 5:26, 7:38, 10:18, etc.). Such a revelation of the etheric forces of the cosmos also took place in the Baptism. It united there with the entrance of the Christ-Sun-'I' in the sign of the Fishes (note the sounds in the Greek *ιχθύς*, 'the fish'). On a higher level the same process is linked with the same sign in the Transfiguration (Mark 9).

The mutual relationship of both, initially revealed in the Jordan-Baptism in the signs of the Virgin and the Fishes, is clear in a special way through a glance at the arrangement of the zodiac signs that allow an overview of the series of individual human members. In the Introduction above, p. 33f., we discussed a comparison with the 'circle of fifths' of the zodiac signs. In this arrangement the sign of the Virgin is linked with the etheric part of the human being, the etheric body, or life-body; to the sign of the Fishes is linked that member known in Indian theosophy as *buddhi*, in Steiner's anthroposophy as *Life-spirit* (the etheric body transformed by the 'I'). The constellation Fishes-Virgin directly reveals the relationship of the etheric body and Life-spirit—as the Christened etheric body, rayed through by the power of Christ's 'I-am'. And where this constellation shines in the cosmic rhythm of Mark's Gospel it reveals to us deep secrets of the Jordan-Baptism, the Feedings, the Last Supper, the Transfiguration and the Resurrection.

We can also call the constellation of the Fishes and the Virgin that of the Holy Grail. The Christian Mysteries of the Grail in pre-Christian

times are prefigured in the Egyptian Mysteries of Isis. Like the radiantly bright star Sirius on the 'Sacred Mount' of the heavens, the star Spica in the Virgin was also a sacred Isis-star. The word Spica means 'sheaf, bread of life' ['ear of wheat, barley']. People experienced in it—and reverenced in it, too, for the direct experience was gradually no longer to be had—the nourishing, enlivening, healing power of the cosmic life-ether, the cosmic power of love, the power of the Tree of Life and the cosmic Tree of Stars whose bearer for the Egyptians was Isis. She was the heavenly Virgin and Mother, the bearer of stellar wisdom. This power of the Tree of Life and the cosmic life-ether gradually becoming lost was renewed through Christ. In the Jordan-Baptism the life-ether, retained when the human being was expelled from Paradise in cosmic heights, was linked again with the Earth. The biblical story of the withdrawal of the fruit of the Tree of Life contains an intimation. With regard to a removal of the 'I' and a suppressing of the 'I', a receiving in the early Mysteries of the influence of the cosmic life-ether, its present renewal through Christ takes place out of the power of the 'I', the Christ-Sun-'I' power in the sign of the Fishes, now uniting with the powers of the Virgin.

This power of Christ also penetrates the lower human being, the dark will-nature susceptible to the forces of evil. In the zodiac these correspond to this 'lower human being', the five lower dark signs from Scorpion down to the Fishes. The latter indeed appears on the human form as the feet. Consequently, Christian initiation that illuminates and purifies, comprehends the lower, dark nature of the human being, and begins significantly with the Washing of the Feet, in the sign of the Fishes. The human form reveals this connection to the Virgin, as the bearer of the subconscious, with the Fishes, the innocent bearer of a deepest subconscious, now linking with the solar 'I'-power of Christ.

In one place, for many people remaining obscure, in his lectures on *John's Gospel in Relation to the other Gospels* (Lecture 10. Cassel. 4 July 1909. GA 112), Rudolf Steiner speaks how the event of the Jordan-Baptism signified something important for the mother of Christ. There

descended on the later mother the maidenly forces of the cosmic Virgin—we recall the child-like, maidenly mother of the child narrated in Luke's Gospel who died young (on the question of the two Jesus children, see R. Steiner *The Spiritual Guidance of Mankind*. GA 15; and the author's *Zarathustra*. Germ. ed. pp. 40-50.[15] This mother [the one who lived on] is actually only the foster-mother [of the Luke-child]. In the constellation standing over the Jordan-Baptism, in the script of the zodiac, the governing context of the Christ-sign of the Fishes with that of the Virgin can be directly seen. Cosmic maidenly forces of the life-ether united at the Jordan with the 'I'-power of the Christ-Sun in the sign of the Fishes. The offering of himself, of the Elijah-John power, is intimately involved in the event. And John himself saw the Mystery of the event in the picture of the hovering dove, which also in the Mystery of the Grail accompanied the event of the Last Supper, the sacrifice of cosmic love into the Earth.

Always when this great Last-Supper constellation (♓–♍) is reached—and from there with its other constellation (♊–♐), forming with it the cross, the etheric Christ-cross, or cross of the Son, similar things are involved. One can say, when we stand in the middle of this Christ-cross—we see in the gospel that the whole 'unity-of-twelve' sacred, heavenly signs is always evident. The unity of twelve zodiac signs always meets us in the twelve disciples, or in other ways. With the Jordan-Baptism, or rather in the section of Mark's Gospel standing in the sign of the Fishes, we find this indication in the words: 'And he was in the desert [loneliness] ... and was with the wild beasts'. In loneliness, again, is to be seen not only as the earthly 'desert', but the loneliness of soul and spirit (in which Buddha after finding enlightenment also remained awhile). And with the 'beasts' to imagine not only the earthly side, in which certainly cosmic astrality is revealed, but rather the 'heavenly wilderness', the 'heavenly beasts' or constellations of the zodiac. The real beings of the zodiacal constellations are real cosmic beings, the heavenly hierarchies, who at the Jordan incline to Christ as in a new

tremendous revelation of the heavenly ladder (John 1:51): 'and the angels ministered unto him' (Mark 1:13).

The different Mystery of the twelve disciples linked with this constellation comes into this section of Mark's Gospel. Following on the Jordan-Baptism, in the sign of the Fishes, the call of the first disciples is narrated. In this calling of the first disciples the preparation of their initiation already begins to form a main theme of Mark's Gospel. In this whole initiation of the disciples, which increasingly becomes the initiation of *one* of them, the actual disciple of Christ, there lives the sacrifice of Elijah-John. Christ does not keep this for Himself, but shares it with the group of disciples. This group is from the beginning meant to carry the great work for which Christ united Himself with the Earth and humanity. The twelve heavenly powers, through which the Sun-Being Christ moves in revealing Himself, is reflected on the Earth in the personalities of the twelve disciples.

John's baptism with water belongs to the sign of the Waterman; the initiation of Christ's disciples belongs to the sign of the Fishes (R. Steiner. *Excursus*. GA 124). Consequently, already over the calling of the first disciples there stands the sign of the Fishes. This calling is narrated in the section with the Jordan-Baptism, arranged in the cosmic rhythm of Mark's Gospel in the sign of the Fishes. This spiritual connection of the calling of the disciples to the zodiac sign of the Fishes is expressed in Mark's Gospel in the picture of fishermen, fishing boats and fishing nets (Mark 1:16-20). More clearly than elsewhere at this point, Mark's Gospel does not narrate stories but Imaginations. John's Gospel, in this case as in some others—though not in all—stands close to the external historical facts (see above, p. 21f.). When it tells of the calling of the first disciples (John 1:35-51), there is nothing about fishermen and fishing boats. The narration of John's Gospel wakens much more the clear and historically credible impression that Christ Jesus gained His first disciples—probably most of them—from the followers of an earlier initiation. Certainly, he who in the initiation became the disciple John cannot have been a mere fisherman. He must have

belonged to the Pharisees or Essenes, a temple priest deeply initiated in the early Mysteries.

In the gospel itself John the disciple appears, as the following discussion will make even clearer, in many ways in the picture of the *rich man*, and we recall the connection of the 'priest-king John' [or 'Prester John'] and the 'rich fisherman' of the Grail legends. Clearly, in the narration of John's Gospel, Christ speaks a language of initiation, a Mystery-language with individuals of the first calling. In conversation with Nathanael—not one of the Twelve—He mentions the symbol of the fig tree, significant for the Buddha-initiation. Steiner, too, emphasizes this relationship in the lecture-cycle on John's Gospel. The later discussion will show when in Mark 11 the fig tree appears again, a similar indication to the clairvoyant forces is meant. Other details of the conversation with Nathanael point to connections to the Mysteries.

Moreover, in the sequence of the calling of the first disciples, the naming of the disciples appears inconsistent. In Mark's Gospel the first called, alongside Andrew, is Simon Peter; in John's Gospel the unnamed—he is never given a name—behind which we can presume the later John. In John's Gospel, Peter only comes in the third place; Philip comes as fourth, who has a role to play in the story of the Feeding. James and John, the 'sons of Zebedee', are mentioned in Mark's Gospel in the third and fourth place. Whoever wants to take the gospel at any cost externally and literally, sees himself placed before insoluble contradictions. The contradictions disappear when we observe the different spiritual viewpoint of the individual evangelists.

The disciple first seen by the spiritual vision of Christ, whom, as it were, he met first spiritually, does not have to be the one who is first met in the flesh. For the spiritual viewpoint of John's Gospel—with all the humble reticence in naming his name—the calling of the disciple John has to stand as the first in the spiritual, probably also in actual, first place. With Mark, on the other hand, we find here a different picture. Behind Peter and Andrew, who as the pillars and carriers of the visible church are first to be mentioned (Peter with the key is associ-

ated with the Roman, or Western Church; Andrew with that of the Greek, or Eastern Church), stand James and John as the carriers of the invisible Church.

We shall not take the calling of the first disciples, as narrated in Mark 1, as merely an outer historical account. Least of all shall we take the narration of fishermen, fishing nets and fishing boats as outer facts but see in them a picture for the spiritual facts, that the initiation of Christ to which that disciples is called, is something new. No longer like the initiation of the Baptist John, in the sign of the Waterman, but—replacing this in the progress of development—it stands in the sign of the Fishes. In this sign the earthly and the heavenly meet in the new meaning realized in Christ. Christ calls His disciples to this great, new work of humanity, which as aim and content is the re-working of everything earthly. The work of humanity stands in the sign of the Fishes, as understood here. All this is expressed in the language of Mark's Gospel in the words in which Christ speaks to those first called: 'Follow me, and I will make you fishers of men.' Here too, there lies in the spiritual meaning meant here, an indication of the zodiac sign of the Fishes.

The Ram: Entering the Forces of the Earth; Entry of Christ into His Earthly Ministry

(Mark 1:21-39)

In reviewing the path so far covered of the cosmic rhythm of Mark's Gospel, we found at the beginning in the mountain Goat the motif of the soul-loneliness of John the Baptist, the heavenly nature and loneliness, the call to change habits of thinking, linking on to the motif of baptism by water in the Waterman as the other Baptist motif. In the descent of Christ in the Jordan-Baptism and the ensuing call of the first disciples, the 'fisherman' is revealed in the transition within the Christ-Sun sign of the Fishes.

The signs of the Goat and the Waterman belong to the completely nocturnally dark signs; the sign of the Fishes likewise still belongs to the night-side of the zodiac. It looks towards those that announce the daylight. Beginning still in the dark, it already leads into the light (see the Figure, p. 364). In the course of the day, it corresponds to the light hour before sunrise. We feel ourselves not quite on the earthly plane; the heavenly [experience] of the night seeks the transition into the earthly experience of the daylight. In the circle of keys, F-major corresponds. Through its key signature of one flat it is allocated to the 'lower keys', but it already carries an element of lighting up in itself.

Everything is not yet actually in the physical sphere, but more in the etheric. In the three crosses, in which the twelve signs of the zodiac can be arranged (see above, p. 34f.), the Fishes and the Virgin both belong to the etheric cross. They belong to the etheric as the Waterman does the astral (knowledge of sin and soul-illumination in the baptism by water), and with the Goat in the physical cross. The Baptist John is but little bound to the physical earth; his being is in the nocturnally darkest of the physical signs of the zodiac.

With the sign of the Ram we enter again into the physical element. It is the sign of the earthly activity in the full light of day, that in the course of the year the first day of spring[16] stands and of Eastertide—we recall the 'Easter lamb'. In the course of the day it corresponds to the sunrise, in music to the 'Let there be light' of the key C-major [Haydn, *The Creation*]. We could describe the Fishes, as it were, as the becoming awake in the early light, in the first shimmer of daylight; the Ram is the real awakening. In the Fishes we become conscious, as it were, of our feet and of our contact with the Earth that [was involved in] creating them; in the Ram, with our head upright we tread the Earth with these feet. The sign of the Ram can be viewed, so that in it can be found the placing of the feet on the ground of the Earth. In this sign Christ appears in the cosmic rhythm of the gospel in the sphere of earthly activity (Mark 1:21ff.).

On the human form, the Ram points to the head raised on high, the forehead turned to the stars, the force of bringing ourselves into the upright dimension. The counter-sign of the Scales is the balance in the hips. In the Ram and the Scales the human form finds its orientation in space, its stance of balance in the earthly sphere. The Christ-statue in the Goetheanum, Dornach, helps us recognize in the upright figure of the Representative of Man the meaning of both these signs in a sublime manner.

From here light is cast on the narration of the healing of those 'possessed', the demoniacs (Mark 1:23 onwards). They form in the rhythm of Mark's Gospel a main motif of the Ram. Who are these demoniacs? They appear as sick, not able to place their soul and spirit properly in the physical body. Into their un-illumined soul, their active astrality, not rightly carried by the 'I', a spiritual world rushes, overwhelming them. Demonic beings inhabiting the astral regions find a bond with the un-illumined soul of each sick person, overpowering them. The not-rightly-incarnated spirit and soul of the sick person, now through Christ, the Representative of Humanity, the ideal of a God-willed incarnation, is brought to a right, normal earthly incarnation in which the demonic being no longer has a place. That is the nature of a healing of a possessed person. And because the motif of this placing into the forces of the earth belongs to the Ram, the healings of those possessed stand in the sign of the Ram.

With this sign of the Ram the counter-sign sounds in sympathy, especially where the viewpoint of the balance of soul stands in the foreground. For reasons that are given in the further course of these studies, the healing of the *one* possessed person [the demoniac 'Legion'] who does not appear in a section devoted primarily to the Ram (see Mark 5), stands significantly in the counter-sign of the Scales.

The healing of the possessed is especially impressively narrated precisely in the cosmic gospel of Mark—the way Christ, not known to the people, is recognized by the demons and addressed by them (cf. Luke 4: 41, one of the remarkable places where in the mouth of a non-human being the name Christ is used that otherwise appears seldom in the gospel). They know of a spiritual world lost to human beings, which in Christ comes down to humanity. Things have progressed so far with humanity that precisely in the cases of visibly grotesque possession and strange pathological conditions a spiritual world is revealed, as its sublime representative, as it were, stands before us, Christ Himself, whose lowest progeny and dregs are these demons, who in the un-illumined soul-element have found a hold in the unstable astrality of these sick people. That which in Christ is the highest purity and sublimity is in them grotesque distortion. Out of the depths of the spirit, out of the Mysteries of resurrection Christ relates to the death and the grave.

With onerous possession, as in Mark 5, we see how the demoniac in gruesome manner seeks a place to live amongst the graves. In Christ the highest cosmic love is revealed. With the naked man running around (cf. Luke 8:27) there is revealed an impure sexual life drawn down into the filth (see Hans Blüher, *Die Aristie des Jesus von Nazareth*, p. 107, which otherwise is far removed from the view of the gospels followed here). But the sublime Archetype—which is the noble motif belonging to Mark's Gospel—is recognizably addressed by the demonic caricature. And in Christ lies the power to rectify what is caricatured in the one possessed. What is incarnated as incorrect and incomplete is led through Christ into rectified, complete incarnation. This incarnation, this proper entry into the earthly forces, takes place in the sign of the Ram.

From Mark 1:32 onwards, the healing of the sick joins the healing of the one possessed, the demoniac, yet this is aligned to the zodiac sign of the Bull, as is shown in the next section. Both motifs progress together, as it were, in vv. 32–9, until in v. 42 the decisive transition to the Bull takes place. Before that, however, in vv. 29–31, a story is told which at first seems to select a simple healing. One would accordingly expect that it would be told in the section belonging to the sign of the Bull. The classification of this story, it could initially be thought, appears to contradict the cosmic rhythm of Mark's Gospel. But this rhythm is in reality carried out with complete clarity and precision. In this context, the construction of Mark's Gospel contains nothing superfluous, nothing to contradict the cosmic rhythm, and in some cases, as in this one, offers a vista into the cosmic rhythm bringing decisive viewpoints to illuminate the gospel.

In progressing through the gospel narrative, it becomes confirmed how at least from Mark 3 onwards, actually everything has something to do with the initiation of the disciples, who ultimately leads to the *one* disciple. The question could arise whether this could not already be the case with the first healing stories. Not as though the fact that Christ Jesus completely achieved the healing of the physically sick should be doubted. No occasion for such a doubt exists for those who only have a distant idea of the nature of spiritual healing. Another question is whether specific individual healings in the gospels are related only as a physical event, or whether what is narrated is at the same time a picture for something different existing in the spirit region—for example, the healing of a deaf-mute is the picture for an initiation event of

the disciples taking place for the awakening of the spiritual word for a 'release of the spiritually tongue-tied' (to use an expression in Emil Bock's *Studies*) (see Intro. p. 20).

The question whether perhaps already the first healings of all—the leper in Chapter 1, the paralytic in Chapter 2, the person with the withered hand in Chapter 3—relate to the disciples' initiation-experiences, or as preparation for these experiences, has here to remain open. But in the case with Simon Peter's mother-in-law (Mark 1:29-31) this viewpoint arises. Matthew (8:14, 15) and Luke (4:38-39) include this event. Of a mother-in-law of Peter, or the fact of his marriage, nothing else is known. Taken as a physical reality, we would feel this fact to be improbable. In the gospels, the 'mother' frequently appears as the representative in the human soul of a revealed spiritual force, the 'atavistic' soul-forces (cf. John 2: 4, the role of the 'mother' at the marriage in Cana, and Mark 10: 35-40 the story of the sons of Zebedee, which we shall discuss later, which in Matt. 10: 35-40 is so narrated that the mother—missing in Mark—is uniquely involved in the event.) Peter was a person still strongly connected with atavistic, 'maternal' forces of an earlier spirituality. With him, however, it is not something normal, but something which disturbs his physical balance, something motherly manifesting in the direction of the luciferic fever-forces. In this sense, the expression 'mother-in-law' is used. It is significant, how with Mark this case directly following the healing of the man possessed, is narrated still with those which belong to this determining sign of the Ram (for in what follows we still meet the possessed; the transition to the pure healing of the sick takes place first in v. 40). In a discrete picture the writer of the gospel expresses how with the inner nature even of Peter, destined to be the 'rock of the Church', something wasn't quite right from the beginning, how Christ has to help even him, similar to the possessed, to a right incarnation, to a right placing himself into the forces of the Earth. Right at the beginning of the narration of the gospels, this story allows us to feel the tragedy of Peter and his easily ignited fever-nature, which later flares up again on all sorts of occasions. The whole explanation of the 'healing of Peter's mother-in-law' is already given by Emil Bock in his *Studies*. Here the attempt was to show how it is confirmed through looking at the zodiac signs and the whole inner rhythm of the gospel narration.

The Bull, the Revelation of the Living Element and the Healing Power of the Divine Word

(Mark 1:40–3:12)

From the sign of the Ram, we enter that of the Bull in the course of the year. After the victory of the light on the first day of spring, in Eastertide, the time of the first blossoms, there follows in May the highest fullness of blooms, the time of lush sprouting and budding when the whole love-life of nature stands at its height. The Bull is allocated on the human form to the larynx, containing the revelation of the power of speech, of the word. In the course of the year the Bull corresponds to the time when in the sprouting fullness of natural life, above all the life-awakening might of the divine creative word is revealed.

In the gospel, too, the Bull is the *sign of the word*, the sign in which the living might of the divine Word is revealed in Christ. To illness Christ brought healing through the living might of the 'I'-carrying word, awakening the 'I'-power in the other. For this reason above all we find the healing of the sick in the section in Mark's Gospel standing under the sign of the Bull. Moreover, in close relationship to these stories of healing there also stands that section of the gospel in which the living word of Christ confronts the dead statutes of the scribes and Pharisees.

We already recognized how the living word of Christ and his healing power is revealed in the Bull, and the dead statutes of Pharisaism is related to the power of death in the Scorpion, which we met in the Introduction (see p. 29) as the counter-sign of the Bull. The clash of the creative, enlivening and healing might of the Bull with the might of death of the Scorpion, in which also the cause of the illness lies, all this is clearly recognizable in the section in the gospel standing in the sign of the Bull. In the Scorpion, so we can also say, is revealed the essence

and cause of the *illness*, in the Bull the essence of *healing*. In the rhythm of the year the two signs correspond. The time of sprouting natural life in the Bull, the month of May, is faced by the time of dying natural life in the Scorpion, in November. In the human organism both signs are so arranged to each other that the forces of speech of the larynx oppose the forces of propagation in the sexual organs. The physiological connection of both areas of forces was already pointed out in the Introduction (p. 29).

In the primordial grounds of existence the secret of creative life and creative love are deeply connected with that of death. In that region from which today because of the Fall of man the forces of death are at work, was once the origin of the Sun-life, as spiritual science teaches. The Scorpion then was still a Sun-Eagle. The meaning of the Johannine, the Christian initiation, is to penetrate with Sun-life again the power of death which has taken over this Sun-sign, and changes the Scorpion again into the Sun-Eagle. As the first and only disciple, John has accomplished this. Consequently, the Eagle belongs to him as evangelist—when according to earlier Church tradition we arrange the four apocalyptic beasts to the four evangelists. In the whole following study, it will be shown how in the constellation (♉–♏) always something decisive for the Johannine initiation, how the creative word lost through the effect of humanity's Fall is regained through John.

The constellation (the Fishes–Virgin) lies in the etheric element; the constellation of the Ram and the Scales in the physical, the earthly cross. We find that of the Bull and the Scorpion in the soul-element, in the astral [cross]. The essence of illness and its healing, its connection with the soul-astral element of the human being is consequently also illumined from the viewpoint of the zodiac (cf. R. Steiner, *Esoteric/ Occult Science*). In Christ there are again the pure life-awakening forces of the Sun and of Love. Through them is overcome what works as a cause of illness and death in man. Through this there appears the enlivening force of the word, of the Bull with

Christ at the same time as the *healing force*. In the Bull, through the power of the divine Word, Christ also becomes the Lord over health and illness, life and death.

We find an understanding of the motif of *healing the sick* in the sections of Mark's Gospel standing under the sign of the Bull. In Mark 1, these healings of the sick are mentioned *besides* the healing of the possessed (Mark 1:32–39). The motifs of the Ram and of the Bull can be found, as it were, still side by side. Only in v. 40, where the 'healing of the man with leprosy' is narrated have we clearly entered into the sign of the Bull. The way the gospel expresses it '*as he spoke*', or in the AV/KJV, '*As soon as he had spoken*, immediately the leprosy departed from him and he was cleansed', brings in a clear and living form the *effective power of the word*. In a comparable manner we are pointed to the power of the word of the Bull when in the beginning of the chapter (Mark 2:2), immediately before the healing of the paralytic, we read 'and he preached the word to them'.

> With the Goat we find the word of changing one's thinking;
> with the Waterman that of the baptism by water;
> with the Fishes the word of the son of the Sun
> ('You are my beloved son…');
> with the Ram (more details later) the words of standing up and standing upright.
> With the Bull we find simply the word 'word' as the expression fashioned in the language of the gospel for the one motif governed by the heavenly sign.

In Mark 1 the healing of the man with leprosy is told, in Mark 2 the paralytic, in Mark 3 the healing of the man with the withered hand. And when we keep in view how the healings concern different members of the human being, how different areas of human nature are apprehended, it is obvious to ask, have these healings not perhaps also some significance for the life of initiation of the disciples? In the progress of these gospels studies, the more it becomes clear what significance this

viewpoint has for the whole of the gospel narration—especially that of Mark—the more the justification illuminates the question.

The external actuality of these healings need not be abandoned when it is pointed out that the gospel narration includes with it, or can include, that other viewpoint. Precisely for Mark's Gospel that other, the imaginative viewpoint increasingly shows itself as truly decisive. Take the healing of the paralytic; how the outer circumstances presented in the narration in John's Gospel, express them perhaps even more clearly than in Mark; in Chapter 5 this healing is narrated as the sick 38-year-old by the pool of Bethesda. Yet also with John this healing is more than the mere outer event. There it forms the third of Christ's seven miraculous 'signs':

- the change of water into wine at the marriage in Cana,
- the healing of the nobleman's son,
- the healing of the paralytic by the pool of Bethesda,
- the Feeding of the Five Thousand,
- the walking on the sea,
- the healing of the man born blind,
- the raising of Lazarus.

These miraculous signs can be inwardly aligned in a certain way to the seven sacraments of the church. The healing at Bethesda with its characteristic emphasis on physical sickness and the sickness of sin (John 5:14)—also of the corresponding context of the constellation ♉–♏—aligns to the Sacrament of Consultation (Confession) and what corresponds to it in the initiation-event of the disciples, or in the preparation for this event. Likewise the 'withered hand' of Mark 3 could point to how the effect of the Fall of man dries up the stream of living strength in humanity. The spiritual side of the hand shrivels up. This stream of strength has to be awakened through the strength of Christ right into the fingertips. Then the hand can again become the expression and the means of a living, spiritual activity. It could also be shown how this 'enlivening the hand' and its stream of living strength has to precede what then begins in Mark 3:13, as the actual

initiation-event of the disciples. Full power and authority is given into their hands.

The narration of the healing of the paralytic in Mark, moreover, strongly emphasizes the connection of the source of the illness with the power of sin: 'Son, your sins are forgiven' [Mark 2:5]. This saying leads to a first clash with the Pharisees and scribes. Here the scribes are mentioned for the first time, whose thoughts Christ sees through. With all these clashes—about eating with tax-collectors (v. 16ff), about fasting (v. 18ff.), and picking the ears of corn on the Sabbath (v. 23ff.)—something moves in the same direction. The living words of Christ face the dead statutes of the Pharisees and scribes. They can all be seen out of the region of ♉–♏. In the Bull is revealed the living word of Christ; out of the Scorpion the might of death is at work. The sayings given to Moses on Sinai belonged to the living divine revelation. They have been allowed to become dead human statutes, rigidly held by the Jews.

In the influence of the paternal forces of Yahweh [Is. 64:8, Jer. 31:9, Mal. 1:6], to whom the Hebrews felt they were connected, lay the fact that these statutes become rigid, that what was once life had to change into death, a one-time freedom into the necessity of laws. Where we today face death and outer necessity—including natural necessity—we are dealing with the 'forces of the Father'. In Christ is revealed that which has become lost through the effect of the Fall of man. This is the 'I', in whose power of the word, death is changed again into life, necessity again into freedom (John 8:51, 5:26ff.; 8:35f. etc.). What today is only an inkling of this secret of the 'I' and the new becoming it harbours for the greater part still lies in the future of development. In this new emergence from the strength of the 'I' the *transition from Father to Son* takes place. The tragedy of Jewry was, and is, that it remains with the Father-principle, not able to find the transition from Father to Son. With the issue of healing on the Sabbath (cf. Mark 2:23ff.) this is expressed at its most decisive and shocking.

What remains over of the experience of the forces of the Father—Emil Bock has written impressively on Solomon's Temple in the

journal *Die Christengemeinschaft*, Vol. 2, No. 6, 167-74—was really only the experience of death. Even the experience of the Mysteries of the high priest in the holy of holies of the Temple—which he entered but once a year—was none other than the experience of the darkness and loneliness of the grave and death (cf. 1 Kings 8:12, 'The Lord said he would dwell in the thick darkness'). In death the majesty of the Father was venerated. And the Sabbath, the day of Saturn, was the sacred day to experience the forces of the Father. So grand, so holy was reverence before the majesty of the Father and of death that even the sick were not allowed to be healed on this day. We are to recognize in all this not only a dark superstition, a dark hypocrisy and sanctimony of the Pharisees, but a certain greatness of religious viewpoints. And the tragedy can be felt how the Jews, as it were, remained stuck with this holiness of the day of Saturn. In Christ's earthly appearance they could not participate in the accomplished advance of the cosmic-hour from Saturday of the Father-forces and forces of death, to Sunday, to the forces of the Son, of life and resurrection.

[Always when we speak of the 'Sun-being' and 'Sun-life' of Christ, of 'Sun-existence' and the 'Sun's day', in contrast to 'Saturn's day', all today's one-sided astronomical notions are to be kept quite distinct. In astronomical ideas Sun-existence is simply earthly ideas transferred to the cosmos. Here the Sun and Sun-existence is meant in a spiritual sense, which includes the essence and secret of the living realm, just as the spiritual sense of 'Earth existence' includes the nature of the mineral realm and of death. In his book *Esoteric/ Occult Science*, Rudolf Steiner shows a spiritual view advancing from a death situation to the living situation. In the greater stages of the context of creation, our earthly existence is differentiated. In four stages of world-becoming—named Ancient Saturn, Ancient Sun, Ancient Moon and the Earth—are evolved the original seed and the original image of the dead mineral kingdom ('physical body'), of the living plant world ('etheric body'), of the conscious animal world ('astral body'), and finally of the self-conscious human realm (the 'I').]

In sanctifying the day of Saturn, we could also say, Jewry was initially correct. The tragedy consists that it did not see how the day of Saturn is now over, and the day of the Sun has dawned. In the Scorpion we feel the might that kept Jewry back to the forces of the day of Saturn, hindering the revelation of the Bull, bringing to its consciousness life-awakening and healing forces. And the power of death of the Scorpion governed the necessity of the law, the rigid adherence to the book of the law, hindering the Sun-experience of freedom. The Jews, held in the constraints of the consciousness-darkening influence of the Scorpion, remained with the Sabbath, with the day of Saturn, with Saturday; not knowing that it has now become Sunday.

The great confrontation between the Bull and the Scorpion, between the powers of life and of death stands in a certain sense in the middle point of Mark's Gospel, permeated by the Johannine initiation. It is a significant fact that when we search in the circle of fifths (in the way explained earlier, p. 33f.) in the zodiac, that is, progress from the first to the sixth, eleventh, fourth sign, and so on, and find therein the relationship to the human supersensory members. In the Bull, we find the *consciousness-soul*, which is determined not by the sensory impressions from without, but by those out of the inner being, out of the 'I', the 'I' in the receptive soul. This development of the consciousness-soul still standing at its beginning today belongs to the Johannine age, to the age of the Christ-future of humanity. Only to the degree that through the Johannine strength of the living word (♉) will the victory over the adverse forces of the death-sign (♏) be achieved and the soul find its true content. Finding this content from stage to stage of inner experience forms one of the most significant motifs of Mark's Gospel.

The Twins, the Sign of the Sacred Mount of Inspiration and Initiation

(Mark 3:13–19)

The transition from the Ram to the Bull happened gradually; for a while the two motifs progressed alongside each other. The point where the narration of Mark's Gospel enters the sign of the Twins is given in all exactness. It happens in 3:13, with the words: 'And he went up the mount ... and called the Twelve'. Some translations have: 'into a mountain' (AV/KJV), 'up on a mountainside' (NIV); but the Gk. *εις το ορος*, and the reconstructed Aramaic original (Torrey) have 'on *the* mountain' [observed in the versions by Darby 'up into the mountain'; Knox 'up on to the mountain-side'; 'up on the mountain' (RSV); 'up the mountain' (NRSV); 'up onto the mountain (NJB); 'up on the hillside' (Amplified Bible); 'up the hill' (Weymouth); 'up into the hill country' (REB)]. In the sign of the Twins we find in the gospel the Sacred Mount upon which Christ calls the twelve disciples around him. Here he gives them the first impulses of spiritual inspiration; he begins the work of initiation that penetrates the whole gospel narration.

In this book, *initiation* is the name given to that spiritual schooling through which the spiritual teacher—in the case of the disciples, Christ Jesus Himself—opens to the pupil the way to knowledge of the spiritual worlds and to work with their forces. (Further details on this and other expressions of Mystery-language are in Rudolf Steiner, *Christianity as Mystical Fact* [GA 8] and many of the later books and lecture-cycles.)

We find ourselves in this sign, as it were, at the high point, the culminating point of the zodiac; above all the others, this point is inwardly related to the *heights of the spirit*. This inner relationship of earthly mountain heights to the heights of the spirit, the impulse of spiritual inspiration and initiation was felt and experienced by the peoples

of the ancient Mysteries, the early Indians, Persians, Chaldeans and Hebrews—we recall the revelation on Sinai. The Psalms often speak of the sacred hills, as do the early Zarathustra documents—or their echo in the Avesta. And we find this holiness of the mountain heights again in the gospels, of the mount of the calling of the disciples, the great experiences of healing and of the Mount of Transfiguration.

In Mark 3, with the appointment of the Twelve marking the beginning of their initiation, it was shown how precisely this sign of the height of the Sacred Mount shines beautifully in the 'starry script', it is really to be seen in the outer starry sky. The Holy Mount of the gospel shines in the sky, in the radiant star-picture of Sirius-Orion, over which the series of bright stellar constellations of the upper zodiac arches in the mid-winter nights till towards spring. (From the viewpoint of the course of the Sun this 'upper' zodiac is in the summer sky—because the Sun moves through them; from the viewpoint of the sky at night the winter zodiac—because visible in the winter sky.) It was pointed out that towards spring, around the end of February, already in the early hours of the night, this aspect invites the gaze to the zenith, high over this 'Holy Mount in the heavens', culminating in the 'heavenly twins' Castor and Pollux. Experiencing this aspect as the 'starry script', one can recall the festive moment in the gospels when Christ on the 'Holy Mount' calls the Twelve around him at the beginning, or carries the initiation further. Already on the first occasion and even more clearly with later visits to the sign of the Twins, amongst the twelve disciples the two 'sons of Zebedee', James and John, in a special manner appear as the 'heavenly twins' of the gospel, the actual sublime impulse of initiation.

With the arrangement of twelve in Mark 3, which forms the point of departure for the initiation, the appearance of the two 'twins' James and John takes place in this way. They are named by Christ 'sons of thunder' (*Bnehargem, υἱοὶ βροντῆς*); through this they are distinguished from the others. At the same opportunity Simon received his name Peter, marking him as the 'rock of the Church'. As with the

first call of the disciples (Mark 1: 16ff.) the four disciples appear first, of whom two (Simon and Andrew) as the carriers or pillars of the visible church, the two others, James and John, who already through the name 'sons of thunder' aligned to the heavenly-cosmic element of the 'heavenly twins', stand as the pillars or carriers of the invisible church and esoteric Christianity. With the call of the disciples in Mark 1, at first Simon and Andrew are called, the bearers of the visible church, after them James and John, the bearers of the invisible church. In Mark 3, at the beginning of the disciples' initiation on the Sacred Mount, the listing names Peter first, Andrew in fourth place, with James and John between. This gives the picture with the two pillars of the invisible church, as it were, in the background, raised over the others of the visible church:

J. J.

P. A.

The same ordering is found in a significant way at the beginning of Mark 13, at the place—as the further course of this study will show—where lies the future secret of the invisible temple of the New Jerusalem raised above and behind the visible temple of old Jerusalem, doomed to destruction. Between the three places in Mark, Chapters 1, 3 and 13, an inner connection can be found. Everywhere Peter and Andrew as bearers of the visible church form, as it were, the earthly foreground, James and John the super-earthly background.

A secret of the super-physical, the cosmic-etheric is expressed in the names given to the sons of Zebedee as the 'heavenly twins', *Bnehargem* (Gk. *Boanerges*). And after having stood in the Ram in the physical, with the Bull in the astral, soul realm, we are now really in the Twins again in the 'cross of the etheric'. The constellation Fishes—Virgin forms the one axis of the etheric cross; the Twins with the counter-sign of the Archer the other axis. At the top of the cross stands the lofty sign of the Twins, the sign of the 'Sacred Mount'; below at the foot stands the death-sign of the Archer. It is the same sign in which with

the 'Transfiguration on the Mount' the death of Christ begins, which is completed on Golgotha. It lies in the nature of the Christian initiation—here beginning in the sign of the Twins—that in a significant way involves this secret of death, of the death of Christ, the Mystery of Golgotha. Seen from the zodiac, with the lofty sign of the Twins we always find the death-sign of the Archer is somehow also stressed. Already at the end of the section under the sign of the Twins, this can be recognized at the end of the listing the disciples (Mark 3:19), in the way the betrayal of Judas is mentioned as the direct precondition for the death of Christ.

With the constellation Fishes–Virgin we already see with this 'cross of the middle' how in a certain manner all twelve sacred heavenly signs shine at the same time. With the constellation Twins–Archer this is even more the case, at the most expressive where with the calling of the disciples standing under the sign of the Twins of Mark 3, significantly all twelve apostles are named. (In different sources the twelve disciples are allocated to the twelve zodiacal signs from various viewpoints in various ways. A decisive solution of this objectively authentic question has to date not yet been found.)

From the mountain-tops on Earth the view is extended, allowing an overview of the land that we could not have as long as we were closed in the narrow valley. The mountain heights of initiation, over which the heavenly Twins shine, opens up a further view of spiritual worlds and their connection with the earthly world. Yet it is not in order to extend the spiritual view that Christ is the Initiator, but with that which Christ now causes to stream over the disciples, connected to specific forces. Two of these forces, the power to heal illness and to banish demons, are particularly named in the gospel (Mark 3:15). This is no coincidence but exactly relates to what was narrated before in the signs of the Ram and the Bull. It allows us to gain a new viewpoint for what has been narrated, allowing us to become ever clearer how everything narrated in Mark's Gospel really has something to do with the initiation of the disciples.

What the disciples had experienced in the signs of the Ram and the Bull, what for them perhaps at the same time was also a picture and sign for specific healings and purifications that they experienced for themselves and in themselves on their own body and soul—the healings of the sick and exorcising of devils—that now itself became a force through which they are able to heal and purify others. An important viewpoint in explaining the gospels—also emphasized by Steiner—is that in the whole earthly ministry of Christ, above all with the healings of the sick and possessed (cf. Mark 9), the group of disciples actively participated. Some of the healings reported of Christ were effected through one of the disciples, according to Steiner, to the eye of the spiritual researcher. And appearing as the bearer of most intimate forces, the more the initiation of the disciples progressed, the pair, as the heavenly Twins, stand as the representatives of the cosmic-spiritual element in the group of disciples—until the initiation increasingly concentrated on one of the two, reaching fulfilment in the person of the *one*.

We enter into the 'heavenly Twins' in the lofty stellar constellation of the zodiac, corresponding to that point in the course of the day of the midday hour (or rather the one leading to the midday hour); in the course of the year the summer heights (or rather the time period leading to the summer heights). If we look at the still greater rhythm of the great cosmic year, in which the Sun in 25,920 years pushes the first day of spring back through all the signs of the zodiac, we find as the *age of the Twins*—that is, the time when the Sun enters the constellation of the Twins on the first day of spring—the age of the great Zarathustra, the original Zarathustra about whom Plutarch writes as living 5000 years before the Trojan War, not the later inspirer of the Avesta documents. In a New Year lecture in Dornach, Rudolf Steiner expressively spoke that in the far past, the old Sun-clairvoyance of humanity, the old Sun-wisdom and stellar wisdom stood at a certain climax, at that time, in this sign of climax of the 'great midday'.

It was really something like a 'great midday' in the evolution of humanity, and in the way Nietzsche attempted to enliven the spirit

of Zarathustra there still lives something of this feeling of the 'great midday'. In Zarathustra lived the great initiator of humanity of the pre-Christian era, and right into the Egyptian-Chaldean Mysteries and into the Hebrew world, all the great initiation-impulses lead back to Zarathustra and his sign of the Twins, and the great midday. Moreover, the great connection to the 'mount of initiation' for the evolution of humanity stands in Zarathustra's lofty sign of the Twins and the great midday. It stands in that time of the Twins which we still recognize in the later Zarathustra religion with its teaching of the duality of light and darkness. Furthermore, the Zarathustra initiation in the way it consciously aligned itself to the Christ-Earth of the future, carries the active element of will in itself, and in a certain way it has taken into itself the impulse to work on and change the earthly out of the spirit. It is the first, in contrast to the ancient Indian initiation wisdom, clearly looking to the earthly fact of Christ, with an inner connection to the later Christian impulses (for further details on all this, see the author's *Zarathustra*).

In the lofty sign of the great midday, on the Sacred Mount of initiation shining over the heavenly Twins, Zarathustra, the great teacher of humanity sending impulses into earthly evolution, is at the same time the great preparer of Christ and His earthly mission. Consequently, great connections are revealed of the evolution of humanity in the way Christ himself on the 'Sacred Mount' shines over the 'heavenly Twins', in Zarathustra's sign of the great midday calling the twelve disciples around him in order with them to begin the great work of Christian initiation, and thereby to give the decisive impulse for the initiation of the future. Over the great calling of the disciples in Mark 3, which forms the growing point for the initiation events, the Zarathustra secret of the 'great midday' shines in the sign of the Twins. And in a significant way this secret of the great midday, as it is completed through Christ in the calling of the disciples, allows us to look over and look below the Mystery of Golgotha towards the opposite sign of the Archer, the concluding secret of the deep midnight.

The Crab as the Sign of the Descent

(Mark 3:20–35)

Lofty experiences of the most tremendous kind are what Christ on the Sacred Mount, the mount of Inspiration and Initiation, opened up to the most intimate, most trusted disciples whom he had gathered around him in order to direct them to mankind's path leading to the future. There they were led high above the notions and imaginations of everyday consciousness into a lofty spiritual consciousness, to a really spiritual mountain height. But the meaning of a Christian initiation did not lie in remaining on such a lofty spiritual mountain height, in order to enjoy life in the heights. It lay in communicating to others what is received in the heights, to carry it down into the darkest depths of humanity, to those needing the light, to allow healing forces to radiate into everything that 'proves to be sick in earthly existence', as the words of the Pentecost Epistle of The Act of Consecration of Man express it.

For this reason, the way down has to follow the ascent to the mountain-top. This way down stands in the same sign that in the course of the year describes the descent of the Sun. After reaching the summer solstice, it turns in the sign of the Crab from the summer heights to the winter depths. In the gospel the sign of the Crab is always bound with the earthly life of humanity's depths and low ground, humanity's blindness and darkness, humanity's inhibitions and sickness.

The transition from the sign of the Twins to that of the Crab signifies a descent, a stepping down from the heights of the spirit into the depths and lowlands of the Earth. Looking at the zodiac, this is expressed in that we found ourselves in the sign of the Twins on the 'etheric heights' of the spirit, really in the 'cross of the etheric plane' (see p. 34f.), whereas the Crab belongs to the 'cross of the physical plane', the earthly cross. It becomes ever more familiar to us when we receive such things into our thinking; the language of the twelve signs of the zodiac appears more vivid and concrete, to correspond to what

we really experience in going through the individual sections of the gospel. The inner logic, the inner rhythm of the zodiac itself leads us from the heights of spiritual life into the earthly depths of humanity's experience.

In life this logic of events is to be found everywhere, this rhythm of events, where the descent to the depths has to follow after the ascent to the heights; world-development is revealed in all the greater and smaller rhythms of world-events. Not first in the New, but already in the Old Testament, we find these contexts. Such a fall of consciousness is to be found in the great rhythm of world-evolution, above all where the human being, created initially as a spiritual being, as the 'image of the gods' (Gen. 1:27), finds the transition from pure spirit-existence into a kind of existence in the senses—still to be thought as more etheric [than later conditions]—where spirituality changes into sensuality. With anthroposophical terminology and divisions of time, this would be the transition from the Hyperborean age (Earth-Sun time) into the early Lemurian age (Earth-Moon age). The hitherto one-gender human being, carrying spiritually both polarities of feminine and masculine (Gen. 1:27) now becomes two genders, revealed outwardly the opposite genders; male and female are divided in the outer appearance. The Bible presents this great fact of world-development in the story picturing Adam's sleep and the creation of Eve out of Adam's rib. In the picture of the 'rib' one can see a hidden, 'occult' hint of the sign of the Crab (♋).

This sign appears here, as it were, initially as the sign of the great Turning Point of Time and World Turning Point, as the sign of involution, following a previous evolution that has attained its climax. Moreover, the sign speaks above all of what the ribs and ribcage signify, of enclosing and confining the chest, of how the evolution of the human form through the solidifying of what is outer becomes an inner including and enclosing—even in the period to which Gen. 2:21, 22 relates, when we have to think that everything was still more in the etheric condition. From the aspect of the soul, the consciousness of

human beings during the stage in question was attuned to the sensory world, in anthroposophical terminology the 'sentient soul'. And it can really be found how, traversing the circle of fifths (described on p. 33 above), seeking the relationship to the supersensory members, the sign of the Crab corresponds to the 'sentient soul'. In the Crab as sign of the sentient soul lies the first indication of a Fall of human nature into sensuality, preceding and preparing the actual [spiritual] event. What we can call the 'lower nature' of man, in a certain way initially appears here.

Connected with this side of the Crab, furthermore, is the tendency of the Crab sign to embrace that in the blood which tends to drag down and cause illness, all tendencies towards dulling and restricting in the blood that counteracts the living flow. That which brings consolidation of structure, leading to growth of tumours in the tissues, has to do with the Crab.

The Crab as the sign of the chest is especially the sign for the mother's breast and earthly maternity in general. The noble aspect of motherhood, that in it which reveals the divine, stands in the sign of the Virgin and cosmic Mother. With the Crab we have more the extant, lowly aspect of maternity, with everything in earthly motherhood that is narrow, cramped, that which encloses the human being and limits in blood relations, grounded in dependence on kinship and love of the bloodline. Precisely at the end of the section of the gospel that belongs here (Mark 3:31-35), we find in this sense the divergence of Christ from His mother and brethren. Facing the cramped love of the bloodline, Christ places the freeing of the comprehensive love of human beings:

> And he answered them, saying, Who is my mother, or my brethren? And he looked round about on them which sat about him, and said, Behold my mother and my brethren! For whosoever shall do the will of God, the same is my brother, and my sister, and mother.

Through all this is also expressed how the experience of humanity, the experience of comprehensive love of people overcoming the bonds of blood, is also precisely presented before the disciples. Christ leads them down with consciousness from the mount of spiritual, lofty experience. They were to experience the whole cramped situation. It is placed there from the side of humanity's preconceptions and connections of the blood against the influence of Christ. In meeting this hindering and cramping, with all the darkness of humanity and blindness of humanity, they are to become aware of the greatness of the task of humanity lying before them.

In this descent into the depths of humanity lay at the same time a *test of the will*. It is not without significance that the 'physical cross'—to which the Ram, the Scales, the Goat and the Crab belong—is at the same time the 'cross of the will' (the astral cross is that of the feelings, the etheric cross that of thinking). In the Goat we found the call to a change in the direction of the will, in the Ram, of the will active in the earthly life. In a similar manner, in the Crab is manifested the will that proves itself against objects of resistance and overcomes them. The Crab is the sign above all—and this is connected to the 'mother' (Lat. *mater*)—also the sign of material and of materialism. (On the relationship of the zodiac to the 'twelve world-conceptions' and the sign of the Crab in the light of this significance, see above p. 31.)

Consequently, the lofty significance of the sign of the Crab touches on the Johannine initiation, of changing (transubstantiating) the earthly element, to spiritualize matter again. Later we shall show more clearly how precisely in this sign of the Crab, the initiation of the disciple John is completed. What here in Mark 3 is initially presented as the more negative side of the Crab is the presupposition and preparation for the later lofty experience of initiation.

The exalted Johannine experience of the sign of the Crab corresponds in the gospel to the words—not in Mark, but in John 3:30: 'He must increase, but I must decrease.' If we look in Mark's Gospel itself for the words aligning to the meaning of the sign of the Crab, we find words that clearly allude to the meaning of descent, of a descent of consciousness. 'He entered a house' [NIV], 'went home' [RSV, V. 19],

which Luther [1534] translates: *'sie kamen zuhause'*, 'they came home'. The words of ascending the mount (v. 13) show the transition into the sign of the Twins; here with the words of coming home the transition takes place into the sign of the Crab. The mountain-heights belong to the lofty sign of the Twins; the descent and sign of turning of the Crab belongs to one's 'own domesticity'. In his lecture-cycle on Mark's Gospel, Rudolf Steiner points out how in the pictorial language of the gospel, different kinds of locality correspond to different kinds of consciousness and stages of consciousness. The mountain-heights correspond to the experience of Inspiration; the lake, or shore of the lake, expanses of water reflecting pictures of the shore, correspond to the experience of Imagination. One's 'own domesticity', being 'at home', corresponds to the daytime consciousness, the condition where devotion, prayer and meditation, a raising to elevated stages of consciousness is the most difficult. In the picture of being 'at home', the cramped and enclosed aspect of the earthly disposition is expressed, of sense-bound ideas and imagination.

Still before the meeting with the brethren, especially characteristic for the sign of the Crab, there appears this sensory-bound imagination facing Christ in the attitude of the Jewish scribes and those belonging to the Jewish folk in general who want to ascribe something ungodly, demonic, to Christ's revelation of the divine. The might of the dark adversary is revealed in this attitude; we feel when we glance at the zodiac something of the dark counter-sign of the Crab, the Goat, which, when it has not become a sign of *change [*or *reversal] of thinking*, which it did achieve with the Baptist, expresses the meaning of dark insubordination, the essence of the dark adversary. To this the words of Christ refer: 'Whoever blasphemes against the Holy Spirit will never be forgiven; he is guilty of an eternal sin' (Mark 3:29). The deepest abyss of mankind, the highest danger for mankind is revealed at this point. The deepest darkening of consciousness and the night of consciousness proceed out of the region of the mountain Goat. Out of the sign of the Crab, in which the Johannine initiation finds its

completion, radiates the light of consciousness, which overcomes the might of the dark adversary, changing and spiritualizing the darkness of matter itself.

At the end of the section standing under the sign of the Crab, Christ meets with His brethren and on that occasion speaks about the comprehensive love of humanity. The disciples of Christ, in approaching the seat of love for those belonging to their bloodline, are to overcome it. Here we sense in the background of this event the Mystery of the Johannine initiation. We feel that the one who receives the great impulse given here to humanity the most strongly and vitally will really become the 'disciple of love'. In the progress of the gospel narration, this becoming of the disciple of love comes increasingly to the light of day, until in a later, higher cycle (octave) he then once again completes the great Sun-rhythm in the sign of the Crab.

The Lion, the Esoteric Sign of the Sun

The zodiac-sign of the Lion stands in the cosmic rhythm of Mark's Gospel differently from the normal arrangement, as already noted in the Introduction (see p. 31f.). It is unlike the other zodiac signs, to which are outwardly allocated specific sections of the gospel. Theological commentators (cf. A. Drews 1921. p. 170) have come across this phenomenon and are of the opinion that here a particular section of the gospel must have been lost. It is of course absolutely possible that the original pure version of the gospel text has not everywhere been retained. Sections could have been inserted or taken out, or their place or the order of words changed. Wherever written words have been handed down, there exists the possibility, through human dealings, that in the handing down possible errors have crept in. A simple glance at the usual editions of the Greek text shows the various deviations of the text. Not seldom you find [against examples favourable] for a spiritual interpretation of the wording, the remark of the philological editor: '*schlechtere Lesart*—less good reading'.

Amongst the many viewpoints significant for this study on the 'cosmic rhythm' to explain Mark's Gospel, that of textual criticism is present, that is, a test of whether and how far a gospel passage is genuine, whether and how much the wording and its position corresponds to what from the spiritual viewpoint is to be expected at this place. Through knowing the cosmic rhythm and through living with it, we are in a certain manner freed from the outer text of the gospel. We read the whole gospel in the manner of a spiritual stellar script. Without being dependent on the mere external text, we can check whether and how far this external wording of Mark's Gospel agrees with what results from reading the stellar script.

But just when we check the cosmic stellar script in this way and out of this the resulting cosmic rhythm of the narration of Mark's Gospel, we will find in the main how little occasion exists to change anything essential in the text as received. And the occasion cannot be supplied

for the external initial opinion that a section for the Lion is missing in the gospel rhythm of the zodiac signs. Far otherwise, we receive the immediate impression this at least apparent absence of the Lion amongst the zodiac signs of Mark's Gospel cannot be a mere external circumstance, a mere chance occurring in handing down the text. And Mark, the Lion evangelist (see p. 22), would not simply pass over the Lion, without some sort of deep reason, some deeper context standing in the background.

Astrologically the Sun and Moon are also regarded as 'planets'. The term applies to all heavenly bodies that, observed from the Earth, take their course in the heavenly zodiac. If we follow the usual allocation of the individual planets to their specific zodiacal 'houses', then in the Lion—as already noted in the Introduction—the Sun is in its own house, there it is 'at home' (*εσω*), in all the other signs it is, as it were, 'outside' (*εξω*). Already in this sense the Lion is the 'esoteric' sign of the Sun-rhythm, the other zodiacal signs are exoteric. Consequently, Mark the Lion evangelist, treats the Lion differently from the other zodiacal signs; he treats it in an esoteric fashion.

We recall how also in the human organism, the Lion is that organ which from within rules the whole course of the rest of the system; the Lion is the *heart*. In his relationship to the heart, too, the Lion can be felt as the esoteric sign. In the Lion—and so the matter appears also for viewing the gospel—the great cosmic rhythm has its heartbeat, its inner pulse. Consequently, the Lion is not like the other zodiac signs to be found on the periphery of the gospel rhythm. We have to seek it much rather in the inner centre of this gospel rhythm. The Lion is the heart for the cosmic rhythm of Mark's Gospel; it acts as a cause and rules from within this cosmic rhythm. And so it cannot in the same way as the other zodiac signs be outwardly shown in the course of the gospel narration.

What the Christ-Sun effects in the most inner region takes place in the sign of the Lion that as we have seen (see p. 33f.) is also the sign of 'Spirit-man'. From this sign the forces from the human 'I' radiate, lay-

ing hold right into the physical, animating and changing this physical human being right into the blood. In this sense, in Mark we also found the Lion as the counter-sign of the Waterman, in the episode with John the Baptist at the beginning of the gospel standing under the sign of the Waterman, where the baptism by water of John is placed facing the spirit-baptism of Christ (the other gospels have 'baptize with the Holy Ghost and with fire'). This passage already clearly shows us how Mark knows about the spiritual meaning of the Lion. The outer Sun in the plant world cooks the blood of grapes, changes water into wine; the Christ-power penetrates the human etheric and astral with the fire of the 'I'. In this connection, it is especially impressive how the Lion-motif with that of the Waterman in John's Gospel, presents the story of changing the water into wine at the marriage of Cana.

Everywhere the 'cosmic rhythm' in Mark's Gospel renders the most significant viewpoints also for explaining John's Gospel. These viewpoints are reserved for an independent study on John's Gospel. In the Lion we touch in a certain way the most inner Christ-Sun sphere, the most inner Sun-secret of Christ, and we can imagine how the presentation of these things was reserved for the actual Christ-gospel (see p. 51). Mark, the Lion evangelist, initially presents only how the John-consciousness develops into these Mysteries of Christ. He consequently attends discreetly and esoterically to what is the most inner concern of Christ Himself in the experiences. He leaves to John as much as he can and wants to reveal of the Mystery of the heart and the Mystery of the Lion.

We are able to arrive in a certain way at a correct view of the sign of the Lion by taking it from the periphery of the circle of zodiac signs and placing it in the centre of the circle. From here we can, for example, so understand the events of the section on the Crab last discussed, that above all the Lion appears as the one who overcomes the negative aspect of the sign of the Crab, that which is dull and stagnant, that which hinders, causing illness in the blood. That which in the Crab tends to pull to the Earth, becomes in the Lion animated, changed and spiritualized.

The Crab, belonging to the cross of physical existence, as this study will show ever more clearly, is a decisive sign for the Johannine initiation. Because this initiation is completed in this sign, it becomes the sign of change and transubstantiation, the re-spiritualizing of matter. By increasingly raising this significance, however, the Lion appears over it and under it, involving the Mystery of Sun-alchemy within itself. The Lion, we can also say, becomes the overcoming and completion of the Crab. The Crab and the Lion can in this sense be seen in Mark's Gospel as belonging together. The Twins, Crab and Lion—and we can include the Bull—then appear as the climax of the Johannine initiation. In the Bull, the sign of the word, the preparation in a certain way is experienced, in the Twins the illumination, in the Crab and the Lion—or, in that the Lion overcomes the Crab—the initiation is completed.

We can also say:

- In the Bull, the word is spoken from the heights; the cosmic *Gospel* is heard.
- On the Holy Mount of the Twins stands the altar of offering; here is the cosmic *Offertory*.
- In the Crab what has been received and heard is brought down to the Earth where it is changed through the power of the Lion, animated and spiritualized. The Crab and Lion become the signs of cosmic change, of metamorphosis, the *Transsubstantiation*.

And as with the Crab, so also with all the other signs, in its working out of the centre of the heart we can recognize the power of the Lion that overcomes and changes what is negative in all these signs—namely, the five lower, dark signs. Out of the centre, of the Lion, in the beat at the heart of the great rhythm, the power of Christ works, Who ultimately changes and spiritualizes everything earthly, allowing it to shine anew and radiate into the fire of the Sun. John, who penetrates the deepest into this Mystery of the heart and the Sun, expresses this in the Apocalypse in the words: 'See, the Lion has triumphed ...' (Rev. 5:5).

The Virgin

(Mark 4:1-34)

We met the Virgin first as the counter-sign of the Fishes at the Jordan-Baptism. With that event the power of the cosmic life-ether in the sign of the Virgin united with the power of the solar-'I' that streamed in from the Fishes. These powers were felt in ancient times as the heavenly provisions on the way, as the bread of life. And when the stellar forces were still experienced, people pointed in the heavenly zodiac to the *Virgin with the sheaf* (Spica) as bearer of the starry bread. In a special way, out of this region people still experienced the nourishing, building forces. And bound up with the forces of the starry life there is the stellar wisdom of higher, clairvoyant vision. We can call also these forces of stellar life and stellar wisdom those of the Holy Grail. Already from the ages before the Christian revelation, the *Virgin* was always the bearer of the Holy Grail. Ancient Egypt revered the heavenly Virgin, the giver of stellar forces of life and stellar forces of love, the bearer of the stellar wisdom, as Isis. The sacred stars of Isis were the resplendent Sirius, which shines on winter nights on the 'Sacred Mount of the heavens' beneath the zodiac, and resplendent Spica shining from the spring into the summer in the constellation of the Virgin in the zodiac itself.

Over the course of time, the old receptivity of the stellar forces and the stellar wisdom progressively decreased; the heavenly bread became ever more scarce for humanity. The story in the Old Testament of Joseph and his brethren shows the attempt of the patriarchs to find once more in the ancient Egyptian Mystery-centres what was lacking. Then even in the Mystery-centres the heavenly provisions declined. Out of the solar heights, out of which Christ descended to Earth in the Jordan-Baptism, He gave himself anew as the living force to the starving earthly existence. From the side of the etheric, earthly life also received afresh a new burst of cosmic life-ether. Innocent, maidenly, paradisal life lost through the Fall of man, held back in Paradise in

the Tree of Life (life-ether and sound-ether)[17] came again to the Earth. However, the forces of the cosmic ether in the sign of the Virgin is now bound with the force of the 'I' in the sign of the Fishes; the source of life now flows out of the 'I', the bread of life is received by the 'I': 'I am the bread of life' [John 6]. In the spiritual primordial creation (Genesis 1:27) the Eternal Feminine and the Eternal Masculine were united; in Christ the force of the heavenly Virgin is bound with the force of the 'I'.

As explained earlier (p. 33f.), the supersensory human members relate to the zodiac. The Virgin unites with the member that carries the etheric—the life-body. The Fishes correspond to the 'Life-spirit', to the human life-body penetrated by the 'I', metamorphosed by the 'I'. Likewise, significant for understanding Mark's Gospel is the arrangement of the 'twelve senses' to the signs of the zodiac. The sense of sight belongs to the sign of the Virgin. This gives the forces of pictorial sight and imagination. Likewise, of the 'twelve world-conceptions', phenomenalism belongs here. (For more details, see R. Steiner, *Human and Cosmic Thought* [GA 151] Lecture-course, Berlin 20-23 Jan. 1914.) Mark 4 in particular includes the secrets of vision, of seeing in pictures, of Imagination (see above p. 18). In that which happens in the sign of the Virgin it becomes especially evident how the events in each of the zodiac signs pass through the stages of Imagination, Inspiration and Imagination in the three rounds of the twelve signs which form the cosmic rhythm of this gospel. The element of Imagination appears especially strongly precisely when the Virgin initially appears. Already the seashore, which is the subject from the beginning, and the sermon from the ship, points to the element of Imagination, whereas the mountain-top corresponds to Inspiration (see above p. 86).

In following the events in the Virgin through the three rounds of the 'cosmic rhythm', we increasingly recognize in it the bearer of heavenly Feeding, of the bread of life, of the cosmic, sacramental nutrition, of the sacred Last-Supper events. The picture of the 'Holy Grail' points in the same direction. Virgin and Fishes, as we mentioned (see p. 67f.),

together form the 'Last-Supper' constellation. This is not some outer cultic event but a self-offering of divine forces of life and of love into the world's becoming, into cosmic evolution. Everything in world-development, all creation in the primordial beginning was the outflowing of such an offering. All world-renewal is recognized as 're-enlivening of the dying earth-existence', as the Creed of The Act of Consecration of Man puts it in the Eucharistic rite of The Christian Community. This rite is a contemporary form of the 'Last-Supper' events, corresponding to today's form of consciousness. To recognize how the seed planted into earth-existence through Christ's deed of love develops further, till the Earth is ripe to pass over into a new form of existence, opens up an understanding for the Mysteries of the Last Supper. Novalis' great hymn to the Last Supper points to these Mysteries. Likewise the same poet's saying, 'Love is the ultimate purpose of world history, the Amen of the universe.' And John the Apocalyptist speaks of the Holy City of the resurrection, lit by no outer temple [Rev. 21:22f.], where no outer cult is celebrated, in which the 'marriage supper of the Lamb' takes place [Rev. 19:9, 17].

In this sense, it is significant how in the third great round of the great rhythm, in Christ's Last Supper itself (Mark 14), the completed event begins in the Virgin with the Parable of the Seed and the Sower in Mark 3. Precisely the stellar constellation makes us aware of the connection of this story with the later story of the Feeding (Mark 8) and the concluding Last-Supper narration (Mark 14). In such cases it is especially evident what is achieved through the whole manner of studying the gospel to attain clarification. Connections that at first glance are not evident then become clear.

Astral mythological research has already pointed out the context of the Parable of the Sower and of the Seed with the sign of the 'Virgin with the sheaf'. To this research it appeared significant that the gospel speaks of grain and corn, corn in the ear, and the mustard seed. But what is decisive here are not simply the outer details of these pictures, but in them the eloquent secrets of change and development, of

the 'Last-Supper event'. In this Last-Supper event, the meaning of the sign of the Virgin revealed, not merely external references to seeds and fruits of the field. Here verse 11 is significant. Christ speaks of how the effect of His words for the disciples is different for those 'that are without':

> And he said to them, To you has been given the secret of the kingdom of God, but for those outside everything is in parables [Mark 4:11, RSV].

The problem with some translations is the added words 'to know' ['to know the mystery ...'] that do not stand in the original. The Greek has only 'to you is (with this) the Mystery (Gk. *μυστηριον* = Lat. *sacramentum*), the sacrament of the kingdom of God (the cosmic Last-Supper event) is given'. The disciples directly receive not merely words but the real substance of a cosmic event. Of harrowing seriousness is the following advice of Christ to those who 'seeing they may not see, and not perceive' (KJV/AV), or 'that they may be ever seeing but never perceiving ...' (Isaiah 6:9, 10, NIV), ever hearing but never understanding, that is, those for whom the pictures and words remains just pictures and words, who do not receive the *power* of the pictures and words as real substance. Already where the 'Last-Supper events' appear here in the first, pictorial stage, it 'divides the spirits'[18] in this sense, leading to the crisis (i.e. literally 'division'), to judgement, until on the third stage (in the Last Supper of Christ, narrated in Mark 19) it is experienced in highest seriousness with His own body, and becomes the most harrowing element of the crisis.

For the disciples, then, the introduction of a picture, the telling of a parable through Christ is taken more than an external reception of a picture or words, but in picture and word there lies a power which as real substance, as the seed of an event working in from the future of the Earth. The words of Christ corresponding to the consciousness of the disciples are genuine *Imaginations* bearing power and reality. Through these there takes place something in the initiation, in the 'becoming' of the disciples. Events of real spiritual development are

thereby released, the secret of cosmic development itself. The event of the cosmic Last Supper—initially as a picture, on the stage of Imagination—sinks into the consciousness of the disciples. And what is presented in the grain of wheat and the growing seed, corresponds cosmically to the heavenly picture of the 'Virgin with the sheaf'.

Christ never spoke in the way we speak today about the abstract concept of 'development'; at that time it could not have been spoken about like that at all. Only in pictures, in parables, could He reveal the secret of the highest things. And when it had to do with the secret of becoming, of growth, self-development, ultimately leading to the 'cosmic Last Supper', that which out of the nature of the thing offers itself as the more eloquent and expressive picture is precisely that of the *growing seed*. In the expression, 'Everything is a growing seed', Novalis speaks of the secret bearing everything in world-events, the secret of unfolding and development, of involution and evolution. We are surrounded everywhere by this 'secret of the growing seed'. Already in the physical world we see—and this really leads to the serious problem at the centre of Mark 4—how everywhere vast quantities of seed go to waste. The few that apparently by chance remain intact and really do become seeds, nevertheless contain and bear the future of the respective species. What is already a truth in the series of visible things, first really becomes a truth in the realm of the invisible, for the 'kingdom of God'. (The expression points in the same direction as the expression '*Abendmahlsgeschehen*—Last-Supper event'. In the Apocalypse of John we note that Mysteries of the future of the Earth meet those of the Last Supper.) Only here it is much more difficult to achieve an overview, demanding other forces of faith and of the heart. The disciples are to receive something tremendous. They are to understand how what initially is only spoken to them in a word contains living power. This really is intended and is able to build up a new future of the Earth and of humanity; the disciples already carry in themselves this future in seed-form.

Christ, at the beginning of the initiation, had led the disciples first of all to the sublime experience on the Mount of Inspiration—which took place in the sign of the Twins. Then He led them deep into the depths of humanity—this took place in the Crab—into the blindness and darkness of humanity, showing the whole need of humanity devoid of the food of life. Now, in the sign of the Virgin, He has to show them, not as a theoretical teaching but in the conscious transfer of power, how in this apparently so needy, unreceptive soil of humanity, the seed of life can nevertheless be planted so that out of it a new, changed Earth will spring forth.

Such powers embracing such knowledge, containing such pictures and Imaginations carrying recognition and strength, planted by Christ Himself, are not only like any harmless, passive reception of some kind of message; it calls the soul to highest activity, to most intensive inner co-working. It awakens storms in the soul, leading it in inner crises of the most earnest kind. Such soul-storms and crises are told in the following section of the gospel (Mark 5:35-41). Not without meaning does this stand in the same chapter. It is to be taken in closest connection with what precedes it, yet it already leads to the next sign, the *Scales*.

The Scales

(Mark 4:35–5:20)

The inner connection of the signs of the zodiac, the whole rhythm governing Mark's Gospel is nowhere more clear than where the constellation Fishes–Virgin leads over to that of the Ram and the Scales. In a series of cases, in themselves characteristically parallel cases, the motif of crossing the Sea of Galilee and stilling the storm follows the motif of the food of life, contained in the Imaginative picture of the Parable of the Sower in Mark 4. This motif stands in the signs of the Ram and the Scales as the other—bread and fishes!—stands in the sign of the Fishes and the Virgin. With the Ram the passing over from night-experience to the awake daytime is more emphasized, from 'the water of the etheric' to the firm land of physical existence. With the Scales, the motif of the crossing over is emphasized, of finding the balance between the Storm on the Lake and the storm in the soul. In both constellations the sign and counter-sign appear closely connected.

In the Introduction, reference was made to the twelve signs relating to the 'twelve senses' taught in anthroposophy. It should be pointed out that the sign of the Scales does not correspond to the 'sense of balance', as one might suppose. That sense, lying completely in the subconscious, is rather allocated to the Archer. To the Scales, still lying in the conscious part of the soul, Rudolf Steiner allocates the sense of taste.

The Scales is the sign of outer and inner balance. The outer sense of balance has to do with positioning in the physical world, in the forces of the earthly body and earthly life. Here it appears as the countersign of the Ram, which expresses attaining the upright position in the earthly realm, of placing oneself in the earthly situation. Where the Scales is the primary sign, beside the emphasis of physical balance, the inner balance appears more strongly. The sign of the Scales has to do with the calming down of the soul-storm, of an inner soul-calm.

We recall how we found, or articulated out of them, certain words in the gospel actually everywhere ascribed to the individual zodiac signs:

- With the *Goat* it was the saying of the change of thinking;
- with the *Waterman* the saying of baptism by water;
- with the *Fishes* the saying concerning the Son of the Sun ('You are my beloved Son... ');
- with the *Ram* the words of resurrection and becoming upright (see especially Mark 9) and of the landing;
- with the *Bull* the word 'word';
- with the *Twins* the saying on the Sacred Mount at the initiation;
- with the *Crab* the saying concerning descending and humbling [of kenosis];
- with the *Lion* the saying concerning the baptism of the spirit and of fire;
- with the *Virgin* the sayings of the bread of life.

What we perceive in this sense from the *Scales* is nothing other than the great 'I-AM' of Christ Himself, Who places Himself into the forces of the Earth (cf. the two stories of the Storm on the Sea and walking on the Sea [of Galilee] John 6:20 and Mark 6:50; although the Scales is not in the first instance emphasized, this sign is sympathetically involved). Through this I-AM, through the strength of the 'I' and the calm in the 'I' the Storm on the Sea and the storm in the soul, the surging unrest of the astral element is brought to rest. In Mark 4 everything is still at the first stage, the stage of Imagination. The I-AM of Christ does not yet sound, everything appears as a picture, in the picture of Christ peacefully asleep in the stern during the midst of the Storm on the Sea—as in the unrest of the astral realm, the 'I' can still be found asleep.

In the sign of the Scales, the human 'I' becomes the great I-AM of Christ, the Lord over the unrest of the astral realm. Here we stand at a point where initially the allocation of the zodiac signs to the human supersensory members that appeared problematic (as mentioned in the Introduction) may be illuminated to some degree. For the 'tone-zodiac', the 'circle of fifths' mentioned there, holding the key for the inner mem-

bering of the human being, points with the sign of the Scales to the 'Spirit-self', or manas in Indian theosophy. But, as Rudolf Steiner has shown, this Spirit-self or manas is the 'astral body' purified and transformed by the 'I', or ego. We recognize how this viewpoint is illuminated precisely by the gospel. There, in the sign of the Scales, through the I-AM of Christ, the unrest of the astral, the waves of the Storm on the Sea of Galilee and the storm of the soul, are brought to rest.

The story of the Storm on the Sea of Galilee and the fear of the disciples—told at the end of Mark 4, to be thought of in the sign of the Scales—of Christ Who brings the storm to silence, is nothing other than the direct result of what previously happened in the sign of the Virgin. An etheric event was played out in that sign belonging to the 'cross of the etheric'. Into the consciousness of the disciples, Christ planted great Imaginations carrying the seed of the future. Through this experience the soul felt raised out of everything in which it felt rooted, firmly bound. Out of the consciousness of the physical, spatial realm, in which hitherto it felt as if securely anchored, it felt now as if thrown out into the waves of the etheric sea of the flow of time. It is really so; in rising to the Imaginative consciousness one enters the surging etheric sea of time. It is then as if suddenly the secure land wavers under the feet. Placed before the secret of becoming and passing away of the flow of the events of time, human beings can only find this 'firm ground' when they find the eternal in all the becoming and passing away, when they find the *'I'* in themselves.

In the everyday consciousness, human beings including those regarded as educated, view plants only according to physical, spatial laws. Whoever really wants to penetrate into the secrets of plant life, into the essence of the etheric realm, has to be able to enter into the time-processes of plant growth. You have to enter into all the transitions of becoming and passing away, of blooming and withering. The metamorphosis of plants involves the whole progression of a plant from the single seed through the germination, the leaf, the bud and flower to the fruit, which then again carries in itself, the seed of a new plant. In his book *Knowledge of the Higher Worlds, How is it Attained?* [GA 10], in the chapter on 'Illumination', Rudolf Steiner gives advice to the meditative observation of a seed, the germinating and the dying, and again the fruiting plant. He does this not only because of certain visions of colour and flames that come about to the beholding consciousness, but in order appropriately to lead the pupil of the spirit advancing out of the physically spatial world into that of the etheric world of time and into the Mysteries revealing world-development there ('everything is a growing seed' [Novalis]), to lead into the world of Imaginative consciousness. It is to be observed in his remarks, how necessary it is that the pupil, precisely with this exercise, takes care that he does not lose the inner balance, that he does not become anxious, that he develop in himself courage and fearlessness. The situation is exactly the same as the presentation in Mark's Gospel of the Christian Johannine path of initiation, where likewise, with the placing of the picture of the single grain in Mark 4, through the resulting entry into the world of Imaginative consciousness, the sudden *fear* now overcomes the consciousness of the disciples, which the Storm on the Sea pictures as the power of fear approaching their souls.

The souls of the disciples, through the Imagination implanted by Christ into their consciousness, felt, as it were, taken out of the firm, physically spatial world into the billowing sea of the etheric element of time. With the picture of the 'storm tossed sea' we see not only the Sea of Galilee. The outer experience of the disciples with their Master may also have played a role, but in the 'etheric sea' we see into the inner experiences in the etheric level of consciousness. To these feelings of fear connected to this transition comes in addition all the insecurity adhering to the soul from the Fall of humanity. This still carries in itself the unquiet element of urges, desires and passions. These are the wind that brings them into disturbance. The secure direction and leadership through the higher 'I' is lacking. The 'sea' corresponds to the etheric, the 'etheric sea'; the 'wind' corresponds to the astral element of passion. We note that the spirit of [the German] language has linked the words *'See'* (sea) and *'Seele'* (soul). Through the billowing wind of passion and longing (the opening motif of Wagner's *Tristan and Isolde* expresses this pain *musically*), through the storm of the soul, the ether-sea becomes transposed into the wild, stormy surge. Upon this surge the ship of the soul—manas, the 'Spirit-self', the higher soul, is frequently seen as the picture of a ship—is tossed hither and thither. Christ, the higher 'I', sleeps in the stern. When called upon by His true believers He quiets the storm; the sea becomes calm. The awakened 'I' soothes the storm of the astral element.

Note:
The physical event of the Storm on the Sea, which of course can never be positively proved, is demanded by those who want to keep hold of the physical side of the occurrence, not wanting to give it up for the sake of this 'Imaginative interpretation'. One can indeed well imagine that some kind of outer occasion, a real sea-storm experienced by the disciples on a sea-voyage with their Master, was taken up and elaborated in the picture-world of Imaginative consciousness. It has only ever and again to be said, that the viewpoint from which the things are presented in Mark's Gospel depends not on this outer side of the—perhaps actual—physical event, but on that which this event expresses as a *picture of a spiritual event.* The Imaginative content of the narration, not the external historical fact, is decisive for Mark's Gospel and the initiation story it contains.

* * *

When we have recognized how the Storm on the Sea in Mark 4 is *Imagination,* is the picture for specific soul-difficulties of the disciples released through the previous parables and the seeds of consciousness in them, then the riddles of Mark 5 can be resolved. Initially there appears to be no connection between the end of Mark 4 and the beginning of Mark 5 with the grotesque narration of the demoniac ['Legion'], and the demons who enter the herd of pigs and drown in the lake. Only

too easily to the superficial glance, the Christian gospels can appear as a colourful series of diverse, unconnected episodes. To a deeper penetration there is revealed here precisely the wonderful connection of all the details and the grandiose construction of the whole, the completely spiritual and artistic composition of the gospel. With Mark's Gospel especially, through the 'cosmic rhythm', through the general relationships of the individual sections with specific heavenly signs, connections not unveiled at first glance become even clearer.

Such a connection exists between the Storm on the Sea in Mark 4 and the Man Possessed in Mark 5. This too belongs to the zodiac sign of the Scales, though motifs also play in from the following sign, the Scorpion. The fact that the story, unlike all the other healings of those possessed in Mark's Gospel, at all events is not allocated to the Ram, stimulates our attention. Likewise, the circumstance that not just any other sign appears but in the place of the Ram the *one* constellation forming with it the counter-sign of the *Scales*. Precisely in this we experience very strongly the logical inner consistency, the inner connection of the individual sections of the great rhythm. And yet on the other hand, the fact is not insignificant that here the healing of 'Legion' cannot stand in the sign of the Ram, the standard sign, but in the counter-sign of the Scales. With the healings of those demoniacs (Mark 1:23-39) in the Ram, the picture strongly appears of Christ working in the physical world, placing Himself and others into the earthly forces. Everything in this sign of the Ram points to Christ's earthly work. Whether these healings at the same time would like to contain the picture of specific preparatory events of the initiation of the disciples (cf. Mark 3:15), they do initially appear as an outer procedure—also if in the individual case, as has to be repeatedly said, the historical moment of the narration can never ultimately be nor should be decisive.

It is different with the narration in Mark 5. As with what has preceded, where we cannot and should not decide in the positive sense, here too we cannot and should not ultimately decide in the negative sense. But at all events it will not be easy to imagine all the details of the

narration as outer events—just think only of the herd of pigs rushing into the sea—to attribute to Christ in this way a grotesque magical trick out of sympathy. (The explanation in this sense offered by the occultist Eliphas Levi is hardly enlightening.) And at the beginning of Mark 5, the continuing influence of the sign of the Ram points the whole event to another sphere than that of the other possession-healings. It points to the self-same sphere in which the previous Storm on the Sea took place. That is, as there, we are dealing here with the soul-events of the disciples and with the way Christ works for the initiation of the disciples' consciousness.

The story in Mark 5 of the demoniac ['Legion']—no matter what perhaps is to be thought about it as an outer event—is even more than the earlier stories of this kind, Imagination, the picture for specific soul-crises evoked through the initiation by Christ in the consciousness of the disciples. After the first pictures of the Seed and the Sower had begun to work, mirrored in their etheric bodies, in the picture of the Storm at Sea they experienced the storm of their soul-life, the unrest of their still impure astral bodies not yet governed by the 'I'. In the picture of the Healing of the Possessed Man, they then experienced something of the deeper origin of this unrest. They received a shocking impression in the whole abyss of human urges, desires and passions; they see how the impure soul becomes the playground of demons, until the 'I' creates order. And they experience the whole disorder with what enters from the sexual region—the source of errors in the love-life. The herd of swine also appears as a picture for everything that propels the impure astrality of the human being. All this can be claimed, no matter how far what is narrated is to be imagined as outer events. With biblical narration, up to a certain point not infrequently everything to do with outer events relates—pending from this point onwards what then is *still* narrated as an outer event—is to be taken in reality as the picture for an inner experience, as Imagination.

Something beyond pointing to outer events in the story of the demoniac in Mark 5 is what is said about the swineherds. In experiencing

the event of the herd of pigs rushing into the water, they were so disturbed that in the end they implored Christ to leave their region (Mark 5:17). But here, too, another interpretation is possible, when we recall how many herdsmen, also in the gospel, appear as bearers of an atavistic vision and have clairvoyant experiences. One can imagine that the Imaginations Christ awakens in the souls of the disciples work so strongly that the consciousness of other personalities tending towards atavistic clairvoyance are, as it were, drawn into the sphere of these pictures. The spiritual atmosphere of the whole region is, as it were, filled with these pictures. We can imagine how the presence of Christ Jesus with the disciples in some region or other signified something tremendous for that region. What perhaps passed over without a trace to the consciousness of people turned merely towards the sensory world, to those, however, who were still connected to the spiritual world, released deeply stirring and deeply disturbing experiences, lying on their souls like a difficult nightmare.

In the demonic pictures of Mark 5—no matter what outer events did or did not happen in the story of the possessed man—the disciples behold what was kindled in their souls by the storm, what hindered the higher Imaginations planted in them by the peaceful influence of Christ. Christ as the Initiator of the disciples, in letting them see in such pictures into the abyss of their still unpurified souls, leads them through a crisis, accomplishing in them a stage of purification that is necessary if the further path of Christ-initiation is able to be found by the disciples. How in particular John—the one becoming-John—is raised by this to a significantly advanced level in soul-education, is revealed in what follows. The surface of the etheric sea, previously wildly disturbed by the astral storm-wind, lies pure and still as a mirror after the demonic herd rush in and are drowned.

All these apparently grotesque, demonic pictures of Mark 5 lie spiritually close to the following sign of the Scorpion, which is of critical importance for the story of the initiation of the disciples.

The Death Sign of the Scorpion

(Mark 5:21-6:6)

In the foregoing narrations of the Storm at Sea (Mark 4:35-41) and of the naked, wandering, possessed man living 'in the tombs', whose demons entered the herd of swine who then rushed into the Sea [of Galilee], we saw the motif of the Scorpion already at work. The meaning of the Scales lies in the way Christ, the initiator, works on the consciousness of the disciples, and how they themselves have to struggle for their inner balance. What inner resistance they experience in this struggle, or inner crisis as the source of inner disturbance and opposition, already brings in the dark shadow of the power of death of the Scorpion. In the Introduction (p. 29f.), we already spoke of how in this sign secrets of the Sun-life and the source of life, the 'creation in light', are linked with secrets of the Fall of man and the sting of death of sensuality. Always when the narration of the gospel enters into this critical sign, the initiation of the disciples comes to an earnest and critical turning point.

The meaning of what is going on generally in the first round of the cosmic rhythm lies in the fact that the context first of all is presented in pictures, as Imagination. Two pictures are shown first, the healing of the woman with the issue of blood who touched Christ's garment, whereby she is healed of her twelve years of suffering, and the waking of Jairus' daughter out of the sleep of death through Christ Jesus. He is accompanied by the three disciples Peter, James and John. That these two events are connected is already recognized by a theological research quite distant from anthroposophy (see Drews 1921/2012). Rudolf Steiner speaks in his lecture-cycles on the gospels as follows. Between the twelve years of sickness of the woman with the issue of blood, and the twelve years of the girl who comes to the boundary of death, a connection exists because the two personalities are bound by destiny, as it were, by a sympathetic connection. Of what the woman with the issue of blood has too much, the girl had too little. Although

the girl had arrived at the years in which in southern lands she should have entered puberty, she was not able in the normal way to reach maturity. And this weakness is present in her physical organism from her birth. Christ heals both cases of illness by balancing out the too-much of the one with the too-little of the other.

In the etheric rhythm of Christ lives the power directly to effect such things. And the power is so strong that the girl is called back to life again out of the sleep of death, or death-like sleep. The rhythmical power of Christ can work right into the rhythmical functions of the human physical basis, right into the secrets of the flow of the blood and the streams of life. The great cosmic rhythm itself, the pulse beat of humanity entire, pulses through Him. All streams in the great sea of etheric life are subject to Him. (Even the 'stilling of the Storm on the Sea' in Mark 4 is ultimately only a picture.) In this great sea of etheric life, all natures are in various differentiated ways connected with each other. In the midst of these streams of disturbed balance, Christ restores not only where the disturbance is going on within one and the same person, but also where it reaches beyond the sphere of one person into that of another.

If one regards it all as mere healing stories, then the question arises why these healings are not simply narrated in the sign of the Bull, but in the counter-sign of the Scorpion. One can first seek the answer by pointing to the special nature of both cases of sickness, as it were, to the 'medical viewpoint'. When we follow Steiner's explanation, we are clearly led to the Scorpion, to the realm of organic functions really governed by the Scorpion. One could add that in the way in which the second of the two cases, that of the twelve-year-old girl, had led her to the border of death, quite especially the might of death of this sign is expressed. We are not dealing here with a mere healing like others, but we see Christ wrestling with the power of death itself and overcoming it.

As far as really being led to the power of death of the Scorpion, there lies something correct in all this. But to understand the context that

can lead us to the 'cosmic rhythm' in Mark's Gospel, we gain decisive viewpoints only when we recognize these stories of healing and awakening are inserted into the governing theme of the disciples' initiation in the narration of Mark's Gospel. None of the twelve heavenly signs is for this initiation more destiny-laden, more decisive, more critical than the death-sign of the Scorpion. This will become completely clear in the ensuing higher [second and third] rounds of the cosmic solar rhythm. Everything then appears on the level of consciousness of Inspiration and Intuition, that is, experienced in the essential depths.

During the first round that is not the case in the same way. Everything still stands at the stage of Imagination. Things stand initially as though only pictures of outer events are presented. But the meaning of these pictures we only grasp when we also recognize what they mean for the consciousness of the disciples. The power of death, which already previously cast its dark shadow on their soul-life, the disciples were to recognize in order to overcome it. And already at this point it is shown that only *one* manages to overcome it. And here once again what has been said is to be understood that through the indication of the Imaginative significance of the events, the outer actuality, or possible outer actuality, should not simply be brushed aside.

That we are dealing with an initiation process, the gospel says with most sufficient clarity with the waking of Jairus' daughter. Already in the way Christ dismisses all the public, and allows only the three most trusted of the Twelve, until then the most valued (Mark 4:37), to follow him, marks the Mystery character of the event. The three are those who remain with Christ during the sacred events on the Mount of Transfiguration. They are Peter, who is seen as the 'rock of the church', and the other two who increasingly play an esoteric role, the 'sons of Zebedee', James and his brother—whom Mark in his presentation simply calls 'John', and whom we call the 'becoming-John'. We stand here above all before the fact that all the awakenings from death narrated in the gospel signify something for the initiation of John. How far this is the case with the 'waking of Lazarus' (John 11), and the 'waking of the youth of Nain' (Luke 7), was touched on in the Introduction (p. 49). Early legends tell of the person deeply connected with the secret of the becoming-John, called in John's Gospel the one who is 'sick', Lazarus. Through the awakening of the youth of Nain, the 'son of the widow', to whom he is deeply bound in his being and in his destiny, he is most deeply moved. This impression increasingly intensifies his own infirmity, all those events described in John's Gospel as the infirmity, the death and raising of Lazarus.

Between the first raising of the dead narrated in Luke and the 'raising of Lazarus' in John's Gospel, comes the raising of the twelve-year-old daughter of Jairus, chronologically taking place between them (Mark 5). The more we penetrate the connections of the gospel, not apparent at first glance, with these stories of awakening, of raising, the more will their inner relationship to John's initiation be seen. The significance of the fact that the becoming-John is present at this Mystery-event of awakening becomes clear. We sense what the whole process means for the consciousness of the one becoming-John, and how this process, without prejudice to its outer actuality, can be seen as a picture for what takes place in John's consciousness.

Mary Magdalene

In a later study on the gospel the share in the Mystery-events, in the sacramental events of John's initiation, of that personality, who in John's Gospel appears as the sister of Lazarus, Mary Magdalene, will become even more apparent. In John's narration (John 12:3ff.) she is the one who, directly after the raising of Lazarus and immediately before the beginning of the Mystery of Golgotha, herself washes the feet of Christ Jesus and dries them with the hair of her head. In the narration of the same event in Mark (Mark 14:3ff.), differing in certain details, the name Mary of Magdala is not mentioned. Now it appears very significant that even Luke contains such a story of washing (Luke 7), likewise without mentioning Mary Magdalene, yet in many—not all—details

clearly recalling the narration in John 12. Chronologically, though, it stands in particular in another context, not following the raising of Lazarus but that of the youth of Nain. Another main difference from the narration in John's Gospel is that there Mary Magdalene accomplishes a sacramental deed on Christ like a high priestess, whereas the woman in Luke 7 who washes the feet of Christ, is there called 'a sinner'.

Let us recall once more what the legends tell of what the results of the 'raising of the youth of Nain' were on the one who was 'sick' (Lazarus), who then, through this experience of consciousness and of the deep shock of consciousness, finds the way to 'become John'. We are able to view as meaningful precisely this diversity of both Magdalene excerpts. The 'sinner' reflects the state of consciousness of him who at the beginning of his 'sickness' felt the whole curse of sin, the curse of Cain on humanity. However, the high priestess, herself taking part at the fulfilment of the Mystery of Golgotha, reflected the state of consciousness of the one who had meanwhile gone through, wrestled through, the grave and resurrection into the fulfilment of his own initiation, into becoming John.

When we seek such a working-through of the sisterly experience also with the middle one of the three raisings from the dead, the raising of Jairus' daughter in Mark 5, it is true we do not find Mary Magdalene. But if we are allowed to follow certain early legends (first pointed out by Emil Bock in his gospel studies), we find the woman with the issue of blood healed through touching Christ's garment, who was sympathetically connected in such a remarkable, deeply psychological way to the twelve-year-old daughter of Jairus. She is none other than Martha, the sister of Mary Magdalene, of whom it is said (John 11), as of Mary and Lazarus, that Christ Jesus loved her (a word in the gospel always pointing to deep Mystery-contexts). Through her relationship to Martha right into the physiological level, the daughter of Jairus also lies in the Mystery-sphere to which Mary Magdalene and Lazarus belong. Through Christ, Mary Magdalene achieves

a change of consciousness (cf. Mark 16:9). Initially—in Luke 7—she is named the 'sinner' (her name 'Mary', like that of 'John', in the gospel is no mere name; it is not mentioned until she actually achieves the Mystery grade of 'Mary'). Then—in John 12—she appears as the holy priestess participating in the Mystery of Golgotha. Her counter-piece is the destiny of her sister Martha. She is healed through Christ of her illness, touching on a soul-background of astrality and related to the Scorpion's power of death.

The power of death of the Scorpion is at work in the one who is 'sick', the invalid. In getting through it, he, the one raised by Christ, finds the Johannine initiation. Through this initiation he becomes the overcomer of the power of death; he finds again the living word of the 'creation in the primordial beginning'. The might of death stands in the dark counter-sign of the Scorpion; the power of life of the word stands in the bright, upper sign of the Bull. Between the Bull and the Scorpion the decisive events of the Johannine initiation take place.

The same power of death of the Scorpion and its overcoming plays into the destiny of the bearer of the Johannine initiation, linked in the Mystery sense with the sisters Martha and Mary. (It has to remain for a later chapter to show how far this destiny with Luke 7 and Mark 16 plays in for Mary—or the later Mary—perhaps also in John 8, strongly overshadowed by the Scorpion's power of death.) And in what happens in the events of Mark 5, a significant part of this power of death is wrested away. In overcoming of this power of death, fulfilled in the raising of Lazarus and the initiation of John, a significant stage is achieved.

For whom, then, will this stage be achieved? Not for the whole circle of the Twelve. In the Storm on the Sea and in the story of the demoniac—as the 'cosmic rhythm' has precisely established—the twelve disciples stand already deep in the crisis effected by the death sign of the Scorpion. Not without reason do most of them remain—as with the Transfiguration—excluded from nine of the Mystery events narrated in Mark 5. They have no part in what happens in the 'raising of the Jairus' daughter'. Peter who is admitted is nevertheless the one

who is unable to remain steadfast against the strong attacks of the adversary, as the gospel narration goes on to relate. He is increasingly laid low through the power of death of the Scorpion. So, despite his presence, he cannot be the 'one who overcomes' in Mark 5. And James, who with the other one, his brother, is linked in the depths of being and the Mystery depths as one of the two 'sons of Zebedee', does not go along the 'way of life', in the sense that John does. According to his destiny he is still on the way of death; without prejudice to his importance otherwise for esoteric Christianity, he does not stand on the same level with John in the 'overcoming of death'. Despite, in a deep Mystery sense, his involvement in all the events, even he is not yet actually the one who overcomes the power of death in Mark 5.

Only with the one becoming-John himself are we able to imagine that he really achieves the stage meant here of overcoming the Scorpion's power of death. For him, and only for him, the events in Mark 5 are not only outer events, but pictures of what now takes place in his own consciousness, his own striving to become John. And getting mixed up with the contexts so full of Mysteries mentioned in the narration, contexts in which both female figures play a role in this chapter—the woman and the girl—this gently points to the sphere of inner events. And here the words which Christ speaks to Jairus' daughter lying in the sleep of death: *Talitha kumi*, 'Maiden, I say to you, arise', reveal to us a new meaning. Apart from the meaning these words have in the outer event that then through Christ took place, or can have taken place, they express an inner event, an inner change taking place in the one becoming-John. The one becoming-a-disciple of Christ here achieves afresh the inner virginity of his being. In himself stands the maidenly virgin-purity.

It has been said (p. 30), that John, overcoming the power of death, changes the Scorpion again into the Sun-Eagle. For this reason in the early ecclesiastical representations of the four evangelists the Eagle was assigned to John. We can, however, also express the completed change in John through another picture. If we remain with the present form

of the zodiac, in which the twelfth sign is the death-sign of the Scorpion, we can recall that an older form of the zodiac had only ten signs. The Virgin and the Scorpion at that time formed *one* sign. In the events that the 'Fall of man' brings about, the deadly arrow of the Archer was turned towards the Virgin. The maidenly quality of the heavenly-etheric fell to the forces of death. Note how the usual signs for the Virgin and the Scorpion (♍ and ♏) are similar. The Scorpion sign ♏ came about when, for itself alone, the 'Archer' arrow expressing death (♐) approached the Virgin from outside. (The form for the sign of the Scorpion is always clear ♏; the sign for the Virgin in the form ♍ emphasizes the inward closing off. The signs should not be confused.)

The sign of the Scorpion points to a one-time virgin-quality that the death-forces laid low. In order to withdraw a part of the realm of the Virgin from the approach of the forces of death, the Scales appeared, dividing and protecting, between the Scorpion and the Virgin. And so ten zodiacal signs became twelve. And when we contemplate the one becoming-John in the light of these cosmic events, we are able to say: by overcoming the sting of death of the Scorpion, the poisoned sting of sin and sensuality, John regains the inner virginity and childlike nature, realizing that which the original sense of his sign was, before it became the Scorpion through the Fall of humanity. He realized in relation to the zodiac sign allotted to him that meaning that it had when there was still *one* sign for the Scorpion and the Virgin. In other words, he stands now in his nature in relation to the zodiac no longer with the Scorpion, but with the Virgin. This cosmic secret is expressed—alongside what otherwise is expressed—in the words '*Talitha kumi*': 'Maiden, I say to you, arise.' The Mystery of the Virgin of John's being is eloquent in these words.

We may not make mistakes when we find somewhere presentations that relate the being of the disciple John to another zodiac sign. What significance precisely the Crab has for this being and John's initiation, will also be shown in detail in the present studies. The problem of arranging the twelve Apostles to the twelve zodiac signs is so difficult because the

individual beings and their position to the cosmos can be seen from such different viewpoints. In the Crab John's initiation was completed but in the Virgin his inmost being is expressed. A light on the whole problem is shed with the four triangles, already touched on (p. 34f.), in which we can think the unity of twelve of the zodiac signs thus divided. They also relate to the essence of the four evangelists. And the three points of John's triangle stand with the sign of the Fishes, the Crab and the Scorpion. This last sign, however, with John is seen from one viewpoint in the Eagle, from another changed back to the Virgin.

***

With the transition from Mark 5 to 6, like that from Mark 4 to 5, the fact to be observed is that the section aligned to the individual zodiac sign is not decided according to the chapter divisions, which do not simply correspond to the divisions of the 'cosmic rhythm'. This is not merely arbitrary or a chance arrangement, for an inner meaning and connection also governs in the whole artistic construction of the individual chapters. An inner connection resulted also between the first part of Mark 5, still under the sign of the Scales, and the following section, to be regarded under the sign of the Scorpion. Likewise the beginning of Mark 6 (vv. 1-6) is still to be thought under the sign of the Scorpion. Nevertheless, it is deeply grounded in the meaningful and artistic construction of Mark's Gospel, that these six verses already are taken into Mark 6. As will be shown in detail, a most significant relationship comes about between this opening and all the others in Mark 6 that will be discussed.

After all that is contained in Mark 5 as the result of the power of death of the Scorpion, something like an echo can be felt in the opening of Mark 6. In everything that is told there of the unbelief of people, of the offence they take to Christ's activities, one feels the working of the power of death in people's hearts. Seen outwardly, this section reminds one in some ways of the section standing in the sign of the Crab, Mark 3:20-35. (We recall the triangular divisions of the zodiac signs; the Crab and the Scorpion are related, since they belong to the

same triangle—see p. 34f.) Through the connection with what has been said hitherto, the opening of Mark 6, however, appears even more as the end of Mark 3, displaced into the sphere of the death-sign of the Scorpion. The 'death in the heart' is to be felt here even more than there. And the indicated failure—or almost complete failure—to heal the sick in v. 5: 'He could not do any miracles there, except lay his hands on a few sick people and heal them', is characteristic for the sign of the Scorpion. By recalling how otherwise in the healings that do occur, the power of the living word in the sign of the Bull is revealed (p. 79ff.), we feel the counter-might of the Scorpion in what faces the healing, the working of the living word.

The Scorpion viewpoint of the opening of Mark 6 becomes understandable especially in its deeper significance, when we recognize how it stands inwardly related to the previous crises of the disciples. The sting of death of sensuality is overcome by the newly acquired virgin purity in the heart of the *one* disciple; the sting remains in the hearts of the others. The events narrated in the opening of Mark 6 are to be brought to their consciousness through what the unsubdued sting of death in the human heart signifies. Everywhere it is the source of inhibitions and oppositions; it stops all the movements of life and healing. Not only what the situation at the opening of Mark 6 is in itself, but what it means for the disciples, is to be felt. And when we take into account everything that the evangelist reports of Christ's activities, including the healings, the disciples were involved in many ways—Rudolf Steiner frequently pointed this out, and Mark's Gospel itself indicates in Mark 3:15—with this sudden failure to heal, this check of the healing activity, we can well imagine how the inner crisis in the group of disciples is a contributing cause. Something depressing lies in this check to the healings, in the whole mood of the opening of Mark 6. In this depressing mood it can be seen how the crisis of the disciples and the power of death of the Scorpion working in the group casts its dark shadow.

The Other Sign of Death: the Archer

(Mark 6:7-11)

Like the Bull that is followed by the sign of the Twins that leads to the midday heights of the daily and annual rhythm, the counter-sign of the Scorpion is followed by the sign of the Archer leading down to the midnight depths. The Scorpion and the Archer are signs closely bound together. Already from this viewpoint the transition of the one into the other in the opening of Mark 6 can appear understandable. They were regarded as *one* sign in early astrology, above all the Assyrian. In the explanation above, where originally the Archer followed the Virgin, the Scorpion came about first through the effect of the Archer's arrow on the Virgin. Its impact on the form of the sign no doubt most correctly expresses the relationship.

The sting of death of the Scorpion was originally connected with the Archer's arrow of death. The rest of the being of this sign—once linked to Mysteries of the Sun-life—was connected with that of the Virgin. Today not only the Scorpion but also the Archer appear as 'signs of death'. With the Scorpion we think more of the origin of death, with the Archer more of the influence of death. This also corresponds to the fact that the Scorpion belongs to the 'cross of the astral element' (see p. 34)—for the deeper origin of illness and death lies in the astral sphere of the soul. The Archer, however, belongs to the 'cross of the etheric element'. This cross reveals the highest manifestations of life (manifestations of the etheric), the cross that embraces the Mystery of the Lord's Supper, sonship with Christ (the Fishes) and the bread of life (the Virgin), which in its apex in the Twins speaks of the 'Sacred Mount', of heights of life and heights of Inspiration and initiation. This cross also bears at its feet the Mystery of death. It is of deep significance that the cross of Golgotha, the death on Golgotha itself, from the viewpoint of the cosmic rhythm, is contained in this cross of the etheric, this Christ-cross of the zodiac. Thereby the death-sign of the Archer in the 'cosmic rhythm' of Mark's

Gospel receives a special festive meaning. The revealed secret of the 'Sacred Mount' in the counter-sign of the Twins is thereby significantly experienced. This clearly appears in the 'Transfiguration on the Mount' and with the death on Golgotha. It is as though here with the Archer one looks from below up to the Sacred Mount, which then in special majesty stands before the spiritual eye as the 'Sacred Mount' Sirius-Orion (see p. 40). The stellar constellation of the Twins shining over it shines at its most festive in the night sky when the Sun itself stands in the sign of the Archer approaching deep winter.

The whole relationship of the Archer to the exalted sign of the Twins, belonging to the 'constellation of the Sacred Mount' clearly appears in the gospel. As at that time in the exalted sign of the Twins (3:13ff.) and now again—this time in the sign of the Archer—Christ calls the Twelve to him (6:7) in order to renew the impulse towards the initiation begun with them then, only the 'Mount', the ascent of the Mount, this time remains unmentioned. It is as though this time in the Archer one looks up to the Sacred Mount, as though one is not above but below, also in the spiritual sense, in the sense of destiny, the whole situation as it exists through the crisis that is apparent in the group of disciples and in the disciples' initiation. A renewal of the impulse to initiation has proved necessary through the previous crisis. This crisis appears as the reason that this renewal does not happen in the heights of the Twins but in the depths of the Archer. Not a sublime mood but a dark feeling governs the events narrated in Mark 6.

In this context, the death-sign of the Archer standing over the section referred to here reveals itself in the way in which a destiny-bearing incident stands in the background of this renewed call of the disciples. Without this incident the renewal of the initiation-impulse through Christ would not have been possible. This destiny-bearing incident is the death of John the Baptist, which, as is to be gathered from v. 14, had already happened at the moment when Christ calls the group of disciples around Him.

The death of the Baptist John was also a sacrificial death. This is to be recognized already from the events with the Jordan-Baptism. John at the Jordan really did sacrifice his whole being, or the angelic part of his being; he sacrificed himself to Christ and into the events around Christ. Herod's deed only completed according to destiny that which out of freedom John had begun at that time. Luke 7, richly full of Mysteries of John, very clearly shows this picture of death in life, of John's living sacrifice. The apparent contradiction of the two places touching so significantly on the Mystery of Elijah in John the Baptist, Matt. 11:14 and John 1:21, are resolved when we remember that between both places there lies in the middle precisely the sacrifice of John-Elijah. The angel of Elijah gives himself, changing from the pre-Christian into the Christian bearer. Elijah-Mysteries and Elijah-forces deeply connected with the sacrifice of John the Baptist are realized and become real in the group of disciples, especially increasingly in the disciples of John. Precisely Mark 6 is full of such Mysteries and influence of Elijah. Through the sacrificial death of the Baptist John, over which the death-sign of the Archer stands, these manifestations gain their strength.

Full of significance and full of destiny, the sacrificial death of John falls at that moment when the initiation of the disciples falters, arriving at an initial check, an initial crisis. Here a darkening of consciousness out of the sign of the Scorpion has led them, so that strength fails them all—except one. Out of the etheric, from the Archer, another influence is at work, which renews the strength of the disciples, that gives Christ Himself the possibility to renew the impulse of initiation. Let us imagine ourselves looking at the zodiac, at the constellation that also stands over the death on Golgotha. With its stars in the mist of the Milky Way the bright shining Archer stands low down near the horizon. Like a heavenly stream of heavenly life the Milky Way shines to escape from the sign of death. And so, still before the event of Golgotha itself has taken place, from the sacrificial death of John out of the spiritual world, a stream of life now takes effect in which the strength

of the disciples can be renewed. Already at the point of failure, they have arrived at the crisis.

Out of the source of death life and strength is renewed. In the way in which these enlivening and renewing forces out of the sacrificial death of John (completed in the sign of the Archer) stream into the activities of the group of disciples, already the prelude and transition from the first to the second round or octave of the great Sun-rhythm is taking place. We shall be looking into the zodiac again, as with the first stage of John's activity, to the sign of the Ram and the Waterman.

PART II

The Second Round of the Sun-Rhythm

Transition to the Second Round in the Goat and the Waterman: New Stage of the Sacrifice of John (Mark 6:12-29)

In the immediate death of the Baptist John through the crime of Herod, effected through the black magic of Herodias, the sacrifice already begun in the Jordan Baptism is completed. The power of Elijah already streaming over into the sphere of Christ at the Jordan now increasingly passes over to the Twelve, renewing for the disciples the impulse of their initiation and the strength of its influence. In both 'Feedings' of Mark 6 and 8, recalling the picture in the stories of Elijah in the Old Testament of the 'increase of bread', this in-streaming is expressed above all in the sacrifice of the power of Elijah.

A theology not based on spiritual research, standing distant from anthroposophy [Drews 1921/2012], has found an indication to the signs of John, the Ram and the Waterman, in a reference to John the Baptist and Elijah (Mark 6:14ff.). The matter, however, is not to be laid hold of so superficially, as though such an indication is already contained in the mere reference to John the Baptist. But in the way in which all that now takes place, one can recognize a new sacrificial presence of John the Baptist out of the spiritual world. The operation already begun at the Jordan through the completion of the sacrificial death, now raised to a new, higher stage, is expressed in the revelation of John's signs, the Goat and the Waterman. Previously, in the first round, John and the effect of his sacrifice stands like another picture before the spiritual eye. Now, in the second round, the sacrifice of John works out of the spiritual world to renew from within the strength and impulse of the group of disciples. In the second round, with reference to the revelation of the individual heavenly signs, we now leave the stage of Imagination and enter that of Inspiration. Into the new phase of initiation-events of the disciples, the power of Elijah-John in the Goat and the Waterman gives itself to a new stage.

In no way are we dealing here with applying some kind of interpretation, but in the language of the gospel itself the things can be found. We recall how we found specific words in the gospel, as it were, written for the individual heavenly signs. Linked to the being of the Goat, where it appears as the sign of John, is the saying of John's sermon 'change your thinking' (Gk. *μετανοειτε*, usually translated 'repent'). Already at the Jordan, the being Elijah-John sacrificed himself into the sphere of Christ. We see, correspondingly, Christ Himself preaching John's sermon to change one's thinking (Mark 1:15). And now, in Mark 6, with the same words the sermon passes over to the group of Twelve (as Emil Bock also points out in his *Studies in the Gospels*). Now the disciples preach the sermon of changing one's mind, one's thinking. (Mark 6:12, NIV: 'They went out and preached that people should repent.') This is preceded by the renewal of the initiation-impulse through Christ in the Archer, in the death-sign of John the Baptist. The word to change one's thinking now sounding out of the mouths of the Twelve marks the transition from the sign of the Archer to the sign of the Goat. With the same words with which the sign of the Goat in the first round of the Sun-rhythm was initially introduced, the same sign returns now in the second round on a higher level.

The sign of changing one's thinking, the dark sign of the Goat, appears in John's activities. Dark self-will, the original meaning of the sign, changes into 'change of mind' towards the Good and the spiritual. This also affects the human form, where it is allocated to the Goat, the knee and the elbow. Initially self-will and self-assertion is expressed; when they bend in prayer, devotion before the divine is expressed.

Full of significance, Mark 6 allows us to look into the deep and the shocking background of historical events of the gospel narration. Alongside the clear meaning of John we also sense the dark meaning of the sign of the Goat. We are allowed to see the immediate connection of John the Baptist and his sacrificial death with the two dark

figures of Herod and Herodias. What hitherto was said about the might of death of the Scorpion-sign and the darkening of the disciples' consciousness proceeding from it, gains a quite new and concrete meaning when we recognize these two forces are, as it were, humanly incorporated in Herod and Herodias and their dark, black sexual magic. The power of the adversary, with which the disciples in their initiation always have to struggle, appears in Herod, even more in Herodias, as if in essence incorporated. Through their criminal act Herod and Herodias immediately conclude the pre-determined death of John. What on the one side appears as one of the darkest crimes in human history, on the other side forms a significant link in the destiny-laden events proceeding from the wise [spiritual] leadership watching over the world.

Herod as shown in Mark 6 stands before us as a knower, as an initiate of deep secrets of the spirit, indeed, as one amongst those living in the Palestine of Christ Jesus, witnessing His earthly life and work, who knew most. He knew, as one of the really few, the being who was working now through the deeds of the disciples and revealing himself in these deeds. Mark 6:13 also indicates the strengthening of the disciples through the sacrifice of Elijah-John. Only one person knew even more—his wife Herodias. Significantly, the gospel quietly expresses this point; if there was anybody who knew the Elijah-secret it was Herodias. We sense we recognize in her a connection to a certain person, indeed identification with that other person in the Old Testament who stands before us as the deadly arch-enemy of Elijah. If we follow the explanation of spiritual science from Rudolf Steiner (Berlin, 14 Dec. 1911. GA 61), she causes the death of that person who at that time was the earthly bearer of the forces of Elijah (gently indicated in the narrated events in I Kings 19 and 21)—*Isabel*[RSV Jezabel], wife of King Ahab. This identification or link of a being is indicated in the Bible itself, in the 'fourth message' of the Apocalypse of John (2:20). It contains special advice to the, at that time, present—the previous 'messages' relate many things about the past. Here Isabel ('Jezabel') is

named as a contemporary. The manner in which this happens clearly points to Herodias and her dark Mysteries.

Isabel fought the forces of Elijah in the person in which at that time those forces manifested; Herodias fought them in John. It is an opposition that drags on through long epochs of humanity's history, the opposition of the dark Moon-forces. This dark enchantment, turning to the lower nature, befogged and dampened down the forces of consciousness through a world of pictures called up out of the abyss. These ensnared and overwhelmed the soul, and the clear forces of consciousness preparing for the solar 'I'-impulse of Christ. The work with the 'I'-forces of consciousness is gently indicated in both the Old and New Testaments in the picture of 'work in the vineyard'. 'Naboth's vineyard', that plays such a role in the Elijah story, points in the same direction as does the vineyard about which Christ speaks in the parables of Matthew's Gospel.

Isabel's name (Isis-Baal) points to the Mysteries of the Moon and the Sun, to the Isis-Mysteries, now become degenerate black magic; she fought the work in the vineyard. She fought the power of Elijah, who is the great forerunner and preparer of the Christ-Sun 'I'-impulse, she fought it in that person whom she recognized through her black-magic knowledge as the bearer of the power of Elijah. And this struggle is not shut within the narrow confines of *one* earthly life; it is a struggle carried out on a level of consciousness from which, as it were, pulls away above the confines of time and space of one earthly life. This struggle continues from life to life, through the whole of earthly history, or extensive epochs of earthly history. Between the free power of the 'I' and the dark coercive powers which overwhelm the soul, opposition exists from the primordial beginning.

Herod and Herodias stand before us, more the latter, as knowers, initiates in hidden knowledge. Their knowledge, however, is a lower knowledge, serving selfish purposes, a black magic that does not baulk before the darkest crimes. In Elijah-John forces of the cosmic life-ether, of the 'heavenly provision', give themselves

to humanity—the 'miracles of feeding' of the Old and the New Testament are the pictorial expression for these events. The black magicians cut off the etheric stream of life of the world and use it for their self-addicted desires. In Elijah-John the clear forces of 'white magic', of the 'Holy Grail', are at work; in Herodias the dark counter-forces are at work. The bloody head on the silver platter is the direct expression for these dark forces of the Moon enclosed in themselves. The 'dark Grail' is the counter-image of the 'Grail of light', the clear Moon vessel carrying in itself the spiritual powers of the Sun. The dark, black-magic side of the being of the Goat is revealed in these pictures.

During the course of the year, Christmas and Epiphany lie in the sign of the Goat. During the time of year of deepest darkness falls the festival of clear heavenly grace, the birth of the child of heaven. In looking at the birth of the heavenly child, the gaze also falls on the dark deed of that other Herod, the child-murderer. Here too both sides of the being of the Goat are revealed.

This Herod who committed the murder of the children of Bethlehem was a forerunner of him who allowed the beheading of the Baptist, told in Mark 6 (cf. Matt. 2:19). His deed, too, can only be understood from viewpoints of the darkest, black-magic evil. Not only against that one child—that in reality was not achieved at all—but against childhood itself this deed was directed, perhaps the most atrocious crime of the whole of earthly history. The black magician wanted to cut off and capture for himself those future-bearing forces of germinating life, at work in the newly born. Through the dark deed of black magic, through the most terrible black-magic crime, the cosmic grace—also felt by the dark initiates—revealed in the heavenly child, in which the highest of all deeds of white magic, the Mystery of Golgotha, was prepared, was, if it were at all possible, to be extinguished. Black magic was supposed to take off the head of white magic. But through a wise leadership the destinies of the world were steered differently from what the black magicians planned.

The later Herod who beheads John the Baptist does not reach the black-magic malice of his sinister predecessor Herod who acted in the history of childhood. We should rather think of him as a weakling without conscience who seeks to satisfy his occult curiosity concerning John the Baptist, as well as later with Christ Jesus Himself (Luke 23:8). He only wants to enrich himself with occult knowledge and, through this, to increase his power. His wife Herodias is far more advanced in this knowledge than he is. She alone truly knows what the death of John the Baptist means for the world and what she, Herodias, wants to achieve with this death. She recognizes the forces of Elijah working in John, which she hates to the depths of her being. Christ through the group of disciples wants to lead the sacrificial forces working in John into world-events. He wants to let them flow into earthly becoming, those forces that she wants to make serviceable to her own egotistic strivings: the forces that belong to the world, Herodias wants for herself.

Then in the events of Mark 6 revealing the Grail-forces of white magic—these she wants to oppose with the black magic of the dark Grail, the bloody head on the silver platter. She also wants through black magic to break the cutting edge of white magic. Not so much in the death of John the Baptist—who indeed wanted to sacrifice himself; he was not afraid of death—does the atrociousness of the deed lie, but the way in which Herodias intends to reap the forces of the sacrifice of this death for herself. The self-offering power of Elijah-John was to be revealed through Christ and the group of disciples. Through the paralyzed, solidified, bloody head the clear images were to be wiped out.

In this black-magic knowledge and intention the weakling Herod was not able to follow his wife Herodias. He, who would dearly like to enrich himself with the presumed knowledge of the mysterious Baptist can only have been disappointed that his wife wanted to take from him this source of enrichment of knowledge. But Herodias is the stronger; it is not difficult for her through her sexual magic arts to break the opposing will of Herod. In the dancing of Herodias' daughter—she is called Salome in later legends—lies the power of enchantment to beguile the heart of the weakling. The head of the Baptist falls. The dark picture of the counter-Grail is effectively placed in the world.

The adversary couple of dark opposition in the Old-Testament story of Elijah appearing as Ahab and Isabel, in the New Testament as Herod and Herodias, appear in the sphere of the Grail legends of the Middle Ages as Klingsor and Iblis. In his *Parsifal,* Wagner has taken up this motif and its connection with the story in the gospels. He lets Kundry, in service to the enemy of the Grail, be 'Herodias' in an earlier life. Not the actual dark Herodias of Mark 6 can be meant. Wagner's female figure can well carry the characteristics of the daughter of Herodias, who in the legends is called Salome. Salome does not stand at the same level of conscious black-magic evil as does her mother Herodias. She is only a serving tool for the purposes of sexual magic, a hierodule [temple slave or prostitute], a medium; the demonic abyss of the female nature appears in her as captivating enchantment. And thus she can still change and be redeemed. In Act II, Wagner expressively presents her meeting with Christ Jesus:

> *Ich sah Ihn – Ihn – und lachte …*
> *da traf mich sein Blick …*
>
> I saw Him—Him—and laughed …
> there his gaze met me ….

Now she seeks from life to life to meet again the redeeming gaze of Christ—which she met at that time as admonishing love and admonishing strictness—but she fails in her search. She has to serve as a tool without a will, a tool of the dark enemies of the Grail. Through her enchantment she even seduces Amfortas, the erring Guardian of the Grail. Only the childish-pure Parsifal resists her. Particularly through this he releases her from Klingsor's fetters:

> *wer dir trotzte, löste dich frei.*
> he who defied you desires your freedom.

On Good Friday morning before the Grail Castle she finds in the eyes of Parsifal the redeeming gaze of Christ. Wagner beheld that deeply within the world-tragedy and the context of world-consciousness of a person already met in the gospel. All of this may be mentioned here because in Mark's Gospel itself we soon meet a scene (Mark 7:25ff.) for which the above-mentioned context offers a key to unlock its riddle.

***

When we look once more at all this from the aspect of the zodiac, including the way Wagner deals with the person met in Mark's Gospel, how the 'dark evil' links to the admonition to 'change your thinking', motifs of the Goat can be found. It is the same sign from which the questionable section in Mark 6 is governed. Both sides of the Goat's being appear expressively in this section, the Johannine, or the Elijah side (5:12, 13), and the opposite, that of dark evil (5: 14-28). What for Herod and Herodias is the execution of their black magic plans, is for John the Baptist the completion of his offering.

As in the first round, the motif of the Waterman unites with that of the Goat. In the first round of the cosmic rhythm this sign helps us to see John's baptism by water, of the waters of the River Jordan, and with this submersion the experience of the etheric world. In the second round everything moves a stage deeper. In the place of the depths of water and of the etheric, the depths of the Earth are met. The motif of the baptism by water becomes that of the deposition in the grave. [We may mention that Rudolf Frieling, *Sacrament and Ritual*, Edinburgh, Floris Books 1988, finds in the funeral service—lying outside the seven sacraments—the 'octave' of the first sacrament,

baptism. What Frieling expresses, purely out of the essence of the rite, independent of the zodiac, does find its confirmation in the zodiac and its reflection in the cosmic rhythm of the gospel.]

First the burial of John the Baptist is narrated. The earthly body of him who in his nature was but loosely connected to the earthly, physical element—he was actually more bound with the etheric element (cf. Mark 1:6)—is committed to an earthly grave. This earthly grave is at the same time a picture for all the depths of matter and of evil into which the Elijah-being of the Baptist offered himself, and through this himself purifying and changing this matter and evil. Here, too, the influence of John the Baptist appears like a preparation for the influence of Christ. He knew that he could not unite so deeply, so completely, as Christ could unite with the earthly element (Mark 1:7). The motive of the Waterman that initially we met in the etheric baptism of John by water, then on a higher level in the deposition of John, is finally met on the highest level in the deposition of Christ Himself.

And so Mark 6:29 stands in the sign of the Waterman, where it is narrated how the disciples of Christ take the body of John the Baptist and lay it in the grave. Here is expressed how they know they are united with him and with his sacrificial death. The whole destiny and sacrificial influence of John the Baptist really is linked to the initiation-events of the disciples. It works on, inspiring from within in the initiation-events of the group of disciples. And with the motif of the Waterman it becomes clear how the cosmic rhythm of Mark's Gospel is raised from the stage of Imagination to that of Inspiration.

The Feeding of the Five Thousand in the Sign of the Fishes

(Mark 6:30-46)
Transition to the Ram (Mark 6:47-54)
and the Bull (Mark 6:55f.)

A critical moment in world-history is recorded in Mark 6. A terrible crime has been committed. Black-magic malice of the dark adversary threatens to divert for itself the flow of blessing that, out of the sacrificial deed of John the Baptist through Christ and the group of disciples, wants to flow into the world. To strengthen its own power and self-seeking, the dark adversary wants to use the bread of life of the power of Elijah, that through Christ and the circle of disciples is intended for hungering humanity. Only through the highest, purest, white magic can the tip of black magic be broken, can curse be changed into blessing. And only with Christ and the disciples can these forces of white magic be found. He alone sees through the events and what it means for world-events. He alone is able to blunt it. And he needs the co-operation of the circle of disciples. As the earthly representatives of the twelve powers of the zodiac, through which the Sun of Christ works, the twelve disciples form a ring around Christ. And the harrowing tragedy of the world-events lies therein, as so often precisely with the most important things, the most decisive occasions fail and leave Christ in the lurch.

With their Master and Initiator the disciples discuss the seriousness of what they have done (Mark 6:30). Christ now knows what to do; He clearly recognizes the demand of the hour. Most translations of v. 31 sound harmless: 'Come with me by yourselves to a quiet place and get some rest.' The original text means: 'Prepare yourselves, each for himself alone (*κατ' ἰδίαν*), to return to the loneliness of soul, and produce the peace of meditation in yourselves.' Here *ἔρημον τόπον*, the 'lonely

place', is really not the outer desert (as Luther translates it), but—a few other places clearly reveal this meaning—the spiritual region of soul-loneliness, of inner deepening and meditation. John the Baptist experienced this spiritual place of spiritual loneliness on Earth as his homeland. There he met Christ—even if seen from outside the meeting took place in the solitude of the Jordan valley.

Now, after he had passed into the spiritual world, this place of spiritual loneliness, the inner peace and meditation remains for each soul the region in which they can meet with the power of Elijah of the great initiates. There—it is the will of Christ—the disciples are to encounter those forces of the Elijah-being, John the Baptist. There they should gain the inner connection to those forces of life, which the impact of black magic of the dark adversary wanted to divert. They should be able to pour them again 'in a right stream' over the world and humanity. Something full of deep significance is expressed in the gospel about the meaning and the power of meditation, of which the popular translations have not the foggiest notion.

Christ recognized what was needed. In the current critical moment of the world, the exertion of all the spiritual forces in the inner calm of meditation was needed, in order to steer back to the Good that which in world-events had sinned.

And everything that follows can only be properly understood by recognizing how it leads us increasingly out of the world of outer events into a spiritual world of pictures. The formula, relevant in so many other cases, where through the Imaginative interpretation and significance of the gospel narration the outer actuality of events is not necessarily denied, no longer suffices for our understanding. It has to be recognized that here around the middle of Mark 6, the narration of a report of outer events (as which we do take the Herod-Herodias story) gently, gradually and increasingly leads over into a playful, dreamlike event, a spiritual (spiritual-astral) beholding of pictures. This is valid even when—but in the narrative manner of the Bible this is everywhere the case—apparently everything continues to be narrated as an

outer event. And it has to be recognized how Christ the Initiator, by spiritually watching over the meditation of the disciples, steers and leads their beholding of pictures. Here the transition is revealed from the element of merely beholding pictures, of Imagination, to that of the second octave of the cosmic rhythm, the determining element of Inspiration.

It belongs to the most significant matters of this book, that everything it contains can only be understood when we know that human *consciousness* is not something that remains the same for all ages. It stands in the flow of development; in earlier ages other more pictorial forms of consciousness existed (our dreams are a decadent remainder of this); and into the future the development of other, newer and higher forms of consciousness is a possibility to be kept in mind. On this basis, we can come to understand what *initiation* is.

So Christ now shows to the disciples—spiritually, in meditation, in the initiation-events—the picture of hungry humanity, needy of help: 6:31b. The many people, of whom it says there that they came and went, that they had no opportunity to eat, we find not true of external events. Having followed the gospel narration up to now, we don't quite understand from where they have all come. Likewise, what follows appears shadowy and dreamy: the way they see the ship depart, carrying the disciples—or Christ (there are variant texts)—to the 'lonely place'; they make their way on foot, and at the 'lonely place' they are suddenly all there again, indeed, they manage more swiftly than those in the ship who apparently take the shorter route. Even the ship, the matter under discussion here, is no longer an outer ship but the ship of the soul, in which the 'lonely place' of meditation is sought. (We recall how in Indian presentations manas, the Spirit-self, is frequently pictured as a ship on the water, as the 'moon boat'.)

The whole style of the gospel narration of the quoted passage, when we intimately live into it, has something of a 'dream-play' quality (recall certain scenes in Strindberg's *A Dream Play* [1901]).

It is no longer the logic of outer events, but those of a more dreamlike event that links together the individual events—which are now no longer outer events but inner pictures. Yet we have not only to think of normal dreams but of a picture-world of a sublime kind, corresponding to the level of the life of initiation. These are initiation-dreams in a grand style, a show of pictures of a tremendous kind, that arise against a background of deep spiritual realities that reach the spiritual eye.

Out of his spiritual research, Rudolf Steiner draws attention to the fact that the people who in what follows were fed with bread and fishes were not at all those of that time but those of our epoch. The number 5000 encapsulates the Mystery of the 'fifth post-Atlantean cultural epoch' of today (in which the Sun rises on the first day of spring in the Fishes). In a tremendous spiritual vision, the disciples were shown the secret of this 'fifth post-Atlantean epoch' and therein the awaited etheric experience of Christ. What the disciples behold is not their present but the future, that is, the present (or near future) today; experiences of the future of humanity are disclosed before their spiritual eyes. They behold everything not with the awake eyes of daytime but in a higher kind of dreaming revealing the future. In this story of the first Feeding, the gospel reports not daytime experiences but nocturnal experiences, a night vision of a most sublime sort. The gospel itself speaks here (Mark 6:35) that 'the time is far passed' (AV/KJV); 'it was late in the day' (NIV), that everything was an experience during the night. This is not to be understood in an outer but in a spiritual sense, as meant here. In the way Christ 'began to teach them many things' (AV) (Mark 6:34: *καὶ ἤρξατο διδάσκειν αὐτοὺς πολλά*), when he feels compassionate towards the hungry folk—does not think about the Feeding—there lies a dreamlike, playful trait, corresponding to a night-experience. It is as if the Sermon on the Mount (Matt. 5–7), once experienced by the disciples, is once more placed before their spiritual eyes, as if they are woven into the picture-vision of the initiation-experience.

(In the Sermon on the Mount too, as Emil Bock has shown in his *Studies in the Gospels*, the human crowds should not be thought as physically present.)

The Mystery of the bread and fishes and its relationship to the heavenly zodiac was pointed out several times in the Introduction (pp. 32f., 36, 42ff.). It was emphasized how the character of the meditation-experience at night, which the first of the two Feedings has, is expressed in the cosmic rhythm governed by the night-side, that is, by the Fishes belonging to the night-side of the zodiac. (This aspect is connected with the other one previously mentioned of the first of spring, in the fifth cultural epoch.) It corresponds to the character of the nightly meditation-experience that bread and fishes are not to be thought of as earthly bread and fishes. In this is revealed the power of Elijah, of the cosmic life-ether. The heavenly provisions for the way pass over to the disciples through the sacrifice of John. Like a heavenly miracle of the Grail, through which He extinguishes the dark picture of the counter-Grail presented through the black magic of Herodias, Christ, the Initiator, lets this picture of heavenly provisions dawn in the disciples' meditation-experience and initiation-experience. The Elijah-power of the bread of life in the sign of the Virgin is linked in this picture with the Christ-power of the 'I' in the sign of the Fishes. In their experience of initiation and meditation, the disciples now also become aware of the power of the Christ-Sun and the Christ-'I', which in the Jordan-Baptism initially began to stream into the earthly sphere.

At the point where in the narration the description of outer events gradually goes over into meditation-experience (Mark 6:30ff.), we have to think of the transition from the sign of the Waterman to that of the Fishes. This sign of the Fishes now also appears in the second octave of the Sun-rhythm, on the stage of Inspiration. What earlier was the external picture, the in-streaming of the power of Christ into the earthly realm is now received by the disciples in their initiation-experience as spiritual power from within.

***

In an increasingly tremendous manner, the picture of the spiritual night-vision is painted. Bread and fishes shine before us as the great Last-Supper constellation in the night sky. It is as if the gospel itself wants to turn our vision, just when the receiving of the bread and fishes is the subject, by allowing Christ to 'look up to heaven' (Mark 6:41). Before us stands the picture of a midsummer night (cf. p. 41). Towards the west shines the stellar constellation of *the Virgin with the Sheaf* (Spica), the heavenly bread; towards the east near the horizon at the other end of the zodiacal arch the constellation of the *Fishes*. In its lesser brightness it almost disappears to view on a summer night. From the constellation of the Virgin actually only the star Spica makes itself seen on a summer night with its mild and comforting, almost feminine light. In the west, we see in the summer night sky the five lower, dark constellations of the zodiac—including the Scales towards the south. In these five dark zodiacal signs (Scorpion, Archer, Ram, Waterman, and Fishes) we recognize at the same time again the picture of the five loaves, which, in the Feeding of the Five Thousand, Christ breaks 'looking up to heaven'. They are deeply connected with the Mystery of this Feeding, which spiritually taken is an event of the fifth post-Atlantean epoch. On the human figure (see p. 32f., 36, 42ff.), they correspond to the five members of the lower human being, down to the feet (the Fishes). Through a Christian initiation of the will, which ends in the fifth cultural period, in the 'age of the five thousand', this lower, dark will-part of human nature, otherwise easily open to be taken hold of by the forces of evil, is changed and purified by the strength of Christ, the strength of a higher consciousness, a higher clear thinking. At first the feet express this higher consciousness. Consequently, Christian initiation begins with the Washing of the Feet. The rhythm of the gospel here again is the constellation of Fishes–Virgin.

For the disciples all this is a vision of the future. This is the initiation-experience in general, that the impact of pictures of the future of humanity gives strength for human work lying in the present. In this sense, the initiation-experience expressed in the picture of

the Feeding of the Five Thousand does but continue that which in the same constellation (only there emphasized from the sign of the Virgin) in the picture of Christ's Parable of the Sower (and the following, related parables) was begun by Christ the Initiator as work on the consciousness of the disciples. The receiving of these parables with their pictures (*Bilde*) lighting up deep Mysteries of the human future for the disciples, meant a reception of active forces into their souls (and in their own 'formative forces', *Bildekräfte*). This is also the case with the meditation-experience of the 'Feeding of the Five Thousand'. Therein begins directly what was begun in the Parable of the Sower. Already the sameness of the constellation reveals the connection (only emphasized in the one case from the day-sign of the Virgin, in the other case from the night-sign of the Fishes). With such examples it becomes increasingly clear how the 'cosmic rhythm' helps us to recognize the whole construction of the gospel and its inner connections.

Not a physical but an etheric experience speaks to us in this mysterious 'Feeding of the Five Thousand'. We feel it inwardly meaningful to be in the middle 'etheric' cross (see p. 36), to which the 'Last-Supper constellation' of Fishes–Virgin indeed belongs. The 'green grass' of Mark 6:39 corresponds to this etheric character of the nocturnal spirit-vision that reveals the etheric forces, taken as an Imagination. Pictures of bursting and burgeoning life are placed before us. Rudolf Steiner speaks (*The Effect of Occult Development*. Lecture-course, The Hague. 20-29 March 1913. GA 145) how this picture of bursting and burgeoning life precisely expresses that which is revealed when we sleep at night. Here, too, in the gospel an emphasis on experiences at night is to be found.

With the enlivening etheric forces, how very much humanity needs at the same time the strength of the Christ-'I' is expressed in the picture of Mark 6:40: 'They sat down in groups of hundreds and fifties.' In the language of the Mysteries the number 'thousand' expressed the whole, what is complete. Here the numbers of arrangement 'hundred'

and 'fifty' were taken as 'incomplete numbers'; they express in human souls that which is still group-orientated, herd-like, not yet penetrated by the 'I'.

The twelve baskets of fragments, or broken pieces, are also significant for the meaning of the future experiences of humanity beheld by the disciples in meditation. The fragments remained after the great feeding (see Introduction, p. 35f.). This Christian initiation of future humanity (today it has already become the near future or the present) also turns to the lower, darker part of human nature, the human being of will (the five loaves and five dark zodiacal signs). This initiation embraces the forces of the total human being, that is, all twelve zodiacal forces (from head to feet). The 'twelve baskets' corresponds to the twelve zodiacal forces, the twelve members of the total human being. In his lecture-courses, Rudolf Steiner conveys this meaning.

Above (p. 89), we discussed how the constellations (cross beam and longitudinal beam) of the middle, etheric cross, the Christ-cross (carrying in it the Last Supper and Golgotha) in a certain way illuminate in various ways all twelve sacred, heavenly signs. And this is the case with the 'Feeding of the Five Thousand' standing in the 'Last-Supper constellation'. The picture of the twelve baskets full of broken pieces remaining at the end of this Feeding correspond to the twelve signs of the zodiac on the human being; we see, as it were, all twelve sacred, heavenly signs light up before us. In a specially expressive manner in the stories of both great Feedings in the gospel, the picture of the heavenly zodiac stands before the spiritual eye.

***

In the picture of the 'Feeding of the Five Thousand' described in the gospel the disciples are placed before a new earnest test in the life of initiation. With this Christian life of initiation, it is a fact that nothing is merely received, is simply given. But in order to

bear proper fruit everything received has to be actively worked on by proactive soul-forces. The disciples have to show whether they really have pressed on to inner hearing and understanding, from Imagination to Inspiration—which corresponds to all the events in the 'second round'. Do they know how to enliven what had been received? Are they really in the position to distribute amongst humanity the bread of life brought about by Christ? What they behold in Mark 6:41 is initially only a picture of the future, not of present activity.

Already, as Christ in the great pictures of the Sower and the Seed planted the future secrets of humanity into the disciples' souls, this test initially passed them by. What they then experienced in their souls is described in the gospel in the picture of the Storm on the Lake and of the fear of the disciples (Mark 4:35ff.). And their present experience is exactly parallel to that previous one—also after the 'Feeding of the Five Thousand' follows the episode of the Storm on the Sea (Mark 6:48-54). On this point, the 'cosmic rhythm' in the gospel is especially clear. Like the 'Parable of the Sower', the 'Feeding of the Five Thousand' also stands in the constellation Fishes–Virgin—only there the Virgin, here the Fishes is primarily emphasized. Like the Storm on the Lake following the story of the Sower standing in the constellation Ram–Scales (linking to the previous one), here, too, the Storm follows the first Feeding-experience, only with the first Storm the Scales, with the second the Ram is the sign primarily emphasized. With the Scales we see more the struggle to attain the inner balance, with the Ram the endeavour to be able to pass from the weaving of the etheric element to the firm ground of the physical element. For the viewpoint of the 'night-experience', with the 'Feeding of the Five Thousand', this is especially important. The change is from the uncontrolled nocturnal consciousness into the 'I'-governed, day-awake condition, from the uncertain impressions of the night and dreamlike initiation pictures into the awake consciousness. The difficulty clearly to carry over the images of nightly dreams to a

clear memory is known to all. By subsiding into the 'physical body', 'etheric' impressions are easily confined to oblivion.

We recognize most clearly the being of the Ram at the end of the Storm episode to be thought of as under this sign, with the words 'they landed at Gennesaret' (NIV); the original has 'they came to land, to Gennesaret'. Like other words to other zodiac-signs, one can conceive this ascribed to the Ram. The Ram as the sign of placing oneself into the forces of the Earth, into the powers of the physical realm and of an awake consciousness, is revealed here in its essence. Also that the experience takes place 'about the fourth watch of the night' (Mark 6:58), towards morning, lies in the indicated direction.

In the whole episode the gospel clearly speaks of the difficulty of the disciples to land what they behold in the experience of the night on to the shore of day-consciousness. Their task is to bring what they behold to an inner understanding, to a real understanding of the heart, to raise Imagination to Inspiration. Here the difficulty arises. Everything said in this sense of inwardly connecting the Storm on the Lake with the experience of the Feeding is not to import some kind of 'meaning' into the gospel. About these things the gospel expresses itself clearly enough. It connects the 'amazement' [*ἐξίσταντο*], the ecstasy over the stilling of the storm, with the non-understanding of the experience of the Feeding [v. 52]: 'for they had not understood about the loaves; their hearts were hardened'—other translations interpret: 'blind', 'dull', 'stupid' (Gk., *πεπωρωμένη*: the pores of their hearts were, as it were, hardened, impermeable). The higher forces in the disciples, the actual forces of the heart, are still unawakened. Like a flower, which should open but still holds its calyx, its cup, closed, the heart of the disciples is closed. This closure of the heart, not a lack of intellectual comprehension, is the actual hindrance where Imagination is already present, standing in the way of Inspiration.

Yet, when we exactly observe the gospel narration, it can nevertheless be recognized how the disciples at least step by step approach the experience of Inspiration. And Christ, the Initiator, guards this whole experience, in which it seems they are left to themselves. For precisely this reason He withdraws for His own meditation to the mountain, the Sacred Mountain of Inspiration (Mark 6:46; the Greek, like 3:13, has the definite article: *τὸ ὄρος*, 'the mountain'), in order to watch over the becoming of Inspiration in those entrusted to Him. He remains spiritually with them, and as long as they believe they are still alone and abandoned. Then they get a degree further in experience, they overcome their feeling of loneliness, they now *behold* that the spirit remains with them. They behold—already close to waking up, in the 'fourth watch'—Christ walking on the waves before them. The previous etheric experience works on in Him. It is an experience of the 'etheric Christ'. In the sacrament of marriage, to which this gospel picture is inwardly related, to the physical fact of marriage a supplement is presented from the etheric. (With the narration of the previous experience of the Feeding the dreamlike nuances in style was pointed out. It may be recalled, how also the picture of Christ walking over the waves in the background of the Storm is to be found as a main picture for the situation of consciousness today in Strindberg's *A Dream Play*.)

In this experience of the etheric, the experience of the 'I' is still missing. What in such a manner is recognized is not yet the spiritual essence, but appears like a phantom, a phantasm (as the Greek original says, *φάντασμά*), a 'ghost'. Everything is still picture-experience, Imagination, similar to that of the Storm on the Lake in Mark 4. And yet there lies in it a higher stage of etheric experience, as they see Christ (initially still appearing as a phantom) no longer in safety in the solid ship, but free and secure walking over the waves. Also with this stage of beholding they don't remain standing. What previously was only a phantom-like picture of Christ begins to speak; they hear the voice of Christ speaking to them (Mark 6:50): 'I am (*ἐγώ εἰμι*). Do not be afraid' ('I AM the I AM' is the actual meaning of the words). 'Then he climbed into the boat with them, and the wind died down.'

A mere phantom-like beholding goes over to an experience of inner hearing, and with this, despite v. 52, still a significant step nearer Inspiration. Still missing is the full recognition of Christ as the higher 'I', yet from within nevertheless the voice of the 'I AM' is heard. Calm and security thereby enters into their soul-ship; the Storm on the Lake and the Storm in the Soul have subsided.

A final stage of the whole experience is then the bringing over what has been seen in the sea-voyage at night to the sure beach and firm land of day-awake consciousness. Here the disciples first recognize Christ, their higher 'I' (NIV, Mark 6:54, 'As soon as they got out of the boat, people recognized Jesus.' AV/KJV: '... they knew him', similarly Luther). Inasmuch as they did not yet possess the strength in the etheric, out-of-the-body experience, it sufficed for them, waking out of spiritual vision, that they are with their 'I' again in physical bodies. Here too the Ram is the sign for placing oneself into physical corporeality. In few passages in the gospel is spiritual experience so clearly described from stage to stage. With the constellation Ram–Scales it was clearly shown how in the second octave of the Sun-rhythm the experience advances from mere beholding to inner hearing, from Imagination towards Inspiration.

Perhaps, to the three degrees of 'I'-experience Imaginatively described here in the episode of the Storm on the Lake in Mark 6, we may also link what Rudolf Steiner in *Anthroposophical Leading Thoughts* says on the three degrees of 'I'-experience:

> On the way of meditation three further forms are to be found in addition to the form in which the 'I' enters in normal consciousness:
>
> (1) In the consciousness, laid hold of by the etheric body, the 'I' appears as a picture, but which at the same time is an active being, and as such lends to the human being form, growth and formative forces.
>
> (2) In the consciousness that the astral body lays hold of, the 'I' is revealed as a member of a spiritual world, from which it draws its strength.

(3) In the consciousness that is simply mentioned as the final stage to be achieved, the 'I' is shown as relatively independent of the spiritual surroundings, an autonomous spiritual being.

These three stages of consciousness mutually relate as Imagination, Inspiration and Intuition.

***

The point we have reached is still not the end of Mark 6. Its final two verses (6:55 & 56) report on some healings of the sick. It reaches over from the Ram into the sphere of the Bull, which is always the sign of healing the sick. The beginning of Mark 6 (see above) still belongs to the previous sign of the Scorpion that continues its influence. Similarly, the end of Chapter 6 belongs to the comprehensive sign of the Bull, embracing the whole of Chapter 7 that follows. Already when we keep in mind the inner relationship of Bull and Scorpion, we recognize in this no coincidence, but it is meaningfully grounded in the construction of the whole chapter. We recall how at the beginning of Mark 6, a connection could be recognized between the check to the narrated healings of the sick—alongside other checks to Christ's activities—and the crises and resistances threatening the initiation of the disciples out of the death-sign of the Scorpion. The tremendous events of Mark 6 taught the disciples how the opposition is incorporated, as it were, in Herod and Herodias and their dark, sexual-magic Mysteries.

Out of the sacrifice of the death of John there streamed the forces of white magic through which with the help of Christ the black magic of the adversary could be overcome. So a renewal of the initiation-impulse was possible that had led to everything in the initiation-event which is narrated in the pictures of the experience of the great Feeding and of the awakening after the Storm on the Lake at night. The power of Elijah, of the cosmic life-ether streaming in after the sacrificial death of John, is revealed in these events. And thus in everything that lies

in the middle between the beginning and the end of Mark 6, in the whole rich events of this chapter, lies the answer to the question why the power of healing the sick, checked in such a depressing manner at the beginning, streams once again unchecked and stronger than ever before (Mark 6:56. Torrey):

> And whenever he entered villages or cities or hamlets, they brought out their sick into the streets, and besought him to let them touch even the border of his garment; and all those who touched him were healed.

More than before, we find ourselves here, where we have stepped again to the day-side of the zodiac, in the realm of physical experience. And yet these physical events at the same time reveal spiritually to the disciples what a sacrificial deed as that of John the Baptist meant for world-events and for their—the disciples'—own process of initiation.

The Bull in the Second Octave as Revelation of the Divine Power of the Word

(Mark 7)

At the end of Mark 6 (vv. 55, 56), the healings of the sick stand in obvious contrast to the checking of healings narrated at the beginning of the chapter. There the power of death of the Scorpion was evident, here the power of the living word in the sign of the Bull. And this, when we look at the whole content of Mark 6, becomes for the disciples an inspiration in which they were to realize the power of Elijah-John, even strengthened through the sacrificial death and with it also the 'meaning of death' which is closely linked with that power. How far they really could realize it will soon be revealed in the progress of the events in the gospel.

In the second octave of the Sun-rhythm, the sign of the Bull, through which the whole of Mark 7 is governed, moves into the viewpoint of the stage of Inspiration, now to be realized in the initiation-events of the disciples. This becomes completely clear with the healing of the deaf-mute at the end of the chapter, which is to be seen as a 'loosening of the spiritual ties on the tongue' of the disciples. The Mystery of the word—and the Bull is the sign of the word—is to be increasingly revealed to the disciples; the strength of the word is to pass over to them. From this viewpoint the content of Mark 7 that precedes the Healing of the Deaf-Mute can also be understood. Therein certain motifs of the Bull return, known from the first octave of the Sun-rhythm but strengthened through other new motifs.

Thus, right at the beginning of Mark 7 'the living word of Christ confronts the dead word, the deceased statutes of the Pharisees and scribes'. It becomes yet more clear on the level now reached that all this has to do with the destiny of the word. The reason for the confrontation in Mark 7 is the disciples' eating with unwashed hands, to which the Pharisees and scribes took offence.

Here Luther—whose translation otherwise we often have to approach with a critical view—has the deeper, one would like to say, cosmic meaning of the whole very clearly, by translating Mark 7:2: '*Und da sie sahen etliche seiner Jünger mit gemeinen, das ist, mit ungewaschenen Händen das brot essen,* versprachen sie es' (1545). The AV/KJV reads like a translation: 'And when they saw some of his disciples eat bread with defiled, that is to say, with unwashed hands, they found fault.' Recent editions have changed the no longer rightly understood word [at the end] to '*tadelten sie es*'. Luther meant '*versprechen*' not in the sense of 'to give a promise', but '*rügen, tadeln, beanstanden*—censure, rebuke, object to'. The Greek has *κατέγνωσαν* or *εμεμψαντο* [1550 Stephanus NT]. Something significant results if you think of '*sich versprechen*' [the reflexive]. On the meaning of the prefix '*ver*', which changes the meaning of a word into its opposite or a deviation, '*versprechen*' would then be the misuse of the word, the deviation of speaking, the death of the living element in the word.

The living word of Christ in the sign of the Bull then places itself against the lost, deceased word of the Pharisees and scribes, violated by the Scorpion's power of death. Because of the Fall of humanity through the Scorpion, the world lost the word—the Old-Testament story of the Tower of Babel and the confusion of tongues shows in pictures this 'loss of the word'. The world has lost the real ability to speak. Only in the appearance of Christ as the 'Word become flesh' is the living speech, the real speaking, here again; the speaking of the others is a speaking without life, a misuse of the word, a '*ver-sprechen*'—a 'mis-speaking'. In all this we can feel how the Bull as the 'sign of the word' stands over the whole passage. (In his translation, Luther was, of course, not conscious of this. It lived unconsciously in him, though objectively in the genius of language that was indeed at work in him. Precisely such discussions lead to the objective appreciation of the context of the zodiac and the role that it plays in the gospel.)

The divine Word once lived in the wisdom of Moses, the living source of inspiration of the early Hebrews. Christ speaks expressively

about this. Out of the divine Word which sees into the heart of human beings, in the interpretation of the Pharisees this had become dead human statutes (Mark 7:6-9). In the heart, the Word has died because the heart itself is closed by the might of death (Luther expressively has '*verstarret*', Mark 6:52, newer editions '*erstarret*', 'was benumbed'; AV 'was hardened'). With this—and the whole passage 7:14-23 belongs here—Christ touches on the innermost point of all revelations of the word and Inspiration—which indeed is always the viewpoint of the present stage of the Sun-rhythm. In the light of this revelation their [human beings'] own hearts were increasingly to open (cf. Mark 6:52).

In the 'lost word' of the Pharisees and scribes that already faced Christ in Mark 2, as now in Mark 7 faced Him again, the death-might of the Scorpion is at work, the counter-sign of the Bull. The whole chapter appears as a confrontation of sign and counter-sign. The might of death is even more terribly revealed, this sting of death of the Scorpion. The word is not simply lost or killed as with the Pharisees, but here it is misused in black magic, as it were, violated. Not for nothing does the story of Herod and Herodias in Mark 6 allow a harrowing insight into the abyss of these black-magic aberrations and its dark Mysteries. And with this insight the disciples, too, are to wake up more fully to the nature of their own adversary. Out of this viewpoint light flows on the further episode (Mark 7:24-30), which initially poses some difficulties to the understanding.

Who has not initially stumbled on first encountering the narration of how Christ, Who otherwise was always ready to heal the infirmities of mankind, is implored by the Syro-Phoenician woman to heal her daughter possessed of a devil, but—and it appears out of nationalist Jewish grounds (Mark 7:27)—the healing is initially rejected? Who is not initially disappointed that here Christ, the Representative of comprehensive love of human beings, allows Himself to be led by such narrow viewpoints? It is surely better fully to admit such an apparent hard saying of the gospel, than, as is the case with many who read the gospels, to leave the feeling in the subconscious. What otherwise

remains felt as a dark hard saying, brought into the light of consciousness and investigated as a question, becomes the path to a new and better understanding of the gospel. The fully conscious attention should be turned to all such hard sayings, of which there are more than a few in the Christian gospel.

The key to understand the problem undoubtedly felt here in Mark 7 is offered by aligning the story of the Syro-Phoenician woman as nearly as possible to the story of Herodias in Mark 6. Running right through the Old Testament is the history of the dark Mysteries and cults of the gods that were practised in the 'high places', especially on the borders of Palestine. They appear at a certain climax in the story of Ahab and Isabel, the dark opponent of Elijah and the Yahveh-'I'-impulse, the forerunner of the Christ-impulse. Always in the Old-Testament stories this impulse sets itself in opposition, working out of these dark Mysteries and cults to wipe out the 'I' and damp down the consciousness. They want to capture the soul in a decadent picture-consciousness, to befog the intellect through a sensory, illusory world of pictures, and to lame the free power of the 'I'. It was the divine mission of the Hebrew people to develop the free power of the 'I'. Not for nothing was it decreed: You shall make no image or any likeness [cf. Ex. 20:4].

Black-magic enchantment, dark sexual magic, was the picture-vision in these obscure, decadent Mysteries, which in earlier, purer Mysteries was still clear Imagination, still divine vision. The story of Herodias and Salome (concerning the names, see p. 138f.) allows us to glance into the dark abyss of this sexual magic and its depraved world of pictures. In the opposition of Herodias against John the Baptist and the group of Christ's disciples we saw the deadly enmity between Isabel and Elijah come to life again.

In *The Fifth Gospel* [GA 148. Lecture-course, Christiania (Oslo), 1-6 October 1913], Rudolf Steiner speaks of how, on his journeys already before the Jordan-Baptism, Jesus of Nazareth came into contact with such lower Mystery-centres. From the controlling demonic beings he received harrowing impressions. In the Syro-Phoenician woman, the female hierophant of such a lower Mystery-centre somehow standing close to Herodias appears before us. So, we can well imagine how and whereby her daughter had fallen to a demonic being. We may think of her as a 'medium', a 'hierodule', in the style of Herodias' daughter. A dampening down of consciousness through abuses and aberrations of sexual magic has led her to demonic possession. Had Christ in this case given Himself without further ado, He would have made the business of that fallen Mystery-centre His own; He would have made a move towards the impulses that attempt to wipe out the 'I'. This, the impulses of the higher 'I' oppose outright: as Representative of the divine 'I', Christ could not do so. He cannot serve the counter-'I'. (In his *Studies in the Gospels*, Emil Bock explains the story in this direction. Here we essentially add the aspect out of the 'cosmic rhythm'.) The representative of the divine Word cannot support the violation, the black magic misuse of the word.

Here a view is expressed that cannot be 'proved' in the usual sense. It can only be presented as a hypothesis. This encounter of Christ with the female hierophant from Syro-Phoenicia is not something subordinate or random, but the dark opponent and black-magic adversary has a hand in this. Her attack to wipe out the white magic of the power of Elijah through the death of the Baptist had misfired. The black-magic effect from the dark counter-picture of the bloody head was countered through the meditation of Christ, allowing the influx of the power of Elijah. This fact is revealed in the experience of the Feeding in Mark 6. But she already launched a new attack against the work of Christ. The Syro-Phoenician woman appears before Christ as someone sent by Herodias and her dark Mysteries. And the attack is shrewd, because this adversary of Christ wants to make Him serviceable to her use precisely through His compassion. She tackles His comprehensive love of humanity.

But Christ sees through the attack. He knows exactly who stands before him. He speaks to the hierophant of the Mystery-centre—even of fallen Mysteries—in the language of the Mysteries. As such we have to take the conversation about 'children' and 'dogs' in Mark 7:27 & 28. It has to do with the contrast of those admitted within and those relegated to the atrium. And in this Mystery-language He tells her why He cannot fulfil her request. The whole meeting in the sign of the word appears to dip into the 'Mystery of the word'.

But here, in this Mystery-language, the surprising and decisive thing occurs. The rejected hierophant and adherent of decadent Mysteries, instigated by others, had a hostile intention in the background with what she asked from Christ. Under the tremendous impression of the Christ standing before her, she experiences a deep inner change. Out of this change of her being she suddenly finds again the right use of the word. The word in her that had fallen to the adversary turns all at once to the divine. It lies perhaps less in the content of what she says, more in the way she says it. She, the destroyer and betrayer of the word, sees at once opposite her the living power of the divine Word in Christ. This performs in her the decisive conversion.

And Christ, who sees to the heart (John 2:25), recognizes this conversion. This gives Him the possibility to take up another position to the woman than that which He took at the beginning. On the other hand, there are now no grounds for Him to take refuge in something like a magic remote healing. That this episode has nothing to do with a usual healing of a possessed person, the cosmic rhythm of the gospel conveys in all clarity. It points in all the events of Mark 7 to the revelation of the word of the Bull—healings of those possessed belong to the Ram. Here, too, the cosmic rhythm can be a real help to find the decisive viewpoints to expound the gospel. It is this: the fact that the Syro-Phoenician woman returns to the divine the 'word' torn and violated by the adversary in her Mystery-centre, means the curse of the lost word also retreats from the youthful hierodule drawn into the corruptions of that Mystery-centre. There is no need for any 'healing of a possession' at all; a healing through Christ is no longer necessary. In the whole event lying in the sphere of the word and the Mysteries of the word, as it has gently and invisibly played between this hierophant

and Christ, the bearer of the living word, the fact has arisen of itself that the demon, that the whole sick damping down of the daughter's consciousness, withdraws.

7:29 *Διὰ τοῦτον τὸν λόγον* ('because of this word')

'Um des Wortes willen' (Luther) literally, 'for the sake of the word',

'For this saying' (AV; Torrey),

'For such a reply' (NIV),

'For saying that' (NEB),

'go your way, the demon has left your daughter'; Christ can now tell the mother as a fact, independent of Himself. In a wonderful and healing manner, a knot of destiny has been so dissolved that the divine aims—not as originally devised for the use of the dark adversary—are thereby realized.

The living word is victorious over the misuse and violation of the word through the dark adversary, over the might of death of the Scorpion. In recognizing the stereotype expression of the individual heavenly signs in the language of the gospel itself, we clearly find indicated precisely at this place the sign of the word of the Bull.

Here, in the manner how on the one side personalities in the sphere of Herodias are looming, and on the other side the encounter with Christ releases a decisive and redemptive change in their being, recalls the whole episode, mentioned above, of the meeting with Christ in Wagner's *Parsifal*, Act II. A similarity of motifs governs here. Like the Syro-Phoenician woman with Christ, Kundry attempts to ensnare Parsifal through a tempting appeal to compassion. (*'Fühlst du im Herzen nur anderer Schmerzen, so fühle jetzt auch die meinen'*, 'If you feel in your heart only others' sorrows, then feel mine too!') A true exposition of the gospel can only gain through the recognition of these deep world-contexts.

***

The revelation of the word of the Bull in the second round of the Sun-rhythm reaches its climax in the Healing of the Deaf and Mute Person through the word of Christ narrated at the end of Mark 7. Already through the previous episodes, the disciples, led ever deeper into the Mysteries of the divine might of the word, arrive here at a decisive point in their life of initiation. It has to be said repeatedly that through the spiritual interpretation of an event narrated in the gospel the external actuality does not necessarily have to be pushed to one side, and that precisely concerning the actuality of the healings effected through Christ are here not at all doubted. Nevertheless, as Bock stresses in his *Studies in the Gospels*, with the narrations of this healing of the deaf-mute, the decisive viewpoint presented is the picture of how Christ loosens, as it were, the spiritual bonds on the tongues of the disciples, conveying the power of the living word to them. Thereby the disciples really move on from the stage of Imagination to that of Inspiration—which is an opening of the forces of the heart revealed in the effect of the word. Everything narrated from the first Feeding onwards, the experiences of the Storm on the Lake, and so on, stage by stage prepares for this.

In the next chapter, the second Feeding is narrated, showing the results. It is to be conceived as a revelation of the power of the living word. The Deaf-Mute Healing shows in a picture how, in the initiation undergone through Christ, the disciples are penetrated in appropriating this living power of the word. At least initially and to a certain degree, they have overcome what hitherto as a 'hardening of the heart' still presented difficulties to its full Inspiration—which is certainly shown in the reception of the divine 'I AM'. The deficient understanding of the heart of the deaf and dumb man which they themselves carried—because he could not understand, he was not able to speak—should now convince the disciples how everything experienced hitherto, everything just experienced in the 'sign of the word', has taken them to the point that Christ can now work on them to 'loosen the spiritual ties on the tongue'. And we can also imagine, if we want to attribute this meaning to the event, that the beholding and participation in an outer event released such spiritual results.

The Twins, Crab and Lion in the Second Octave

The whole content of Mark 7 right to the end, under the viewpoint of the revelation of the power of the word standing in the sign of the Bull, becomes wholly clear from the last words, Mark 7:37: 'He even makes the deaf hear and the mute speak.' Now, we would expect out of the 'cosmic rhythm' the ascent to the spiritual heights of the Mount in the Twins, in the Crab then somehow the descent to further effects in humanity. We already know that the Lion, unlike the other signs, is not aligned to specific outer sections of the gospel. In Mark the Lion belongs more to the centre than the periphery of the circle.

We already met many stereotype sayings in the gospel connected with the meaning of the individual signs. With the Twins the words are: 'And he went up the mountain ...' (cf. Mark 3:13; 'the' not 'a' mountain); in so far as it refers to the Mount of Inspiration and Initiation, to the 'arrangement of twelve' in the sign of Initiation. We look for these words here in Mark and do not find them. After Mark 7 clearly ends in the sign of the Bull, Mark 8 begins immediately with the narration of the 'Feeding of the Four Thousand', which just as clearly points to the 'Last-Supper constellation' Fishes–Virgin, yet so that this time dealing with a daytime experience, the day-sign of the Virgin is primarily emphasized. The 'Feeding of the Five Thousand' stands in the night-sign of the Fishes.

So, for an outer contemplation, it appears as though, apart from the Lion, the Twins and the Crab are simply missing, and one asks the reason for this phenomenon. Let it be noted straight away that at this place the only omission of this sort, or at least apparent omission, in the text of Mark's Gospel is to be observed. Simply to insist on this fact is more correct than to try artificially to establish the rhythm for which one searches through some kind of new interpretation of individual passages. One could come to the notion that perhaps a part of the text

is missing. This is theoretically possible, but for relevant inner reasons nevertheless improbable. It looks much rather as if the missing signs, which in the spiritual events, in the cosmic rhythm, in the starry script *are* really to be found, only when the presentation in outer words are purposely left out and for a reason. This will be substantiated in more detail in what follows.

We find the missing words between Mark 7 and 8, initially concerning the Twins, in actual fact at the corresponding place in Matt. 15:29, between the narrated episode there of the Syro-Phoenician woman and the Feeding of the Four Thousand. Especially in connection with the omission of these words in Mark, their presence in Matthew appears all the more impressive and significant. The objective of the 'cosmic rhythm' is rather enhanced than mitigated by this circumstance. It is as though something like the possibility of an understanding of the gospel purely out of the spirit lights up immediately out of the starry script and stands before us independent of the written word.

Let us look once more at Mark's presentation. We recall how in Mark 7, immediately preceding, the experience of the word to be conceived in the sign of the Bull was a picture of how in the disciples Inspiration was finally to be awoken. If the word-experience belonging to the Bull is not explained away, we are there, in a certain sense we really have come to the 'Mount of Inspiration'. We have also the picture how Christ renews once more on this spiritual mountain height the impulse of the initiation of the disciples (similar to the time before, with the 'Feeding of the Five Thousand', Mark 6:7-11). What happened afterwards, the successful work of the disciples in the 'Feeding of the Four Thousand', points very much to such a renewal of the impulse to initiation. That for the presentation in outer words much is here omitted, is simply because the main concern of the writer of the gospel in the Feeding of the Four Thousand was to have recognized the previous 'loosening of the spiritual ties on the tongue'. We follow Bock's explanation in his *Studies in the Gospels*, that it was an activity of the word, a kind of word-communion.

What is narrated in Mark 7 leads directly into that described in Mark 8. Moreover, certain intermediate aspects or steps present in the cosmic rhythm are omitted in the outer presentation. If the ascent of the Mount remains unmentioned—yet spiritually present in a certain sense, in Matthew even indicated in words—it logically follows that the descent will also remain unmentioned. The external omission of the Twins means as a logical consequence that of the Crab, the sign of descent, is also omitted. This descent is also spiritually present—the experience of humanity of the 'Feeding of the Four Thousand' would not be possible at all unless the disciples had again descended from the previous achieved heights of spiritual Inspiration, turning towards the plain of spiritually hungering humanity. And the victor over the Crab, the Lion, is what gives to them, in this plain of the material element, the power in the ensuing experience of Feeding and the experience of the Last Supper revealed in the 'transformation, or metamorphosis, of matter'. And so the three signs, although suppressed in the account, are nevertheless spiritually present. They are, as it were, to be found in the spiritual interval between Mark 7 and 8. The 'cosmic rhythm' is here almost a resource for the inner completion of the gospel, correctly to intimate and supplement its contexts.

Apart from the reasons already discussed that the writer of the gospel had to shorten the course of the narration between chapter 7 and 8, it is absolutely so that in the second round of the cosmic rhythm a certain shortening should appear. These rounds of the cosmic rhythm are like spirals that contract as they ascend. In the Introduction it was emphasized that the 'rounds' are not simply repeats but a return always at a higher level. This corresponds to the picture of 'spirals' as well as to that of the musical octave.

It would be possible that the shortening especially with the second spiral is connected with the fact that here on the stage of Inspiration, a planetary viewpoint joins that of the zodiac. This involves a question that would have to be followed up independently, and has initially to remain open.

In his study, *The Ninth Century and the Holy Grail* [Temple Lodge Publishing 2009], which [first] appeared after the present work had gone to press, Walter Johannes Stein shows the cosmic rhythm of the zodiac also applies to the Grail legends. He also finds three rounds, which Stein likens to spirals. With the second spiral, also shortened, alongside the viewpoint of the zodiac-signs he finds those of the seven planets.

The Feeding of the Four Thousand

The Virgin and the Scales in the Second Octave (Mark 8:1-9; 8: 10-26)

The perceptible influence of the power of Elijah-John in the group of disciples reaches a climax in the 'Feeding of the Four Thousand', in which the disciples take a decisively active part (Mark 8:6, 7). The characteristic power of the 'increase of bread' already in the Old Testament (1 Chron. 17) now passes over to the group of disciples around Christ, who know Christ as their centre. Only here too not earthly bread and earthly fish are to be thought but again the 'starry bread', the living power of the cosmic ether in the word. This bread, like a 'heavenly provision' or Grail food, is given to human beings, even if the *picture* may have been present of the distribution of bread and fishes by the disciples, as with those who receive the food. The power of Elijah of John Baptist's sacrifice, which Herodias through black magic wanted to receive for her own use, nevertheless through the white magic of Christ has now found its way to human beings, its real stream-bed.

The difference of this Feeding from the 'Feeding of the Five Thousand' narrated in Mark 6, lies in this: The latter was a pure spirit-vision and vision of the future, a night-experience and meditation experience, concerning the crowds of human beings, a dreamlike beholding of the 'coming race'. The 'Feeding of the Four Thousand' was an experience of the present, of the daytime. It was a deed really carried out by the disciples amongst their bodily-present contemporaries. For this reason it stands in the day-sign of the Virgin. The Fishes appear only as the counter-sign, also standing back in the gospel narration, Mark 8:7. This night-constellation is the sign primarily emphasized in the 'Feeding of the Five Thousand'. Even the number 4000 with the second Feeding (see the Introduction, p. 36) indicates the secret of the 'fourth post-Atlantean epoch', at that time the present.

The 'Feeding of the Five Thousand' contains the inner preparation for what took place in the 'Feeding of the Four Thousand'. In the meditation-experience, in spirit-vision, the disciples gain from within the inner power with which they are able to work outwardly into the reality of the day. And the cosmic rhythm of the zodiac makes so evident this governing connection of inner and outer, night and day between both Feedings—both times the same constellation, the great 'Last-Supper constellation' of the Christ-centre. Only in the one case the night-side (♓) is emphasized, and in the other (♍) the day-side. Thus the Feeding of the Five Thousand, seen from the [viewpoint of the great] rhythm, takes place exactly in the middle of the way that leads from the first appearance of the Last-Supper sign of the Virgin that already shone over the Parable of the Growing Seed, right to its shining again in the second octave. Between the Parable of the Sower (Mark 4) and the Feeding of the Four Thousand (Mark 8) stands the Feeding of the Five Thousand (Mark 6), rhythmically exactly in the middle.

That which in the sign of the Virgin in the picture of the grain of growing seed was initially contained as a nucleus—we recall the phrase of Novalis: 'Everything is a growing seed'—meanwhile has gone through an inner development. It has unfolded as on a higher stage after the cosmic rhythm in the second octave has arrived again in the sign of the Virgin. It has now become a real power in the hearts of the disciples, with which it can work in the world. With this is indicated the inmost Mystery of the sign of the Virgin, the 'Virgin with the Sheaf' (Spica), the 'starry bread'. In our language today we can call it the 'secret, or Mystery of cosmic development', in religion the 'secret, or Mystery of the Last Supper' (see p. 103f.), the 'secret, or Mystery of the human future'. In the language Christ Jesus speaks to the disciples in the gospels, it is called the 'secret, or Mystery, of the kingdom of God' [e.g. Mark 4:11], *μυστήριον τῆς βασιλείας τοῦ θεοῦ*. The Greek word *μυστήριον* is none other than the Latin *sacramentum*, which once again hints at the 'meaning of the Last Supper'. When we look at the development leading from the Parable of the Growing

Seed via the 'Feeding of the Five Thousand' to the 'Feeding of the Four Thousand', Last-Supper events of humanity stand before us in tremendous pictures.

Let us glance back at this development. In pictures bearing the future and bearing power, Christ has first planted this Mystery of the Last-Supper events into the hearts of the disciples, in the picture of the Sower and the Seed, in the picture of the Feeding at night. Already the reception of the first picture, the first nucleus of soul-development, was followed by the first inner difficulty, the first inner crisis that is bound up with every inner development. Already many refuse these forces. They already threaten to stop the initiation at a critical point. Already the healing forces fail to appear for the people. Here the sacrificial death of the Baptist leads to a new enlivening of the impulse of initiation through Christ. He could cause the disciples to see into dark human abysses, allowing new human tasks to arise before them. In earnest inner concentration, in devoted meditation, He allows all this to be experienced.

In tremendous pictures of the future ('Feeding of the Five Thousand') He places the Mystery of the Last Supper of the events of humanity before them. Forces of Elijah-John, forces of the Grail-Feeding of humanity, thereby stream into the hearts of the disciples. And they have to go through new inner crises and Storms on the Lake, until they inwardly hear the 'I-AM' of Christ, until they increasingly open their hearts to the Mystery of the spiritual power of the word and of the 'I'. The Last-Supper events in the picture of the Sower experienced still as Imagination are now increasingly Inspiration, working from within as under their own power. The meaning of the sign of the Virgin, which in Mark 4, with the Parable of the Sower was seen still as Imagination, is now in the second octave of the Sun-rhythm, with the experience of the Feeding in Mark 8 raised to the stage of Inspiration. What was received earlier becomes effective power in the hearts of the disciples. From receiving they have moved on to giving; they are now able themselves to distribute to other people the bread of life of the

etheric forces. And with the bread still 'a few small fish'—the Christ-power of the 'I' at least in its first, humble beginnings …

A real advance is achieved compared to what took place in the 'Feeding of the Five Thousand'. As *picture* this 'Feeding of the Five Thousand' signifies indeed something more. With the 'five loaves' also the lower, dark will-part, that is, the forces of the *total* human being are taken hold, which is why *twelve basketfuls* remain over. All twelve zodiac-powers of the total human being remain over with this Feeding. The 'seven loaves' of the other Feeding (also discussed in the Introduction, p. 36f.) express here that initially only the forces of the upper human being, the *conscious* forces are laid hold of, the forces of day-consciousness, corresponding to the seven upper 'bright' zodiac pictures. The 'five loaves' of the later Feeding are the five lower, 'dark' zodiac signs.

Consequently, after the second Feeding only seven baskets remain over with the remaining fragments. This relates to the fact that only those forces can be laid hold of, those of the upper human being and of the day-consciousness. Seen in this way, the 'Feeding of the Four Thousand' signifies something 'less'. But the 'something more' of the first Feeding is simply a 'more' of the future. Initially, it is an inner vision, a prophecy looking to such a 'more of the future'. It is that which gives to the human being the necessary forces for the present. It is the countenance of the night. The 'Feeding of the Four Thousand', seen as a picture is less, yet it is an experience of the daytime, a real experience of the present. It reveals a real ability; it is active giving, a really achieved work for humanity. In so far, it is something 'more' compared to what took place with the 'Feeding of the Five Thousand'.

***

With the 'Feeding of the Four Thousand' the initiation of the group of disciples, which already before was in a kind of crisis, reaches a climax. 'This time,' we could say, 'everything proceeds well.' And from the sacrificial death of John the Baptist we understand how those forces stream, making it possible that after all the previous vacillations, checks

and crises this turning towards the Good could now enter. Here the Scales in which the cosmic rhythm now enters, express a real—at least transitional—achieved balance, whereas earlier it expressed a struggle for balance.

We recall how always with the transition from the Fishes–Virgin into the following constellation the Ram–Scales, the rhythm of the gospel narration was especially clear. After the 'Parable of the Sower' in Mark 4, and after the 'Feeding of the Five Thousand' in Mark 6, we see the Storm on the Lake follows. After the narration of the 'Feeding of the Four Thousand' in Mark 8, we could now ask, 'Why no Storm on the Lake this time?' In the sense of what meanwhile has been achieved and revealed in the 'Feeding of the Four Thousand', it seems the disciples now succeed to keep inner calm in the midst of the great experiences of initiation. They manage to keep back and overcome the fear and unrest of the astral realm of the soul, that otherwise in such circumstances wants to assail. Had they not themselves achieved a certain degree of inner calm, they would never have found the strength in the 'Feeding of the Four Thousand', as they did, to strengthen and enliven others. To a higher degree than it was possible for them earlier, in the inner calm and clarity of the astral element in their souls, they have now developed *Spirit-self* (manas) through the higher 'I'. We recall how in the rhythm of the zodiac, to which the supersensory human members can be related, Spirit-self, the astral body transformed by the 'I', leads to the sign of the Scales (see p. 33f.). In this 'creating the Spirit-self' out of the inner calm of the soul, the disciples have now realized the *meaning of the Scales* on a higher stage than earlier. Also in relation to the sign of the Scales, we recognize how the cosmic rhythm, now in the second octave of the Sun-rhythm, enters the stage of Inspiration. (Earlier, in the stage of Imagination, the disciples see the picture of the ship of the soul, tossed by the billows on the lake, as if from outside; now they have the 'spiritual balance' within.)

Thus the inner logic of the gospel events corresponds, so that there is no talk of a 'Storm on the Lake'. The rhythm of the gospel, otherwise

in this series of constellations so clearly evident, is nevertheless here too preserved, for after the Feeding there follows again a crossing of the Lake (Mark 8:10), but this time the voyage occurs smoothly. The calm voyage appears as the picture of the now achieved calm of soul. And this calm voyage stands exactly at the point where earlier the stormy voyage was experienced.

Yet precisely here, where initially a certain height, a certain advance at least is achieved, the earnestness of the initiation can be felt. Even in here the critical sign of death of the Scorpion casts its dark shadow. While reading the brief simplicity of the gospel narration we frequently pass over, in individual, apparently harmless or subordinate phrases, something deeply shocking. Such a phrase in the passage from Mark 8:13, following the voyage on the Lake that begins 8:10, appears in 8:14: 'The disciples had forgotten to bring bread, except for *one* loaf they had with them in the boat.' And we hear how the disciples in association with Christ were involved in the 'miracle of the increase of bread', how they distributed the bread of life to other people, how the enlivening ether-forces flowed abundantly. Now at one stroke there was a dearth of bread, the ether-forces were scarce. What has happened, what is at the bottom of this?

In the whole pictorial manner of the gospel narration lies the clear answer. The Imaginative character of Mark's Gospel (see pp. 18f., 23f.) is clearly evident here. Whence comes in 8:11 this short dream-like playful episode of the Pharisees? Are they really flesh-and-blood Pharisees here, with whom a discussion takes place, or is everything but a picture, an Imagination? Are the disciples only now to achieve conscious Inspiration, at least for the time being? The essential might of human nature is incorporated in this, which against their (the disciples') development and influence the opposition always places itself. The might of the death-sign of the Scorpion always wants to kill the living word (cf. in this sense everything said about Mark 7). It is the poisoned sting of death of the Scorpion, which in the 'dead statutes' of the scribes and Pharisees has killed the living word.

And still more threatening and terrible than what comes from the Scorpion's sting of death of the Pharisees is the whole sexual magic of the black-magic Mysteries of Herod and of Herodias, recognized in Mark 6 in such a ghastly manner. Here the disciples see the actual fiend of death to their and to Christ's work. Here they see the arch-enemy incorporated in flesh and blood, who wants to rob, reap and take for himself the John-Elijah power of the living bread, the ether-forces intended to flow into the stream-bed of the development of humanity. Here they look into the corner out of which come all their frequently riddling, incomprehensible difficulties and vexations, the 'forces of Klingsor', which always oppose and obstruct the clear forces of the Grail.

Here we understand all at once the earnest saying Christ speaks to the disciples (Mark 8:15 NIV): 'Be careful,' Jesus warned them. 'Watch out for the yeast (leaven) of the Pharisees and that of Herod.' Suddenly it is clear why the 'bread of life' has become so scarce. It is no usual, harmless yeast, or leaven, to which He refers. But the 'leaven of the Pharisees' is an old leaven that has become bad; the 'leaven of Herod' moreover a poisoned leaven, a dark foreign substance, which poisons the pure bread of life of the cosmic ether-forces. The poison from the sting of Scorpion is at work in this substance. Consequently, above all Christ warns the disciples of this poison. For this they were allowed to experience all the previous events of Mark 6 and 7, so that they should also receive into their consciousness of Inspiration the nature and danger of this most terrible of all poisons.

And the Inspiration will repeatedly be denied, will repeatedly dwindle. In this spiritual area it is a fact that what has been wrested does not remain fixed and won, it has to be wrested from subtle forces of opposition. Consequently words of warning from Christ have to be delivered to the disciples, whether they still bear a 'hardened heart' (Mark 8:17). These are the same words with which on a previous occasion (Mark 6:52), after the first Feeding and the Storm on the Lake, the closed hearts, this inability to permeate Imagination by Inspiration, are expressed in the gospel. We notice how at the place in Mark 8,

where the disciples are reprimanded with all the pictures of both Feeding-experiences, how He now also exerts them to understand the pictures, really anchored in inner depths, not only a transitional simulated understanding—that means, however, to pass from Imagination to Inspiration. 'Do you still not understand?' (Mark 8:21).

***

Ever-new inhibitions and hindrances are placed against the initiation, in the understanding of those undergoing it. Christ, the initiator, seeks ever-new ways to help the disciples to overcome these inhibitions, to awaken their closed senses. The Healing of the Deaf-Mute was a picture of how Christ seeks to bring the disciples to inner hearing and spiritual understanding—which still remains elusive to them—and to awaken the inner power of the word. In the same way He now seeks to awaken in them yet a final, purest, highest sense, the sense of spiritual seeing itself, the sense of a beholding that is more than a mere beholding of Imaginative 'astral' pictures.[19] Only with this would the stage of 'Inspiration' be completed. This is a beholding of spiritual reality itself.

Therewith, 'Inspiration' would be fulfilled. Regarding inner hearing—that cannot stand for itself alone—the true spiritual beholding has to be added. The picture for the development of inner hearing is that of the Healing of the Deaf-Mute. The picture for that of higher vision is the picture of the *Healing of the Blind Man*. Already in the physical world the sense of sight is the highest, the purest, the maidenly-innocent sense. And in all this it is also a picture and parable for what is meant here as 'spiritual beholding'. In the Introduction, p. 20f., we discussed the spiritual meaning of the Healing of the Blind Man, its relation of this spiritual seeing to the externals of the event. And we mentioned the relationship of the episode in Mark 8:23-26 to John 9.

In the picture of the story of healing the blind man in Mark, we can observe (Mark 8:24, 25) how Christ step by step awakens the spiritual sense. That the blind man initially 'sees men as though he saw trees' till he then can see everything in sharp focus, is on the one hand a clear

description of the outer event of such a healing—regardless whether we take it as such in this case or not. But it is also a picture for how spiritual vision progresses from the mere physical, initially to the etheric plant-like, living element, then raises itself to beholding the higher spiritual reality, the spiritual human being, the 'I'. Only when this is beheld, is the spiritual blindness taken from the eye.

Even the 'Healing of the Blind Man' is still to be thought of in the sign of the Scales (a detailed reason for this connection is given in the study on John's Gospel). In this sign Christ works on the consciousness of the disciples, in order to develop in them the Spirit-self and the higher senses. The Scales stands in the middle, forming the transition between the bright sign of the Virgin (to which of the 'twelve senses' the sense of sight is allocated) and the dark sign of the Scorpion, the sign of spiritual darkening. Likewise for those for whom blindness is the outer picture, the Healing of the Blind Man is also the process through which the previously closed eyes of the sighted person are opened to the light. The relationship to the zodiacal sign becomes completely clear when we recall (see p. 123) how earlier the Virgin and the Scorpion were *one* sign. In other words, Scorpion first came about when the arrow of the Archer hit the Virgin. The Scales is placed as the divider and protector between the Scorpion and the Virgin. This description, to do not with astronomical but with spiritual facts, should require no further emphasis.

On the one hand, the event of the Healing of the Blind Man in its relation to the sense of sight allows us recognize the presence of the sign of the Virgin. On the other hand, already the dusky shadow, the spiritual darkening is felt, connected to the being of the Scorpion. The cosmic rhythm has again arrived at the borders of this dark and critical sign. Christ sees the whole danger, the completely new crisis from this sign of death threatening the initiation of the group of disciples. In order to meet this danger, He searches in the initiation-event of the Healing of the Blind Man a final, highest expedient, a final most effective remedy for the disciples. How the use of this remedy works on the group of disciples, especially on Peter, is revealed in the chapter directly following. Therein will also be shown, how despite this 'opening of the spiritual eyes' a new darkening, a new crisis in the death-sign of the Scorpion descends on the group of disciples, and in particular on Peter. What we could call the 'tragedy of the Apostle Peter' forms the actual end of the initiation-events in the second round of the Sun-rhythm.

The Death-Signs of the Scorpion and the Archer in the Second Octave. Peter's Denial

(Mark 8:27-33; 8:34–9:1)

At the point to which we have arrived in the gospel narration and the initiation of the disciples, the figure of the Apostle Peter stands in the foreground. We spoke of the 'tragedy' of this apostle and there is more soon to come. So it appears necessary also to point to his greatness. It was the leading of destiny that allowed him to be the first—outwardly seen—to meet Christ. He was the first, or amongst the first, of the Twelve to be called. Not without reason, but just because he was chosen by destiny, Christ appointed him as Rock of the Church (Matt. 16: 18-19; Mark 3:16). But the greatest in world-events suffer their own tragedy. The tragedy of the Apostle Peter belongs to all that is most deeply distressing in world-events, carrying the most difficult consequences and destiny. It is also bound to the tragedy of the Church and its whole history.

We recall how already at the beginning of the gospel story (Mark 1: 30, 31) the healing of 'Simon's mother-in-law' of fever stands as a picture how Christ has to straighten something of the spiritual being of Simon-Peter himself. He endeavours to put right something that wants too much to flare up, has too much the 'strength of spiritual fever' in it. He possesses certain powers that bind him too much to the human past, 'atavistic' forces, especially strong magical powers of the word, which repeatedly pose a danger right into the Acts of the Apostles. Right into the rites of the [Roman] Catholic Church today something is shown of this atavistic and magical use of the word based originally on Peter's being. Also with what is shown in Mark 8 of Peter, this side of his being now steps into the picture.

Not at least with reference to Peter, the appointed 'Rock of the Church', did Christ accomplish the 'healing of spiritual blindness'

of the disciples. The hope of something decisive, a test at the same time, lay in this deed. And really precisely for Peter this 'Healing of the Blind Man' signifies a climax of his whole initiation, the highest degree of the advance he reached, immediately before his denial, his tragic crisis. For him the climax itself became a crisis. This is revealed in a clear, most shocking manner here, entering again in the Scorpion, in the sign of darkening and the sign of crisis in the 'cosmic rhythm' of Mark's Gospel.

The whole scene at Caesarea Philippi (Mark 8:27ff.) stands in this sign of crisis. Matthew narrates the event (Matt. 16:15ff.), appearing as the main moment of Peter's recognition of Christ, making him the 'Rock of the Church'. With Mark, who also narrates all this, the cosmic rhythm revealing the decisive viewpoint is not the fact of confession as such, but the situation. Immediately after this shining confession of Christ, the darkening of Peter's consciousness approaches. This hinders him from laying hold of what would have actually been the main thing; this is what the Christ first and foremost wants and must lead the disciples in their initiation towards realizing: the meaning of Christ's sacrificial death, the Mystery of Golgotha. Only through this is this understanding possible that in a quite specific sense the might of death—working from the Scorpion—is overcome within. And at this point we see Peter failing. The death-might of the Scorpion is what darkens his consciousness. For this reason the whole episode of Caesarea Philippi in Mark stands in this sign.

Initially Peter's understanding appears far in advance of all the others (8:29, 30). To the question concerning that personality, who otherwise in the gospels—with the exception of a few significant passages to mention the word 'Christ'[20]—is always named only as 'Jesus': 'Who do people say that I am?' Peter gives as in a magical illumination the answer, 'You are the Christ.' He speaks the name, which in the gospel is not spoken lightly as we do today, but always sounding very important like a Mystery of initiation. And we may imagine how hitherto in the group of disciples the name not yet spoken would be experienced

as something tremendous, above all something magical. It embraces after all the highest Sun-Mysteries of the cosmos, a name containing the most secret Mystery-word of the primordial human Mysteries,[21] the name in which all the secrets of the stones and of the stars are illuminated, of the earthly and of the heavenly and their mutual relationships. Here it is not important what language Peter spoke, and whether he really used the word '*Christos*', but what he said and how he said it was understood as a revelation of the Mystery of the Christ as Sun-Being.

Hitherto, this Mystery only few high initiates, like John the Baptist and Simeon (Luke 2:26) had seen as a presentiment; super-human beings, such as the angels, had announced to the shepherds in the fields, or the demons of those possessed [who had recognized this] (Luke 4:41). Even Herod, the knowing one, did not know it (Mark 6:16); the disciples knew it even less. But now with Peter, the 'Healing of the Blind Man' through Christ Himself, in connection with what had begun to work as the Elijah-power of John the Baptist through the disciples, and through his strong atavistic forces to which he was especially open, was to lead him as a magical lightning to the knowledge of the great secret of the Sun-being Christ shining and flashing through. And the flaming, fiery power of the word, allows him also to find the word through which he expresses the great recognition of Christ in the group of disciples.

At this point let us look from the figure of Peter to that of the other disciple, of whose actual ascent, if we correctly understand the heavenly language, something may be sensed for the first time at that point where Christ awoke the daughter of Jairus out of the sleep of death. Here, in overcoming the sting of death in the Scorpion, that disciple re-found the childlike innocence of his own being, an important stage in his development to become John. In a certain sense he stood apart from the others. They had already come to an inner crisis at the critical corner of this sign of death at that time—at least the gospel gently indicates this—in order later at the same point to plunge ever more deeply into it.

Caesarea Philippi in particular becomes a special crisis for Peter who had just given a shining confession of Christ. At this moment of Peter's confession, how was it with the One 'becoming John'? Why did he not express the great recognition of Christ, the Sun-being, he who had penetrated most deeply into the secrets of the great Sun-rhythm? In this connection we recall the picture of the early legend (see p. 49f.) that tells of the deep impression this disciple received of the raising of the youth of Nain, which he witnessed. He fell into chronic illness which found its ending in the 'illness' of Lazarus told in John 11 [v. 1 'Now a man was ill, Lazarus of Bethany']. He exchanged his earlier riches for poverty; from then on he became the 'silent disciple'. Through poverty, the grave and death, the path leads him to life, through deepest silence, to regain the creative creator-word that was lost to humanity through the Fall of man.

If we seek to enliven the spiritual picture of this disciple, for instance in that moment when Christ questions the disciples about the Mystery of His own being (Mark 8:29), we find him silent, pensive, sunk in himself, in deep melancholy. Perhaps it is not too much to say that he walked about like a shadow. The once so winning impression of his personality was then nothing less than imposing. Even in the group of disciples many possibly passed by this lonely, silent, still disciple. Only Christ knew what was in him. He, the One becoming John already possibly divined the Mystery of the Christ-Sun, the most deeply of anybody, but he could not have put it into words. He would have been the least able to give such an answer to Christ's question as Peter did. Like a gift from above, a blessing from heaven comes to Peter; the enlightening recognition, a fiery, magical power of the word carried by atavistic forces, allows him almost too early to speak a word, the weight of which he could not yet grasp in his own soul (cf. Matt. 16:17).

In what the other, the disciple becoming John, then already carried in his soul as recognition or a divined recognition, there lived—even if he, the silent disciple, was not able to express it—the divining of the

great Mystery of death (with which, then, his own path of initiation brought him into such a close connection, when Christ-Jesus awoke him out of the sleep of the grave), and in his recognition there was something more akin to death than in the recognition of Peter, which just at this point has its snag. For a true confession of Christ is only that which precisely embraces this secret, the meaning of death. Today, *after* the Mystery of Golgotha and in possession of all that which has flowed towards us of knowledge out of the substance of this Mystery from great teachers and leaders of humanity, we should not imagine that the task placed on Peter was an easy one. He was deeply connected with the wisdom of pre-Christian Mysteries. But exactly for this ancient Mystery-wisdom such a human deed, not the deed of an initiate, like the earthly death of Christ, the humiliating death on the cross, was something unheard of, unimaginable, as a smack in the face. One knew only the 'initiate' was lifted above everything earthly, and had no actual connection to it. Basically, it is the same snag on which later—also in the Scorpion—we see Pilate fail in such a tragic manner that yet was a world-necessity. Unlike Pilate and Judas, Peter fails in this 'world-necessity'. We always receive the impression he could have done better.

Precisely through this divesting of the earthly element, ultimately the ancient Mystery-wisdom increasingly succumbed to the might of death. The mysterious 'way of life' (cf. Matt. 7:14. The counter-statement in v. 13, according to the original text, *ἀπώλειαν*, is literally 'of loss', or 'of digression', not 'way of damnation' [tr. of Luther; most Eng. trans. have: 'destruction']), which John was the first to go, first made it possible that a God, a being from that world in which death was *not* known, out of free decision and free deed of love, went through earthly death. A God had to die on the earthly plane, in order that the human being could *live* in Him. In order to take hold of this new fact, never existing before, the wisdom of the early Mysteries, as they existed in the time of the Mystery of Golgotha, no longer sufficed. All the concepts of the existing Mysteries broke up at the Mystery of

Golgotha. It is not a contradiction that in their heyday the pre-Christian mysteries, including that of Zarathustra, foretold the Christ-event of the future, that these Mysteries originally looked towards the Mystery of Golgotha.

The Mystery of Golgotha, as a world-necessity and as the world's Turning Point, Christ had to suffer alone, misunderstood by human beings. In that sense it was tragic. Only the *one* soul could understand it, which in a unique world-historical manner in its initiation came into contact with the great Mystery of death itself, the soul that then also worked into that poet [Novalis] who, out of the deep revelation of these Mysteries of the night and of death, bequeathed to us the *Hymns to the Night*. These speak of the 'mysterious youth' and from him the words are found:

> *Im Tode ward das ew'ge Leben kund,*
> *du bist der Tod und machst uns erst gesund.*
> In Death, eternal Life hath been revealed:
> And thou art Death, by thee we first are healed.

It was possible only for the Johannine soul to lay hold of such insights. This soul had overcome the sting of death of the Scorpion. In its re-won inner virginity it had the possibility to penetrate the pure origins of the solar life and to find again there the lost Creator-Word of the primordial creation.

To Peter and all the others who had not overcome the sting of death of the Scorpion, access to this Mystery was prohibited. In vain had Christ warned the disciples of the leaven of the Pharisees and of Herod, in vain—in this warning—pointing to the danger of this sting of death and sting of poison. In vain too he had taken the blindness from their eyes, the blindness from Peter's eyes. As this blindness was taken from him, Peter was able to recognize a presentiment of the solar magnificence of Christ, as on the Mount of Transfiguration, indeed was able to *behold* it in highest cosmic glory. But the actual secret of the Sun-life bound with the profundity of death was revealed

to him neither on the one nor the other occasion. Consequently, the actual secret of Christ's being, that he prematurely and impetuously expressed, was closed to him. This is also the reason why Christ forbade the disciples so strictly to reveal this secret (8:30). They would only have revealed what basically still remained a secret for them and what expressed in *this* way would only have worked against the fulfilment of the Mystery of Golgotha.

The clarity with which the breaking in of the crisis, the arrival at the darkened might of death to Peter's consciousness as described in the gospel, is deeply moving. The transition from the sphere of the 'light-bringer' into the power of darkness can in this be experienced as tragic. Christ sees in this power of darkness, Ahriman's being [the 'Spirit of darkness'] standing behind Peter. The words, 'Get behind me Satan! You do not have in mind the things of God, but the things of men' [8:33], apply here. But the region of the zodiac from where that power of darkness always works, that power of death darkening the consciousness, is the Scorpion. Through Peter's failure in the sign of the Scorpion, all the disciples—except the one—are swept along (about the special position of James, beside John, there is more to say).

Once more, Christ speaks earnestly to the disciples—this time in such a way that they can all hear it—on the meaning of the sacrifice of death, which Peter could not grasp. And we can imagine that the presence of the folk, of humanity, during this event is a spiritual experience of him who is becoming John, who now is the one who grows ever more deeply into the understanding of the Mystery of death. Here we stand immediately before the 'Transfiguration', at a point where the narrated events begin to be removed ever further from the sphere of outer happenings. The earnestness of the second 'announcement of death' (Mark 8:34-38, and 9:1) allows us to feel how we now stand at the point where the dying of Christ has already begun. This is revealed in full clarity in the story of the Transfiguration immediately following this. With this we have already entered the death-sign of the

Archer that governs the beginning of the Transfiguration as well as the death on Golgotha.

The transition from the second to the third round of the Sun-rhythm takes place by building on the death-sign of the Archer and beginning in it. The events on the Mount of Transfiguration through the John-Elijah sign lead from the Goat and Aquarius into the Sun-depths of the Christ-sign of the Fishes. In it we move from Inspiration to what in the inner depths of the being is grasped and experienced, to *Intuition*. Here the presentation of the initiation-event becomes increasingly a presentation of the initiation-experience of the one becoming John. John's initiation and the way it is connected with the Mystery of Golgotha forms the third octave of the cosmic rhythm of Mark's Gospel.

PART III

The Third Round of the Sun-Rhythm

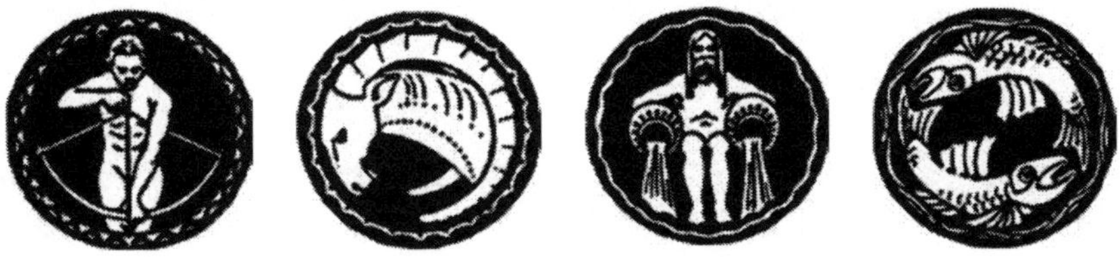

Initiation of John
The Mystery of Golgotha
Transition from the Death-Signs of the Archer in the
Third Octave:
The Goat, the Waterman, the Fishes:
The Transfiguration of Christ on the Mount
(Mark 9:1–13)

Transition in the Ram
(Mark 9:14–30)

With the 'Transfiguration of Christ on the Mount', as with Golgotha itself, it is especially clear that the 'course of the Christ-Sun through the twelve heavenly signs' does not simply relate only to the course of the outer Sun. From month to month the outer Sun moves on from sign to sign; a single sign always embraces the events of a month. The 'Christ-Sun' spoken of here is a *spiritual Sun*. The rhythm studied here is spiritual, more independent of earthly events and earthly time periods. (Only in individual cases does a possible meeting of the spiritual rhythm occur with the outer position of the Sun and the corresponding earthly events: cf. the reference to the Feeding of the Five Thousand on p. 21.)

Above all, the event of the 'Transfiguration', without detriment to the profound and real significance and effect that it has for everything earthly, is completely removed from the sphere of earthly-sensory consciousness with its spatial and temporal conditions. Here the Eternal shines into the realm of time, yet in the temporal realm the course is no longer graspable with earthly categories of time. In the realm of temporal phenomena, only the lightning is a picture for how the Eternal shines in and strikes into the realm of time. What is seen as a temporal event, like the lightning appearing as a fraction of a moment, seen from the Eternal is a world-wide, world-embracing event of extensive

periods of time that cannot be determined only with the measurements of earthly time. So it can be that the *Transfiguration on the Mount* in the heavenly starry language spans a whole arch of four signs of the heavenly zodiac. And yet, in the earthly sphere four months do not pass; everything that occurs is packed into a moment, into a point, into an earthly-temporal 'nothing'.

The Transfiguration on the Mount begins (cf. Mark 9:1) in the sign of the Archer, the sign of death and of the 'deep midnight', from which we look up to the Twins, the exalted sign of the 'great midday', the 'Sacred Mount'. The Archer and the Twins, we could say, together form the 'constellation of the Sacred Mount' that bears in itself both the most sacred events and Mysteries of the Transfiguration and the Death on Golgotha. Death and Transfiguration lie in the same heavenly signs. As will be shown more clearly, with the Transfiguration the great Mystery of death begins. The beginning and ending of the death of Christ lies in the sign of the Archer. Transfiguration as well as Golgotha lead through the Goat and the Waterman to the sign of the Fishes.

We stand spiritually not only at the beginning but also the end of the heavenly arch spanning the 'Transfiguration' when we think of the twelve heavenly signs in three separate crosses, as explained earlier (see Fig., p. 364). We stand in the middle of three crosses, in the cross of the etheric or of the Son, in the Christ-cross. Its crossbeam consists of the 'Last-Supper constellation' Fishes–Virgin, and the longitudinal beam of the constellation of the Sacred Mount and of the Death on Golgotha, Twins–Archer. We can also name the whole cross as that of the great Last-Supper event of humanity. Then, in the three crosses of the Son (♓ ♍ ♊♐), of the Father (♈ ♎ ♋ ♑) and of the Spirit (♉♏ ♒ ♌)—which in other contexts appears as the cross of the etheric, of the physical, and of the astral—the 'three crosses on Golgotha' shine before us. And we recognize all three crosses as a heavenly arch spanning the event of the Transfiguration, from the Archer to the Fishes (how and in so far the Transfiguration spans four signs will become

clearer in the further contemplations). Then, similar to Golgotha itself, all three crosses then appear in the 'three crosses on Golgotha', yet in such a way that the whole event is spanned by the middle, etheric, Christ-cross.

The death-sign of the Archer, in which the Transfiguration begins, still appears like a conclusion to the second octave, whereas with the Goat and the Waterman, with the event of the Transfiguration, the 'prelude' already begins to the 'third octave' (round, or spiral) of the great Sun-rhythm. If we stand in the Archer, in the second octave, still at the level of Inspiration the neighbouring signs already appear on the level of Intuition. The sacrifice of death, which on the first level in the sign of the Archer with the death of John the Baptist is still presented as a *picture* (Imagination), now becomes on the second level innermost Inspiration, to the one becoming John whose initiation now moves towards its completion. He, the one becoming John, can now in the depths of his being engage with the sacrificial being of Elijah. Consequently, both Elijah-signs ♑ ♒ appear on the level of Intuition, which also in the gospel narration is clearly expressed. Elijah is now, as it were, incarnate—even if etherically incarnate (cf. Mark 9:4). This incarnate existence always belongs to the essence of the level of Intuition. As always, both John-Elijah ♑ ♒ signs form the prelude to the octave, to the new (third) octave of the Sun-rhythm, designating a new stage of the sacrifice of Elijah.

Not only because this sign belongs to the 'constellation of the Sacred Mount', does the 'Transfiguration of Christ on the Mount' begin in the death-sign of the Archer. (As mentioned earlier, the Scorpion is more the sign of the origin of death, the Archer more the completion of death. The two signs today relate as cause and effect.) But above all because the whole event of the Transfiguration has already to do with the dying of Christ; therein the actual 'Mystery of Golgotha' is already prepared. Not for nothing in what came before (Mark 8:31ff.) did Christ Jesus speak to the disciples of the essence of this Mystery of Golgotha and of the necessity of the sacrifice of death (Mark 8:35, RSV: 'For whoever

would save his life will lose it; and whoever loses his life for my sake and the gospels will save it'). He speaks as of an event already imminent. With Buddha a similar process took place as the Transfiguration of Christ, to which it is inwardly connected, a supernatural illumination of the garments in temporal proximity of death, of the Buddha's passing over into *nirvāṇa* [for details on this event, cf. the author's German translation, *Der Hingang des Vollendeten*. 102; Eng. tr. TL forthcoming].

And yet the significance of the event of the Transfiguration has to do with the life of Christ, not only His earthly dying. Rudolf Steiner gives a key for a deeper understanding by indicating how in Christ a Sun-existence, that in the primeval times departed from the Earth (see above pp. 33, 64), united again with it. This process began in the Jordan-Baptism. The end is accomplished in the Mystery of Golgotha. In the entombment of Christ, a seed was planted in the Earth bearing the future events of the Earth ('that the Earth too may one day become Sun'—Chr. Morgenstern, from the poem 'Licht ist Liebe' in *Wir fanden einen Pfad*), referred to in John's Gospel (John 12:24). Here Christ, the Sun-being, becomes the 'Spirit of the Earth' and the Earth itself the 'physical body' of Christ. The Transfiguration in this (not chronological) sense forms the middle between the Jordan-Baptism and Golgotha.

And the uniting with the Earth, the dying of Christ into the Earth, is only the *one* side of the event. United with this dying *into* the Earth, is the other side of the event, the departure from the Sun, the *dying, by coming* from *the Sun-existence*. An understanding of all these things is only possible when one can imagine 'Sun-existence' not only astronomically but spiritually. Not only on the Earth does Christ's being go through a death, a real earthly and human death, but—following Steiner's presentation of these things—also its leaving, departing from the Sun had for the Sun-existence the character of a dying, a sublime death of a God. With His whole being, with all His supersensory members—as spiritual research[22] relates—Christ died to the Sun-existence. The event did not take

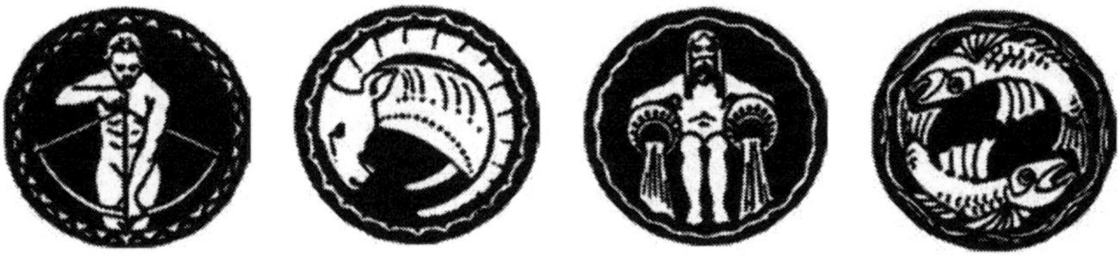

place all of a sudden, but was stretched over the three years of Christ's earthly life. Only, from the viewpoint of the human supersensory members, the highest supersensory member, 'Spirit-man' (*atman*), Christ leaves behind on the Sun. The higher etheric, 'Life-spirit' (buddhi) becomes the highest of Christ's members to leave the Sun and unite with the Earth.

From here we understand the event of the *Transfiguration* in a higher light. The dying of Christ, coming from the Sun-existence that only began in the Jordan-Baptism, was completed in the 'Transfiguration', finding therein its ending. In its departure the higher supersensory member was also completed in the manner the higher etheric (Life-spirit, buddhi) of Christ also united with the Earth. The higher etheric of Christ, in which the whole spiritual Sun-splendour shines, the 'etheric aura of the spiritual Sun' comes down to Earth with the 'Transfiguration'. That is the inexpressible splendour and sublimity, the fullness of blinding light, which also could still be felt so strongly in the actual spiritual context of what is not yet known with the Transfiguration story of the three 'synoptic' gospels (Matt. 17, Mark 9, Luke 9). It is the highest Sun-splendour itself, which now in Christ turned to the Earth, dying to itself in order to incarnate into it. In the death on Golgotha, in the deposition, this Sun-splendour of Christ, this etheric aura of the Sun, as it were, was magically transformed and buried into the Earth. This happened in order—working from within, out of the heart of the Earth, and revealing this working in human hearts—for the Earth to be led in the far future again to the Sun-existence. Consequently, the darkness with Golgotha; the shining light with the Transfiguration.

The *Transfiguration on the Mount* to a certain extent keeps hold of the moment when this etheric aura of the Sun had already left the Sun but had not yet entered into the depths of the Earth; it so to speak still hovered and radiated from the circumference of the Earth. The etheric of Christ is revealed in the splendour of the clouds (Mark 9:7). The radiance of the garments (Mark 9:3), recalling Buddha's

enlightenment (see p. 33f.), characterizes the beginning, the 'cloud splendour' the end of the Transfiguration. A new stage of the revelation of the Christ-Sun is achieved, of the earthly becoming of Christ. As already in the Jordan event, this revelation of the Christ-Sun stands in the sign of the Fishes, in which indeed the Transfiguration beginning in the death-sign of the Archer finds its conclusion. With reference to the revelation of the Fishes, what began earlier in the picture of the descending dove [the Baptism] is completed now in human depths; we have moved on from the stage of Imagination to that of Intuition. The gospel describes this relationship of both revelations, corresponding to the same zodiacal sign, through the quite similar words of the returning voice from the cosmic heights, 'This is my beloved Son ...' (earlier, 'You are my beloved Son ...'). The difference corresponds to the different *stage* of the same experience. As to other heavenly signs there belong certain words of the gospel, *this* saying, the 'word of the Son of the Sun', as we could also call it, belongs to the sign of the Fishes.

If we turn now to the key given earlier, frequently used and found useful, which leads from the zodiacal sign to the human supersensory members (Introduction, p. 36f.), from here on we find: to the sign of the Virgin the etheric member is allocated, and to the sign lying opposite the sign of the Fishes, the higher, transformed etheric (buddhi, Life-spirit). On the one hand, what was found about the descent of the etheric Sun-life and the Life-spirit of Christ in the Transfiguration is also illumined from the side of the zodiac. On the other hand, what was said about the significance of the zodiacal sign of the Fishes adds a new important viewpoint. Some evidence is gained through all this about this key itself of the zodiac signs and the supersensory members.

In this whole approach [the Transfiguration from the viewpoint of the Sun-rhythm] there lies a harmony with the experience of Zarathustra. On the one hand we looked up in the experience of the Transfiguration from the death-sign of the Archer, the sign

of the 'deep midnight', to the opposite exalted sign of the Twins (see Fig., p. 364). This is the sign of the 'Sacred Mount'—appearing here as the 'Mount of Transfiguration'—and of the 'great midday' of Zarathustra. On the other hand, we looked from that death-sign and midnight sign of the Archer leading over via the Goat and Waterman into the sign of the Christ-Sun of the Fishes. In all this, there lies a harmony with the great Mystery-experience of Zarathustra, the Sun-Initiate, which in the language of the Mysteries was called 'beholding the Sun at midnight'.[23] But now, in the 'Transfiguration of Christ on the Mount', the secret of the spiritual Sun-existence shone so that it becomes a reality not only for the individuals beholding it, but for the whole Earth itself. The secret of the early Sun-splendour is now about to unite itself with the Earth itself. And the Mystery of the spiritual splendour of the Sun includes in itself the Mystery of the deep midnight.

The event of the Transfiguration, revealing the splendour of the Sun and at the same time the beginning of the dying of Christ, lies significantly within the 'Christ cross' (the 'etheric cross'). The event lies between the death-sign of the Archer, the sign of 'deep midnight' and the Christ-Sun sign of the Fishes. Apart from a short indication at the beginning of Mark 9, nothing is spoken about the two transitional signs lying between, the Goat and the Waterman, always linked in Mark's Gospel with the influence of Elijah and his sacrifice and John [the Baptist's] being. Here, too, in the transition into the third octave of the Sun-rhythm, these two signs together always signify the prelude to the octave—the 'Elijah-John prelude' to the revelation of Christ. That is why (Mark 9:4) Elijah is revealed in his being next to Moses at the Transfiguration with the revelation of Christ, now on the level of Intuition. In this connection Christ speaks clearly about the Elijah-John Mystery itself (Mark 9:12, 13; even more clearly in Matt. 17:10-13; cf. also Matt. 11: 13, 14). The Elijah-John sacrifice is now fulfilled in its human depths, on the level of Intuition of the Sun-rhythm.

John

Elijah's being, the Elijah-angel of John, sacrifices itself, as it were, in essence into that disciple of Christ. The more the initiation of the others breaks down, he becomes the actual and only bearer of the event of initiation. As with *Peter* at the feet of Jesus, who himself appears as the earthly bearer of the celestial splendour of Christ, we see in the Transfiguration *James* at the feet of the super-earthly appearance of Moses. We see *John*—the disciple becoming John—however, with Elijah, who spiritually links himself to him in his human depths. 'The secret of the two Johns' is significantly revealed precisely in the event of the Transfiguration (Introduction, p. 49). To him who has himself become 'virginal', the super-earthly being combines from above, the 'angel' combines with 'child'.

Thus the events of the Transfiguration, apart from what it meant for Christ Himself and for the Earth, present an important moment, an important stage for the disciple of Christ who is becoming John. Ever more inward, ever more deeply he combines himself with the being who bears in himself the secret of the rhythm of the Christ-Sun. Ever more he penetrates into the Sun-revelation of the Transfiguration-experience with the secrets of this rhythm. Ever greater the 'realm of the angels' is revealed, about which the beginning of Mark's Gospel speaks. And in this inner penetrating himself with the Elijah-John being, the angel of Elijah-John, there lies at the same time the ever-deeper comprehension of what Peter in Caesarea Philippi could not understand—the meaning of the Mystery of death.

Furthermore, the two zodiacal signs, the Goat and the Waterman also point to this. These are the signs of the 'heavenly death', with which the Elijah-John-consciousness knows it is so deeply connected. In it are revealed secrets of the night and of death, which also so deeply inspired the soul of the poet Novalis in his *Hymns to the Night*. Novalis, in the most sublime sense of the word, was 'related to death'. The Elijah-John soul stands before us as if it has its homeland in that realm, as if it has to force itself into earthly

life, only able with effort to maintain the connection. In this sense, inspiring him who was becoming John, it revealed itself on the Mount of Transfiguration. It united there its raying with that of the Sun-splendour of Christ.

It is the angelic being of Elijah-John, who now in the Transfiguration so deeply overshadowed and penetrated the initiation of the disciple maturing to become John. This angelic being, who now also prophesied the death on Golgotha, the departure [*ἔξοδον—exodon*: 'exodus'] at Jerusalem (Luke 9:31 with Mark 9:1), in a very sublime and sacred sense is also really the angel of death. But for the One becoming John, by taking this angel of death into himself, it became in him the angel of life. In the depths of death, in the 'Transfiguration' preparing the Mystery of Golgotha, the Mystery of life was revealed to him. So John became the first who found the 'way of life' (cf. Matt. 7:14).

Peter

Let us turn our attention from John to the two others with him on the Mount of Transfiguration beholding the Sun-magnificence of Christ, and first to Peter. We can become deeply aware that not without reason, not without deep meaning did Christ open the spiritual eye precisely of Peter. He, who out of the past was richly blessed, for the future was to be called to high things, was now permitted to *behold* the Sun-splendour of Christ, which despite his failure in Caesarea Philippi he so clearly recognized and luminously proclaimed. In his confession lay the strength that gave him before the spiritual world the full power also now to *behold* what he recognized, to be present at the beholding. In beholding the event that signified the beginning of Christ's earthly dying, the possibility was given to him, Peter, to grasp at the last hour the meaning of the sacrifice of death, of which earlier he could not lay hold. And his tragedy was that here, too, he could not grasp it.

All three disciples were deeply transported, in a consciousness that is awakened in people by lightning (this is the sense of the Greek

ἔκφοβοι—ekphoboi, Mark 9:6 ['frightened' NIV; 'sore afraid' AV/KJV; 'terrified' NRSV]). For John, the silent one, the transport became a deep revelation. Peter, however, who liked so much to speak at the wrong time, spoke here, too, but 'he knew not what he said' (9:6); the excess of the beholding blinded him, darkening his consciousness. Yet what he spoke without knowing, revealed his most inner self. In beholding the Sun-magnificence of Christ on the Mount all the forces awoke in him that he wanted to release over the Earth, those forces that always were his danger. Quite transported by the solar splendour of Christ, he wanted most to tarry in the cosmic heights, always to remain, spiritually, on the Mount:

> Peter said to Jesus, 'Master, it is well that we are here; let us make three booths—one for you, and one for Moses. Let us put up three booths—one for you, and one for Moses and one for Elijah' [Mark 9:5. RSV].

In the event of the Transfiguration, he only saw the magnificence of the Sun-existence, not the earthly meaning. He wanted to keep hold of that magnificence where he saw it. He does not see how it sacrifices itself for the Earth, disappearing by dying into the Earth in order to raise the Earth itself one day again into a Sun-condition. And with that aspect of the Transfiguration so deeply and directly bound with Golgotha—he didn't understand Golgotha. It is the tragedy of Peter, a tragedy which—when we understand the meaning of the 'booths/shelters', the 'tabernacles'—does not dispense with its greatness. Even Peter wants to say to the moment: 'Linger awhile, thou art so fair!' [cf. Faust]. Thereby he falls to the power of darkness, which in the moment of denial altogether wipes out the 'I'.

In the zodiac, a behind-the-times, self-willed holding-fast of old powers of vision which we find in Herod in a far worse sense than with Peter (see above p. 136f.) is allotted to the Goat, the sign of the 'light-bringer', from which the consciousness of egotistical endeavour so easily passes over into the power of the 'dark adversary'. John the Baptist reveals the positive side of the Goat, the 'change your

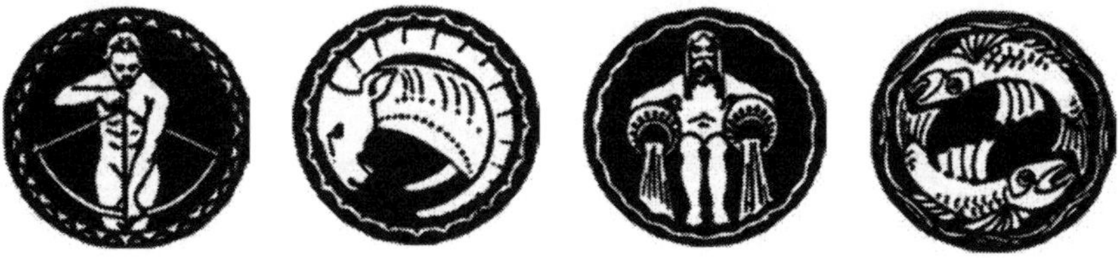

thinking'; Peter shows the negative, the 'self-will'. The problem of aligning the twelve apostles to the signs of the zodiac was touched on earlier. So we find:

> Peter, the denier, with the Goat;
> Thomas, the doubter, with the Twins;
> Judas, the betrayer, with the Scorpion.

These are three signs that reveal a highest and a lowest at the same time.

James

Our gaze turns from Peter to the third disciple alongside John together with Christ on the 'Mount of Transfiguration', to James, the other of the two 'sons of Zebedee'. (In his *Studies in the Gospels,* Emil Bock points out that the expression 'sons of Zebedee' refers rather to a relationship to the Mysteries than to a physical, bodily relationship; that 'Zebedee' was a physical, earthly person is questionable.) John, that is, the one becoming John, in the gospel is always closely linked to James. Already this relationship appears with the calling of the Twelve on the Mount, the beginning of the initiation of the disciples (Mark 3:17). Both carry the name *Bnehargem,* 'sons of thunder' [AV/KJV], that is, 'sons of the heavenly ether'. The name expresses that the pair in a special way are a vessel for the revelation of the cosmic ether. Consequently, they are a vessel also for the revelation of the cosmic Sun-splendour of Christ in the Transfiguration. We see them both on the Mount of Transfiguration, standing on either side of the Sun-splendour of Christ shining over Jesus of Nazareth.

This, however, does not simply mean their equal position. The gospel clearly says that John ultimately stands alone, alone he achieves the aim of initiation, alone he finds the way of life, that he as the only one of the Twelve stands under the cross, experiencing Golgotha in

himself. In this relationship, James stands with the others who did not pass the sign of death, have not overcome the sting of death, all of whom still go on the 'way of death' (cf. in this connection also the final chapter of John's Gospel, which in 21:23 points to the secret of John as the only disciple who 'does not die', who does not go the 'way of death').

Only an outer picture of this fact, not the essence of the matter itself, is shown in the martyr's death of all the disciples, but not John—though the traditions fluctuate. James, the first martyr of the Twelve, as it were, supplies for the others an ideal of the way of martyrdom (Acts 12:2). John helps the others, especially Peter, and the early Church through his living existence; James helps through his death. It is to be noted how with the death of James the influence of the Apostle Paul begins, so decisive for the becoming of the Church (Acts 12 and 13). Without the silent, spiritual help of John and without the activity of Paul, the Church, outer Christianity, would never have arisen. When we properly consider everything that lies in these facts, we gain from Mark the picture, frequently presented, of the significance of Peter and Andrew as pillars of the visible church, and James and John as pillars of the invisible Church (p. 88).

James and John

In *consciousness*—as we could also express it—in what they consciously achieve, James and John are very different; in their *being* and essence they are deeply connected. The one works consciously, the other more unconsciously. Even if James does not achieve the aim of the initiation as his spiritual twin-brother, merely his being present [during the initiation process] signifies something for the 'invisible Church', standing as a pillar before us. As the 'two trees' in Paradise (Gen. 2:9), as the two pillars in Solomon's Temple (I Kings 7:21; see R. Steiner. *Culture and the Individual* [GA 169]. Lecture 3. Berlin, 20 June 1916, 'The Twelve Human Senses'), as life and death—which in sub-earthly depths bear

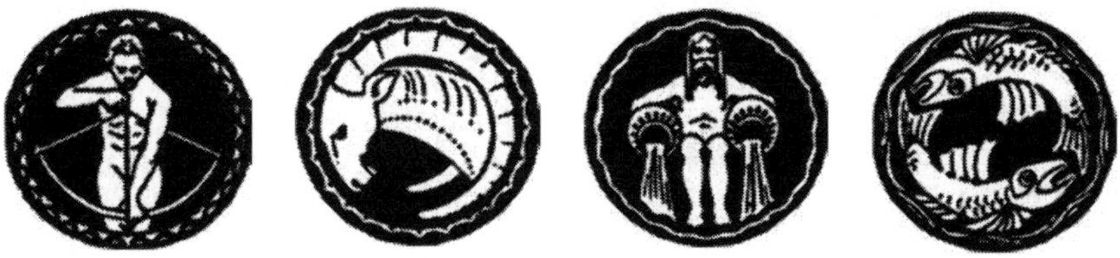

and determine each other—both 'heavenly twins' James and John, though also different are yet linked in the depths of their being.

This difference is precisely expressed in the gospel. In the Transfiguration, James is spiritually seen with the super-earthly appearance of Moses, John with that of Elijah. It does not need to stand in the text to the last literal detail, yet for the spiritual view it clearly stands there. Through James, forces work which also worked through Moses. He had to give his people the 'I'-impulse of earthly thinking as preparation for the great Christ 'I'-impulse. These forces also appear in Genesis in the picture of one of the two trees in Paradise, the Tree of Knowledge. To humanity, through the Fall of man, this became the Tree of Death. Through John, who is becoming the disciple John, the more he works further in his initiation, his 'becoming John', advancing inwardly united with Elijah-John, the more the Elijah-forces of the cosmic life-ether appear—in the picture in Genesis, the other tree of Paradise, the *Tree of Life*. These are the same forces which pour over humanity in the two great starry-feedings, or Grail-feedings, with the starry-bread of life, Mark 6 and 8—the first of which relates to our present epoch of humanity—as later in the 'Holy Grail' itself.

Speaking in the pictorial language of Genesis, the Tree of Knowledge and the Tree of Life in Paradise form *one* being, bowing their crowns to each other. They were pulled apart through the Fall of man. The upper life-ether as the 'Tree of Life' was saved from the might of death, yet was thereby removed from the human being, fallen into the might of death (Gen. 3:22-24).[24]

In the stellar script of the zodiac these facts are expressed (mentioned above, pp. 123) in the relationship of the signs ♍, ♐ and ♏ and the ♎ that steps in between♍, and ♏, after ♍, has become ♏ through ♐. Only through Christ, in the continuing penetration of the human being with the forces of Christ, is the meaning slowly removed of that divine commandment not to eat from the Tree of Life. As we have seen, the feeding of the 5000 that carries within it the secret of the present 'fifth post-Atlantean epoch', points towards that first renewed

eating of the starry bread of life that has become possible again only through Christ.

Still speaking pictorially, the way the 'two trees' in Paradise are pulled apart through the Fall of man, and how through this the human being itself becomes split, is mirrored in the Bible in the deeply meaningful story of Cain and Abel (Gen. 4)—to be taken as Imagination. The one part remains with the divine, heavenly powers. It escapes by returning into the upper element, but thereby loses the earthly element (like Abel who is slain by the earthly-powerful brother). The other part, remaining with the earthly element, masters the earthly forces, but initially loses the heavenly element (which he, Cain, seeks to regain out of his own strength). Here lies the 'Mystery of the sons of Cain', gently referred to at the end of Genesis 4. It plays a role significantly in the story of Solomon's Temple and its master-builder (cf. Gen. 4:22 and 1Kings 7:14), in the story of the waking of the 'young man of Nain' and the initiation of Lazarus-John. [Cf. the author's little book on *Genesis*, published in English with *From the Mysteries*, TL 2020, p. 44.]

The upper forces, turning towards the heavens, are only loosely connected with the earthly element. They also live with the being of Elijah and its later bearer, John the Baptist, who again for this reason is only loosely connected with the earthly element. In the one who in his initiation takes up into himself those Elijah-John forces and becomes the *Christian John*—we can also say, in Lazarus—there live the original forces of the other human substance, the forces of Cain.[25] Through Christ, through that which in the initiation of John was accomplished through Christ, those sundered human forces increasingly come together again. The last decisive event takes place over the 'grave of Lazarus' (John 11). The Tree of Life and the Tree of Knowledge, which once in the Paradise of humanity bowed their crowns to each other, are newly connected through Christ.

Out of this consideration, the picture of the 'Transfiguration of Christ on the Mount' receives a new and wonderful, deep meaning. It is really, alongside all the other things that otherwise lie in it, the whole picture

of the Paradise of Genesis. In the picture of the two Trees in Paradise—presented by Moses and Elijah—the gospel picture of the Transfiguration receives shining over it the glory of the primordial light. And yet in that which here is seen through the spiritual eyes (cf. Mark 8:22f.) opened through Christ, more is to be found than only the old Paradisal glory. Between the Tree of Knowledge (Moses) and the Tree of Life (Elijah) (to which identification Rudolf Steiner already points, cf. *The Apocalypse of St John* [GA 104], Lecture 9. Nuremberg, 26 June 1908; also *Bilder okkulter Siegel und Säulen*. GA 284. *Einleitung* / Introduction), there stands now the Christ-Sun of highest cosmic love, uniting again what has split apart in humanity through the Fall of man.

On the Mount of Transfiguration between Moses and Elijah, the Sun-Glory of Christ now shines. Moses appears, who in the Paradise story of Genesis [as traditional author] tells humanity of its primordial beginning, as the representative of humanity's past. Elijah appears like a preparer of the way for the human future that is completed in Christ. In the picture of the Transfiguration, the paradisal primordial past of mankind and the farthest human future shine before the spiritual eye. Significantly, the figure of Christ stands between humanity's past and humanity's future. In the lightning flash of the Eternal all the secrets of the becoming of time are illuminated. As in an instant, the secret of the whole of humanity's becoming crowds into the event of the Transfiguration, no longer graspable in an earthly measure of time. Alongside the Death on Golgotha itself, it is the most sublime instant in the whole gospel. Both instants are most intimately bound together; they stand indeed in the same constellation, under the same heavenly sign. In their external revelation they are both very different. The deep darkness of Golgotha (Mark 15:33) forcefully contrasts with the blinding, shining light of the Transfiguration (Mark 9:3) and its Sun-Glory.

John himself—the one becoming John—in that flash of light of the Transfiguration shining over Eternities, takes in the meaning of the Deed of Death on Golgotha, the Christ-meaning of the whole history of the Earth. For him here Inspiration becomes Intuition.

Here the question could arise: if witnessing the Transfiguration of Christ was really so decisive for the John-initiation, why then precisely in John's Gospel is no mention made of the Transfiguration, as in the three other gospels? As with the meaning revealed by Emil Bock (*Studies in the Gospels*) of the 'walking on the waves' narrated in Matthew, Mark and John, it too is not narrated in Luke's Gospel. Precisely because this experience of the etheric Christ is poured out like a substance over the whole of Luke's Gospel, the event is not expressly told. Likewise the 'Transfiguration on the Mount' in John's Gospel is not expressly told, because the 'Sun-glory of the Transfiguration' is poured out like a substance over the whole of John's Gospel.

***

To conclude, let us look again to the zodiac, to the arch spanning four heavenly signs with the Transfiguration event. We recall how with each of the zodiac signs always in a certain sense the respective 'counter-sign' (i.e. standing opposite, six signs further removed—see the Fig., p. 364) sympathetically resonates. Thus the gaze moves from the sign of the Archer, in which the Transfiguration begins, to the opposite sign of the Twins in the heights, to the sign of the 'Sacred Mount', here the Mount of Transfiguration. The gaze moves from both Elijah-John signs in the middle, the Goat and the Waterman, to the opposite signs of the Crab and the Lion as the signs of change, of transubstantiation, in the sense that it is revealed in the John-initiation, soon to be completed.

And from the Christ-Sun-sign of the Fishes, in which the Transfiguration ends, and has its climax, we look over to the etheric sign of the Virgin, the giver of the Bread of Life, the bearer of the Holy Grail. And like the events of the Jordan-Baptism, also lying in the Christ-Sun-sign of the Fishes—think of the descending dove—and the Feeding of the Five Thousand, the 'Transfiguration on the Mount' becomes a great Grail-event, the greatest and most sacred Grail-event, a Last-Supper event of humanity, taking hold of and embracing the whole Earth.

Christ Jesus was Himself transubstantiated into a shining host, which in the Mystery of Golgotha is given to sinful humanity as the Bread of Life. (Here 'transubstantiated himself' is the literal translation of the Greek, Mark 9:2 [*μετεμορφώθη—metemor phōthē*], usually translated 'was transfigured'. Instead, for this section, we could say: 'is transformed', 'is metamorphosed', 'is transubstantiated'. The beautiful picture of the 'shining host' was first used in a sermon by our friend, Rudolf Frieling.)

* * *

The picture of the 'Transfiguration' is still not complete if we only look on the spiritual-etheric event up there on the mountain heights, where Christ tarries with the three disciples, if we do not also look on those who remain below. And Mark's Gospel shows us (Mark 9:14-30) the shocking picture of the possessed boy whom the nine disciples could not heal (Mark 9:18 and 29). With this section the transition occurs of the events in the gospel into the sign of the Ram, in which (or in the constellation Ram–Scales) the healings of the possessed—here too the possessed boy is then healed through Christ—always take place.

The passage in question (Mark 9:18 and 29) belongs to those whose significance and tragedy are so easily overlooked in everyday gospel reading. We recall how already an earlier crisis entering into the initiation of the disciples (Mark 6, beginning) caused the healings of the sick to stop. The power passed on by Christ to the disciples in their initiation, to heal the sick and possessed (Mark 3:15), dwindles to nothing. Now through the failure of Peter in Caesarea Philippi the crisis—and for the others, who are drawn in—is renewed and aggravated. As we have seen, witnessing the Transfiguration has changed nothing for Peter. The story of the possessed man in Mark 5 has shown how far such a case and its healing can also stand as a picture for that which occurs in the souls of the disciples and also on the disciples through Christ. With the story of the possessed boy in Mark 9 many things speak for the reality of its outer occurrence. The zodiac sign of

the Ram, more than if this were the case with the Scales, also points in this direction.

Nevertheless, what is narrated in Mark 9, an especially difficult case of possession, *at the same time* is a shocking picture for what is taking place in the souls of those nine disciples who were not permitted to witness the Transfiguration, whose spiritual strengths were faltering. And beyond this, we can still see a picture within it for the whole critical situation of humanity, for those who suffer in the lowlands of the Earth far from the spiritual world and who cannot imagine spiritual experience, the people ill with the sickness of sin and wounded by the sting of the Scorpion. This contrasts so tragically with the sublimity and glory of the Transfiguration-experience on the Mount.

The descent from the Mount of Transfiguration is for Christ and the three disciples (cf. Mark 9:6) at the same time the re-entering of normal, awake consciousness. This transition takes place indeed in the sign of the Ram, belonging to the physical cross. As became clear in earlier cases (p. 74f.), with the healings of the possessed, the Ram expresses how those who are ill due to a disordered incarnation, into whose unstable consciousness demonic beings could find entry, are properly placed into their physical bodies through Christ. The Ram and the Scales are the signs of the orientation of the human being in space, in the physical realm.

This becomes especially clear with the healing of the possessed boy in Mark 9. Mark's Gospel vividly describes how the possessed boy is thrown on to the floor by demons (v. 20), how he loses the power of the upright ♈, which distinguishes the human being from the animals, how he no longer has a proper relationship to the Earth (v. 22), where it is told how the demon repeatedly throws him 'into fire or water'. It is said of Christ Who, because of the failure of the disciples, has to take up the healing Himself, 'He lifted him to his feet' (v. 27), and of the boy it is said, 'he stood up'. These words of getting up and standing up are in the language of the gospels, especially those of the Ram (see pp. 62f., 109).

Several things in the narration of the gospel can be taken as a picture for something spiritual, without detriment to the possible outer

actuality of the occurrence, when we look at this whole case of someone possessed as a picture of the crisis of the disciples and the crisis of humanity, which it is *as well*. In particular, why is the possessed person this time a boy? The virginal, child-like element (♍), as it is resurrected in John (Mark 5:41, the episode in Mark 9:35, where Christ places the child in the midst of the disciples also relates to this), also wants to be resurrected in the other disciples, in all people, but it thereby experiences difficulties (♏); things don't turn out as expected, as we say. Instead of the connection with the angel—which otherwise is natural for the being of children, with John this connection of the child, or regained childhood, and with the angel, really does occur—the connection with the demon occurs. Hence the case in point of the possessed boy appears so uncanny.

In addition to this, there is the whole strange role the father of the child plays in the story—he steps in for the son and, imploring, confesses his imperfections before Christ (v. 24). Does it not appear like a picture for the condition of humanity, where the human being cannot properly be aware of his ego-forces, his son-forces? These son-forces are still tied up, appearing as paralyzed, where the human being still expects everything from the father, from the outer natural necessity and resigns himself to it. Through this is expressed the standing still of humanity with the Father-principle, the forces of death, not finding the Son, the transition from the Father to the Son, to the source of life in the 'I'.

The answer given by Christ to the question of the disciples for the reason of their powerlessness (v. 29) stands connected to what was said of the process of the Transfiguration as the beginning of the dying of Christ. As long as Christ the Bridegroom is with them they do not need to fast (Mark 2:19). But now, when the Bridegroom decides to leave His people, their own forces have to be engaged; it requires meditation (praying) and will-exercises (renunciation-) exercises in order to reach that which, during the time of the presence of the Master was possible through grace.

The Bull in the Third Octave

Transition of the Word to John (Mark 9:31–10:31)

In the story of the possessed boy told in Mark 9, we could see a picture for the crisis that occurred through the failure of Peter, the darkening of Peter's consciousness at Caesarea Philippi within the group of disciples and in the initiation of the disciples. Crisis [*κρίση*] means 'separation'. In John's Gospel Christ Jesus Himself repeatedly uses the word for the separation of the spirits through the Christ-'I' where it is introduced into humanity (Luther translates as '*Gericht*'; AV/KJV as 'judgement').[26]

In the group of disciples, too, the Christ-'I' effects such a 'crisis', such a separation, which produces the effect that the paths of the others separate from the path of the *one* disciple who now reaches initiation. He now approaches actually becoming John. The initiation-event forming the content of Mark's Gospel at the point at which we stand, takes on more or less exclusively the character of the initiation of the one, whereas the initiation of the others breaks down.

Yet in their crisis, too, the others remain connected with Christ, the Initiator. Christ's 'farewell discourses' in John's Gospel, which terminate (John 16:32) by pointing to the crisis of the disciples, the climax of which is formed by their flight, and the 'Great Intercession', 'High-priestly Prayer' (John 17), are the most gripping testimonies to this connection. Christ inwardly carries further those who stay connected in their *being*, who only failed in their *consciousness*, who could not inwardly follow Him further in their consciousness. He takes up their failing consciousness into His never-failing, embracing consciousness. In this way He carefully leads them through their crisis until, at a later moment awakened by cosmic grace, they will awaken. In this way through Christ they are saved for their future activities, their future tasks for the Earth and for humanity.

The Pentecost event—Rudolf Steiner also mentions this—is the awakening of the disciples from their sleep of consciousness.

The power of the word, which they do not find out of their own strength on the path of initiation shown through Christ, is given to them from above. John, the one becoming John—this which especially forms the content of the present sign of the *word,* of this section standing in the sign of the Bull—the one initiated by Christ, finds the word out of his own strength, out of the 'I', or ego. He becomes the re-gainer, the re-bringer of the lost Creator-Word. And John, too, who finds in his consciousness what the others initially could not find, finds it not only for himself but also for the others. He is gone before them in the initiation, not in order to supersede them or place them in the shadow, but later the more effectively to ray out helping forces to them for the fulfilment of their earthly tasks. We see John, right into the Acts of the Apostles, in a commanding position as the carrier of the invisible Church, helping and protecting the visible Church, whose rock is Peter.

This already appears with all clarity in the Act of the Apostles, Chapter 1—see, for example, Acts 3 right at the beginning, and Acts 4. At many places where the phrase 'Peter and John' is found, one has the impression that John stands not only physically but especially spiritually behind Peter. The sections, as in Acts 5, where Peter is working on his own, make a very different impression. A completely different, not always a wholesome power, then appears to shine out of his deeds.

Of particular interest for the viewpoint of this work appears to be the role that, alongside the original John [the Baptist], the other John also plays, who is the writer of Mark's Gospel [John Mark], see Acts 12:12, 12:25, 13:5, etc. Here too one feels how the forces of initiation, helping and protecting, rule over the early Church in its becoming.

***

The Spokesman

In the gospel events, the transition to the Bull, the sign of the word, takes place in Mark 9:31 (AV/KJV): 'For he taught his disciples, and

saith unto them ...', and becomes especially clear in v. 32. Here within the third degree of the cosmic rhythm, initiation, it would have had to do with the disciples in their initiation fully receiving into themselves the word, the spiritual power of the word. They would have united in the depths of their being with it, that they become one with the Creator-Word. However, only the one was able to do this—who now gradually achieves it. The others are not able *to receive the word into themselves* (v. 32).

Who alone is able to take up the word into himself, in the sense meant here? Only he who through overcoming the commanding death-sting of sensuality in the counter-sign of the word (♏ the counter-sign of ♉; see the Fig., p. 364), by re-finding the maidenly, childlike quality (♍) of primordial human nature. For this reason Christ places a child amongst the disciples (9:36). This is the larger meaning of this Imagination, pointing to that which now takes place in the initiation of John, or rather what has taken place (see what was said earlier on Mark 5:41, p. 118f.). Likewise, Christ's saying (9:35) on the relationship of Peter and John that, since Caesarea Philippi, has got out of step in such a decisive manner. This saying already prepares for 10:31: 'But many who are first shall be last, and the last first.' The whole 'argument about who was the greatest' is no small argument, but a question that through the recent events, especially the participation of some at the Transfiguration and the exclusion of others, had to be presented to them as a necessity.

The inability of the disciples to receive the word (9:32) is expressively and significantly presented, contrasting in what follows (9:38) with the one who has kept silent for so long. On his search for the path of initiation, from the moment of the decisive turning point of his life (see p. 49, [the raising of the young man of Nain]), he became the *silent disciple*. Now, as the *one becoming John, he finds the word,* and now as John becomes the spokesman. Peter, who always speaks too early, the last time in Caesarea Philippi, thereby lost the word. The other, who knew how to keep silent, now finds the word and is in command. The decisive viewpoint is not that the content of the words was not yet rightly given by Christ, but that the one becoming John here for the first time speaks. His voice has achieved the power to speak before the presence of the master, Christ, and that the word which was hitherto led by another is now transferred to him. One would easily miss the significant bearing of the whole passage, would overlook something all-important, if one were not led to that decisive viewpoint—standing in the centre of these contemplations—through the *cosmic rhythm* of the gospel, pointing here so clearly to the *sign of the word*. Such passages reveal especially clearly what research of the cosmic rhythm of the zodiacal signs in the gospel not only signifies as a question of knowledge for itself, but what it can achieve for the whole context of the gospel in general.

That the content of Christ's words puts the situation straight—John wants to forbid another working in the name of Christ—points to different, not unimportant, deeper contexts necessary to understand the whole situation. Initially, we see how in their crisis the force to drive out demons, lost to the disciples (Mark 9: 18, 28), is now exercised by others. These forces suddenly appear in the vicinity, passing over to outsiders. Not only are the other disciples not in agreement, but John too wants to oppose it for a deeper reason [involving Elijah]. The power of Elijah, when Elijah himself appears, above all in witnessing the Transfiguration, this power that was in John the Baptist, increasingly passes over to the one becoming John. We get to know this power in the whole Elijah story of the Old Testament. Its climax is when Elijah 'calls down fire from heaven', when he puts a spoke in the wheel of the priests of Baal. Rudolf Steiner has shown how the 'slaughter of the priests of Baal' is not to be taken literally, but as the Imagination of how the mighty word-magic of Elijah reveals before all the people the impotence of the others.

And what John in Mark 9:38 means with 'forbid' is no harmless objection, but a magically effective banning, that, as one might think, removes the wrongly exerted force from the other. The disciples want

to erect a kind of Elijah-court of judgement against that outsider. But Christ teaches His own [disciples] that the time is now passed for such Elijah-courts—which in the pre-Christian era were justified. The influence of Christ is one in grace and freedom for all people, not only for preferred individuals or for closed groups. Moreover, the power of Elijah, where it is renewed in Christ, is now something new, its effect more sublime in grace, no longer in 'wrath'. The 'wrath of God' belongs to the Father; freedom, love and grace belong to the 'Son'. And for the one becoming John an obstacle lies here around which he has to negotiate. And in what follows, we shall soon experience how certain crises, which he too has still to get through, are inwardly connected with it. Whereas Peter cannot get loose from his past, the one becoming John, from the moment of that soul-change that brought him to tread the path of initiation, knows how he can overcome all that is past and how he has to abandon it. But even for him, who from the beginning basically sees, knows and wants the right thing, the actual carrying out in the individual case can still be difficult. From this angle, we understand the episode, soon to be met, of the 'rich young man'. In particular, taking up the Elijah-forces places him now before the test of dealing with the new power, not in the former pre-Christian manner but now truly in its new, Christian, meaning.

Life v. Death

The teaching of Christ forming the end of Mark 9 is to be thought of primarily as experienced in John's consciousness. This is increasingly the case in what follows. The end of Mark 9 contains clear echoes of the Sermon on the Mount of Matthew's Gospel (Mark 9:43ff., cf. Matt. 5:29ff.; Mark 9:49, cf. Matt. 5:13). The chronological contradiction with the narration of Matthew's Gospel disappears when it is recognized how what was heard by all the disciples, but not yet understood in its final depths, now achieves full understanding in the initiation of the one becoming John. The struggle of the might of life (♉) with the

might of death (♏), the overcoming of death through what is alive is the clear motive of this teaching. Increasingly the Mysteries of the 'path of life' arise in the consciousness of the one becoming John, who has now found the 'word'.[27]

And in the salt (Mark 9:49, 50) bearing the formative forces of the life-ether (cf. Günter Wachsmuth, *The Etheric Formative Forces*, p. 43), the secrets of life are revealed. When in applying the key of the zodiac signs to the supersensory human members, we find the Bull is also the sign of the 'consciousness-soul'—which is not stimulated through outer sense-impressions but from within by the determining human soul—we recognize even more clearly how the contents of this and of the following sections of Mark's Gospel lie in the direction of the *development of the consciousness-soul*, of Johannine initiation. Inner experiences of the consciousness, insights arising from within consciousness, are told in these sections of Mark's Gospel.

***

This is also valid above all for the many deep riddles and secrets contained in the content of Mark 10, whose first half (till v. 31) is to be conceived under the sign of the Bull. We will advance in our understanding only by reminding ourselves that, since the initiation of Lazarus-John will now be led through to its completion, the content and language of the gospel will become ever more mysterious. These things become increasingly further removed from taking the content of the gospel as corresponding to what is conveyed by a mere outer meaning of the words. Chapters 10-13 of Mark's Gospel are initiation chapters, *κατ'εξοχην* [pre-eminently] Mystery chapters.

From its beginning, Mark 10 stands in the sign of the word: '... as was his custom, he taught them' (10:1). And then, in v. 2 as a 'testing with the Pharisees', one motif in the whole contemplation on the Bull, already become the most familiar, follows: the living word (♉) in Christ is opposed by (♏) the might killing the living element of words, the dead leaven of the Pharisees. And yet one has to ask, is this whole confrontation with the Pharisees to be conceived as an outer event, a normal discussion? Are the 'crowds' (v. 1) really physically present? One has to listen intimately to the words of v. 1, 'as was his custom' (ὡς εἰώθει). The whole manner, as frequently in earlier times Christ Jesus taught the people gathered around him, how it then came to arguments with scribes and Pharisees—now this arises *out of the memory*. In whose memory? In the memory of him now becoming the bearer of the life of initiation, the one becoming John. Here everything is pictorial, Imagination. And the spiritual content of the words of Christ taken in this teaching and the discussions, is now inner experience of the consciousness-soul, the *Intuition* of the one becoming John.

In the Sermon on the Mount of Matthew's Gospel the crowds mentioned there (Matt. 4:25, 5:1) are not to be thought of as physically present (see p. 145). Only the disciples were present as listeners. And yet the crowds of people are mentioned in the gospel, because the words of Christ, even when they do not reach the ears of people, are received into the heart of humanity. In the *way* they are spoken, somehow they do reach human souls. And this is the case here in Mark's Gospel (Mark 10:1ff.). Initially only the consciousness of John perceives everything in a purely spiritual manner. Yet for him it becomes an *experience of humanity*; he is aware the words in the last resort are for all human beings, they are spoken for humanity itself. On spiritual paths sooner or later humanity will have to attain them. John consequently really does see in spiritual experience the crowds of human beings in the pictures before him.

As little as we are to think of the 'crowds' mentioned in 10:1 as physically present, as little is this the case with the Pharisees in v. 2. The time is past when Christ Jesus, still unthreatened by scribes and Pharisees, could still have shown himself in public. This is clearly stated in John 11:54ff., the gospel that often emphasizes the external facts most directly. And with the events narrated in Mark 10ff. we are already quite near to what forms the content of John 11. Here too it is as it is everywhere: the 'confrontation with the Pharisees' earlier so

often experienced as purely outer events, the way that the living word in Christ opposes the dead words of the Pharisees, now becomes the inner experience of the consciousness-soul. It becomes Intuition for the one who is becoming John, who is becoming ripe for his initiation. Out of the 'harmless' sermon on divorce (as the beginning of Mark 10 is sometimes called) something different, deeply Johannine emerges. Deepest secrets of the earlier wisdom of Moses and the ancient Mystery wisdom, out of which the wisdom of Moses had arisen, are touched on by Christ.

The Primordial Human Being

We note how the centre of this teaching of Christ is formed by a verse (Gen. 1:27) full of deep meaning. Its meaning (completely blurred in most translations) announces how human beings were originally spiritually created (*ἀρχή κτίσις*) in the image of the divine as 'male-female' (*zakhar neqebah, ἄρσεν καὶ θῆλυ*) how the contrast of feminine-masculine is spiritually united (see the author's monograph, *Genesis*, in *From the Mysteries*). In this sentence in Genesis lies primordial wisdom, the wisdom of the primordial human Mysteries that still contain a memory of the lost divine, primordial consciousness of the human being. An echo of this primordial wisdom lived in the Egyptian Mysteries of Isis, whose initiate—though no longer in its time of primordial blossoming—was Moses.

In Isis, the eternal feminine, the Egyptians revered the enlivening cosmic power of the Virgin, the power of the cosmic life-ether—which in the gospel with the experiences of the Feedings and Last Supper appears as the bread of life in the sign of the Virgin. The enlivening power working in the [depths of] *being*, Isis, the eternal feminine, connects itself with the power working in the *consciousness*, with Osiris, the eternal masculine. It is at the same time the enlivening source for this power, in the same way as the light of the lamp is nourished and contained by the oil. (See Rudolf Steiner, *The Mysteries of the East and*

Christianity, GA 144. Lecture 3. Berlin, 5 Feb. 1913—for the secrets of 'oil and lamp', the parable at the beginning of Matt. 25 is also important.) The original pure essence of this connection is not fully expressed through any earthly picture. Isis is sister and spouse of Osiris; at the same time she is 'Mother and Virgin who gives birth in eternity to the Son, the creative cosmic Word'. Osiris, consequently, is at the same time son, spouse and brother of Isis. Primordial secrets of the human being and human nature are expressed in these pictures. Gen. 1:27 echoes Egyptian Mystery-wisdom.

[Gen. 1:27: And God made man, according to the image of God he made him, male-female he made them.]

Gen. 1:27 LXX: *καὶ ἐποίησεν ὁ θεὸς τὸν ἄνθρωπον, κατ' εἰκόνα θεοῦ ἐποίησεν αὐτόν, ἄρσεν καὶ θῆλυ ἐποίησεν αὐτούς.*

Yet this wisdom, however great and sublime it is, carries a critical, double-edged moment in itself—only the pure, innocent soul can properly receive it. For this primordial knowledge, fallen human nature is an unsuitable, cloudy vessel. Through purification and trials of all sorts the initiates of the early Mysteries sought again for a pure, serviceable vessel to receive this knowledge. Only in the earliest times, in the primordial flowering of the Mysteries, did this really transpire. When Moses led the Hebrews out of Egypt, the Mysteries there had long overstepped their highpoint. They fell ever further into decadence. The sublime divine wisdom of Isis and Osiris, of the union of female and male in the lap of the Godhead, became progressively pulled down into the abysses of lower human nature with its urges, desires and passions. Isis, the ruler of the highest, virginally purest life-forces and maternal healing-forces of love, became the demonic being of human sexual urges and aberrations. The one-time 'starry queen' and later 'lotus queen' became 'queen of serpents'.

The Mysteries, already mentioned in this exposition of the gospel, the Mysteries of Isabel in the Old Testament (already the name, Isis-Baal, points to the context of the Mysteries of Isis—Herodias in the New Testament with her ghastly sexual magic, in whose abysses Mark 6 concedes an earnest glimpse) are degenerate residues of these Egyptian Mysteries of Isis, fallen into ever deeper decadence, and their neighbouring Assyrian-Chaldean Mysteries of Istar-Astarte (Astaroth). The vessel of human nature was no longer pure enough to guard the purity of this originally pure and lofty Mystery-knowledge. The 'word', the divine creative-word, Osiris, was 'lost' in these Mysteries. Only he, led by Christ, won back the original virginal purity and innocence of human nature, was able to re-find it. From this we understand how significant it is that everything touched on in this section stands in the *sign of the word* (♉).

The mouth of no initiate before John would at that time have been pure enough to express this sublime *primordial knowledge* of the human race reflected in Gen. 1:27, which in Egypt was called that of *Isis and Osiris;* none even of the highest initiated Pharisees or Essenes was still able to lay hold of it. Only the *One* Mouth was able to express it, from which the one becoming John now perceives it in his initiation—perhaps only spiritually spoken—the sublime Mouth, in which the Word, lost to humanity, in the divine sense is re-enlivened, the Mouth in whom the Creator-Word in the primordial beginning itself became flesh, the *Mouth of Christ*. And only John, the one become virginal and childlike once more, is able to lay hold of it. To him there sounds in spiritual listening out of the Mouth of Him Who initiates him, there sounds the lost primordial wisdom of the Mysteries, the sublime secret of Isis and Osiris.

Because he awoke the Virgin in himself (Mark 5:41), had found and received the child in himself (Mark 9:37), he is able to receive Christ into himself, to lay hold of the word of Christ of most lofty spiritual wisdom. The others who hindered the child to enter themselves are unable to do this. So the episode of Mark 10:10-16 (together with 9:34–37) becomes a picture of how the path of initiation of the one becoming John separates itself from the paths of the others. It belongs to the most moving, beautiful and weighty themes of the gospel, how

immediately after the most sublime of all teaching the picture of the little child and its blessing through Christ is placed before us.

The sublime pictures of the Egyptian Isis-wisdom arise again in him, the one becoming John, taught by Christ. Because of this he is able later in the Apocalypse (Rev. 12) so expressively to present that picture, created out of the depths of the primordial Mysteries of Egypt. It is the picture of the starry Queen, the Mother and Virgin who gives birth to the Son of the Sun, and with it also the picture of the other might, the might of the dragon, which eradicates the lofty revelation of the stars in human consciousness. The Egyptian speaks of Seth—originally the word meant 'serpent'—the dark brother of Osiris, who murders his shining brother during the month when the Sun stands in the Scorpion. All the secrets of the constellation ♉–♏ that have been touched upon above now light up before us. The secret of the constellation ♉–♏ is revealed in the deepest meaning of all, that of Christ. For John, in experiencing the Johannine initiation, the dead wisdom of Moses, the Mystery knowledge that has died, through Christ has again become a living primordial wisdom and wisdom of the future.

***

The 'Rich Young Man'

The episode of 'the story of the rich young man' (Mark 10:17-27, cf. Matt. 19:16-30) shows how from the achieved heights the Johannine consciousness also leads through crises and tests. The episode taken only as an outer event belongs to the greatest hard things of the gospel. However, taken in the Mystery sense it belongs to the greatest and most moving events contained in the gospel. We can be made deeply aware of the earnestness of the Christ-initiation, the entire difficulty of finding and going on the 'path of life' (Matt. 7:14), by recognizing how difficult it also was for those who first found and went on this path. This 'finding the path of life' is indicated straightaway in the first question of all that the young man poses most clearly to the 'Master', to Christ the Initiator (Mark 10:17).

Who is the 'rich young man' who suddenly stands before us? We know it is a 'young man' (Gk. *νεανίσκος*) from the parallel narration in Matthew's Gospel (Matt. 19:22). Suddenly, and precisely with Mark, presented with a certain dreamlike playful realism, he meets Christ on the way and kneels before him. 'And when he was gone forth into the way, there came *one* (Gk. *εἷς*) running, and kneeled to him, ...' [Mark 10:17 AV/KJV]. In the course of the exposition—initially, of course, everything is only an hypothesis—it will show itself ever more clearly that here we have to translate the Greek *εἷς* (the name for the number one) as 'the one', as in another passage (Mark 13:1), most significant for the fact of the John-initiation and the Lazarus-John Mystery. Or rather we simply allow the translation 'one', but make ourselves aware of what lies between the lines. According to the Mystery-meaning we have to understand as 'the one', he who is the subject of discussion, who has become the one and only carrier of the initiation events after the initiation of the others has collapsed. He is *the one disciple* of whom in John's Gospel it is always said, the Lord 'loved him' (John 11:5, 13:23, 20:2, 21:20)—about whom also in this episode in Mark's Gospel it is said so significantly that Jesus 'loved him' (10:21). The word in the original text *ἀγαπᾶν*—here the aorist *ἠγάπησεν*—is the same as in the first two and the last of the four passages listed above. The word 'loved' is never used of Christ in the gospels as something ordinary, but used only very seldom and always in a certain profound Mystery-meaning.

'Son of the Widow'

Still, it would be an error to conceive in a one-sided way that John or the 'one becoming John' was the one who ran into Christ on the path, asked the questions and then, disappointed at Christ's answer, went

away feeling downcast. Taken as an outer event, the whole episode would be even less understandable than it would with another interpretation. We have to imagine these things in yet another way, lying in quite a different sphere of consciousness—more dreamlike, to do with the Mysteries.

In case we *do* want to imagine this episode as an 'outer' event, one principle harshness in the gospel narration of the 'rich young man' would be this. We are to imagine a person striving towards the spiritual heights. Even if he is not the disciple John, yet in relationship to the 'love' on Christ's side he stands on a line with the disciple John. In addition, this person has the unique destiny in his earthly life to meet Christ-Jesus Himself on His earthly journeys. We are to imagine he is not able finally to get away from his outer riches. But because he cannot renounce his external wealth, i.e. eventually for the sake of pitiful earthly belongings he fails to connect with the spiritual Representative of Humanity. However, it will emerge ever more clearly—initially, as mentioned, all this is presented only as a hypothesis—that we are dealing neither with a mere outer occurrence, nor with clinging to the mere outer riches, to earthly belongings.

We recall the often-mentioned legend telling how the person, which later as 'Lazarus' is re-awakened by Christ out of the slumber of the grave, was once a rich, temple-ruler, also rich with treasures of primordial temple wisdom. This person becomes a witness of the initiation event, through whom Christ awakens from death the 'son of the widow' of Nain (Luke 7). This impression was so profoundly moving that the previously 'rich' person—also rich in a spiritual sense—decides to sacrifice all this richness in order to go like that young man through the narrowest of all gates (Matt. 7:14), through the gates of the greatest poverty, through the grave and death, to find the path of life. From then on he falls chronically sick, increasingly moving towards death as narrated in John 11. The once rich person becomes 'sick', the invalid Lazarus, whom Christ re-awakens from death.

We immediately feel it significant when that 'rich young man', who in Mark is only called 'one', or 'the one', and in Matthew 'young man', appears in the parallel narration of Luke's Gospel (18:18-30) as the temple 'ruler' (*ἄρχων*, as in John 3:1, the meeting with Nicodemus). We see here not a contradiction, but a wonderful supplement of various spiritual viewpoints (Introduction, p. 22). The expression 'son of the widow', which points towards a connection between the young man of Nain, who was awoken earlier by Christ, and the later awakened Lazarus, are linked through a hidden Mystery-connection and only slightly touched on in the Bible to be spiritually read between the lines. This expression can also be found in 1 Kings (7:14), of the builder of Solomon's Temple, of Hiram, the artistic master-builder from Tyre whom, with everything he expressed as symbols in the Temple (1 Kings 6 and 7), we have also to imagine as the possessor of secret wisdom, as an initiate of some Mysteries. The expression used of him, 'cunning to work all works in brass' (1 Kings 7:14 AV) ('highly skilled and experienced in all kinds of bronze work' NIV), can also be found in a quite similar version in Genesis 4, rich in secrets [cf. *Genesis*, chapter 'Cain', in *From the Mysteries*, TL 2020, 44-9], where the wisdom and artistry of the sons of Cain are mentioned. This allows us to feel in which direction the relationships lie, connecting from the figure of the great building-master on the one hand into the primordial past and on the other hand into the future towards the initiation of John-Lazarus.[28]

To the expression 'son of the widow', Rudolf Steiner (*Mysteries of the East and Christianity*, GA 144. Lecture 3. Berlin, 5 Feb. 1913) mentions that the phrase was used of the initiates in the Egyptian Mysteries. At that time of the decline of those Mysteries, the word was lost; the revelation of Osiris and the birth of Osiris the sounding of the divine word had vanished from the Mystery-centres. The initiates experienced Isis only as the silent, mourning widow. Certain connections pointing to the Isis-Mysteries have been mentioned in this section.

The 'riches'

Perhaps at this point it has become in some ways clearer in which direction to search for the 'riches'. With the gospel story of the 'rich young man' the mentioned 'trials of the soul' play a role. Who is the person who saw himself placed before these soul-trials on the path of initiation? In essence this path leads into the future, the future development of humanity. On this path one has to separate oneself from everything connecting the soul in a one-sided way with the past, including treasures of the highest Mysteries. He who in his time received such a deeply moving, soul-changing impression of Christ at Nain, knew in a spontaneous intuition that in order to take the 'path of life' shown here through Christ's deed as a path leading into the future, he had completely to separate himself from the connections to his own past and that of humanity. The whole picture of the silent and sick person in which he is presented in the midst of the process of initiation taking place through Christ in the group of disciples, shows with what earnestness, with what sacrificial devotion he had taken up this path of complete renunciation.

Through this he is distinguished especially from Peter, who is richly blessed with gifts and forces of his own past and that of humanity. Peter is *not* able to separate himself from what connects him to the past; for him this richness of the past becomes the stumbling block. This leads to the decisive turn from Caesarea Philippi. Peter, inspired by the old magical forces of the words of humanity's past, always speaks too soon. Here, too, he spoke too soon; in this way he 'lost the word'. And the other, silent for so long developing through the silent renunciation the right soul-forces, 'found' the word. From this moment onwards he becomes the leader of the word (Mark 9:38). In seeking for the path of life, he found the *living power of the word.*

However, this living power of the word (♉) is always placed facing the other might wanting to kill what lives in the word ♏). It is the might that works through the scribes and Pharisees, who always

want to abide with the Saturn-day of the past (see above, p. 84), with the Father-forces of death and the necessity of the law, who do not see and understand that now in Christ the world Sun-day has dawned, the day of the Son and of freedom. In the early Mysteries, as those of Ephesus, people looked to the seven spiritual mights of the planets, seeing in 'Saturn' the guardian of humanity's primordial memories, of the Earth's past (the '*weltenalten Geist-Innigkeit*', 'ancient cosmic spirit-inwardness', as Rudolf Steiner beautifully expressed it in a verse relating to the Ephesian Mysteries). These were called 'riches' (*πλουτος*).

In Rev. 5:12, in seven listed qualities of the Lamb, the seven Ephesian planetary virtues are hidden:

- *δύναμις*, power, relates to the *Moon;*
- *πλοῦτος*, riches, to *Saturn;*
- *σοφία*, wisdom, to *Jupiter;*
- *ἰσχὺς*, strength, to the *Sun;*
- *τιμή*, honour, evaluation of worth, to *Mercury;*
- *δόξα*, glory, light of revelation, to *Venus;*
- *εὐλογία*, blessing, ability to speak beautifully, to *Mars.*

The present work has to be limited to the viewpoint of the 'twelve zodiacal signs'; the 'seven planets' may at least quietly chime here.

That might, then, which in the case with the situation where the Pharisees and Hebrewdom in general wants to hold the soul fast with Saturn and its kingdom of the past, even when the epoch of the Sun has dawned, is called from the viewpoint of the zodiac, the Scorpion (♏). Precisely in the moment when the one becoming John found the word, penetrated to the power of the word (♉), he sees the strength and essence of the counter-sign (♏) opposing as a might of temptation. In so far as this might expresses itself as the poisoned sting of sensuality, he had already overcome it earlier (Mark 5:41, cf. 9:36f., 10:15f. and what was said at that point about ♏ and ♍). But he has to struggle with it again, where precisely after he becomes master of the power of the word in ♉, it wants to establish the Saturn-impulse of the

past against the Sun-impulse of the future. Here this might wants to hold him fast, tempting him with his own rich past.

And so he who from the beginning was prepared to offer everything, had decided to loosen himself from everything that still could bind him to the past, experiences a moment when it could appear as if it were no longer possible for him to offer the ultimate, to reach the complete zero-point of consciousness, to find the way through the narrow gate, which alone leads to the way of life. In a stirring manner he, the inheritor of rich Mystery and temple riches of the past, has to become aware how all these treasures of the past only bar him the way to the true Christ-initiation, the path of life. In some hidden corner of his being, which hitherto he had most likely not brought to consciousness, he felt himself still belonging to the powers of death. He still feels not completely ripe and inwardly strong enough to cross the mysterious 'threshold'. He still sees there the sinister, crouching Guardian of the Threshold bearing the countenance of the powers of death. And it appears to him as if the other, sublime, bright Guardian of the Threshold, as if Christ the Initiator Himself, still sends him back from the threshold. In his innermost consciousness the one walking on the path of initiation, the path of life, the seeker, still feels sent back (Mark 10:22, 24, 25).

And everything that he experiences in his innermost consciousness as 'trials of the soul', clothes itself for him in pictures. His higher soul-faculties (Imagination, Inspiration and Intuition) are already awoken through the path of initiation. The pictures flit past him like pictures in a dream. Not pictures of outer events of the physical world but a dreamlike experience that passes by the soul in pictures is in the episode narrated in Mark 10:17-22. One can then take everything quite literally if one understands the things in such a way as they stand in Mark's Gospel—the whole picture of the person suddenly appearing as if out of nowhere, crossing Christ's path, posing his questions and feels he is sent back, and moves away disappointed, and so on. Only here, we have to do not with usual dream-pictures, but initiation dreams of a higher kind. The one becoming John-Lazarus sees himself in these dreams like a strange person. And yet it is the experience of his own soul that is mirrored in these pictures. Such an experience, as happens on the path of initiation especially with the meeting of the Guardian of the Threshold, is called a 'splitting of the personality'.[29]

In that moment, when he is finding the path leading into the future and towards life, the one becoming John sees in the dreams and visions of his initiation-experience how a strange personality, removed from him, that part of his being which thinks it cannot separate itself from any remnants from the past, is still in some instances connected to, still fallen, in pawn to the power of death. Once more he experiences before the final victory the whole darkness of the abyss, of despair, the whole curse of Cain, the curse on humanity, the whole bitterness of feeling excluded from the nearness of Christ and the true heights of life. He experiences the whole earnest confrontation between the might of life and the might of death (♉–♏), as it has to be mastered on the Christian path of initiation. In the splitting of the personality, the one becoming John has also to pass through a final crisis in his initiation. But with him this crisis does not lead, as with the others, to a breakdown in the initiation. As will be shown in what follows, he finds the strength to overcome it. The episode following the one with the rich young man, which is also to be thought of as a spiritual experience (Mark 12:28-34), shows the point where the one who felt he had been refused by the Master and Teacher hears now the comforting encouragement of the Teacher, the Initiator: 'You are not far from the kingdom of God' (12:34).

***

Dives and Lazarus

We cannot leave this whole theme in the recognized episode of the 'rich young man' as the *trial of the soul on the path of initiation*, without noticing how this 'splitting of the personality', which we are discussing, also sounds in apparently the strangest puzzle and hard sayings in a section of another gospel (Luke 16:19-31), the 'story of the rich man and the poor Lazarus'. Who has not been pulled up by the whole mode here, at least at first appearance, of how the contrast of poor and rich is presented? How is it, in the context of the wisdom of Abraham (Luke 16:25), that one only because here he had 'received good things', over yonder is consequently tormented, but the other one, who had 'received bad things' (was it not the destiny of his deeds, his karma?), over yonder is consequently 'comforted' and enjoys good things? Here too nothing else is presented than that initiation-crisis of the 'splitting of the personality'. The 'rich young man' and the poor 'beggar' Lazarus are one and the same person!

Whoever, through such an explanation, feels at first as if he had run into a cul-de-sac, or into a brick wall, will understand, if he is not biased, how through this the differences of the four gospels appear in quite a new light, illuminating, complementing and supporting each other. Indeed, Lazarus in Luke (Luke 16:20) is basically none other than the 'sick' man, the 'invalid' of John's Gospel, whom we have known for a while now as the bearer of the Johannine initiation. In the initiation-narration of Mark's Gospel he is not called by this name, it is true, but he is meant. And the 'great chasm' (*χάσμα μέγα*) Abraham mentions (Luke 16:26) is basically the same as that which opens up in the 'splitting of the personality'. This again appears as an image and reflection of the great split in humanity, torn apart through the Fall of man, revealed in Cain's fratricide. It is the cleavage between that substantial part of humanity that has to feel alienated in order to preserve the heavenly, and that other substantial part who in making themselves serviceable to the earthly consequently lose the heavenly; this cleavage gapes between the realm of eternal life and the earthly realm of death.

The whole primordial split of sinful humanity, the primordial contrast between the bright and the dark brother, between Abel and Cain, gapes at each critical point of the life of initiation in the soul of John-Lazarus. He sees his own being torn apart in two. The one, the earthly part, he sees, as it were, with Cain, the original ancestor, the fire-core of the Earth (cf. the expressive Scene 6 in Albert Steffen's drama *Hiram und Salomo*). There he sees all the riches and treasures, all the intellectual treasures which he, the heir to the proud earthly wisdom of the Mysteries of Cain, collected and consumed by burning fire. With that which he sees there consumed as a part of his own being, he suffers the cleansing torment of fire. Everything in him still belonging to sensuality (these are the 'five brothers', Mark 10:28 [the traditional five senses]), he sees fall to this fate.

And above, in the realm of the 'bright brother', he now sees the other, 'Lazarus', the 'invalid', which he himself had become on Earth. His earthly part looks towards the Elijah-power that has sacrificed itself in him, the invalid, who now has become a personality foreign to him. He sees him, the part of his own being that is becoming John, above, in the lofty realm of life. Yet his gaze is still troubled by ancient Hebrew wisdom, with which he was once united. Up there in the realm of life he does not yet see Christ, the Reconciler, spanning the great chasm of humanity, but he sees the patriarch Abraham, who precisely is *not* able to bridge the great divide. Abraham, the bearer of what is past, cannot do what Christ, the Lord of the future, the new Creation, alone is able to do. Where, though, does it happen that Christ helps to bridge the primordial chasm of humanity? (One recalls in Dante's *Divine Comedy*, Inferno 32, the 'Cain-chasm', or the 'Cain-layer').[30] It happened precisely in the initiation of Lazarus-John, about which everything discussed here relates. Abel and Cain are reconciled over the *grave of Lazarus* that opens to the words of Christ (John 11:43).

(For the individual person, this reconciliation of Abel and Cain is only real in as far as it is experienced in that individual's soul. Everything discussed about the path of Christian initiation has to be found and experienced in the *'I' of the individual*. However, it happened objectively in the Mystery of Golgotha and in the initiation of Lazarus-John directly linked to this Mystery. Only through the fact that it happened is it possible for individual souls to experience it.)

That the reconciliation could take place, Lazarus, the son of Cain, had to die, work right through death and the grave to find resurrection. What from then onwards lived on resurrected in him was the bright, higher, Elijah-part of his being. That was *John*—for 'Lazarus' had died. And he now stands *before* this final experience of the completed initiation; he has to work through the final agonizing crises, temptations and trials of the experience of initiation; he has to overcome the final most serious struggles of the soul. He senses this, sees all this at once in his own 'I'. In his own Intuition he finds the solution of the great riddles and knots of destiny, and he expresses it to the sublime world-powers facing him. This is the lofty meaning of Luke 16:30 with 31, so lightly overlooked by a 'harmless reading of the gospel'. Lazarus-John now knows that it all depends that 'one should rise from the dead'. That Abraham does not understand this (Luke16:31), does not believe in this possibility, proves nothing contrary to the rightness of his Intuition. For what is meant and what it is all about here can only be known and performed by Christ. That actually was indeed the test of the 'rich young man', to loosen himself from everything, even the last residue of his own past—including all the wisdom of Abraham. He had to strip off everything external, clinging to him from the past. He had to penetrate through the inner null-point, his own 'I', or ego, the most narrow of all narrow entrances, the 'eye of a needle' (Mark 10:25).

(The saying about the camel and the eye of the needle [Mark 10:25] is written in 'Mystery-language', and can only be understood out of the language of the Mysteries. The difficulties of the saying are perhaps solved from the zodiac—taking all that is discussed here initially only as a hypothesis. In the zodiac we behold the contrast of the two neighbouring signs of the Scales and the Scorpion. The latter is the power of death that wants to clutch the 'rich man', wants to hold him fast with the riches of the past. It is the most difficult to overcome. The overcoming, the finding of the way of life, is easier in the sign of the Scales. As the sign of inner balance—in the gospel, too, pictured in the ship and the voyage on the Lake—it is the sign of 'Spirit-self' [manas; see above p. 110]. On the other hand, the camel—the 'ship of the desert'—plays an important role in Zarathustrian esotericism, as also with John the Baptist [Mark 1:6, 'clothed with camel's hair']. Here the forces of the camel appear as the forces of the Scales, of inner balance, of the 'Spirit-self', the purified astral element. The difficult saying [Mark 10:25] would likewise relate to the experience of the 'splitting of the personality' of the one becoming John. It would express that the Elijah-John part of his being experiences less difficulty to penetrate through the narrow door of the 'I', or ego, than the once 'rich man', the Lazarus-Cain part of his being. In this moment, the latter has a difficult struggle, wanting to doubt the victory. The one part of his being can, as it were, easily find his way with the Scales, whereas the other part has to struggle on the difficult passage with the Scorpion.)[31]

In the 'rich man' of Luke's Gospel we see only the son of Cain and the rich heritage of ancient Mystery-wisdom; in the 'rich young man' (Mark 10 taken with Matt. 19) this rich man has already bound the past with the childlike-youthful, childlike-virginal element, that the one becoming John in his initiation had already awoken in himself (Mark 5:41, 10:37). Both mutually struggle (♏–♍). Accordingly, the 'rich young man' experiences the inner crisis, the 'splitting of the personality'; he has to struggle. In the expression 'rich young man' itself there lies this splitting of the personality (♏–♍), this inner struggle (♉–♏). The pure-virginal, the 'child', after stripping off all the riches of the past, finally achieves the victory, the victory in the sign of the 'living word' (♉).

***

In immediate connection with the crisis of splitting, which is experienced in the picture of the episode of the 'rich young man' (Mark 10:17ff.) of the one becoming John in his initiation, there stands the following conversation with Peter (Mark 10:28ff.). Such crises as the one suffered by Lazarus-John here, are at the same time a wrestling for self-knowledge. By becoming painfully conscious of the Cain-portion in his being, of certain remnants from his past that are not overcome, he gains self-knowledge that is absolutely essential to find initiation. Peter misses this self-knowledge, otherwise he would not claim to Christ's face that he had sacrificed everything, whereas, as we have seen, he was the one who could not let go of certain remnants of his past. For the Christian path of initiation, the complete letting go of the past in absolute renunciation is taken for granted. To boast to the Teacher and Initiator about such renunciation—especially of an imagined one—as of a personal achievement, as Peter does here, means nothing else than to exclude oneself from any further possibility to reach initiation, as does happen to Peter. Crises of self-recognition, as here the one becoming John has to experience in such a painful manner, signify basically only an advance in development. With Peter we see the growing darkening of consciousness spreading; it began in Caesarea Philippi and reaches its climax in Gethsemane.

Incidentally, it would make sense and would fit to the Mystery-character of the whole chapter also to think about 'Peter's discussion' simply as spiritual experience, as the initiation-experience of John-Lazarus. In that he worked through to self-knowledge, he also achieves the intuition how the whole relationship between him and Peter, now out of step, has come to John's advantage. The first is the last, the last has become the first (10:31); the one always speaking too early has lost the word; he speaks awry. The one always silent has become the leader of the word, has found the word. In the way this recognition as an inner insight is confirmed for him through Christ, the Initiator (10:31), there lies at the same time for the one becoming John the overcoming of his last crisis.

The Twins in the Third Octave

The 'Sons of Zebedee' (Mark 10:32-45)

'Victorious overcoming' follows the sublime experience of the 'Sacred Mount' in the sign of the Twins, which always shines over this 'Mount of the Heavens'. From what was said earlier, we know how here the motif of the Twins always incorporates in a special manner the 'two sons of Zebedee', the 'heavenly twins' James and John. And now on this third stage of Intuition of the Sun-rhythm this 'motif of the two sons of Zebedee', who bring their concern, their request, to Christ (Mark 10:35ff.), becomes a controlling and decisive motif of this sign. The words connected to going 'up the mountain', 'and taking the Twelve again' (Mark 10:32) (otherwise: 'appointed twelve', Mark 3:14), always appear with the lofty experience of the Twins, and likewise here.

The motif of the sacred mountain heights, which always plays a role with the 'Twins', is here not only indicated in the phrase 'going *up* to Jerusalem' (10:32), although this phrase also signifies something in this direction. This is especially when related to the other phrase 'and they came to Jericho' (10:46) with the transition to the Crab, and thereby the geography of Palestine is imagined. But here on the third stage of Intuition, the really decisive thing for the manner in which the 'Sacred Mount' is expressed in the sign of the Twins, is the whole relationship in which the episode narrated here stands to the experience of the 'Mount of Transfiguration' in Chapter 9. Here the twins James and John, who approach Christ with their request to be allowed to sit at the right and at the left in his 'glory' (*δόξα*', 'light of revelation, splendour of revelation' is the 'Sun-splendour' of Christ, discussed in the chapter on the Transfiguration).

In the Transfiguration it is the same pair who in the revelation of the Sun-splendour of Christ are really seen to his right and left (9:2). Although the gospel doesn't state it directly, over James the etheric figure of Moses and over John that of Elijah are seen. It is simply

nothing other than the whole picture of the 'Transfiguration on the Mount' appearing once more here in the Twins, in the sign of the Sacred Mount from another viewpoint, into the spiritual field of vision. The 'Transfiguration' begins in the Archer, the counter-sign of the Twins. The Twins, as the 'sign of the Sacred Mount', begins at the same time sympathetically to vibrate and to chime in. Similarly, the whole episode narrated in Mark 10:32-45, in a certain sense the spiritual inversion of the experience of the Transfiguration, becomes set in motion through the experience of the Transfiguration with inner logical consistency.

With this episode, more clearly than anywhere else, the character of the 'stage of Intuition' is to be borne in mind, and, less than anywhere else, the physical reality of an outer event. Already with the 'calling of the Twelve' in v. 32, it is doubtful whether it can have been an outer event. It is of course conceivable. And yet, after the Initiation of the other disciples had broken down, it is improbable that now such a 'calling' takes place on the physical plane. The words rather suggest a recollection. We recall how the initiation of the Twelve began with these words in the sign of the Twins in Mark 3:13. In the same sign the initiation of the *one*, which ultimately developed out of that of the Twelve, is led to its ending. Its actual end is not found in the heights of the Twins, but in the earthly and human depths, in the depths of the grave itself, in the descending sign of the Crab. Yet the end, as each new degree of initiation, is always preceded by the lofty experience in the sign of the Twins. It also shines over the initiation of John, which now moves towards its approaching end.

In the consciousness of the one, the memory remains how earlier the Twelve always gathered on such occasions around their Master. And now they are *spiritually present*. For what the one, who initially became the bearer of the initiation process, works through, he gains for the others. In their *being* the others remain connected with him and with Christ and with the whole initiation process, even though in their *consciousness* they are not able to follow.

In this sense we also understand the repeated 'announcement of death' (Mark 10:33, 34). It may be that precisely these words were repeatedly spoken to the other disciples. But the 'cosmic rhythm' speaks here for the experience of Intuition, the purely inner experience. According to this viewpoint the previous 'announcements of death' are aligned in individual cases to different heavenly signs.

- With the announcement of death in Mark 8:31 the viewpoint is of the approaching might (♏) darkening the consciousness of Peter—it stands in the Scorpion.
- With the immediately following teaching on death (Mark 9:34-38) the viewpoint of the immediate approach of Christ's death in the Transfiguration itself (♐).
- With the announcement of death Mark 9:31 the inability of the disciples to receive the *word* (♉).

This present announcement of death [Mark 10:33, 34] stands as an experience of highest and most inward Intuition, in that lofty sign of the Twins that lies opposite the death-sign of the Archer. The Mystery of death on Golgotha is now appropriated in its innermost Mystery-depths by the one becoming John, the unique further bearer of the Christ-initiation, understood and embraced in his essential depths. On the Mount of Transfiguration, what in so far as the death sign (♐) came into question, was yet still an etheric experience, Inspiration—for the stage of Intuition first begins with ♑ ♒ ♓—now in the episode of Chapter 10 has become most inward spiritual experience, *Intuition.* The experience on the 'Mount of Transformation' (Mark 9) is of etheric-spiritual nature; the experience in Mark 10:35-45 (if not 32-45) is of pure spiritual nature. And only the one becoming John experiences it in the full, bright clarity of consciousness.

But why only the one? Considering v. 35—'And James and John, the sons of Zebedee, came forward to him, and said to him ...'—should not at least two, should not James be thought of as one participating in the experience? If the whole thing is to be conceived as a physical event, then the objection without more ado would be valid. It falls away if

we are dealing with a spiritual experience. In that which John experiences in spirit, his twin brother James, who in his *being* was so closely bound to him, was involved, as indeed he was present on the 'Mount of Transfiguration'. And so, as that whole picture of the 'Mount of Transfiguration' rises up here intuitively before the consciousness of John, of course the other, the spiritual twin brother, has to play a part in this experience. But he who experienced *consciously*—as we may imagine the event—was alone the one becoming John. *He* experienced in inner vision how he, and with him the other, James, goes to Christ with the request. For James all these things are present in *being*, in the more unconscious depths of his being. But he does not experience it in full consciousness as John does. James does not take part so *actively* in the initiation process as John does (cf. what was said about the relationship of James and John, p. 199ff.).

'But'—the 'simple reader of the gospels' will object—'why interpret so much of the gospel, why not just take the things simply as outer events? Why should everything be only a "spiritual experience", and to top it all a spiritual experience only of the One becoming John? Where is all this stated in the gospel?' This question, too, could be answered when we look at the parallel narration of the whole episode in Matthew 20:20-28. There it will be immediately noticed that the request to Christ by the 'sons of Zebedee' is put by their mother. Especially, if we understand the gospel in such a way as the 'simple reader of the gospel' wants, as a purely externally report, we stand before one of the well-known contradictions of the gospel (cf. Introduction, pp. 16 and 22). Even when it has to do, as it could seem at first, with something 'subsidiary', the 'contradiction' remains. Especially where the two parallel narrations coincide so beautifully, this one contradiction should be noted.

It is resolved out of the spirit, when we recall how the 'mother' in the gospel, the female element in general (think, for example, of Peter's mother-in-law, Mark 1:30, 31—see above, p. 77—also the role the 'mother of Jesus' plays in the wedding in Cana in John's Gospel),

frequently stands for the soul-element, for the magical or intuitive visionary power that holds sway in the higher soul-forces. That which such forces from pre-birth, coming from the 'atavistic' side, effect in the human blood, appears here often as the mother. Matthew, besides the more Imaginative elements that he has in common with Mark, possibly brings more outer historical matters than Mark. But with the episode of the sons of Zebedee Matthew had reasons to emphasize that here we are *not* dealing with an outer event. These reasons did not exist in the same way for the author of the cosmic gospel of Mark, from the beginning more conformed to the Imaginative element. And Matthew emphasizes this in the way he introduces the 'mother' here. That the birth-mother should be dragged into the most intimate occasion between Christ and the trusted disciples, taken as an outer event, is quite unlikely; its improbability is easily seen. Precisely in such passages, with such 'contradictions' one has to be aware to penetrate deeper into the secrets of the language of the gospel and into the methods with which it is to be read and understood.

The meaning and the being of the whole event told in the section Mark 10:35-45 (or 32-45), a climax of the spiritual experience forming the initiation of John, is basically easy to understand out of the whole progress of the gospel narration. The initiation of Lazarus-John has come to a decisive point with the experience on the 'Mount of Transfiguration' (Mark 9). It has entered the stage of Intuition; the One becoming John himself in inner activity takes things in hand; as spokesman he 'finds the word'. The actual one becoming John in the narrow sense, who is directly overshadowed by the power of Elijah-John, begins with the Transfiguration. Through all possible inner crises and trials that have to be passed (much of which is the matter of Mark 10), this deeply inspiring experience of the Transfiguration works further on the consciousness of the one becoming John.

From this moment onwards, when the inner trials and crises are passed and overcome (10:31), he has to present himself renewed in his whole splendour and in enhanced significance before the spiritual

eyes of the disciples undergoing their initiation. After he had beheld the spirit-forms of Moses and Elijah on the Mount of Transfiguration, the picture of Paradise (see above p. 203) contained in the picture of the Transfiguration appearing before his soul must have appeared to him now especially strong and luminous. By seeing himself[32] with Elijah, his twin brother with Moses, he beheld in this picture at the same time the picture of both Trees in Paradise, the Tree of Life and the Tree of Knowledge. He beheld the one to the right and the other to the left of Christ (10:37)—everything comes now out of *his* consciousness, but clothing itself in the picture, as if the request was presented before him *and from James.*

This is actually nothing else than the etheric-spiritual fact already beheld on the Mount of Transfiguration. Only what is beheld by him, who is just now completely overshadowed by the power of Elijah, is still loaded with a certain one-sidedness. He sees too one-sidedly only in the picture of Paradise pointing to the past, not yet fully recognizing the significance of the Christ-Sun of love pointing to the future that appears here between the Tree of Knowledge and the Tree of Life, between Moses and Elijah, between James and John. And over the meaning of the great sacrifice of love, Christ, the Initiator, now teaches in pictures the two disciples, that is, to the consciousness of the one becoming John. Enlightenment is now given him as a decisive Intuition. He hears now in spiritual hearing through Christ:

> 'The Father planted in Paradise the Tree of Life and the Tree of Knowledge. How and where they stand, is determined by the eternal primordial law. The deed, however, which I now do in offering my Blood, is a Deed of free Love. Only he who follows me in this Deed of offering in love and out of inner freedom, whoever with me drinks the cup that I drink, and is baptized with the baptism with which I will be baptized, is worthy to sit at my right and at my left throughout Eternity[, through all cycles of time to come].'

The deep meaning of participation in the Passion, of the Mystery of Golgotha, directly following the completion of the initiation, is revealed at this point of his initiation process, to the one becoming John.

Moreover, it is revealed to him, who is far in advance of the others in initiation, how his whole relationship to these others should be fashioned and developed in the future. Only a picture in the spiritual events is indicated in 10:41: they were, 'greatly displeased' about the pair, as it could appear, who are so very much preferred. (The whole existing contrast between the 'visible' and the 'invisible church'—whose two pillars are John and James—does not manifest at all as spiritually objective, but only appears here in the earthly human sphere.) We can well imagine the situation, that similar scenes have often enough taken place in the physical world. *This time* it has to do with a spiritual experience. And John, the far advanced, recognizes how the correct, forthcoming imitation of Christ for the Christian disciple consists in allowing those riches that he had received before the others to radiate all the more helping and serving forces to the others who, being weaker, are still in need of help (vv. 42-45).

The Crab and the Lion in the Third Octave

The Completion of the one becoming John and the making of the Apocalyptist (Mark 10:46-52, Mark 11–13)

(In a certain way, the Crab and the Lion join their influence with the sign of the Twins in this section as the lofty signs of initiation. See endnote 35.)

In the now concluding initiation of John, the ascent of the Mount is followed, as earlier, by the descent. The experience on the heights of the Mount is always followed by the experience in the depths, of the lowlands of humanity. Here is found the darkness and the blindness of humanity, the whole picture of the inhibitions and obstacles which humanity places against Christ's great task [within] humanity. And this descent, this experience of the depths, this setback against the spiritual experience of the heights, this experience of the darkness and blindness of humanity always takes place in that sign in which the Sun, after reaching its height in the summer, begins its descent in the sign of the Crab. In this experience, the blindness and darkness of humanity reveal to a certain extent the *negative side* of the sign of the Crab. We are impressively aware of *the cross of the physical [plane]*, to which this sign belongs (see p. 30f. and the Fig., p. 364).

The character and the significance of the Healing of the Blind Man at the end of Mark 10 (v. 46ff.) have already been indicated by Rudolf Steiner. He spoke clearly enough of the actualities of the Healing of the Blind Man and the nature of the power out of which Christ accomplished such healings (see the first lecture-cycle on John's Gospel, Lecture 7 [GA 103]). With the story of blind Bartimaeus in Mark 10, he explains, the essential viewpoint is not that here a blind person is healed, but the fact that a blind person in a certain way recognized Christ. He addresses Him as the 'one healing through God', as *Jesus* [Saviour]; he cries after Him on the road: 'Jesus, Son of David, have mercy on me!' The motive of the 'seer who is blind' in the midst of

'blind sighted people' is the theme here. The whole nature of the blindness of humanity could not be more effectively presented than with this blind man, who felt the divine power of Christ in the midst of humanity. Not even among its most wise and perspicacious representatives, with all the clever Pharisees and scribes, did any recognize Christ walking in their midst. Furthermore, as earlier the whole group of disciples were led before the experience of the blindness of humanity (Mark 3:20-25, also at that time in the sign of the Crab), so now for John as he makes for the ending of his becoming, still working through a 'spiritual elevated experience' (Mark 10:35-45), this experience of the depths of humanity is again brought to his consciousness in an especially moving way.

One should note how the descent into the depths of humanity, which during an earlier episode, to be thought of in the sign of the Crab, was expressed through the words (Mark 3:20 [Luther 1534]): '*Und sie kamen zuhause*—and they came home'; Luther 1545: *nach Hause* [Gk. *Καὶ ἔρχεται εἰς οἶκον*—'And he comes into a house'; most Eng. translations render, 'they entered a house'.] (See p. 95f.) Here on the third stage of Intuition of the cosmic rhythm, it is expressed in such a way that we really look thereby into the earthly conditions, into the whole configuration of the earthly element. With Intuition we are always dealing with a level of experience that directly encompasses the spiritual in the earthly element.

Earlier, in the phrase 'they came home', an even more spiritual picture was presented. Now, on the level of Intuition, the meaning of the descending sign of the Crab is expressed in a quite earthly, geographical manner with the words, 'Then they came to Jericho' (Mark 10:46). Jerusalem is situated on the heights of a mountain, or rather a high plateau 800 metres above sea level. The 'Moon city' (from the Hebrew, *jareach*, 'Moon') lies much deeper below sea level, near the depression of the Jordan valley. (It has a similar meaningful connection with the origins of Christianity as the highest plateaus of the Earth in central Asia have with certain manifestations of Buddhism.) Right into the

physical, geographical level we can experience here the descent from the spiritual mountain heights of the Twins into the human lowlands of the Crab. And in the spiritual element of the Moon (which astrologically is 'at home' in the Crab) expressed in the name 'Jericho', there lies the hardening forces that have condensed the one-time etheric element into the earthly-physical (further details in this connection in Rudolf Steiner, *Esoteric/ Occult Science;* see also p. 84, final paragraph). As we can look at the 'cross of the etheric' to which the Twins belong as the *Sun-cross*, we can see the 'physical cross' to which the Crab belongs, as the *Moon-cross* (see p. 34ff.; Appendix 1 and the Fig., p. 364).

It is the descent from the heights of the Sun to the depths of the Moon—all this, of course, to be understood not astronomically, but in a spiritual sense—which we can experience in a certain sense with the descent to Jericho at the end of Mark 10. With this we have especially pointed to the 'occult [hidden]' element of an experience, which the one becoming John, moving towards the completion of his initiation, has still to go through. It is deeply significant for the essence of the Christian Johannine initiation that it finds its completion, not on the spiritual heights of the mountain in the lofty sign of the Twins, but in the descent to the lowlands of humanity in the Moon-sign of the Crab. This spiritual viewpoint remains even if we wanted to presume that in real outer events—which we can never prove—Christ-Jesus went with his disciples into the lowlands from Jerusalem to Jericho.

***

Through the fact that the John-initiation is completed in him, in addition to what we have seen so far as the 'negative' side of this sign, the Moon-sign of the Crab, a completely new 'positive' meaning is still revealed at the end of Mark 10. The impulse of initiation from the spiritual heights of the Mount over which the 'heavenly Twins' shine is carried down into the earthly lowlands. Here in the 'cross of the physical' the effects and power of the Crab is revealed. This earthly element does not remain as it is, or was before. It is changed in its being through the

powers of the heights of the spiritual-etheric, which it now assimilates as spiritualized, purified and illumined. Through this transformation the earthly element becomes aware again of its primordial connection with the spiritual element and the cosmos. It is returned to its primordial condition.

A Christian Johannine initiation is not a one-sided impulse to spiritualization by turning away from or stripping off the earthly element. *Its impulse is to transform the earthly* right into the depths of matter. This is why this initiation does not remain on the spiritual heights of the Mount, but descends into the earthly-physical realm. It carries out, speaking in the sense of the 'cosmic rhythm' of the zodiac, the transition from the sign of the heights and 'Sun-sign' of the Twins into the descending 'Moon-sign' of the Crab.

On the Sacred Mount over which the heavenly Twins are shining—to express it in a religious-cultic manner—there stands the sacrificial altar of the great 'Offertory'. The human being, the one who is being initiated, offers his own being to the divine world-powers as a [living] sacrifice. But the change, or 'Transubstantiation', that follows the sacrifice, the great Offertory, does not take place on the spiritual height of the Mount, but in the depths of the Earth. The Earth itself, penetrated and shone through by the forces from the heights, is transformed and spiritualized. Christ Himself in the 'Mystery of Golgotha' incorporates, actualizes the sublime meaning of the cosmic Offering of the Mass. The one becoming John, who moves towards the completion of his initiation, consciously takes up the meaning of this sacred event.

This 'transformation of matter', or 'transubstantiation', now takes place in the sign of the Crab, belonging to the 'earthly cross', the 'cross of the physical', revealed in its deepest meaning on Golgotha. What is low and tends to lowness in the sign of the Crab is overcome in this 'change of the earthly'. Again, in this overcoming—in Mark expressly emphasized—the Lion is revealed in the spiritual background of the Crab. We can also see the Crab and the Lion in this their connection as the signs of 'transformation of matter', of

metamorphosis, or 'transubstantiation'. The Crab combining with the Lion reveals the 'alchemical meaning' of both signs. And the Johannine initiation, completed in the Crab—behind it the Lion can be spiritually perceived—means absolutely this alchemical change of the earthly, of transubstantiation. The secret of Johannine initiation includes the secret of the highest 'white and red alchemy'. In this sense, in the Crab and the Lion are revealed at the same time the secret of the Moon and the Sun, of silver and gold.

At this point we recall the twelve world-conceptions in contemplating the 'cosmic rhythm' of the zodiacal signs (cf. R. Steiner, *Human and Cosmic Thought*. GA 151. Lecture-course, Berlin, 20-23 Jan. 1914). In the Crab, [the philosophy of] *materialism* is revealed. We only recognize its low side as 'thinking bound to sensuality'. The Johannine initiation allows us to re-think in the deepest sense precisely the essence of this materialism. It raises this 'thinking bound to sensuality' to a real penetration of the *Mysteries of matter*, that remain closed, locked up in a thinking bound to sensuality. In penetrating its secret, matter changes into spirit; here it reveals itself, in a certain sense, as the deepest and most secret of all revelations of the spirit. Only in initiation, in the Christian Johannine initiation, is the actual, the alchemical secret of earthly matter revealed. For the materialists of today this remains a 'book with seven seals'. This then is the true, higher, Johannine, alchemical materialism. Therein is revealed the higher, positive side of the sign of the Crab, as in the lower sensuality, in the thinking bound to sensuality, the lower, negative side of the sign of the Crab is revealed.

In Mark's Gospel, we first met the negative side of the sign of the Crab. The Johannine initiation and therein the realized 'transformation of matter', changes the meaning of the sign of the Crab into its positive side. On the third stage of Intuition, embracing the earthly element, this sense of transforming the Earth of the sign of the Crab is actualized in the initiation of John.

We searched in the gospel for specific words for the other signs, linked to the meaning of a specific sign. If we search for this higher,

positive meaning of the sign of the Crab, we may not only look for the words to do with ascent and descent, which we do meet in Mark's Gospel (3:20, 10:46). We will find this higher, positive meaning of the sign of the Crab in words no longer standing in Mark's, but in John's Gospel, 'He must increase, but I must decrease' (John 3:30). (In the sequel on John's Gospel it will be shown how this whole chapter, John 3, is to be considered in the constellation of the Goat–Crab.)

These words not only refer to the relationship of John the Baptist to Christ, but also of the Baptist to the disciple John. Indeed, they refer to the relationship of Christ, walking to His earthly death, to the disciple John, who takes up in himself the spiritual future of the Earth—as has become possible through the death of Christ. The words refer to the whole relationship of the earthly and the spiritual; in the dying and in the decreasing of the earthly element, the spiritual resurrects. In the dying away and breaking up of what is past the future can be fashioned and develops. In the same way in the course of the year, when, after attaining the mid-summer heights in the sign of the Crab, the Sun turns to the descent, we, in the dwindling of the revelation of the senses, increasingly live towards this revelation of the spiritual nature of the Earth. This climaxes [with the spiritual birth in mid-winter] at Christmas.

***

During the course of the year, the Crab is experienced as the sign of the turning point of the year. In Mark's Gospel, in the 'third round' of the cosmic rhythm (Chapters 11–13) it appears as the sign of the great *Turning Point of Time* and *Turning Point of the World*, actualized in the death of Christ in the 'Mystery of Golgotha'. Inasmuch as we see the presentation of John's becoming, the initiation of John, especially here in the 'third octave', this is expressed in these Chapters (11–13), as well as the experience of Christ Himself. The becoming John, now approaching ripeness for initiation into the highest Intuition, assimilates in the deepest depths of his own being this meaning in the death

of Christ, which manifests itself as the great Turning Point of Time and Turning Point of the World.

Essentially, the meaning of everything is indicated of what is carried out in an abundance of individual motifs and episodes in Mark 11–13. More than anywhere else we shall find in these chapters how looking up to the cosmic rhythm, to that heavenly sign determining a whole section of the gospel, helps us to find the inner connection, the embracing viewpoint of the single motifs and episodes, in themselves so different and apparently without a uniting context.

Already the outer figure of the sign of the Crab, ♋, very clearly reveals this meaning. In it we see, as it were, how one spiral of development, a specific impulse of development, ends in a specific point, as it were, spirals-in on itself (involution). Where this curling-in happens to the one spiral, the other, new spiral uncurls (evolution). The end of the one, old impulse of development is taken as the start of another, new impulse.

If we relate all this to the Turning Point of Time and the Turning Point of the World, realized in the Mystery of Golgotha, witnessed by John in his initiation now approaching completion, there stands before us as the meaning of the sign of the Crab in this third octave of the Sun-rhythm (Mark 11-13), the great theme of death and resurrection, of the becoming of the new in the passing of the old, of the rising again of a future in the crumbling and break-up of a past. And we behold as the old, which now passes away, the Earth itself, as it has become through its past, through the 'Fall of man'. And with the Earth at the same time the new transformed Earth, of the body formed out of earthly material, woven with the past of the Earth, inherited from Adam as the new body that is to become and to resurrect. John the Apocalyptist speaks in Rev. 21 of the new, transformed Earth, and with it the new, transfigured resurrection body, which in Christ raised itself for the first time out of the grave of Golgotha.

Already the Parable of the Sower (Mark 4) revealed to us how in the transitory world through Christ the seed of the new becoming is sown.

Thus it belongs to the deepest insights of the Johannine initiation how the old body, inherited from Adam, through Christ and through the resurrection of Christ can receive into itself the seed of the new, of the resurrection body. It receives with it the seed of the becoming of the new Earth, the resurrection future of the Earth itself. The old body inherited from Adam is subject to the might of death and the might of the past; the new inherited from Christ carries in itself the forces of the unfolding of the future.

And this whole relationship of past and future revealed in the sign of the Crab, of the old Earth and the new Earth, old body and new body—a decisive perspective, furthermore, for understanding Mark 11–13—is expressed once again in a sublime cosmic symbolism in the connection of the old Jerusalem to the 'new Jerusalem' (Rev. 21:10), of the 'old temple' in Jerusalem destined for destruction, destroyed by the Romans under Titus, to the resurrection temple, to the new Jerusalem. Everywhere the *temple* appears in the gospel as the noble symbol of the human body. The old temple corresponds to the old body inherited from Adam; the resurrection temple corresponds to the new body, the resurrection body. In John's Gospel (John 2:21) this is openly presented; in Mark's Gospel (Mark 11–13) it lives as a hidden symbolism.

What Peter did not comprehend at Caesarea Philippi—also afterwards in the 'Transfiguration on the Mount'—what John in his initiation then increasingly did comprehend, is this, that only through death is the resurrection possible. In the passing of what is old and past, the new, the future, the becoming can be realized. Christ consequently has to want and to be resolved on His own death, the sacrificial death on Golgotha. In the Transfiguration, where Peter wanted one-sidedly to retain the exalted experience (see p. 198), is revealed to the becoming John the deep meaning, the lofty cosmic meaning of Christ's death. In this moment, the Elijah-angel, who overshadowed him and with whom he was completely united, had revealed this meaning.

To the realized completion of this meaning, standing precisely in the sign of the Crab, there now belongs, besides the cosmic understanding, still the earthly understanding of the Mystery of Golgotha, the whole earthly and historical connections which have led to the death of Christ on the Earth. To the one becoming John there is revealed in the Transfiguration and finally in the lofty sign of the Twins, so far as this sign is inwardly connected with the experience of the Transfiguration, the exalted cosmic meaning of the Mystery of Golgotha. Now in the earthly sign of the Crab, its earthly meaning is revealed, the whole riddle of its earthly, historic connections.

It is significant for the whole essence of the Christian, Johannine initiation, that it embraces not only the cosmic heights, but also the earthly depths, penetrating not only in the essence of the cosmic connections but also those of the Earth. How world-destiny operates in earthly destiny, right into the political and legal viewpoints, woven into the purely external, historical events, is now revealed to the one becoming John in his initiation in the sign of the Crab.

John has to see into the whole knot of destiny existing between Jews and Romans, in order now also to find the purely earthly foundations of the great event of Golgotha, already recognized previously in the Transfiguration in the depths of its spiritual context. In the episode of:

the Cleansing of the Temple (Mark 11:15-18), likewise in that of:
the discussion with the Pharisees (11:27-33), and
the question of tax to Caesar (12:13-17),

we see directly into this earthly foundation of the Mystery of Golgotha.

On the other hand, the episode of the Cursing of the Fig Tree (11:12-14, 11:19-26)—in which that of the 'Cleansing of the Temple' is strangely inserted—shows the inwardly entangled story of the 'Entry into Jerusalem' (11:1-11), how certain hindering moments, which stand in the way of the causative forces bringing about the death on Golgotha, have to be removed through Christ Himself. Thus, also the Parable of the Vineyard (12:1-12, see especially v. 12) the unequivocal

expression by Christ Himself of His decision to die. The motifs and episodes contained in addition in Chapter 12:

> the conversation with the Sadducees about the resurrection (12:18-27),
> the questions of the teachers of the law (12:28-35),
> the teaching about the Christ (12:35-40), and finally
> the poor widow's offering (12:41-44),

are connected directly, as the previous narration is connected indirectly, with the initiation of Lazarus-John. Chapter 13, however, already contains an indication of the 'making of the Apocalyptist' following the initiation of John.

***

In his lecture-cycle *Building-Stones for an Understanding of the Mystery of Golgotha* [GA 175. Berlin, 27 March–8 May 1917] Rudolf Steiner speaks on the ruling relationships of the time between Romanism and Judaism, in which is to be sought above all the earthly cause of the destiny of the death of Christ Jesus. (The relationships are also impressively presented in Emil Bock's observations on Matthew in his *Studies in the Gospels.*) Steiner points out how the Romans were mostly tolerant towards all the possible cults, religions and Mysteries of the various peoples in their wide Empire. They included the foreign gods and cults within their realm, into their own 'Olympus of the gods', but in such a way that the Roman Caesars, who themselves, as obscurely dark initiates enforced initiation in an unlawful manner, made the cults of those gods and knowledge of their Mysteries to serve themselves. It was the policy of Imperial Rome to seek to rake in everything for themselves. The Roman Caesar had made himself to be venerated as a god. Above all the cults of the gods there stood the cult of the Caesars. The bust of the Roman Caesar was placed in the midst of the foreign gods.

The Jews under Judas Maccabaeus had invited the Romans into their land but had grown increasingly dependant on the mighty Empire.

They were anxious for their Temple, their sanctuary; they were afraid that even there a bust of the Roman Emperor would be placed and a Caesar-cult installed (which really happened under Caligula). In his gospel studies, Bock shows how monetary dealings for the Romans were something sacred and cultic, for them a kind of cult of Caesar. Regarding the money-changing tables in the ante-room of the Temple in Jerusalem, he points out, the issue has to do with nothing less (Mark 2:15, John 2:13, 14); permission for this from the side of the Jews signified a kind of compromise with the Romans. Giving over the forecourt to that Roman Caesar cult and cult of Mammon, the Jews sought to protect the most holy sanctuary of the Temple from intrusion by the Roman cult of Caesar.

Through His whole conduct in the matter of Cleansing the Temple—whether what is described in Mark 11:15-18 should be directly taken as an outer occurrence or perhaps only a picture for outer occurrences—Christ Jesus destroys the compromise that existed between the Jews and the Romans. The answer given by Christ to the tax of a denarius payable to Caesar lies in the same direction. With all clarity, Christ explains that no compromise can exist between the divine and the counter-divine power of the Roman Caesar. He knows He seals His death with this conduct and this answer. For surrendering Christ to the Romans forced the Romans to make Him responsible for what had happened, for the whole embarrassing—and for the Romans most difficult—disturbance of the compromise. The Jews could divert the consequences from themselves and from their so carefully protected sanctuary, the Temple—but not for ever, as history shows.

The tragedy of Judaism lies in the whole way it has to be anxious about that which ultimately does not hinder what has inevitably and inexorably to come. It is as if, held captivated by the power of death to what is past, it has to be anxious about the destiny of the old, indeed of the Temple destined for destruction. As if for the sake of this past destined for destruction, it has to cause the Bringer of the new, the freedom of the resurrection-temple of the future, it has to cause Christ

Himself to die. In these impulses of Judaism the unsurmounted sting of death holds sway, the might of death that holds people fast with the Saturn-impulses and Father-impulses of the past, causing it not to find the Son-impulse of freedom and of the future, the Son-'I', or Son-ego, impulse of Christ.

Here, where Judaism and Romanism are completely under the spell of the might of death of what has passed, standing under constraints of earthly necessity, we see, moreover—and again this at the same time is one of the most significant insights, which the one becoming John now gains in his initiation—how Christ, the sublime human Pattern, the Representative of Humanity and bearer of its future, living in the kingdom of unconditional freedom, resolves on His own death out of the most complete innermost freedom, 'to redeem the Earth, for humanity to attain freedom and to progress' (Rudolf Steiner's words). He knows that now the God has to die, so that human beings can live again. And this secure knowledge is present concerning His imminent earthly death, in His steadfast decision to die, as well as in the whole conduct in the occasion of the Cleansing of the Temple, in the answer to the question of paying taxes to Caesar, also in the way Christ deals with the Jewish rulers in that discussion with the high-priests and scribes (Mark 11:27-33)—it is all one whether at that particular time such a discussion is to be thought an outer event or not. And this knowledge and this decision is present in an unambiguous manner, as He says in the Parable of the Vineyard (Mark 12:1-12), concerning His knowledge about His destined death in the face of both His enemies and His followers (v. 12). Christ knows exactly what the work 'in the vineyard of humanity' signifies, that is, to pledge oneself for the 'I'-impulse of freedom and of progress amongst the variety of human beings today [i.e. within humanity]. And all of this, in the process of initiation towards which John is travelling, becomes at the same time an intuitive insight for the becoming Christ-disciple into deep secrets of humanity and of Christ, into profound human contexts.

Only *one* circumstance stands in the way of realizing what stands before Christ Jesus, the destiny of death wanted and chosen by Him. By touching on it, we approach the Mystery governing the section at the beginning of the Crab-sign, the story of the 'Entry into Jerusalem' (Mark 11:1-11), and the story standing in close connection with it, of the 'Cursing of the Fig Tree' (Mark 11:12-14, 11:19-26). This section belongs to the more difficult, indeed most difficult parts of the gospel, at the same time it belongs to those from which we are able to gain especially much about the way the gospel is to be read and understood. The story of the Entry into Jerusalem and the Cursing of the Fig Tree is in a special way characteristic for the meaning of the sign of the Crab, as already recognized in a certain way by theological expositors, and shown in a more spiritual manner by Rudolf Steiner.

Are these stories—or how far are these stories—to be thought as 'outer events'? With the other motifs and episodes of Mark 11, partly also Mark 12—think especially of the question of paying tax—we have seen that the earthly and historical sphere is touched. This is especially strong, and at this point it also connects precisely with the meaning of the initiation of John. Whether the details of the Cleansing of the Temple, the story of paying tax to Caesar, and so on, are purely outer events or only pictures for such, has of course to remain open. Moreover, there is the question whether discussions as those narrated at the end of Mark 11 or at the beginning of Mark 12 are conceivable *at that time* as outer events. It is certain that all these events are based on real historical backgrounds, in the sense that Christ Jesus through His conduct shattered the compromises between Judaism and Romanism, thereby sealing His death. But in this connection how does it stand with the Entry into Jerusalem, and even with the Cursing of the Fig Tree?

Concerning the Entry into Jerusalem, we have first to point out, that this episode is also related in John's Gospel (John 12:12-16) in a quite different chronological context. It belongs to the few episodes in which all four evangelists are 'synoptic'. And yet it shows, as

otherwise among what are called the 'synoptic gospels', the most remarkable 'contradictions' in the presentations of the individual gospels. In John the episode is told *after* the re-awakening of Lazarus, that is, it is told after the events ending John's initiation, whereas at the beginning of Mark 11 we find ourselves approaching these events, but still at an earlier moment. Here other events follow in which the initiation of John then finds its conclusion. Already these facts suggest that the story of the Entry into Jerusalem told in the different gospels (Matt. 21:1-11, Mark 11:1-10, Luke 19:29-41, John 12:12-16), at least not in all their details, cannot be 'external events' of a physically real occasion. It may also be pointed out how in Matthew's account two asses are mentioned ('ass and colt') with the Entry into Jerusalem, whereas the other gospels only mention the colt. One could say, 'this is an unimportant circumstance,' yet still it remains, if everything written in the gospel is taken purely literally as an outer event, a contradiction. But can we take the whole somewhat grotesque story of Christ's Entry into Jerusalem on a donkey merely as an outer event? Who would not have felt slightly taken aback by this scene, perhaps unconsciously within, as long as he thought it had to be understood in such a way?

Apart from certain inner reasons that carry great weight a glance at John's Gospel (John 12:12-16) teaches that here with the 'Entry into Jerusalem' it is hardly to be thought of as an outer occurrence of a physical reality. Already in the Introduction (p. 21) it was emphasized that precisely John's Gospel, by many regarded as a one-sided spiritual gospel, of all the gospels is in many cases the one that shows us most clearly what is an outer occurrence and what is not. (Also in Hans Blüher, *Die Aristie des Jesus von Nazareth*, though it does not reach the actual spirituality of the problem, the fact is recognized [p. 35ff.] with a particular inner certainty.) Let us look at the dreamy, playful manner in which John briefly narrates the event (John 12:12-16), in the midst of other events, which in the other gospels is described in detail, by Matthew and Mark at the beginning of the respective chapters. Let us look further at the narration in

John 12:54ff. which carries weight in a historical sense, that Jesus at that time—it comes after the raising of Lazarus that caused a tremendous stir all around—could no longer walk freely amongst the Jews, could not longer show himself to the high-priests and scribes but had to seek lonely, hidden places. Is it not said clearly that the subsequent story told in John 12 is not an outer event? How could it have been that Christ Jesus, if He had shown Himself in such a grotesque way publicly before all the people in the capital city, would not have been arrested by the Jewish authorities? Finally, let us look at the important verse, in Luther's translation [and others] not quite understandable, and consequently in its importance and bearing mostly overlooked: John 12:16. This says literally that the disciples with their recognizing consciousness did not receive (*οὐκ ἔγνωσαν*: 'knew not') what took place at the time, but only later, when Jesus revealed Himself in the Resurrection and Ascension, did it ripen in their consciousness what was written in the prophets (Zech. 9:9 is meant) about Him, and what happened at the time.

The events that took place were such that they withdrew from the perception of the disciples. And according to the other evangelists (Matt. 21:1-3, 6:7, Mark 9:1-7, Luke 19:29-35, 37-39), would not the disciples have directly shared in what took place? How can we resolve this contradiction? Of what kind were the events that took place at that time?

The key is given again by John. He diverges from the other evangelists, narrating the occasion precisely *after* that event told in John 11 as the 're-awakening, or raising of Lazarus'. If we are to understand the episode of John 12:12-16, it has really to be taken with John 11:53-57. The deed of 'raising Lazarus' affected the people far and wide and the Jewish authorities, so that Jesus was no longer free to show Himself among the Jews. The witnesses of the 'raising of Lazarus' had all experienced something tremendous—we shall soon see more clearly how with the initiation of John it inwardly connects to the middle-point of Mark's account.

What they had experienced was a shock in their deepest consciousness. Deeply hidden powers of vision were suddenly released in their souls, the 'supersensory world' lay open in a moment, lighting up like lightning for their beholding consciousness. As with all the problems discussed in these contemplations, one has to imagine that human consciousness was different from that of today. It was not so abstract as it is today. In earlier epochs certain human faculties of a higher (Imaginative) pictorial consciousness were more strongly developed; even the decadent remains of such faculties of consciousness still slumbered in the soul. It only needed an external occasion for the slumbering 'atavistic' (that is, based on older inherited [gifts]) soul-faculties to awaken out of their slumber. Such an occasion of the most tremendous, unnerving kind was the 'raising of Lazarus' out of the sleep of the grave through Christ Jesus. The witnesses of this event were as if illumined by a sudden stroke of lightning; they beheld sudden supersensory realities. Above all, they beheld the Reality of all spiritual realities, the mysterious-supersensory nature of Christ Himself, who revealed Himself so tremendously in this deed. And because they were still constrained within atavistic forces, standing within Jewish maternal inheritance and Jewish esoteric ideas, what they beheld was linked to pictures in which the prophecy of Zechariah (9:9 NIV) clad the future revelation of Christ's being:

> Rejoice greatly, Daughter of Zion!
> Shout, Daughter of Jerusalem!
> See, your king comes to you,
> righteous and victorious,
> lowly and riding on a donkey,
> on a colt, the foal of a donkey.

(Some versions have '*and* on a colt ...', which is physically and literally impossible; Matthew, however, everywhere linking to the older Jewish tradition, the Old Testament, sets it forth exactly like that—Matt. 21:7. He, who, similar to John, who respects what is historical, perhaps emphasizes in his way that the event is *not* a physical one.)

Therewith the riddle presented by John is solved, why precisely the disciples perceived nothing of everything that so many did perceive at that time. Through their failure, their crisis through the breakdown of their initiation, they found themselves in a deep sleep of consciousness. Their ability in supersensory vision and recognition—always excepting the one becoming John—was at that time caught in a deep lethargy out of which they only awoke in the event of Pentecost. If the 'Entry into Jerusalem' was about an 'external event', it would be incomprehensible why they had not perceived it.

With this manner of contemplation the necessity—and actually also the possibility—to imagine the whole story of the Entry into Jerusalem as an 'external event' falls away. We recognize that it has to do with an atavistic, clairvoyant experience available to many people of the time. The difficulty presented by the above-mentioned 'contradiction' disappears between Matthew's account and those of the other gospels—with Matthew two donkeys, or asses—an ass and the foal of an ass; with Mark, Luke and John only the 'young ass', the foal. For where the whole matter has to do with an event of clairvoyant picture-vision, it is clear that with the 'foal of an ass' (or 'both asses'), we do indeed have to see before everything else a *picture*, an Imagination. And here we are led to a point where again we are led very much to the graphic *sign of the Crab* (♋), with which we should consider the whole section. (Here too is a point to which the earlier theology has paid attention.) Who is the donkey, or rather, who are the 'two donkeys', about which there is this discourse initially in Zechariah's prophecy and also in Matthew's Gospel that links to the earlier Hebrew document? (In his lecture-cycle on Mark's Gospel, Dr. Steiner indicated the viewpoints touched on in what follows.)

The Double Sign of Evolution

This contemplation shows how in the sign of the Crab two unfolding spirals, two impulses of development, come into contact. Here in the sign of the turning point of the year, also the Turning Point of Time and

Turning Point of the World, are experienced. A past comes to its end; a future stands at the point of its beginning and seeding. An old world destined to decline is destroyed; a new world and humanity come about initially in delicate, youthful beginnings. All this stands before us in this whole chapter in the picture of the old Jerusalem and the old Temple moving towards its destruction. And in the background of the old Temple destined for destruction, the new Temple, the resurrection-temple already arises in the spiritual distance. Both the old and the new Temple are at the same time a picture for the old body, inherited from Adam, fallen to the power of death, and the new body inherited from Christ, the shining resurrection-body of the future.

With this, it is already said how we have to think of the 'two asses' of Zechariah's prophecy and Matthew's account. They stand as a *picture* for the old visible body, inherited from Adam, carrying in itself the results of the 'Fall of man'. The 'ageing body' subject to the forces of illness and death is the 'old donkey'. The other, the new, the future resurrection-body, which, in so far as we are inwardly connected to Christ, is initially invisible, but yet carried as a real seed inwardly felt as spiritually developing, guaranteeing an inner youthfulness. This, inwardly becoming and growing body in the midst of the destruction of the old body, is the other, the 'young donkey', the donkey colt. Resurrection-impulses and resurrection realities are what is hinted at with a wonderfully delicacy in the pictures of the gospel.

The key is also given why the three other evangelists, Mark, Luke and John, only mention the young donkey, the donkey colt. For them it has only to do with the young Christ-impulse, the future-impulse of resurrection, whereas Mathew, as everywhere, still builds bridges to the past, the Old Testament. Consequently the two impulses, the lapsed and the growing and becoming, the old and the new body, the old and the young donkey, are placed side by side. And for Christ Jesus, too, the matter is such that He now offers the body inherited from Adam and Abraham, artistically prepared through three times fourteen generations (see Matt. 1), which He had taken over in order

to insert the becoming, the resurrection-body as an individual seed, a seed of mankind's future development. The Jews were anxious about their old Temple, the work of art of stone and bronze. But not only does this old Temple put together out of stone and bronze in its original form (but not kept pure) from Hiram, the wise master-builder of King Solomon, have to fall. Another, higher, more artistic temple, the miraculous building of the human earthly body, the 'work of art of the heavenly Hierarchies', built and worked on by Divine Beings through cosmic-ages, has also to fall, so that what the counter-forces have spoiled of this temple of the body can be overcome in order that a still higher temple, a 'shining resurrection body' in the future can arise.

Theological research (Drews, *Markus-Evangelium*), has pointed out that in the stellar constellation of the Crab two stars are found which carry the names 'the northern donkey' and 'the southern donkey' [known today as γ and δ Cancri], and it considers that the gospel story has simply to do with these two 'donkey stars'.[33] At this point it can become especially clear how a certain, in our sense 'materialistic', direction of research is differentiated from the spiritual manner of contemplation meant here. The story of the two donkeys has got into the gospel narration as it is found especially in Matthew, not in some kind of arbitrary manner from the star-map. One has rather to imagine how an old consciousness of humanity saw the connection of the spiritual events described in Mark 11 (or Chapters 11–13) with the spiritual essence of the zodiac. The significant picture of both donkeys, deeply linked to the spiritual meaning of the sign of the Crab—as the double impulse of development—was now placed into the outer picture of the corresponding stellar constellation. When we consider how the Christian Mysteries were indicated everywhere in the old pre-Christian Mysteries, it could confirm the indicated context here, even if it should be demonstrated that already in pre-Christian ages the 'two donkey stars' in the stellar constellation of the Crab were known.

***

The 'contradiction' of the story of 'two donkeys' in Matthew's Gospel, as against *one* donkey, or foal, in the other gospels, is easily and simply solved when we take the whole, as we did, not as an outer event but as a clairvoyant, pictorial experience. We imagine how the one evangelist saw more of both sides of the spiritual event, the three others emphasize more the *one* side, the future side. Thus we arrive here, proceeding from the same presuppositions and reach beyond the chronological contradictions between the narration of Mark (similarly with Matthew and Luke) and that of John, in so far as the latter reports the event *after* the re-awakening of Lazarus, that is, after the completion of the initiation of John, whereas with Mark it is narrated in the midst of those episodes that still relate to the process of becoming of the disciple John. The whole disturbing business of the 'contradictions' falls away when we remind ourselves that, for Mark, Chapter 11 and those following, we have to do with how the whole complex of outer causes, which then lead to the death of Christ Jesus, to the Mystery of Golgotha, not only exist on the objective level, but *how it comes to the consciousness of the disciple becoming John in his initiation*. It also belongs to the, so to speak, entire (so far as one can at all say 'entire' of a world-encompassing Mystery that reaches beyond all human notions), or all-round understanding of the Mystery of Golgotha, that is, the understanding of its earthly causes and context, with the essence of the initiation of John.

He who is now making his way through this initiation, stands directly in the middle-point of the events described in John 11. For him this experience with all its effects is in a certain manner a present reality. He still sees something of the old forces of consciousness present in humanity, which, when called by a process like that of the 're-awakening of Lazarus' out of slumber effected through Christ, must awaken in extensive groups of people such an impression of the calibre and power of Christ's being. This impression would work against the execution of the plans and attacks against the life of Christ Jesus of the Jewish authorities who are concerned about their sacred sanctuary, the Temple. They would be hindered by the people standing

on the side of Christ, carried away by the divine greatness and power of Christ. But then precisely the Mystery of Golgotha, necessary for the future and progress of the Earth and humanity, would remain without effect. Christ, Who wants this Mystery out of a free decision of love, who takes on Himself the cross out of free decision, and, as the Parable of the Vineyard (Mark 12:1-12) and as the contemplation of other motifs and episodes contained in Mark 11 and 12 have already shown, has long since made the firm resolve for death, must consequently clear away those hindrances in the human soul that stand in the way of the Mystery of Golgotha. This and nothing other Mark places Imaginatively there in the way he narrates the 'Cursing of the Fig Tree', meaningful in itself, woven in with the episode of Cleansing the Temple, just after the 'Entry into Jerusalem' (Mark 11:12-14, 19-26).

One could still object against the 'interpretation' given here of Mark 11:1-11 as a 'clairvoyant experience', that it is 'far-fetched', that it does violence to the 'simple gospel narration', which also with the Entry into Jerusalem simply speaks of an outer event, that really nowhere in Mark's Gospel, even at this place, should there be some indication of 'clairvoyant experience', unless it would be in clear connection with the Cursing of the Fig Tree following it.

The Cursing of the Fig Tree

Here firstly the question has to be placed: Do we want to take this grotesque 'Cursing of the Fig Tree' told in Mark 11 simply as an 'outer event'? Are we really satisfied that Christ Jesus, the Representative of Humanity, Who upholds comprehensive love of humanity and harmony, during a season in the natural year when a fig tree cannot bear fruit, and has none (11:13), is cursed for that reason? Does Christ use his spiritual powers for some kind of grotesque sympathetic magic, with the effect that the cursed fig tree no longer bore any leaves, that it withered to its roots? (v. 20). Why is a divine power, as it appears at

first sight, placed here in such a pointless way in the service of breaking the laws of nature?

But all this is not the case here. More clearly than in any other episode of the gospel, the Cursing of the Fig Tree is not about an external, but an Imaginative event, about a *picture for a spiritual event.* Unlike some other cases, we cannot say here that what is reported, alongside what it signifies as an Imagination, can *also* exist as an outer event. Here we have to seek for the whole meaning of what happened in a sphere other than that of outer events. What is the fig tree, the subject of discussion here, and what can we make of its cursing, and why is this spoken curse from Christ so effective (vv. 21, 22)?

The 'language of the Mysteries'—often mentioned in these contemplations—belongs here to the 'fig tree', as elsewhere in the gospels (John 1:48, the episode with Nathanael—see R. Steiner's lecture-cycles on John's Gospel). The Buddha sat under a 'fig tree', the 'sacred fig tree' (*Ashvattha, ficus religiosa*) of the Indian, during a night decisive for his life and influence, when in deep meditation he found 'enlightenment' (*bodhi*). This raised him from Bodhisattva to Buddhahood. (See H. Beckh, *Buddha's Life and Teaching*, 88ff., where it is said that Buddha on that night, following the custom of the Indian ascetics, perhaps sat under a real fig tree. The decisive meaning, nevertheless, stems from the fact that the fig tree stands here as an image for the clairvoyant process of finding the Buddha-knowledge.)

Moreover, the legend tells that the sacred fig tree for a last time became verdant, a rich ornamentation of leaves, when Buddha received enlightenment under it. Later the sacred tree, which today is still shown to visitors [at the Mahabodhi Temple] in Bodh Gaya in northern India, did wither. It can appear to us as the Tree of Paradise, of which the people in India also know. The forces of the Tree of Life lost through the Fall of man—not lost at once, but gradually fading away—still lives in him. When Buddha in meditation found his enlightenment, the Tree of Life and the Tree of Knowledge were once more united, as once in Paradise, resulting in the rich ornamentation

of leaves of the Tree of Knowledge of the Bodhi-tree (in the Indian language '*bodhi*' means 'knowledge').

In Mark's Gospel the fig tree, although it carries no fruit—for the time of actual fruit in a spiritual sense is over—but still bears leaves, stands for that which as a remnant of ancient clairvoyant forces in human souls was still alive during the time when Christ walked the Earth. In the story of Peter and John we have seen how in the consciousness of Peter certain remains of ancient, atavistic, human forces do not always play a healthy role. It became Peter's fate, his crisis, that he could not separate himself once and for all from those forces of the past. The other disciple, who could also look back on a rich spiritual past, knows that he has to relinquish this remnant of the past. In the story of the rich young man, we found this expressed in his having to undergo hurdles, crises and tests. But he, the disciple of Christ, knows and sees with ever greater clarity that the path of Christ is a path into the future that consequently demands the complete dying and sacrifice of everything from the past. The real 'passage through the narrow gate', through the complete zero-point of consciousness, is at the same time the ego-point.

In this sense, too, the Christ-event signifies the Turning Point of the World, the sign of which in the zodiac, as well as for the turning of the year in the yearly cycle, is the Crab, which governs this whole section. An earlier consciousness of humanity has now reached its justified end. As far as individual persons are still connected to such earlier, atavistic forces, they appear as decadent residues. A completely new human consciousness has to be achieved out of the zero-point of consciousness of the 'I'. This will re-awaken in itself clairvoyant forces of Imagination, Inspiration and Intuition. The 'lost Tree of Life' has to be re-won and brought to a new verdant growth. 'The dwindling of the earlier clairvoyance; the seed-like beginnings of new forces of consciousness'—this too is one of the motifs with which we can describe the meaning of the sign of the Crab (♋) governing the whole section.

At a decisive point in world-events, the Christ has, consequently, to extinguish the then still appearing remnants of earlier clairvoyant forces of consciousness. He does this in the 'Cursing of the Fig Tree', because these forces if retained would at the time have hindered the whole meaning of the Mystery of Golgotha, even the possibility to carry the Mystery into effect. The older, atavistic clairvoyant forces were the ones called up in human souls through the shock of witnessing the re-awakening of Lazarus and which called up the 'mood of Hosanna' (Mark 11:9). If this mood of Hosanna had spread to further groups of people, then the Jewish authorities would not have been able to execute their plans to bring about the death of Jesus Christ. But we have seen how Christ Himself inwardly resolved on this Mystery of Death, how—from Mark 8 onwards—He seeks to instruct and prepare the disciples in their initiation into the earnestness of this Mystery of Death. We have found how the becoming John takes up ever more deeply—and at first he himself is completely alone—the meaning and earnestness of this Mystery of Death into his consciousness. The whole varied content of Mark 11 and 12 with all the richness of the individual motifs and episodes can be understood under this viewpoint. And so he now realizes—and in this all the already-mentioned episodes inwardly merge with the beginning of Mark 11 and the Cursing of the Fig Tree—what causes that mood of Hosanna in many souls, why it is not allowed to remain if the Mystery of Death should become effective, why therefore Christ Himself extinguishes it in the souls of the people, comparable to the Cursing of the Fig Tree. The tremendous knowledge gained by the one becoming John at this point in his initiation is this: through the Cursing of the Fig Tree, which as such is only a 'picture', Christ Himself changes the 'Hosanna!' of the crowd into 'Crucify!'

The objection that the 'interpretation' of the 'Entry into Jerusalem' as a clairvoyant occurrence does violence to the 'simple narration' of Mark's Gospel can no longer be upheld. The story of the Fig Tree, clearly pointing to the sphere of clairvoyant events and pictorial

happenings, directly follows the 'Entry into Jerusalem'. Mark's Gospel expresses how the somewhat grotesque event of the Entry, taken as a physical occurrence, has rather to be looked for in the sphere of a more spiritual happening and of clairvoyant forces.

These forces at that time flared up once more at an untimely moment. The fig tree stands here, as in the legend of the Buddha, as the picture of the old forces of humanity, of the forces of the early clairvoyance. Their day, at Christ's Turning Point of the World, has now expired. This tree that for a long time bore no actual fruit, should also now no longer bear leaves. It should wither completely, until through Christ's sacrificial death, the dead wood of the cross—which, as the legend tells, was taken from the stem of the Tree of Life—will sprout with new life. This new life will also bear in itself future forces of a new clairvoyant vision in humanity.

***

Once more with the contemplation of the Mystery of the fig tree in the gospel, we recall here the picture of Buddha meditating under the Bodhi tree and awakening to enlightenment. In the deep night, in a condition of consciousness that is contrary to that of the day-awake consciousness, Buddha finds the highest knowledge and enlightenment. If we contemplate the 'cosmic rhythm', as it can also be found in the Indian narration of the life of the Buddha, 'Buddha's enlightenment' under the fig tree is to be thought of in the sign of the Goat. As an experience at night in the nocturnal sign of the Goat the Mystery of Buddha's initiation takes place. And we recall how the pre-Christian John, the other great pre-Christian initiate, like the Baptist, was inwardly united to the meaning of the sign of the Goat (p. 58f.). The Christian initiation of the disciple John takes place in the counter-sign of the Goat, in the day-sign of the Crab. This is the sign of bright day-consciousness, and the consciousness of full light. In music (see p. 26f.) it is found in bright A-major, in Wagner [*Lohengrin*] the 'key of the Grail'. On a particular degree of humanity's initiation this 'bright day-consciousness' leads to

'materialism', which then in the Johannine initiation, in the 'transformation of matter', is once again overcome. A deeply significant difference between pre-Christian and Christian initiation is also revealed to us in the cosmic rhythm of the signs of the zodiac. We are allowed to see into weighty problems of the development of the consciousness of humanity.

(With the present contemplations on the gospel it is not possible to pursue the question, in itself interesting, of the 'cosmic rhythm' in the life of the Buddha. Suffice it to say that the 'circle of fifths of the zodiacal signs', mentioned a few times here (e.g. p. 33f.), plays a role. The first of the 'twelve aspects of Buddha's life', the 'descent to the earth', is to be conceived in the Ram [the sign of earthly incarnation]. [On the twelve aspects, see H. Beckh, *Buddha's Life and Teaching*. 29ff.] The 'entry into his mother's body' takes place in the sign of the Mother and Virgin, the birth—in which the 'two streams of water' play a role—in the sign of the Waterman (♒), the first childhood meditation experience under the lotus tree in the Crab, the fifth aspect, of 'Bowshot in the battle for the bride', really in the sign of the Archer. If we follow the events in the rhythm further, we meet the 'enlightenment' in the Ram, the sign of the 'light bearer' [Lucifer].)

***

'One of the scribes'

'Christ Jesus Himself resolves on His own death, out of unconditional love; to redeem the Earth, [and] to attain freedom and progress for humanity. He decides to go through the Mystery of Golgotha' [R. Steiner]—this can be recognized as the motif summarizing the content of all the episodes of the whole section contemplated up to now (Mark 11:1–12:17). Furthermore, as has already been said, this knowledge, placed into the whole initiation-story forming the actual content of Mark's Gospel—as all of this is equally to be grasped—represents a

decisive insight, a decisive Intuition as part of the initiation of the one becoming John. The earnest meaning of this Mystery of Death and also its whole earthly context, not grasped by Peter at Caesarea Philippi, becomes increasingly clear to the disciple John. In the Mystery of [this] Death, he comprehended at the same time the Mystery of Life, of resurrection. He recognized how the resurrection, which in Christ became reality, is not something one-sidedly reserved for yonder existence. But already on this Earth in the midst of the dying of the past, the seed of the new life of the future is growing and developing. In dying, in the destruction of the old body inherited from Adam, itself fallen to the power of death, the individual seed of Christ is taken into the soul. Here initially like a seed, an invisible becoming of the new, youthful, resurrection body takes place. (In the two spirals of the sign of the Crab that stands over this whole section, everything of this is expressed graphically.)

Therewith, the disciple of Christ in-the-making recognizes in his initiation a completely new, 'Christ-ened' meaning of the Mystery of resurrection. It is not as though before Christ this Mystery of resurrection was not already known. These things were spoken about in Jewish esotericism, most likely by the Essenes. The Sadducees were those who countered such theories; they taught there was no resurrection (Mark 12:18). Resurrection in Jewish esotericism was only imagined as something one-sidedly belonging to yonder existence. The Sadducees turned against it. The earthly meaning of resurrection only realized in Christ could not be grasped. After everything that we have hitherto heard concerning the historical background of the contemporary situation (see again John 11:54-57), it is not improbable that at that time discussions took place between Jesus and the Sadducees on issues concerning resurrection. But what with regard to Mark 11:18-37, for the one becoming John in his initiation process, what was clothed in such a discussion with the Sadducees is the whole process that comes to consciousness in the depths of his being, of the meaning of the resurrection of Christ for the Earth. In this insight he now feels falling away

from him everything that was still clinging to him from earlier on—older notions of Jewish esotericism and bygone Mysteries of humanity. He saw before him all these riches of ancient wisdom previously in that test of the 'rich young man' (Mark 10:17-23, Matt. 19:16-24) as tempting riches; he had definitively sacrificed them, let them go. He now knows definitively that only through the 'narrow gate', the gate of death, the complete zero-point of consciousness, that only by penetrating through the 'I' into the true meaning given by Christ, can he experience the resurrection, realizing it by manifesting it.

Thus, the passage under discussion (Mark 12:18-27) of the Johannine experience of initiation stands in a clear relationship to the 'story of the rich young man' (see p. 218). What earlier could prepare him to undergo a final challenge, a final test of the soul of the once rich young man, who now prepares to go through the Christ-gate of complete poverty, what was a final crisis and 'splitting of the personality' for the disciple of Christ in-the-making in his experience of initiation, is now overcome. It is like scales falling from the eyes of the disciple who makes towards the daylight of the Sun of Christ right through the sleep of the grave—for we now approach ever nearer the events described in John 11, finding ourselves perhaps already in the midst of them. The pupil of initiation, who once in a final difficult crisis felt rejected by the Teacher and Initiator (Mark 10:22), has now passed the test.

And this 'passing of the test' is now clothed in a picture that in many details has to remind us directly of that last crisis, the 'trial of the rich young man' (Mark 10). Without the context of everything else, how basically insignificant would be the episode of the 'discussion with the scribes' (Mark 12:28-34), if we wanted to imagine it simply only as an 'external event'. How deeply meaningful it becomes, how richly it enters into the whole context of the Johannine initiation-experience when we relate it to what is indicated by the episode of the 'rich young man'.

The person of the 'rich young man' standing as the focus of the earlier episode (Mark 10:17-24) should not cause confusion. 'Young man'

is only mentioned in Matt. 19:20. In the present episode, he is the person who meets Christ, called 'one of the scribes' (Mark 12:28, 32). If we look at the parallel 'story of the rich young man' in Luke (18:18ff.), the person in question there is called a Temple ruler (*ἄρχων*, archon). The 'contradictions' only demonstrate once again that here it cannot concern an outer event. In this initiation-experience, in this initiation-dream of a higher kind, it is no different from normal dreams. In the 'splitting of the personality', which the soul experiences, the individuality appears torn apart into different personalities.

Here all the different characters that meet us—the mysterious *εἷς* 'one' who 'came running', and the rich young man of Mark (10:17), also the 'rich young man' of Luke 16, the 'young man' of Matthew, the Temple ruler in Luke, and again 'one of the scribes' (Mark 12:28)—they supplement and complete the picture of the mysterious person always standing in the middle point of the initiation process. He was the 'rich young man', at one time in a spiritual sense the inheritor of rich treasures of temple wisdom and the wisdom of the ancient Mysteries. He is the spiritual descendant of Hiram, the great master-builder, and of those primeval, strange Mysteries of Cain, which the end of Genesis 4 gently points towards.

He was a young man in years, a 'young man' especially in the sense that he had re-won the inner virginity and childlike quality of his own being (Mark 5:41, 9:35-37, 10:13-16). In outer profession he was a 'ruler of the temple', an *Archon*, who ruled in the temple created in its archetypal picture by Hiram his spiritual forebear. In this capacity he stood near to the esoteric circles of Pharisees and Essenes. We have to think of him as the most read of the 'scribes' of the time. Everywhere it is really the 'one' who approaches us in the picture of the various characters in the various places (Mark 10, Matt. 19, Luke 16 & 18, Mark 12), and especially now, having overcome in the lower sense all the '-isms'—Pharisaism, Essenism, Sadducism and scholastic Legalism—he appears in the 'higher dreams' of the initiation-experience once more as 'one of the scribes'.

Everything of the past has fallen off for good from him who has found the way, or is about to find the way, through the 'narrow gate', the path into the future realm of Christ, the path of life. The more explicit description of the events is contained in John 11. Shortly before he still saw himself as the rich youth wavering at the abyss, at the threshold. The path of life appeared then a hopeless possibility. For him it had to appear as if he were rejected without hope by Christ the Initiator. Now in his innermost experience, he is allowed to hear out of the mouth of the Master and Teacher the comforting phrase: You have passed the test. 'You are not far from the kingdom of God' (Mark 12:34).

Conversations like that in Mark 12:28-34 reported between Christ and the 'scribe', conversations between the 'pupil' of initiation and his 'Teacher', were really not always only conducted as 'outer events' on the 'physical plane', but—here is an important point to comprehend—often exactly as 'spiritual conversations' and inner dialogues. Especially when we can grasp the inner connection of the episode of the scribe with that of the 'rich young man', we will understand that Mark 12:28-34 has to do with such a 'spiritual dialogue' of the 'pupil' with the 'Teacher'. The pupil, seen placed here in the picture of the scribe, who he once was, is the one becoming John; the Teacher and Initiator is Christ.

Let us look briefly at the contents of this spiritual dialogue, at the point where above all it allows us to understand why the whole meeting can end with this comforting and hopeful encouragement of the Teacher and Initiator. We find a viewpoint that shows us how far the initiation of John is fulfilled precisely in the Crab, and also why precisely this conversation with 'one of the scribes' is to be thought of in this sign. We recall from the first round of the Sun-rhythm (Mark 3:20ff., esp. 31-35), how in the meeting of Christ with his mother and brethren, the constriction of love for blood-relations and members of family appears as the negative of the sign of the Crab. Christ, the Representative of Humanity, places comprehensive love of humanity

facing the confining love of blood relations (Mark 3:34, 35). The exalted, apocalyptic meaning of the sign of the Crab is connected, as now, with the passage of the dialogue with 'one of the scribes'. To John approaching the end of his initiation, this comprehensive human love and love of humanity (Mark 12:33) lights up in the deepest depths of his consciousness. In due course, the picture presented by Christ in the Imagination becomes for him Intuition.

(Here we are repeatedly aware of the difference of the three 'rounds', 'spirals' or 'octaves' of the Sun-rhythm. The first round has to do with pictures, *Imagination*. In this case [Mark 3:31-35], it concerns the picture of Christ's kindred placing themselves against that of the Representative of comprehensive, unconditional love for mankind. On the second stage of *Inspiration*, the picture is internalized. Out of this internalization, at that time the disciples could carry out the deed for humanity, the 'Feeding of the Four Thousand' [Mark 8]. Now, on the third stage [Mark 12], the one becoming John embraces all this in the depths of his being, thereby raising himself to the stage of *Intuition*.)

John is just about to penetrate right through the 'narrow gate', in the zero-point of the 'I', to experience the world afresh in the sense of resurrection and out of the 'nothing' to build anew. He is at the point, where he too freshly experiences the Mystery of love in its comprehensive meaning for the world and mankind. In the secret of divine love, there opens for him the secret of comprehensive human love and love for humanity, the 'love for the other' in its real earnestness and inner difficulty. He stands at that point where the word for love is no longer a phrase—so often misused or taken lightly by people—but becomes a more active, more effective reality. Already this passage causes us to feel how the one becoming John, moving towards his initiation, is just about to find the fulfilment of knowledge, at the same time being on the way to become the 'disciple of love'.[34]

Thus the dialogue with 'one of the scribes' (Mark 12:28-34), which as an 'outer event' ripped out of the context of the whole could appear as a somewhat insignificant episode, becomes a Johannine

initiation-experience and an experience of humanity of comprehensive significance and deep meaning. This meaning touches significantly on the matter of the episode with the fig tree (Mark 11:20-26), likewise to be conceived as an initiation-experience, lighting up for the one becoming John as a central insight of initiation. We note how in this 'dialogue'—it is again a 'spirit-dialogue', a purely inner dialogue—Peter (11:21) appears as the one who is unable to understand. He, who still cannot and will not break away from the old forces of humanity's past, is deeply unsettled through the 'Cursing of the Fig Tree'—as we have seen, the dissolution by Christ of those forces of humanity's past. The one becoming John, however, recognizes in deep intuition the comprehensive omnipotence, full of wisdom and love, of Christ's cosmic will in the 'I'. This 'I', when it touches the innermost inwardness, the inner centre of existence, is really almighty. This omnipotence, if it is not to destroy the world and itself, is only to be used when and in so far as it stands in deepest loving harmony with the whole of life and the whole of humanity (Mark 11:25, 26).

Something tremendous, a Mystery carefully shielded from the understanding of those not called, is hidden in what is announced here of the 'power of prayer' through Christ, that is, it is experienced by the disciple John-in-the-making. Because he experiences such things now in his initiation, this could allow the disciple John to find for this secret the words in his gospel to flow in such a significant manner (John 14:13, 15:7, 16:23-27)—allowing Christ to speak to the group of disciples in the 'Farewell Discourses of Jesus'. Such passages can repeatedly make us aware of the inner connection of Mark's Gospel and John's Gospel.

A most profound *understanding of Christ* is opened up to the disciple John in this recognition and appropriation of the great love of humanity, in the way the comprehensive love of humanity is revealed to him, as within the Mystery of divine love is the Mystery of the 'love of the other' (Mark 12:33). Therein conjoins for him the Mystery of death and the sacrifice of death (this understanding as a common motif runs

through all the episodes of Mark 11 & 12) with the understanding of the comprehensive love of humanity and the love of Christ. And only in such understanding of the Mysteries of death and of love is a real understanding of Christ possible. On this point, how very much the discovered recognition of Christ differs from that found by Peter as the first of the disciples. This prompted him to that splendid and surprising, and yet thereby premature and hasty, confession of Christ at Caesarea Philippi (Mark 8:29). The shining confession was immediately followed by a darkening of consciousness—his failure to understand the decisive point, upon which precisely a true understanding of Christ would depend—his non-understanding of the sacrificial death on Golgotha. What Peter could not understand, John now in the depths of his being has understood and assimilated. Understanding the Mystery of death opened for him at the same time the Mystery of the comprehensive divine love and the love of humanity.

In understanding both these Mysteries, he who was once the silent one, only slow to understand—towered over and outrun, as it seemed, by Peter—has now gained an understanding of Christ from which everything falls away that previously still clung to him from the vestige of old ideas from the past. Therewith we understand at the same time the meaning of that episode (Mark 12:35-40) adjoining not only outwardly but also inwardly the conversation with 'one of the scribes'. This episode, ripped out of context as a mere 'outer event' for itself alone, can once again make a somewhat insignificant impression. In fact, the revealed recognition, his recognition of Christ above all now rightly crowns the ending of the initiation of the one becoming John.

From this Johannine confession of Christ everything falls away that could still adhere as the remains of past imaginations—one thinks of Peter and the 'test of the rich young man'—everything, which could somehow have to do with the passing wisdom of the Pharisees and scribes with that wisdom that remains standing with the Saturn-impulses of the Father, and cannot find the actual Sun-impulse of the Christ 'I'. This old Jewish wisdom of the Pharisees and scribes could

only imagine Christ—or rather Messiah—as a blood relation, a descendant of David and Abraham, as the end of a series of generations. They could only conceive Christ's nature as a physical, blood relationship in space and time. The true nature and Mystery of Christ's Person, as it now opens to John in his initiation, can only be understood out of the Eternal, out of that which was before Abraham and David. And this Mystery-secret of His Person is clothed in a sermon by Christ, even if now no longer (John 11:54), yet earlier was perhaps often held for the edification of many (Mark 11:37).

Christ, so understood, is recognized as 'David's Lord, not David's son' (Mark 12:35-37). And he who now found this confession as an initiation-confession, in his gospel placed the great saying of Christ: 'Truly, truly, I say unto you, before Abraham was, I am' (John 8:58). And here, in the initiation story of Mark's Gospel the profundity of the true confession of Christ arises. At the same time, there is revealed how subtly all that clings to the past in Pharisaism and the legalism of the scribes obstructs the Sun-filled confession of Christ and the love of Christ. He sees the inner hollowness of the Pharisee's clericalism. What he experiences is clad in severe words, which Christ had for this Pharisaism, which He only could express with this severity. The disciple of Christ experienced on the heights of his initiation confession that the judgement in these words is not as a human judgement but as a valuation given through the spiritual world itself. And such a 'final reckoning' belongs to what is experienced in stepping through the portal of initiation.

***

End of the Initiation: The Widow's Mite

What now follows as the crowning last stage summarizing the whole process, in its magnitude hardly imagined by the consciousness of humanity today, leads beyond 'knowledge' into the centre of life itself.

It is the passage through the ‘narrow gate’, which leads to the ‘way of life’ (Mark 10:23-27, cf. Matt. 7:14) already indicated in the ‘trial of the rich young man’, so difficult to do and difficult to bear as destiny. Through the portal of deepest poverty, through the ‘zero point of consciousness’ (or of the ‘I’), through the grave, this most difficult of all initiation-processes is clothed in Mark's Gospel in the most simple of all pictures, in the picture of the ‘poor widow’ who offers her ‘two mites which make a farthing’ [Mark 12:42. KJV/AV], her two last tiny copper coins, into the Temple treasury.

In its simplicity the episode touches the heart (Mark 12:41-44), the exact opposite picture to that of the ‘test of the rich young man’, who still lived in the imagination, who precisely could *not* offer up the experienced treasures out of the past in order to find the ‘way of life’, the connection to the unfolding future. What appears there still as a test not passed, an unfulfilled remnant of the past, an outstanding debt before the spiritual world, is here paid to the last farthing. In the simple, gripping picture in Mark's Gospel of the poor widow, who places her last mites into the Temple treasury, the initiation of John is completed. John's Gospel, that which alone can and may speak more clearly on these things, tells in Chapter 11 of the events as the ‘awakening’, or ‘raising, of Lazarus’ out of the slumber of the grave through Christ.

(Rudolf Steiner shows how it has to do with a transition from the ‘old’ to the ‘new’` initiation. Through a kind of sleep of death that was normal in pre-Christian initiation, Christ, the Initiator, led the disciple, ‘whom he loved’, as the first bearer of the new, the Christian initiation. And we may assume that this ‘sleep of death’ with Lazarus really did lead to the border of bodily death.)

The whole construction of the initiation story in Mark's Gospel also raises the ‘story of the poor widow’ into the sphere of spiritual events, which also includes the ‘trial of the rich young man’ and the conversation with ‘one of the scribes’. Whoever objects here that such an ‘interpretation’ does violence to the ‘simplicity of the gospel narration’

may be consoled with the consideration that just as pictures of normal dreams take their material somehow from the experiences of the day-consciousness, this can indeed be the case also with experiences of the higher consciousness of initiation (cf. here the Introduction, p. 18.). In the whole episode there is nothing that could not also have been an 'outer event'—with the possible exception of v. 41, actually bearing the physiognomy of a dream-experience rather than an awake experience. At all times, and mostly in times of an uplifting religious experience, there have certainly been examples of such willingness to sacrifice. And we could imagine that some event really experienced in day-consciousness by the higher 'I' then is meaningfully woven into the drama of the life of initiation—as also otherwise some experience in waking life is woven into the drama of our dreams. Ultimately, to decide on such things lies outside the possibilities of the present work. Only this can be said in all certainty, that the decisive viewpoint to understand Mark's Gospel for this passage is not that directed to the outer event, but to that of the *picture*. As a picture the whole story of the widow offering her last farthing appears for that which Lazarus, the 'son of the widow' in stepping through the portal of the poverty of the grave, the 'zero point of consciousness', lives through: the actual end of his [initiation-process of] becoming John.

***

'The Little Apocalypse'

From the point reached here in the narration of Mark's Gospel, where the 'becoming John' of the 'disciple whom the Lord loved', the one-time 'invalid' (Lazarus) and 'son of the widow', finds its conclusion, his initiation through Christ comes to an end. Our glance turns back to the beginning of this great initiation-experience. As often discussed (firstly in the Introduction p. 49), we search for meaning in the old legends where the beloved disciple, himself later awoken through Christ

from the slumber of the grave, becomes a witness to that earlier awakening of the 'young man of Nain' (Luke 7:11-15). The gospel itself gently suggests the connection in the way the young man—who in the story of the initiation plays a significant role later—is also called a 'son of the widow'. Rudolf Steiner points out (*The Mysteries of the East and of Christianity.* GA 144. Lecture 3, Berlin. 5 Feb. 1913) how this expression in Mystery-language belongs to how a grade in the Mysteries, a Mystery-experience was expressed, which at the time of the decline and fall of the pre-Christian Mysteries was still possible, as when the sacred places, with regard to the earlier divine revelation, the revelation of the Son, of the cosmic word, remained orphaned. This is found in a certain remarkable passage in the Old Testament. Initially one thinks of the story told in I Kings 17, how Elijah awoke the son of the widow at Zarepath. In I Kings 7:14 Hiram of Tyre, the skilful builder of Solomon's Temple, is called a 'son of the widow'.

All these echoes appear significant when we recall how that disciple, led through the Johannine initiation, out of the grave at Bethany (John 11:43) was in the Mystery-sense related by choice, a kindred spirit, related by destiny, was related inwardly and outwardly to Solomon's Temple and to the temple Mysteries (cf. Luke 18:18 in connection with Mark 10:17). Furthermore, in his Christ-initiation itself, what he experienced in the slumber of the grave of Bethany—active initiation-events in a specific sense even if on a much higher level—appears as a parallel of what Elijah effected in Zarepath. In *both* cases the forces of Elijah played a decisive role. The 'son of the widow' is always the one whose forces fail and die away, who sinks into the sleep of death, whereas in the forces of Elijah—which in the New Testament are led and accompanied by Christ—lies the element of re-enlivening. The invalid (Lazarus) and 'son of the widow' dies; he who is overshadowed by the Elijah-John power, penetrated by the Elijah-John being experiences the resurrection. (Here too we recognize the revelation of the meaning of the sign of the Crab ♋: 'He must increase, but I must decrease.')

It is not the intention immediately to press connections, as the above might suggest, into some kind of notion and theory, but far rather that one can learn in a certain inner silence to repose with them. (The connections referred to form the spiritual background to Albert Steffen's play *Hiram and Solomon*.) Such an inner silence would then reveal much to the soul. If we have once understood or could feel how the story of Hiram of Tyre, the 'son of the widow' and master-builder of Solomon's Temple, how the story of the waking of the 'son of the widow' through Elijah and finally that of the wakening of the 'young man of Nain', who once again is called a 'son of the widow', how there is formed through Christ in their inward connection a spiritual background of the John-initiation, the initiation of John-Lazarus, then we can also recognize this as significant, when the narration—presented veiled but still approachable—of this initiation in Mark's Gospel finds its completion in the picture of the 'story of the poor widow'. Here the final remains of that Mystery-past are settled; here the widow appears as the 'spiritual mother' of him who lives through the initiation. In the gospel, the mother so often stands as the picture of the soul-force and the inner soul (cf. p. 77). Here the 'poor mother' or 'poor widow' becomes the picture of the soul of John who now in his initiation steps through the 'I'-zero point of consciousness.

Only gently, in a kind of Mystery-language, can the writer of Mark's Gospel indicate the actual climax of the initiation of John that like a main theme goes right through the whole narration of this gospel. To present it more clearly remained reserved for him who in his own life was linked to these events, to the writer of John's Gospel himself. In an incomparable manner all understanding of the gospel is deepened when the connections of the individual gospels are rightly seen here. (Luke's Gospel, too, plays in significantly, as has been shown—see Chapters 7 and 16.) For it can also be recognized how for the climax presented in John's Gospel (Chapter 11) as the 'raising of Lazarus', this initiation in Mark is indicated, where at the end of Mark 12 the 'story of the poor widow' is told, so also the 'raising of Lazarus' is to be

thought of in a certain way in the transition between the end of Mark 12 and the beginning of Mark 13.

***

At this point of the gospel narration we enter the ground of one of the most holy events to take place in the concealed sanctuary in the most inner part of the soul. And the writer of Mark's Gospel himself spreads silence over this most holy event. Only when we ourselves, as mentioned above, have learnt to ruminate in silence on these things are we able at this point to follow him in his account of the great initiation, thereby enabled to find the transition to the secrets of Mark 13. This is called the 'Little Apocalypse' of Mark's Gospel; it develops out of what lies in the middle between Mark 12 and 13.

We step up to the beginning of Mark 13 recalling everything concerning the connection of what has led by this time to the conclusion of John's initiation with the 'awakening' or 'raising of Lazarus', narrated in John 11. We recall, too, everything that was found as 'spiritual background' to this initiation process. This actually answers the question of who the one disciple (*εἷς τῶν μαθητῶν*) is, who in view of the Temple asks Christ: 'Look, Teacher, what wonderful stones and what wonderful buildings!' (Mark 13:1. In his *Studies in the Gospels*, Emil Bock also points to this significant moment in Mark's Gospel.) It is the *one* disciple who always was, and is, the one who has now passed right through the initiation. There was a time—as in Mark 6:12—that concerned the initiation-event of the Twelve, a matter of the circle of Twelve. Now, after the initiation of the others has collapsed, it concentrates on the *one*. Fundamentally it is the same 'one', who in the 'story of the rich young man' is called with this numerical word (*εἷς*) (Mark 10:17). The initiation of the Twelve has now become that of the *one*. Translations are not always accurate; for example, not 'a man ran up' (RSV, NIV) or 'a stranger' (RNEB) but '*the one disciple*' is now spoken about, 'there came one running' (KJV/AV), *προσδραμὼν εἷς, καὶ γονυπετήσας*

αὐτὸν', 'running-to one, and kneeling to him...', who since Mark 9:38 has become the spokesman; he also speaks here.

The picture stands before us of the one awoken by Christ out of the grave at Bethany, the picture of the invalid ('Lazarus'), now the disciple of Christ and Christ-initiate. Still bound with bandages (John 11:44), the grave-clothes—everything of this not meant as outwardly physical, but spiritually real—we see him standing before us. ('Lazarus' died; he rose and in John 12 is consequently called 'John', although immediately after the event of awakening he is still called 'the invalid', Lazarus.) In this moment, one half manifests as someone resurrected, spiritually transfigured, the other half still as a corpse; corpse and resurrected form meet in the appearance of this one ascended from the grave. And here the remarkable question concerning the Temple, before which he is standing with Christ: 'Look, Teacher, what wonderful stones and what wonderful buildings!' This Temple and the Holy City of Jerusalem, had he not known them for a long time? Did he not at that time walk there daily with his Lord and Master? What is the meaning of his question?

The consciousness of one who has just risen from the grave, still bound with those bandages, lives no longer in the world. This world, for the man of the senses, is the only real one, the world in which we, laying hold of the stones with our hands, experience 'reality'. This 'world of reality' is like a scattered dream to one who has passed right through the depths of the grave. It is a world of the past with which he inwardly has finished; he has now become the one awoken from the slumber of the grave. And in his consciousness he already carries a new world of becoming, a world of the future. (One notes how in all these motifs, also the apocalyptical meaning of this whole section reveals the governing sign of the Crab.)

Still unclear in the dawning distance, this world stands before his spiritual eye, 'still dazzled by the shining day'.[35] And what happens here can shock us in the inner depths of consciousness. He, who so often has beheld this Temple in the sensory world, often walked over it with his Master and Initiator, the whole destiny of his life so deeply

bound with the destiny of this Temple and its Mysteries, he, who—however we want to describe the secret with words and concepts—in the depths of his being linked to the great builder himself of this Temple, he, as the 'son of the widow' himself carried the Mystery-grade of the great master builder, *he, Lazarus-John, no longer recognized the Temple*. Because before his eyes, before the spiritual eyes of the initiated one risen from the grave, there already shines in the twilit distances of the future another, a spiritual temple. This is the bright resurrection temple of the 'New Jerusalem', the future of the Earth which, as the Apocalyptist in-the-making that he has now become, he is called to describe (Rev. 21 & 22. What concerns us here is not the philological question, who, seen externally, is the 'author' of the Book of Revelation, the Apocalypse, but only the fact that perhaps we would not possess today the sketchy fragment that is called 'the Apocalypse of John' if it did not somehow flow out of the inspiration of the great disciple of Christ.)

Have not all the pictures of Mark 11 and 12 told us how the one becoming John understands that the old Temple of the past, the temple of stone and bronze, similar to the body of the Earth, is doomed to pass away, that it has to fall into ruin and be destroyed? And another, a new, no longer subject to decay, no longer dedicated to ruin, a bright resurrection temple—and resurrection body—of the future rises out of the ruin of the old? This resurrection temple of the future, the bright temple of New Jerusalem, appears now in the distant twilight before the spiritual eyes of that disciple of Christ who has become new.

At this point of Mark's Gospel, where in such a decisive manner the motif of the old and of the new temple—of the visible Temple of stone and bronze fated for ruin, and the invisible temple of the spiritual, future Earth—stands in the focal point, it is significant that there appear again the names of the four disciples (13:3), who are always linked to the *Mystery* of the 'temple of the past' and the 'temple of the future', *the visible and the invisible Church*. Peter and Andrew always appear as the bearers and pillars of the earthly temple of the past, the

visible Church. James and John appear as the bearers of the spiritual temple of the future, the 'invisible Church'. Already with the calling of the twelve disciples at the beginning of the disciples' initiation (Mark 3:16-18), we met this picture (see p. 87f.). James and John, the two pillars of the invisible Church, are, as it were, in the background raised above those of the visible Church. Here (Mark 13:3) this motif that runs through the whole of Mark's Gospel appears in its cosmic and apocalyptic greatness. The revelation of the apocalyptic meaning of the sign of the Crab appears here at its climax.

With this at the same time we have presented the viewpoint as regards content to understand the whole of Mark 13, which is called, also by theologians, the 'Little Apocalypse' [also 'Olivet discourse' and 'Olivet prophecy'] that has its parallels with the two other 'Synoptic Gospels' (Matt. 24, and Luke 21). What appears in this 'apocalyptic chapter' like a prophecy of Christ in the Synoptic Gospels is recognized as actually the digest of the Apocalypse of John. The present contemplation does not aim to expound the details of the content. This has to remain for an exposition of the Apocalypse of John. Apart from the strikingly significant approach to this chapter from world-backgrounds, what is important here is only the picture of the great disciple John, who precisely through the completion of his initiation has become the Christ-initiate and disciple of Christ—in the narrower sense—standing just before becoming the Apocalyptist of the future. We recognize how the prophecy of the future through Christ, which, seen externally, forms the content of the chapter, is spiritually suggested to him in an Intuition, now bestowed as a new future task, bearing the future.

The apocalyptic meaning of the sign of the Crab, of the sign of the Turning Point of Time and Turning Point of the World, stands over the whole content of this Chapter 13. The narration of Mark's Gospel has to do with presenting the crises and birth-pangs of the initiation of the disciple, of the becoming of the Christ-initiate. The Apocalypse of John has to do with a participation of the whole future fate of the Earth, of

the crises of development and birth-pangs of the future becoming of the Earth and of humanity. It is clear in Mark 13 how in the ruin of everything physical, which as such, past all hope, is dedicated to ruin, the Apocalyptist-in-the-making experiences the becoming and development of the etheric, indeed of an ethereally penetrated and changed new super-earthly physical world. The cosmic character of Mark's Gospel (aligned to the human etheric body, see Introduction, p. 22) appears here above all (13:25: 'and the stars will fall from heaven, and the powers of the heavens will be shaken'—that is, the etheric power of the stars will be revealed in the earthly physical world).

And the reference to the 'lesson from the fig tree' (13:28) points to how new clairvoyant powers, new etheric powers of humanity, will develop out of the collapse of the physical and all the old forces. In the most significant, the spiritual and apocalyptic meaning, revealing the sign of the Crab, this combines with what was said above on the decline and disappearance of the old forces in the symbol of the withered fig tree (Mark 11:12-21). The old and the new body, the old and the new Temple, the old and the new Earth are symbolized in the two spirals of the sign of the Crab. Moreover, the old and the new forces of humanity are symbolized in the withered fig tree and its new leafing time in summer (Mark 13:28).

Towards the end of Chapter 13, the more the resurrection glory of Christ is presented, the more there lights up the overcoming of the past and the creation of the future out of Eternal Being, out of the power of the eternal cosmic Word. 'Heaven and earth will pass away but my words will not pass away' (13:31). And we see all the more the sign of the Crab as the sign of the Turning Point of the World go over to the sign of the Lion that overcomes. Both signs in the apocalyptic, alchemical sense, are closely linked as signs of change and transformation (cf. Rev. 5:5: 'lo, the Lion ... has conquered.') We know that the Lion, unlike the other signs of the zodiac, is not outwardly given its own section in the narration of Mark's Gospel. Yet as the 'esoteric sign' of the Sun, the heart of the great Sun-rhythm, it

governs the cosmic rhythm of Mark's Gospel from within. It contains the power through which it helps to change the negative side of the other signs—in this case what is negative within the sign of the Crab—in the spirit of Christ.

And so, the two signs of the Crab and the Lion appear closely connected, once again combined even with the exalted sign of the Twins,[36] precisely in Mark 11-13, and especially with the way at the end the 'master of the house' is mentioned (13:35). This warns how Christ, the great Sun of the world, the spiritual Sun, is at home in the 'sign of the Lion'. Ultimately it is *the forces of the heart* through which the Eternal is revealed, that overcomes everything of the essence of space and time and of the earthly physical level.

The Virgin and the Last Supper

(Mark 14:1-31)

The fulfilment of the initiation, as presented in the previous section, means that John, as also otherwise, does not merely contemplate some achieved point or other, but sets out on new experiences and new tasks. It is a characteristic of the 'path', of the way into the spiritual worlds, that it doesn't simply end somewhere but moves on ever further. John, the disciple of Christ, is that person whose Mystery met us in various characters in the Bible: the rich man, the ruler of the temple, the young man, and the invalid (Lazarus), through all the various, previously presented experiences and crises, trials and victories that have now taken place. Through further experiences, tests and tasks that now meet him, he increasingly becomes the 'disciple of love'. He has taken into his heart the destiny of the whole Earth and of mankind. Consequently, in long, gradual maturing he becomes the Apocalyptist of the future. He is called to present prophetically the whole future fate of the Earth and of humanity in that great painting the Apocalypse, the whole birth pains and crises of development of the future of the Earth. With the apocalyptical content of Mark 13 as such we already have an indication of the becoming of the future Apocalyptist.

The first task that appears to be set for him who now has become John, at the same time, is the most earnest task and test that has ever been set for a great initiate of humanity. It could be set only once in the entire history of the Earth. It is *to participate in the Mystery of Golgotha* itself. Through this John is raised to a new stage of existence; he becomes in the fullest sense the *disciple of love*. A tremendous and comprehensive life's task begins, bestowed during the time after the Pentecost event, to help and foster those who initially failed in their initiation and remained behind. This is shown in the whole manner, as carrier of the forces of the 'invisible Church', through his silent spiritual influence, he helps Peter and the others in their work to build up

the visible Church. After this, years later, as the mature fruit of his life and great deed for humanity, there is given from Ephesus the great testament of humanity, in the creation or creative inspiration[37] of the greatest and most profound of all the documents of humanity, of *John's Gospel*, of the one pure gospel of Christ. And the *Apocalypse* itself is included, still shrouded in the dawning of the future, which we have already mentioned.

Alongside the other task of what the immediate experience of Christ is, or what approaches such, John's one task, which is presented in the next chapters (Mark 14 & 15), is *to witness in the Mystery of Golgotha*, personally to share in the whole *suffering of Christ*. As we have seen the death of Christ began in the *Transfiguration*. Already at that time, the one becoming John witnessed this dying. He was immediately involved in working through the great Mystery of dying. Significantly, Christ repeatedly pointed the disciples to the earnestness of this Mystery of death to the disciples (Mark 8:31, 8: 34-38, 9:12, 10:32-34, whereby this last announcement of death may perhaps have been taken from John's memory). The meaning of the whole initiation of the disciples as originally planned by Christ was actually that they grasp that they should themselves actively witness the Mystery of Golgotha. It was the original will of the world-destiny that Christ should effect this Mystery in the circle of the Twelve, carried by the strength of the Twelve. From the greatness and the pressure of their task we see the disciples fail, except for the one who stood under the cross (John 19:26). The flight in Gethsemane (Mark 14:50) sealed the great crisis. So, it lay to the one, standing under the cross, completely alone, to accomplish what according to the will of world-destiny was actually the task of the Twelve. Only the Christ-initiate has the strength to stand up to the pressure of this task. The others, whose initiation had already collapsed into itself, fail.

The experience of the 'Transfiguration on the Mount' had prepared the Mystery of Golgotha. This Mystery actually begins in Mark at the beginning of Chapter 14. The initiation of John ends with Mark 12 and 13. Directly after that the Mystery of Golgotha begins, but in such

a way, if we correctly understand the Mystery of Golgotha, that we can recognize how John is involved in the carrying out of this Mystery. How is this initially expressed in the narration of Mark 14? How and where is the beginning of the 'Mystery of Golgotha' described?

The beginning of this Mystery is already revealed in what was done to Christ Jesus—the anointing scene as a sacramental deed through a woman, Mary Magdalene. The name 'Mary Magdalene' is not used by Mark; it stands only with John who, with some differences, likewise tells the event (John 12:3-8). But here we should notice an important point. Where the account of John's initiation ends and passes on to that of the Mystery of Golgotha, John's Gospel and Mark's Gospel are much more similar than they hitherto were. And the 'cosmic rhythm', which at the beginning of John's Gospel is completely different from that of Mark's Gospel (followed up in detail in the sequel: Beckh 1930), completely agrees in the final chapters, in the 'Mystery of Golgotha', with those of Mark's Gospel. In a certain sense and up to a certain point—for in the details enough differences remain—in the account of the 'Mystery of Golgotha' all four gospels are 'synoptic'. In this Mark's Gospel in particular is more so, since it is already the case that it is a Gospel of John (see Introduction, p. 51). And one sees in the presentation of the events, that even when these initially relate to Mark's Gospel, yet one continuously needs to refer to John's Gospel.

What is John's part in the sacramental event, like a 'last anointing', opening the Mystery of Golgotha, when this is carried out by a woman, through Mary Magdalene, as she is expressly called in John's Gospel (John 12:3), that is, the sister of John-Lazarus? Here we have to recall the whole role the feminine, the sister-soul, always plays in the experience of initiation and spiritual deeds of John and the one becoming John. It is not as though the physical reality of Mary Magdalene and also of the deeds narrated in Mark 14 and John 12—which precisely in John's account awakens most of all the impression of outer reality—somehow draw doubts. From other sources we know even more

clearly who Mary Magdalene actually was and what role she played as head of a certain esoteric group in the events of the time.

But alongside all this there is also another aspect that has a claim to be heard. The way she appears in the events of John and the events of Christ, is perhaps at the same time a picture for that which is the soul-activity, the spiritual influence of the great disciple of Christ himself. In a significant way she, or even her spiritual sphere, is bound up with the three 'awakenings from the dead', which form at the same time milestones of the Johannine initiation, John's initiation-experience.

With the now often-mentioned events presented in Luke's Gospel (Luke 7:11-14), which at the same time point to the first beginning of John's initiation (Introduction, p. 49), with the awakening of the young man of Nain, she appears in a scene (Luke 7:36-50), which in many details very much recalls Mark 14:1-9 and John 12:1-8. Here too, similar to John's narration, she anoints the feet of Christ Jesus and dries them with the hair of her head (Luke 7:38). On the other hand, she is not called Mary, precisely because she has not yet become Mary. Here she is called the 'sinner' (v. 37), and this absolutely reflects the whole soul-situation at the time of John-Lazarus, who still felt burdened with the heritage of Cain, Cain's curse on humanity, the human fault of sin, the sickness of sin. And the 'tears' which in Luke 7 the 'sinner' sheds clearly point in this direction.

Now, the narration John 12:1-8 alongside what she expresses as a 'picture', at the same time strongly awakens the impression of external actuality. In Luke 7, though, where the event is indeed also transposed to another chronological period, the impression is much more of a spiritual experience. (The whole of Luke 7 is full of Mystery-contexts, which all somehow relate to the secret of John and the initiation of John-Lazarus.) Moreover, the mentioning of the 'Pharisee' in Luke 7 and the role it plays there, one could take—of course this is only a hypothesis—in the sense where elsewhere (see p. 225ff.) concerning the 'splitting of the personality' with the one becoming John in his

initiation, it was said: the one part, striving for initiation in Christ, his sinful guilt is revealed to the conscious part of his being, in the picture of the 'sinner' with her deep contrition. The other part sees itself still as the 'Pharisee' (to whose circles John-Lazarus indeed stood close), which the repentant soul will haughtily oppose.

This anointing of the feet of Christ through the weeping 'sinner' in Luke 7 shows the soul-condition of the one becoming John at the beginning of his initiation. This portrays the fulfilment of the initiation reflected in John 12 (and similarly Mark 14), the soul-condition of John having penetrated right through the initiation. He is now himself actively called to participate in the Mystery of Golgotha. Here the former sinner acts now like a sacred priestess, here is no more talk of tears, here she has become 'Mary'. The first anointing of the feet follows the 'awakening of the young man of Nain'; the other follows on the 'awakening of Lazarus' (John 11), in which the initiation of John is fulfilled. Between these two 'awakenings from the dead' lies a third, narrated as the 'awakening of Jairus' daughter' in Mark 5:35-43. With this daughter of Jairus we have seen (p. 120) how it has a profound inner relationship to the 'woman with an issue of blood', who according to the legends is Martha, the sister of Mary Magdalene. So, the spiritual sphere of Mary Magdalene somehow plays into this event too, a milestone in 'awakening the dead' forming the initiation-experience of John-Lazarus. In this awakening of Jairus' daughter, as we saw (p. 122f.), lies the point where the one becoming John overcomes the sting of death of sin and sensuality, where in inner virginity he wins back his being. Here the 'sinner' so to speak ceases to be a sinner, here she prepares to become Mary.

So, alongside what the whole thing as an external event signifies, the stories told in Mark 14 and John 12 are to be seen as a picture for how the *soul of John* from now on is itself actively involved in all the events of Christ's life, as they are completed in the Mystery of Golgotha. The other disciples that have failed in the initiation, are excluded from this emotional sympathy. This is revealed in the almost shocking way: out

of narrow social reasons, they oppose the pouring out of the costly ointment—in John here Judas speaks alone; more clearly than Mark, Matthew 26:8 relates how the disciples were involved in the dissension. And Christ has to tell them how the great sacrifice for humanity has nothing to do with narrowly material, 'social' viewpoints: 'For you always have the poor with you, and whenever you will, you can do good to them; but you will not always have me' (Mark 14:7).

He has to tell them they have not the slightest notion Whom they have in their midst and what is going on in their midst, that their sleep of consciousness is so deep, their darkening of consciousness has become so complete, that they know and feel nothing of the meaning and content of the great World-Mystery and of the divine Love revealed in Him. The whole incident shows how deeply the disciples have already sunk, how deep their fall, their crisis, has become. For that reason in Mark too the reference to the betrayal by Judas (Mark 14:10, 11) follows immediately, in which the darkening of consciousness and the crisis of the disciples finds its climax.

In Mark the anointing of the head is narrated (Mark 14:3), in John the anointing of the feet (John 12:3). The former, more Imaginative, narration in Mark is more the sacramental aspect of the 'last rites', the 'last anointing' (see also Mark 14:8); John emphasizes more the 'washing of the feet', of 'Christian initiation' (which begins with 'washing the feet'). (Whoever is stuck with the outer wording, may find consolation that Mark perhaps narrates the one, John the other part of the event. Moreover, as the head points to the region of the Ram, the feet to that of the Fishes, and taking into account the aspect of the 'four gospel triangles' developed in more detail in the Appendix, with Mark we really find the sign of the Ram, and with John that of the Fishes.) The 'washing of the feet' has not only to do with what is narrated in John 13, with what Christ performs on the disciples, but it concerns a sacramental deed first performed on Him, which Christ then passes on.

The whole event lies fully in the sphere of that deed that we have always called here the 'Last-Supper event', the sacrifice of divine love

for the future development of the Earth and of humanity (cf. also, Mark 14:9). For this reason, too, it stands directly connected with the great Last Supper which Christ celebrates with His disciples, portrayed in what follows (Mark 14:12-31). The event of the Last Supper stands in the cosmic 'rhythm' always in the *sign of the Virgin*. After the previous chapters (11-13) that progress in the sign of the Crab—alongside which ultimately the spiritual background is increasing felt—with the beginning of Chapter 14 we enter the sign of the Virgin. The Virgin first appeared in the pictures and Parables of the Sower and the Individual Seed, through which Christ plants in the hearts of the disciples the germ of the great Last-Supper event of the 'kingdom of God'. Here the Last-Supper event stands in the sign of the Virgin on the first stage, that of Imagination (Mark 4). In Mark 8, as the disciples in the 'Feeding of the Four Thousand' are able to pass on the bread of life broken by Christ to their contemporaries, this Last-Supper event in the sign of the Virgin has moved to the stage of Inspiration. What was initially seen as but an external picture becomes here a power working and inspiring from within. Already here something of the Last Supper of humanity, a communion of humanity, is brought about by the disciples. The starry Virgin, the bearer of the bread of life, is here experienced within.

Meanwhile, the initiation of the Twelve has collapsed on itself. John, the initiated disciple of Christ, is now the only *conscious* carrier of the sacred events, though it is meaningful and a world-necessity that *all* twelve disciples take part in the Last Supper—the darkening of their consciousness precisely on this occasion is quite obvious, cf. Mark 14:19 and John 31:27-30. In this way, the disciples are inwardly carried further and prepared for their future tasks according to destiny. Now the great Last-Supper event is revealed in the sign of the Virgin on the third stage, that of Intuition. Here it is not only received working in the depths of the heart, but embraced by the total human being in the essential depths, right into the depths of earthly corporeality. It goes—if an expression may be ventured—right into the bones. Here there

shines over the Last Supper the whole earnestness of the cross on Golgotha, from whose force all the disciples inwardly fall apart—except for the one, who then really did stand under the cross (John 19:26).

Here the Last-Supper event of humanity appears on the stage of Intuition as the *communion of the disciples with Christ Himself*. But they do not appreciate the earnestness of this stage; they fall apart at the re-constituting power of this experience. Judas becomes the betrayer—the direct connection precisely of his deed to the Last Supper is clearly indicated in the gospel (Mark 14:18-21, John 13:21-30). Peter denies. For the others, the flight in Gethsemane (Mark 14:50) is prepared. This communion with Christ Himself becomes for the disciples a darkening of consciousness, a crisis, a judgement. Only *one* experiences it fully awake, precisely he who then stood under the cross, and under the cross is united with His mother. This awareness is clearest in John's Gospel, in the picture of the disciple 'whom the Lord loved' leaning on the breast of Christ Jesus (John 13:23, 25; 21:20).

But also the participation of the sister-soul at the Last-Supper event (Mark 14: 1-9, John 12:1-8), alongside what the whole thing as an outer event signifies, or can signify, is at the same time a picture for this direct, intimate part of John at the Last-Supper event, in which the 'Mystery of Golgotha' itself already begins. John is the only one who consciously assimilates at the level of Intuition the great event in the essential depths of his total human nature. With him we recognize how Intuition and communion itself are essentially united. He is essentially at one with the great Christ-event and event of humanity. For this reason the Virgin, who is always the bearer of the cosmic Last-Supper feeding, of the Holy Grail, appears, here not only as the constellation in the stars, but now, on the level of Intuition, she herself bodily appears on Earth in Mary Magdalene, in the sister and sister-soul of him who witnesses the Last-Supper events at first hand.

John is the only one consciously to experience the communion in the great Last Supper of Christ. Yet he does so not for himself alone, but at the same time for the others, who only in the Pentecost event awaken

out of their sleep of consciousness. The Last Supper really is, in this sense, a 'love feast' for those whose consciousness is too weak now to assimilate the great Event in its full virtue, until that moment of waking up carried by the love of Christ, who for them and for humanity went through death. This is the 'love to the end', that is, till the completion of consecration, mentioned in John 13:1. And in this 'carrying love' of Christ, the one who went in advance of the others, *John*, took a conscious part. With precisely what love he poured his Inspiration, his Initiation-experiences into his Gospel, John expresses in the 'Farewell Discourses of Christ' (John 13–16) and above all in the 'High-priestly Prayer', the 'Great Intercession' (John 17). Over this whole chapter of John's Gospel there clearly lies the mood of the 'sacred Last Supper', even if the details of this Last Supper are not narrated as with the other evangelists.

***

With the great Last-Supper event that Mark 14 begins to narrate, the body of Christ Himself is the heavenly Host (Mark 14:22). In the time of the primordial human Mysteries the Host was the starry bread (the starry power of the cosmic life-ether), its bearer the starry Virgin, Isis of the Egyptians. The Indians called the etheric starry-nourishment the heavenly soma; at the same time the crescent Moon was the picture of the heavenly Grail events. Soma in the Indian language also signifies the Moon. Subsequently, when the forces of the stars were no longer experienced, the Host was still the etheric of plants, which the soma name carried. Then everything fell into the earthly, physical realm, where it lost this connection to the heavenly forces. Through Christ this connection of the earthly with the heavenly forces was re-established. The body of Christ Himself (*σώμα, soma*, in Greek means 'body') has now become the heavenly Host. Its earthly bearer is called Mary.

The Scales: Gethsemane

(Mark 14:32-42)

The 'cosmic rhythm' leads from the etheric sign of the Virgin to the physical sign of the Scales (cf. the Appendix and the three crosses in Fig., p. 364). In the earlier rounds the events of the 'Last-Supper events' (the Parable of the Sower and the two 'miracles of Feeding') in the sign of the Virgin, or rather the constellation *Fishes–Virgin*, moved over to the Scales, or rather the constellation *Ram–Scales*. We saw the disciples in this constellation struggle for their balance of soul. The reason for this has to do with bringing etheric experience to the secure shore of daytime consciousness. All the new forces of the soul are to be securely upheld in the earthly, physical realm. The *Ram* always was the sign for the correct placing of oneself in the earthly sphere, and the *Scales* for the struggle for balance. For this reason most of the healings of those possessed lie in the sign of the Ram; the healing in Mark 5, appearing in a particular meaning as a picture for the disciples' inner struggle and opposition of soul, stands in the sign of the Scales.

This meaning of the sign of the Scales finds a tremendous intensification on the third round of the Sun-rhythm, at the stage of Intuition. Here it has no longer to do with Christ inwardly rectifying others, whether those possessed, or those disciples involved in the crisis of struggling to find their balance. But it has to do with the most terrifying of all world-moments for Christ Himself, struggling for His balance in the earthly realm, for His ability to hold Himself in the forces of the Earth. Here He had to affirm His balance right into the physical, in the midst of the most awful, threatening dread. The words standing over the whole section, 'Watch and pray', to which Christ calls His own disciples, are deeply connected to the meaning of the sign of the Scales. The bloody drops of sweat of Christ Jesus in Gethsemane (Luke 22:44) do not refer to the usual fear of death; they cannot refer to a human quaking before the martyrdom of the cross. After what

resulted from the free resolve of Christ to go through death in Mark Chapters 9–12, this should actually go without saying. Rudolf Steiner first showed this most clearly, and Emil Bock in his *Studies in the Gospels* convincingly argues this viewpoint. Here we have only to throw light on what is already recognized from the aspect of the rhythm of the signs of the zodiac. What then was the actual reason that Christ squeezed 'great drops of blood' from his brow?

In his book *The Spiritual Guidance of Humanity* [GA 15], Rudolf Steiner shows how in the first three years of life, young children still live in direct feeling with the realm of the angels. The beings of the higher hierarchies work directly into the child's organism. This stimulates the forces of growth, the forces to stand upright, to think and to speak. As a direct connection this can last for three years but not longer, 'otherwise', Steiner expresses it, 'under the holiness of these forces our organism languishes'. The case is not seen as different for the connection of the cosmic Christ, of the Sun-being, with the earthly vehicle of Jesus of Nazareth. The earthly life of Christ, too, His inhabiting the human, bodily vehicle of Jesus of Nazareth, could not last more than three years.

(The 'three years' of the life of Christ resulting from spiritual research is not directly verified from the gospels, as has already been mentioned [p. 45]. The Easter festival mentioned three times in John's Gospel does not without more ado establish the conclusion of three full years. But in the 'cosmic rhythm' of Mark's Gospel the three years are hidden, even if, as has repeatedly to be emphasized, the individual events ordering the respective zodiacal sign are not to be so understood as if the respective events would span a calendar month [see Introduction, p. 20].)

Some kind of event through world-destiny would inevitably enter, setting the end to the earthly life of Christ Jesus; it would be bound to disrupt the connection between the cosmic Christ and the earthly figure of Jesus. In various lectures, especially those held in Christiania, Rudolf Steiner emphasized how difficult it was for Christ to maintain this connection intact, with the bodily sheaths of Jesus of Nazareth becoming increasingly fragile. Towards the end of the three years it became increasingly difficult for the bodily sheaths. This exposed bodily shell, carrying in itself the God, the Christ, and at the same time keeping contact with everything earthly and human, increasingly 'languished' from the connection. It became thereby increasingly shadowy, like a phantom.

(In *The Fifth Gospel.* Lecture-course, Christiania [Oslo], 1-6 Oct. 1913. GA 148, Rudolf Steiner has pointed out how in these circumstances lies the reason for the betrayal of Judas, which in no way sheds light without more ado. Then why, one could ask, was a betrayer necessary to mark out Christ Jesus for His captors; had they not known Him already for a long time? But, according to Steiner, it was like this because His body was becoming increasingly shadowy, increasingly difficult to recognize in the midst of the disciples. The longer the intercourse with the group of disciples lasted, the more similar even the individual disciples in their outer appearance began to look; it became ever more difficult to single out the one from the group.)

From here a whole new light also falls on the connection of Christ to the disciples, to the group of Twelve, which we have compared during the course of these considerations with the relationship of the Sun in the midst moving through the twelve signs of the zodiac. As the earthly representative of the twelve world-powers, the disciples were to form a ring around the spiritual Sun in their midst, around Christ. Combining their earthly forces with the divine forces of Christ—as these, for example, were expressed with the 'Feeding of the Four Thousand'—was to enable the God through three years to maintain a connection with the earthly and human relationships, as never in this manner hitherto had a member of the higher hierarchies taken on itself—had never been able to do so. The initiation-story forming the content of Mark's Gospel shows with great clarity how the disciples were never able to keep to their task. They repeatedly fail, until, with

Peter as the first, they finally land in a complete crisis. The initiation of the group of Twelve collapses on itself. Out of the beginnings of an initiation of the Twelve intended by Christ, there emerges the one. The crisis was, as it were, still latent with the waking of Jairus' daughter, it more fully burst out in Caesarea Philippi, and it now reaches its climax in Gethsemane.

Now, just as He approaches the end of the three years on Earth, He has to summon all His strength to keep Himself in earthly life so that He can accomplish the Mystery of Golgotha. Now, where He more than ever is dependent on the strength of the group of Twelve, who should form a ring around Him, in this moment precisely the Twelve leave Him in the lurch. The deed of Judas is clearly expressed, which Mark not for nothing points out precisely in this connection (Mark 14:10, 11); the ring that the Twelve should form around Christ is blown. Only three of them can He take into the Garden of Gethsemane, to the place where the decisive struggle is played out. These actual three disciples were also present at the waking of Jairus' daughter and are near Him on the Mount of Transfiguration. But these three, too, are not able to keep awake in the face of the tremendous spiritual tension of these most earnest, critical, and most terrifying of all world-moments.

Not an earthly, human fear of death forced those bloody drops of sweat to fall from the brow of Christ Jesus, but precisely the fear no longer to experience the hour of death on Golgotha. The forces that should make it possible to connect with the Earth during the course of the three years had become ever weaker. He feared to have to leave the earthly body beforehand because those forces fail. The future destiny of the Earth and of humanity lay in the balance; a God trembled for the sake of the fate of a world to which He was bound in love. For had the Mystery of Golgotha no longer been able to come to effect, the Earth and humanity would have been lost. They would have fallen to the power of the abyss; the Power of Darkness would have been victorious. And even in the face of this result, in its scope no longer to be measured in a human, but only by a divine consciousness, the divine love in Christ, who knows it is one with the future fate of the Earth and mankind, still finds the inner balance, in order then, looking up to the Fatherly primordial Ground of the Existence, to speak these words: 'Not what I will, but what you will' (Mark 14:36).

There is only *one* moment in the whole spiritual history of the Earth, which recalls from afar—even if not quite adequate—this critical world-earnestness, the impending world's fear of Christ struggle in Gethsemane. This is the moment narrated in the story of the Buddha's death.[38] After the signs of a mortal illness had appeared, his favourite disciple Ananda came to speak to the Holy One, of the possibility through magical power to extend his remaining on the Earth, even if it were to the end of the ages of the world. Because Ananda is beguiled (these words stand so expressively in the Indian text) by the tempter, by the power of darkness (Māra), he fails to make the decisive request to the master. Three times the Buddha gives him the chance; three times Ananda becomes obdurate in silence. So the Buddha decides to dissolve the connection with the Earth and to enter *nirvāṇa*, the land of no return. Even at that time a fate of the Earth lay in the balance. The Holy One, who 'for the salvation of many beings, for the happiness of many beings, out of compassion for the world, for the salvation, for the happiness of gods and men' was willing to connect himself with the earthly life from now on. But he who by the fate of the world was called to make the decision, did not choose the Buddha's life, and so the tip of the scales of death was deflected steeply downward. In those who read the Indian narrative with an inner sympathy, the description of that decisive world-fateful hour can induce a complete horror of death. And yet we clearly feel that the deflection of the world-scales at the time could have been no other, because the Earth and humanity were not sufficiently mature for the Buddha's intended connection, that of the Holy One with the Earth. Only through Christ and in the meaning He gives—that is, in another time and also in another way than as the Buddha meant in his time. This connection is possible, not through prolonging the earthly life, but precisely through a real earthly death—Buddha's *nirvāṇa* is something essentially different from the earthly death of Christ. Five hundred years earlier, in the time of the Buddha, the Earth was not yet mature enough for the Mystery of Golgotha. This Mystery was not possible for an earlier time, but also not for a later time. If Christ had not succeeded in keeping Himself in His earthly body till the hour of Golgotha, then the possibility of this Mystery to take effect would have been missed.

***

A remarkably significant moment—also to understand Christ in Gethsemane—of the Indian narration is the passage where we read of Ananda, that he failed to ask the decisive question for the whole fate of the earth, *because the power of darkness darkened his consciousness.* In this context, how does it stand with the disciples of Christ?

Not for nothing does Christ Jesus warn His disciples immediately before Gethsemane of that power of darkness: 'Simon, Simon, behold, Satan demanded to have you, that he might sift you like wheat' (Luke 22:31). We recall how the power darkening the consciousness releasing the crisis of the disciples always came to them in the sign of the Scorpion. At that place in the second round of the cosmic rhythm standing in the sign of the Scales, directly after the successful climax of the disciples' work in the 'Feeding of the Four Thousand', the 'bread', that is, the cosmic ether-forces, threatened to run out, Christ warns them in fateful, earnest words of the 'leaven of the Pharisees and the leaven of Herod' (Mark 8:15). We discussed (p. 174) what is to be understood with this 'leaven', especially that of Herod. A poisoned leaven is to be understood, from the poisoned sting of the Scorpion's power of death. Through this the forces of the bread of life are poisoned, changing into something bringing death. The evangelist has shown what a terrible role this Scorpion sting of death played in the dark Mysteries of Herod

and of Herodias. These are the adversaries of Christ's work on the Earth, the deadly enemies of the group of disciples, as they are previously of the Baptist John. It is the same power of Elijah, which initially works through the Baptist John, then through the Twelve, finally through the disciple John.

So it is not some kind of 'interpretation' dragged into the gospel, but actually is quite clearly expressed by Christ Himself. This power wants to darken the consciousness of people and not least the disciples of Christ. This power of the Scorpion's sting of death and the Scorpion's sting of poison is essentially embodied in Herod and Herodias and their dark Mysteries. It is not some kind of indistinct, abstract 'consciousness darkening' that comes to Peter in Caesarea Philippi (Mark 8:32, 33), then again on the 'Mount of Transfiguration' (Mark 9:5) and in his words (Mark 10:28), also no mere 'demonic powers' alone are working here, but incorporated right into human beings the Adversary of the Good and Adversary of Christ plays his hand in the black-magic 'control of the forces of thought'. We mentioned (p. 138) how powers of the Adversary in the Old Testament incorporated in Ahab and Isabel, in the New Testament in Herod and Herodias, play a role in the Grail story as Klingsor and Iblis. After their earlier attack against the work of Christ on Earth miscarried (see comments on Mark 6 & 7, p. 159ff.), this power goes all out for a decisive strike in the most decisive of all world-moments, where really the whole future fate of the Earth and humanity lies in the balance. In no moment in the entire events on Earth does this power of the Adversary raise itself, this Herodias-Klingsor power of dark Satanic Mysteries, to a more terrible straining of power than in the moment of Christ's struggle with Death in Gethsemane.

These powers cannot penetrate into the consciousness of Christ Himself. No suggestion may arise, for instance, that Christ trembled in His soul before the cross of Golgotha. But certainly they could penetrate into the group of disciples, who now should close the ring around Christ; from their determination it then would depend whether Christ would succeed to remain until the hour of Golgotha in the earthly body that was becoming ever more fragile. Already with the deed of Judas (Mark 14:10, 11) the ring is burst. And even the three most trusted disciples, who in the hour of greatest alarm should support Christ (Mark 14:33), struggle with the influence stifling their consciousness. They sink into slumber (Mark 14:37, 40). Better than all the Pharisees and scribes, Herodias knows what is now happening in world-events and what is at stake.

In greatest need, Christ Jesus sees Himself abandoned by His own disciples. He sees Himself left completely to His own strength, that means in this case, dependent on the strength of the earthly body getting ever weaker, ever more powerless. He has still to hold up to the end the connection with this earthly body until the hour on Golgotha, to the last final exertion. His Spirit is willing to accomplish the Mystery of Golgotha, but 'the flesh is weak' (Mark 14:38); the languishing earthly body, pining away from the holiness of Christ's strength, threatens prematurely to break up before the Mystery of Death can be accomplished. And it looks as if Hell has now achieved the greatest and the most decisive of all its victories.

In the whole terror and critical tension of this hour, something completely unique in world-events has to happen. In the most extreme hour of decision, when the balance of the world wavers and shudders, He has to attempt from human beings—also from the closest and beloved disciple, who initially at least had the appearance of having left Christ in the lurch—through the power of prayer, to constrain all the hierarchies of the angelic ranks to send down assistance (as most expressively described by Luke). Through the concentrated power of white magic, He has to attempt to break the tip of black magic that would annihilate His earthly work. 'And there appeared to him an angel from heaven, strengthening him' (Luke 22:43). Just in this moment, when Judas with the squad, the band [of security forces], entered (Luke 22:47, Mark 14:43), the decisive victory is accomplished. The Mystery of Golgotha can now be accomplished to redeem the

Earth and humanity. The white magic of heaven has overcome the black magic of hell.

Once more our gaze turns from here to the three trusted disciples, overcome by sleep in Gethsemane. Was not also John, the disciple of Christ who did go through initiation amongst those who slept then? Did the black magic of Herodias also wield its power over him? Where was his active witness and participating help for the Mystery of Golgotha? Did he too refuse so hastily, after having achieved the greatest of all victories, as initiated by Christ for the greatest and most decisive of all tasks for effective earthly influence? Can we really imagine all this after what had previously taken place?

Really to imagine this means actually to doubt the spiritual power of Christ Himself, Who called the one out of the slumber of death in Bethany, lent him the name of the highest victor, gave him the greatest of all earthly tasks. And nevertheless it would not be good to interpret awry the clear text of the gospel, according to which even John slept in Gethsemane. Probably he also slept, but he slept as the only initiated one of the three. When the initiated one sleeps, his sleep is somewhat different from the sleep of others whose consciousness has not yet crossed the threshold of initiation. He did not sink like the others into complete dullness of consciousness, but when he slept, he was awake and worked in his angelic part. For this reason the spoken admonition in Mark 14:37 is for Peter, not John. Even as the physical body of the disciple John succumbed to sleep as the consequence of the colossal tension of the spiritual atmosphere in that hour of Gethsemane, his angel was awake and active. Do we find nothing about this activity of the angel of John in the gospel?

Already the beginning of Mark's Gospel emphasizes the angel-secret in John the Baptist that once again is one with the secret of the spiritual being of Elijah. It worked in the Baptist and later in the disciple John, after the Jordan baptism in a certain manner it also sacrificed itself to Christ Himself. The spiritual nature of Christ's being is essentially, as clearly said in John 1:51, the whole heavenly ladder of the

hierarchies, right up to the sublime Trinity. The lowest rung, however, of this 'heavenly ladder' is, as it were, the angel. Since through the angelic part of their being John and Christ Jesus are closely united, the angel of John is in a certain sense also the angel of Christ.

With this the question is already answered, who the angel was who in Gethsemane strengthened Christ Jesus in his struggle with Death, empowering Him to keep in balance the earthly existence and the earthly body (Luke 22:43). Emil Bock has found and expressed as one of the most significant results of his gospel research, that *none other than the angel John himself was awake and worked while the earthly body of John lay in slumber*. This is the third case where Luke's Gospel, also otherwise showing itself as a mine of intimate esoteric information, contains an indication of the most intimate Johannine Mysteries. The first was the 'waking of the young man of Nain' in Luke 7, the other the story of the 'rich man and the beggar, Lazarus' in Luke 16 (see p. 225ff.).

The story of Gethsemane forms one of the many stages of the working of John which can be surveyed. This particular working of John as the one initiated by Christ, whom he has now become, takes an active part in the Mystery of Golgotha decisive for the future of the Earth and humanity. In this hour of highest alarm for the world, in which the balance of the world wavers and shudders, he helps to produce the balance, by making it possible through his angelic strength for Christ Jesus Himself to remain in his earthly body until the hour of Golgotha, and thus to accomplish the Mystery of Death for the healing, the redemption of the Earth and humanity.

***

This great moment for the world and for Christ stands in the Scales. The decisive hour for the fate and the future of the world, the hour of Christ's struggle in Gethsemane, is inwardly related to another hour for the world in the Old Testament, spiritually recognizable likewise as standing in the sign of the Scales. This is the nocturnal hour when the patriarch Jacob at the ford Jabok, later the town of Peniel ['the face of God'] struggled with 'the angel' (Gen. 32:21-32). Here too it has to do with a significant milestone in the development of human consciousness and the 'I'-consciousness. Through the personal 'I', with whose impulses Jacob-Israel, as later Moses and the whole development of the Hebrew people are connected, the balance of the Scales of the world and of humanity is brought out of centre—but yet in a necessary manner to advance the world. The 'hollow of the thigh' that was 'put out of joint' (v. 25) corresponds to the zodiacal sign of the Scales (Introduction, p. 28).

At that same point when the balance was disturbed in the development of Old-Testament times, it was re-constituted in New-Testament times through Christ. In the most alarming moment for the world, Christ struggles for the balance of the world in His own balance of body and soul. The hour of Christ's struggle in Gethsemane is that moment for the world when the necessity of the disturbed balance of the world is restored.

(The connection between Old and New Testament indicated here also appears in Kurt Piper's poem 'Pniel und Gethsemane', in *Zwischen Welt und Geist: Schwellenbilder als Totenamt für Rudolf Steiner*. Dornach: Goetheanum-Verlag 1925. 66f. [see Appendix 6 below]. The night of Gethsemane in the 'cosmic rhythm' through the zodiacal sign of the Scales inwardly aligns with the night of Peniel. The completion of John's initiation in the Crab inwardly aligns to the human primordial past indicated in Genesis 2:22, the story of the creation of Eve out of Adam's rib, over which the sign of the Crab likewise stands. Yet it has to do with the indication of the first beginnings of the antithesis of gender—including the female and the male, as meant in Gen. 1:27—out of the original divine primordial unity of the spiritual human being. In John's initiation, however, as in the 'becoming of Spirit-man' this duality and polarity of the human being is in a certain way overcome. This takes place ultimately under the Cross, John 19:26, 27. The three

signs—the Twins, Crab and Lion—standing over the chapter of John's initiation [pp. 238-81] pictorially express this Mystery.)

Christ's restoring the balance does not signify that for every human soul from now on this balance would be guaranteed and achieved without the individual's own struggle. The facts shown by life itself are sufficient to indicate otherwise. But from now on it is possible in an inner meditative connection to Gethsemane for every human soul to find in itself this new balance carried by the Christ-impulse.

The End of the Crisis in the Scorpion: Judas, Peter and Pilate

(Mark 14:43–15:19)

To understand the gospel, it is important to recognize—here the 'cosmic rhythm' can be a valuable help—how the 'crisis of the disciples' comes to a final climax in Judas' betrayal, in Peter's denial, and in the flight of the disciples in Gethsemane (Mark 14:50). The crisis is gradually prepared right through the whole gospel narration. In a certain way it always becomes acute when in the 'cosmic rhythm' the sign of the Scorpion appears, in whose 'sting of death' the essence and the cause of this crisis is revealed in a pictorial manifestation. And it is always in the Scales, in the sign of struggle for inner balance, that the first signs of the 'crisis' are to be faintly felt.

Already in the first round of the Sun-rhythm, at the end of Mark 4, straight after the reception of the first seed of the new life is experienced by the disciples, these symptoms are expressed in the picture of the Storm on the Lake and connected with it the grotesque pictorial world of Mark 5. This explains why with the 'waking of Jairus' daughter' only three disciples are present, and we can surmise how also from these three only one—only the one—has arrived at the stage of inner conscious experience of which this wakening is the outer picture. Also in the check to the healings of the sick, and other symptoms, in the beginning of Mark 6, the first crisis is expressed, or the preparation for the crisis.

The first signs of this crisis follow through various dispensations and guidance of destiny, in which the sacrificial death of John the Baptist plays a decisive role. Like a rousing impetus and a more intensive advance this comes to a climax in Mark 8 where the 'Feeding of the Four Thousand' is narrated. The disciples, advancing for the first time from receiving to giving, are able to distribute the

bread of life administered by Christ to hungry humanity. Immediately following this climax, again in the sign of the Scales, symptoms of a new crisis—the bread of life becomes scarce again (Mark 8:14), and Christ has to warn the disciples of the 'leaven', or 'yeast', of the Pharisees and of Herod (v. 15). We have seen how this picture points to the might of the sting of death and sting of poison at work in the Scorpion.

The crisis already announced here is fully manifest in Peter's failure at Caesarea Philippi, in that passage which according to the cosmic rhythm stands in the sign of the Scorpion. The sudden change is distressing, from the 'light bringer' who inspires Peter's impetuous confession of Christ, to the 'power of darkness' which straightway darkens his consciousness when it has to do with understanding the Mystery of Golgotha. This is the power, to which Christ addresses the words: 'Get behind me, Satan (Ahriman)! You do not have in mind the things of God, but the things of men.' In the story of the possessed [epileptic] boy, immediately following the 'Transfiguration on the Mount', whom the disciples could no longer heal, there is the shocking picture of the situation of those remaining below the Mount, excluded from the sublime experience. It shows that the 'crisis of the disciples' has already reached a certain height.

At the same time we stand here at the point where the one disciple treading the path towards initiation clearly separates from that of the other disciples. Thus the betrayal by Judas (Mark 14:10, 11), the flight of the disciples in Gethsemane (Mark 14:50) and Peter's denial (Mark 14:66-72) are described as but the final decisive climax of a crisis which was already there, preparing itself. It was already indicated (p. 288f.) how this final decisive highpoint is to be thought of as standing in an inner connection with the spiritual influence of Christ's Last Supper, the communion of Christ.

After all this, it is understandable, with the outbreak of this final decisive crisis, that we are standing in the death-sign of the Scorpion. With the arrival of the squad [of security forces]—in which, as

we have seen, Christ's victory in Gethsemane concludes in a decisive manner—the transition of the cosmic rhythm from the sign of the Scales to that of the Scorpion takes place. We are able to give the exact verse where the transition from the one sign to the other takes place. What happens here is not actually the meaning of the death sign of the Scorpion. In Judas' betrayal and the entry of the squad, the *outer* cause for the speedy earthly death of Christ Jesus is given. The meaning of the sign of the Scorpion lies rather in the manner how, in the betrayal and in what then follows, the great crisis of the disciples—and the crisis of humanity—concludes. If we want to understand correctly the meaning of the death sign of the Scorpion in this moment, we have to look not at all so much to Christ Jesus, but to [those members of] humanity who surround Him.

In what follows, there lies here as elsewhere a difference of viewpoints, which all point to the meaning of the *one* sign. So we are slightly reminded of the sphere of the Scorpion in the manner, by disclosing certain intimate formalities on which rested the seal of the Mysteries, Judas betrays Christ Jesus through a kiss.

Judas

The whole figure of Judas belongs directly to this sphere of the Scorpion; we have to seek in no other sign in the zodiac than this for the spiritual essence of Judas. (Already above, p. 89, we mentioned how the relationship of the twelve disciples to the twelve signs of the zodiac, which as a whole is beyond doubt, but in detail difficult to fix. One relationship to the Scorpion exists with John, but only in so far as he is the one who has transformed this sign to its original meaning of Sun-Eagle. If we seek to find John within the twelve signs of the zodiac today, after he has overcome the sting of death, we will have to seek in what remains after overcoming the sting of death of the Scorpion—this, however, is the Virgin. For the ruling spiritual relationships here it is also interesting, as for the spiritual side of the question touched

on here, in Leonardo's vitally important picture of 'The Last Supper', Judas, Peter and John together form a group.)

Not for nothing does Judas bear this name. Like his great Old-Testament forebear, Judas Maccabaeus, who made an alliance with the Romans, he is bound in his whole being with the most inner impulses of Judaism (I Macc. 8:2, 1 Macc. 11:34-38). What were these impulses of Judaism? Ultimately those we know out of the whole contemplation of the gospel: tenaciously holding on to the old, to what has been handed down, to what is past and has become, remaining with what at a particular historical time in world-history was also the right thing, but then not recognizing that this historical time is now over. A new age demands new impulses. Earlier in these contemplations (p. 83) there was developed the *transition from the impulse of the Father to that of the Son,* from the fixed necessity of lawfulness to the impulses of grace and freedom in the 'I'. With the appearance of Christ on the Earth something new and living was placed into the events and development on a world-scale. This is what the Jews could not recognize, in which they could not and did not want to participate.

What they retained with such might with the old, past, ultimately with what is dedicated to be destroyed, is fear. What met us in the contemplation of Mark 11 (p. 247) as fear of the Romans, fear to preserve their holy of holies, concerning the whole fate of their Temple, which ultimately could not be saved from the hands of the Romans, that is, always fear of that which is unavoidable. In this fear essentially lives the might of darkness, Ahriman, that same might which darkened the consciousness of Peter in Caesarea Philippi (Mark 8:33). In the zodiac we find this darkening might, wanting wrongly to fasten the human soul to the past, as the might working out of the sign of the Scorpion. Looking at the planetary aspect, we can speak of the impulse of ancient Saturn that cannot find the transition to the Sun-impulse of the Son, to Christ.

In the confrontation of Christ with the Pharisees and the scribes this might of Jewish impulses set against the living advance

(Mark 2:6-8, 2:16-20, 2:24-28, 3:1-6, 7:1-13, 8:11-15, etc.). In the first of the cited passages (similar to 10:1-9) we saw the 'living word of Christ' (in ♉) confront the 'dead leaven of the Pharisees', in which the sting of death of the Scorpion was at work.

This governing spirit of the Scorpion's sting of death lived concentrated in Judas Iscariot, the spiritual descendant of Judas Maccabaeus. Not as though he too were not a staunch, and in his way a true 'partisan' of Christ Jesus. (The passage in John 12:6 is probably not to be taken externally and literally, but would mean that he adhered to money, like Judas Maccabaeus who was impressed with the gold and silver work of the Romans [I Macc. 8:3]. He was not really able to discriminate between the aspect of the divine from that of 'Mammon' [Matt. 6:24, Mark 12:17], especially when the latter was masked for him as 'social thinking'.)

It is the tragedy of 'partisanship' that there is in it a failure to appreciate true discipleship that is solely based on impulses of deepest love. In his partisanship there lives the Jewish impulse that should be overcome by that of Christ. Yet Judas wanted the power and greatness of Christ, but he wanted it in the wrong way, the wrong Jewish, Messianic sense indicated in John 6:15. He wanted to place the outer kingdom in the place of the inner kingdom, founded alone on the *'I'*. He was always waiting for a revelation of this Messianic splendour of Christ. He is also convinced of the magical power, perhaps veering towards superstition. Perhaps he had only arranged the scene of betrayal to force Christ to reveal this might against his captors, to bring about through violence the hour of the long-awaited Messianic kingdom. If so, then Judas is the one in Gethsemane who experienced the most shocking of all shocks, allowing him to appear as the most tragic person in the whole history of the Earth (cf. Matt. 27:3-8).

One could put the question, why had Christ accepted him into the group of disciples? Had he not seen through him from the beginning? But such basically vain questions should not be put to an event like that of the 'betrayal by Judas' that is so deeply anchored in the depths

of world-history. With overpowering greatness the presentation of John's Gospel points to this context (John 13:21-30).

In the lectures, variously translated as *Inner Realities of Evolution/ Evolution in the Aspect of Realities/ Inner Experiences of Evolution* [GA 132. Berlin, 31 Oct.–5 Dec. 1911] Rudolf Steiner points to the tremendous artistic manner Leonardo expresses these things. In the primordial depths, the 'origin of evil' in the evolution of the world is to be traced back to the Mystery of resignation, of the resigned attitude of the advanced 'good' powers. It is reflected in the way Christ Jesus invites the traitor himself to do his deed through the 'dipped morsel' (John 13:26, 27). Far beyond all questions, whether Christ Jesus didn't see through Judas leads to the consideration that without the betrayal by Judas the whole Mystery of Golgotha, necessary for the healing and advance of the Earth and of humanity, would not have been able to take effect. (Why this betrayal of Judas was necessary, in quite an outer sense, not immediately understandable, is discussed above, p. 293.)

The deed, seen from the periphery of world-events appears as the most horrendous and above all most tragic of all human offences. Seen from the centre of world-events it increasingly takes on the characteristic of a sacrifice—as do all [that results from] the 'origin of evil in world-events', to which Steiner traces back the meaning of sacrifice, to [all] deeds of sacrifice, of sacrificial acts for the world. Thus Christ Himself includes in His consciousness the deed of Judas in His 'High-priestly Prayer', the 'Great Intercession' (John 17:12). All viewpoints of human judgement and human notions in general fall away into nothing before the unimaginable greatness of the governing world-contexts here. Only the Christ-consciousness itself, or the initiate-consciousness of a John, is still able to assimilate such contexts. All theological and philosophical speculation about it is useless.

How Judas commits his betrayal in deep darkening of consciousness (cf. also John 13:30), and how this darkening takes hold of the

whole group of disciples is quite clear from Mark's account (Mark 14:18-21). The question 'Is it I?' can only arise out of such an already deep darkening of consciousness. It is this 'Is it I?' (*μετ' ἐμοῦ*, actually, 'Surely you don't mean me?' [NIV]), already a preliminary stage to the later *οὐκ εἰμί* (literally, 'I am not'; John 18:17), Peter's denial. And we see how *all* the disciples have a part in this soul-condition of Peter's 'I am not'. (How far it was different for John needs no repeating here. On this point, precisely the gospels standing next to the gospels of Mark and John show a delicate and loving reticence, not only out of consideration for the growing Church but also because they have flowed out of the genuine Johannine spirit. At the decisive place, however, as we shall shortly see, that upon which it depends is said with utmost clarity.)

***

Peter

If we turn now from Judas, the betrayer, to Peter, the denier, it is already clear with reference to the earlier episode of Caesarea Philippi how also with him the darkening of consciousness flows out of the might of death of the Scorpion's sting. It is not as though Peter, as it is with Judas, is to be assigned with his whole being to the whole nature of this sign. If we would raise the question in which way the twelve disciples correspond to the signs of the zodiac, we would have to assign him to the Goat. With the nocturnal sign of the Goat we find the earlier pre-Christian initiation, whether concerning the sublime initiation of a Buddha or John the Baptist (as initiates both stand in the Goat, see pp. 58 and 262f.), or whether it concerns the black-magic initiation into the dark mysteries of Herod and Herodias (see p. 136f.). The Goat is the sign of the Sacred Night in which the Buddha finds enlightenment—in this sense then also of the 'light bearer' (Lucifer); it is the sign of the

consecrated 'Holy Night', and in this sense the sign of Christmas. The reverse side of this sign and this sacred time of night is the dark offence of the first Herod.

And of Peter we have heard how the substance of all pre-Christian initiation and old atavistic human forces are mightily present in him, how his strength flows from the magical use of the word. His mistake is that he cannot rely on these forces of the past. The Christian initiation that John achieved, taking place in the Crab, the bright counter-sign of the Goat, in the sign of the bright midday heights of consciousness, Peter consequently did not reach. He remained standing with the forces of the Goat, and those powers once again which operate that he remain standing there is the consciousness-darkening might of the Scorpion's sting of death. John had already in Mark 5 overcome this sting; Peter could not overcome it. The warning of Christ of the leaven of the Pharisees and of Herod (Mark 8:15) was lost on him—likewise the penetrating warning of the might of darkness, which Christ still immediately before Gethsemane addressed to Simon Peter (Luke 22:31).

In this glittering but yet premature and hasty confession of Christ by Peter at Caesarea Philippi (Mark 8:29) is revealed the might and inspiration of the 'bearer of light' (Lucifer) linked to the essence of the sign of the Ram. It is the logic of world-statutes that such a hasty and one-sided placing of oneself in the might of the 'bringer of light' also leads to the premature extinguishing of the light. The 'power of darkness' (Ahriman, cf. Mark 8:33) is called into these world-events. Ahriman is the 'karmic equalizer' of Lucifer. Peter had to experience in a world-historic harrowing manner this transition from the sphere of the 'bearer of light' (Lucifer) into that of the 'power of darkness'. Not only his 'denial' but his whole conduct in Gethsemane renders a tragic testimonial. Already Christ's question in Gethsemane (Mark 14:37), meaningfully and significantly addressed only to Peter, not to John, points in this direction: 'Simon, are you asleep? Could you not keep awake for one hour?'

Let us allow the whole picture of the arrest of Christ Jesus in Gethsemane to affect us (Mark 22:43-50, John 18:1-11). The deed of Judas, with all the awfulness and tragedy attached to it, seen from the human side, was nevertheless anchored in the depths of world-events. It was necessary for the completion of the Mystery of Golgotha. How does it stand in this context with Peter's behaviour in the Garden of Gethsemane? We hear of the high-priest's servant, and the ear that Peter cut off and then was healed by Christ (Luke 22:51)—in Mark the name of Peter is here respectfully withheld; John's Gospel written later names him, as it does the servant Malchus. We leave it open whether the story is to be outwardly taken as literal, or whether to go with Emil Bock. He explains in his *Studies in the Gospels* the sword stands here as the picture for the 'sword of the mouth', for the atavistic and magical use of the power of the word. That has much to say for itself; Peter wants, as it were, to thunder into the ground the captors of Christ through word-magic. One might compare the tremendous narration in John's Gospel (John 18:6), how the 'I-AM' of Christ works in this connection.

In any case, he wants to use forces that, if it were possible, would hinder the Mystery of Golgotha. This means, what he had not understood in Caesarea Philippi (Mark 8:32), also on the Mount of Transfiguration could not yet understand (Mark 9:5), he still did not understand here. He doesn't understand, but through his actions he will counteract Christ, prevent him from fulfilling the Mystery of Golgotha. One should consider the effect of all this. In Gethsemane, in the most terrifying, most critical of all moments for the world, Christ is left in the lurch by His own disciples, especially Peter (Mark 14:37). He has to engage all the [spiritual] powers of the world in order to keep Himself in His earthly body until the hour of Golgotha, in order to defeat the onslaught of hell through the white magic of heaven. Finally the tough, strained struggle, unique in world-history, in which the tip of the scale inclines now to one side, now to the other, and the bloody drops of sweat from the brow of

Christ fall to the ground, ends in victory for Christ. That moment when Judas with the squad storm in, the victory is achieved.

What does Peter do? If it were possible, even now he would reverse this highest and most difficult of all victories in the whole history of the world. He would hinder Christ in His necessary work to heal and advance the Earth and mankind. In this hour when Christ stands at the end of His physical, earthly forces, requiring His last exertion to effect the highest, most inconceivable of all martyrdoms, to fulfil a permanent deed for the world in complete uniqueness, it was necessary to direct strength to make reparation for the committed folly that could have annihilated the whole future of the world (Luke 22:51, cf. also John 18:11).

All this says in a tragically clear way how Peter's deed stands alongside that of Judas. One will receive the feeling how 'Peter's denial' (Mark 14:66-72, John 18:15-18, 25-27) basically is not at all so far removed from 'Judas' betrayal' as one perhaps believed. One could somewhat trivially say: Peter had the good fortune to be able to outlive his deed, which Judas did not manage to do (Matt. 27:5); for him it was a moral impossibility. The truth, most expressively portrayed by John, is that in the behaviour of Peter in the *οὐκ εἰμί* ('I am not') that he says there (John 18:25), the complete negation of the I-am, expresses the darkening of conscious leading as far as the extinguishing of consciousness. But this darkening of consciousness also manifests in Judas. According to human 'criminal' viewpoints we can make neither the one nor the other responsible for his deed. We can only look on, shocked, at what the most terrible of the powers of death (♏) is able to cause in human consciousness, in the consciousness of the best, the most chosen. Peter too would have belonged to those who wanted the greatness of Christ in the Jewish Messianic sense (John 6:15 leads to this conclusion). In Gethsemane he experiences the most terrible of all disappointments regarding Christ that simply robbed him of his 'I'-consciousness. Most tragically, it showed how far removed his confession of Christ at Caesarea Philippi was from a real confession of Christ. Neither Judas nor Peter basically had an inkling of what spiritual Being was sojourning with them and what the earthly tasks of this Being were.

The passage in Mark 11:21 stands in a very significant inner connection with the behaviour of Peter in Gethsemane. Christ curses the 'fig tree' because the time of old 'atavistic', magical clairvoyant human forces in now past (see p. 259f.), but Peter holds on; because he does not understand this, he would still like to work with such forces of the past.

***

As we have discussed, Mark portrays in the most obvious manner, how much the darkening of the consciousness of Peter and Judas darkens the spiritual atmosphere lying over the *whole* group of disciples. Judas' betrayal and Peter's denial in themselves prepare and carry this (Mark 14:18-20, cf. John 13:21-26). With the earlier crises, the whole group became involved. Mark 8 tells initially only of Peter's crisis. But through the story of the possessed boy in Mark 9, whom the disciples could no longer heal, it becomes clear to what degree the other disciples are drawn into this crisis.

Thus it is also with the ending of the group of disciples in Mark 14. Not only Judas—who takes another exit from the situation he produced—and Peter are as though overthrown by what happened, right to the complete extinguishing of their individual 'I'. It is the same with the group of disciples as a whole. The earlier-mentioned initiation of the Twelve has indeed long ago collapsed on itself through the episode of the possessed boy—whether we are dealing with a real earthly event, or the pictorial portrayal of a spiritual event (we adopted both viewpoints: see p. 206f.). It showed in full clarity that nothing remains over from this initiation, that a complete chaos of consciousness, a complete dissolution of consciousness has come about. Through the events of Gethsemane this dissolution becomes completely

acute; inner dissolution is joined by outer dissolution. The substance of the group of twelve, the earthly, physical as well as the spiritual and psychological marrow is dissolved; they are scattered to all the winds. These things are most clearly told in John's Gospel, at the end of the 'Farewell Discourses'. After directing quite the most deeply stirring words of love at the disciples, Christ prophesises how they will soon abandon Him: 'But a time is coming, and has come, when you will be scattered, each to his own home. You will leave me all alone' (John 16:32).

In this 'flight of the disciples' the might of the Scorpion's sting of death is revealed. It is the might that rips the human soul out of its connection with Christ's divine 'I'. It consigns scattering, isolation and abandonment in the isolation. The Greek word for this 'becoming scattered' is *σκορπισθῆτε*, from *σκορπισθζειν*. Its sounding (skorpizein) in harmony with the Scorpion points directly to the presence of this might of death that scatters, isolates and causes sinful apostasy (in German '*Sünde*' comes from '*sondern*'—in English 'sin' comes from 'sunder'). In John 10, speaking of the wolf and the sheep, where 'The wolf attacks the flock and *scatters* it' (John 10:12), we find the word *σκορπίζειν*. The 'wolf' referred to in this chapter is the earlier, pre-Christian impulse dissolving the 'I', that wants to replace the 'I'-impulse of Christ and the initiation resting on Him (John 10:8).

The souls striving towards the 'I'-impulse are the 'sheep', the 'I'-hostile adversary is the 'wolf'. In the case of the disciples, Herod and Herodias with their dark, 'I'-hostile Mysteries are the 'wolf'. They extinguish the consciousness of the disciples in Gethsemane. The disciples, disappointed in all their expectations, in all they imagine, have hit a brick wall through the events and no longer know who they are and what they want; they leave their Master in the lurch. Mark 14:50: 'Then everyone deserted him and fled.' In this tragically shattering sentence lies the tragically shattering event of the whole gospel story.

The black magic of the adversary did not reach Christ Himself. The preparatory and enabling victory of Gethsemane prevailed against its hindering the Mystery of Golgotha. It could succeed to darken the consciousness of the group of disciples and in this darkening to extinguish a part of Christ's earthly work. For a part of Christ's work on Earth at that time, despite all later Pentecostal experiences and other events, *was* extinguished. Through the 'leaven of Herod', about which Christ warned the disciples in vain (Mark 8:15), the bread of life of humanity became poisoned. Even the subsequent Church, despite all the Pentecostal experiences, the experiences of Paul and Paul's deeds, never more became what it could have become without this darkening of consciousness of Peter and the others. A dusky shadow of that darkening of consciousness lay over its whole history; in it too the sting of death of the Scorpion has not been overcome ...

***

John

Yet a great hope and confidence in Christ lived then and still lives today for the future of the Earth and of humanity—its name is *John* (cf. John 21:23). Referring back to the narration of Mark's Gospel, we have to ask, Where did John tarry when the disciples in Gethsemane fled? Did he also join the flight? But if this, as it appears, cannot be the case with him as Christ's initiate, if John was not amongst those fleeing, where is this stated in the gospel?

The first thing that has to be pointed out, is in so far as we take the 'flight' as an outer event—incidentally, it is something different, as will be shown—apparently Peter also made a tremendous effort to pull himself together consciously, to return to Christ and at least follow at a distance (Mark 14:54). Only thereby would the whole scene of denial be possible. The attempt still to hold on to himself, followed all the more by a deep fall, as with all Peter's previous assertions (Mark 14:20, Luke 22:33) that spring from his hot, premature enthusiasm, later only attract all the more the darkening of consciousness ('from Lucifer to Ahriman', see p. 310). With the narration of the 'denial', it is still discussed who apart from Peter went into the high-priest's palace as 'the other disciple' (John 18:15) in John's Gospel. Behind this phrase—in John's Gospel he is never named—we can presume it was John. The main point is and still remains, that John actually—whether physically or spiritually, or both—stood under the cross (John 19:26); as the Christ-initiate he had the task to witness the Mystery of Golgotha, and he did witness it. So he could not have fled, unlike the others who left Christ in the lurch.

However, this fact is also absolutely to be taken from the narration of Mark 14. Moreover, we come to the point where Mark's Gospel is revealed at its clearest as the actual Gospel of John (Introduction p. 51). John's initiation itself is presented in Mark's Gospel; the present exposition shows this in detail. After his becoming the initiate of Christ, he now has the task to witness the Mystery of Golgotha and, in a certain sense, assist. This begins already in the beginning of Mark 14 with the narrated 'last anointing'. This, however, is presented as the Johannine experience more clearly in John's Gospel (John 12). Thereby the special role ends, which John himself played in Christ's Last Supper, as the only one who consciously experiences communion with Christ. This, however, is directly narrated—that is, in an abundantly clear picture—only in John's Gospel (John 13:23, 25). Thereupon, there follows as something very significant, a 'Johannine deed in higher worlds', the angelic help of Gethsemane. This, however, is only narrated in Luke's Gospel (Luke 22:43).

But now, when it concerns whether he took part, or didn't take part, in the 'flight of the disciples', there follows the very decisive point for the whole Mystery of John, narrated only in Mark, and not in any other of the four gospels, 'unique material' *κατ᾽ἐξοχήν* (= eminently) of Mark's Gospel. It permits us to recognize Mark's Gospel as the 'Gospel of John' in the sense meant here. This is hidden in the picture of the story (Mark 14:51, 52) that introduces yet another aspect: 'A young man, wearing nothing but a linen garment, was following Jesus. When they seized him, he fled naked, leaving his garment behind.' Rudolf Steiner has already pointed to it, if we understand his indications correctly, and Emil Bock has developed it in his *Studies in the Gospels* [Vol. 2, Chap. 14].

That the disciples in Gethsemane 'fled' (Mark 14:50), contains a double meaning. It means not only, though it signifies this too, that they left the Master in the lurch, but also relates spiritually that through the force of the experience they were completely beside themselves. In a certain sense their soul and spirit left their physical bodies. They fell into a condition of complete transport. Only the experience of Pentecost (Acts 2) resolved this. Then the disciples awoke as out of a dream. In a certain sense it can be said of John—who certainly did not leave Christ Jesus in the lurch, did not join the flight—that he had a part in the spiritual flight, this 'leaving the body', because of the force of events. But it is here similar to the 'slumber in Gethsemane'. The initiate, who had crossed the threshold of initiation, left the body in such cases differently from those who were uninitiated. For the latter, this leaving is a 'fleeing' in darkening of consciousness. In his 'flight'—understanding the word in the spiritual sense—the death sign of the Scorpion governs. An initiate, in leaving his body, consciously steps into the light of the spiritual world. Over him the sting of death has no more power.

This distinction, too, is not, for instance, only 'dragged into' the gospel, but Christ speaks of it in Chapter 13, the 'apocalyptic' chapter of Mark's Gospel, which in its details we have neglected. One dark saying is Christ's words: 'But pray ye that this flight be not in the winter' [Mark 13:18 KJV/AV]. What is meant here?

Instead of the picture of this distinction of day-consciousness and night-consciousness in leaving the body (in 'becoming free of the body'), we could use another picture, that of the summer and the winter. As the day in the rhythm of the year corresponds to the summer, the night does to the winter (cf. Introduction, p. 25). If we take in this

sense not 'four seasons' of the year, but only 'summer and winter', similar to 'day and night', when does winter begin? Not yet in the beginning of the autumn, but at all events when in late autumn the leaves from the tree fall, when the life of nature dies. (For the essence of the matter, always take such considerations in the context of the 'temperate zone' [of the Northern Hemisphere], if possible somewhere in its middle.) This death in nature happens in November, when the Sun stands in the sign of the Scorpion. The gospel saying of Christ, of the 'flight in winter', is none other than the impression of the seal of the word for the activity of the Scorpion's might of death. As for the other signs which in these considerations touch on other sayings in the gospel, that of the 'flight in winter' stands for the essence of the Scorpion, for its consciousness darkening and consciousness-extinguishing sting.

What Christ in Mark 13—whether in outer teaching or in the spiritual experience of John—still placed as a warning and danger for the disciples, as something about which they should pray, that it should not happen to them, that is ultimately that which in reality did happen, after the crisis had come. It is exactly as with the warning about the 'leaven of Herod' [Mark 8:15], which in the end did poison the 'bread of life'. They leave their bodies in Gethsemane, at the height of the crisis, become free of the body, but this occurs in the deep night-consciousness and darkening of consciousness. Their flight is toward the 'flight in winter', in the sign of the Scorpion. But in the nocturnal encompassing of their consciousness—or does only the initiate-consciousness of John behold the whole event?—they still have the vision of the one. The 'might of darkness' has no part in this consciousness. He did not leave the body in the consciousness-darkening and nocturnal encompassing of consciousness, but consciously entered the light of the spiritual world. When he did leave the body, it was not 'in winter'; he did not 'flee' under the lordship of the consciousness-darkening sign of death.

In the midst of the black darkness, in which the others stand, the one [John] appears, who follows Christ.[39] Already now he bears the impulse of Christ's resurrection, as the 'youth with the [white] linen garment' (Mark 14:51). His path of destiny had now decisively separated him from that of the others; they were no longer able to keep him with them: 'When they seized him, he fled naked, leaving his garment behind.' Already with the 'youth with the [white] linen garment', we are not to think perchance on the outer figure of John, but on his spiritual-etheric being[40]—the appearance told in the chapter on the resurrection (Mark 16:5) lies in a quite similar sphere. Moreover, 14:52 has a pure pictorial, playful, dreamlike and shadow-like quality. The 'playful, dreamlike' trait that surfaces here and there in Mark's narration (cf. p. 144f.) appears here to a marked degree. We stand before one of the most important secrets, before one of the most decisive passages of the whole of Mark's Gospel.

***

The crisis ending now in the Scorpion takes hold not only of the group of disciples, the Eleven, but enters many other groups. This can be more clearly recognized in John's Gospel, where the description of pure facts is so often shown to be the more reliable than the other three gospels (Introduction, p. 20f.). In John 6, where the group of disciples is first mentioned, other groups of disciples are mentioned, who doubting the word of Christ and the 'I' of Christ, leave the Master (John 6:66). Christ then asks the Twelve whether they also want to leave, and Peter ardently replies with his confession. The situation approximately corresponds to that of Mark 8. The end of the chapter (John 6:70-71) significantly contains the indication of Judas' betrayal.

The following chapters (John 7-11: for a detailed exposition of these things see the sequel on John's Gospel) then shows how the crisis becomes a crisis of humanity. The Christ-'I', placing itself among humanity in human souls awakes the contradiction, the schism, the crisis. All this then breaks out in shrill discords, in terrible conflicts. To be sure, this 'crisis of humanity' was revealed initially only in the

Jewish people, but it would have happened exactly the same anywhere else. The group of disciples are a partial manifestation of the great *crisis of humanity*, the part revealed in the direct company of Christ. And this crisis of humanity is released through nothing other than that the true human 'I' lost in the Fall of man, has been placed among humanity in Christ. This demands all the might of the adversary lurking and slumbering in the human soul. John's Gospel alone portrays this crisis of humanity in its complete extent, tragedy and terror. And this portrayal is once again important to understand the other gospels and the Mystery of Golgotha. The expression always used here, 'crisis', is no 'invention' or something arbitrary dragged into the gospel, but (as already mentioned on p. 208) used always in this sense by Christ precisely in John's Gospel. *κρίνειν* (from which the word *κρίοις* (*krisis*), 'crisis' derives) means 'divide, separate', and that 'I' in Christ placed into humanity, its own, lost, divine 'I', is that which causes the division of spirits, the division of light and darkness (John 3:19 and many other places).

In Mark's Gospel (Mark 14:51, 52), the vision so peculiarly presented of the fleeing, white youth is a picture for that which in the crisis of the group of disciples now divides into light and darkness. John flees into the light of the spiritual worlds, the others fall to the might of darkness. Mark places in Chapter 14:51, 52 the John-experience of the crisis of the disciples. This Johannine experience depicted by Mark then flows into the tremendous presentation of the crisis of humanity over Christ in John's Gospel. The whole presentation of Mark's Gospel, including the final chapters, is most rightly understood, when you say to yourself: it does not have to do with the mere telling of Judas' betrayal, Peter's denial, and so on. But it has to do with how the initiate-consciousness of John assimilates all these things, so that John later can become the helper and support of the Church, struggling so hard for its existence, already in its beginnings and point of departure threatened by the powers of the abyss.

***

Pontius Pilate

Although the presentation of the actual 'crisis of humanity', as it is portrayed particularly in John's Gospel, has to remain reserved for the exposition of John's Gospel, nevertheless it has at least to be mentioned in the exposition of Mark's Gospel. Without this viewpoint it is not possible to understand the Mystery of Golgotha. It reaches its climax in the call of the crowd to 'Crucify!' (Mark 15:13, 14), contrasting so shockingly with the previous mood of 'Hosanna'. We have seen how the will of Christ Himself is at work in this sudden change (see p. 248ff., 257ff.).

In these contemplations on Mark's Gospel we have to touch on the crisis of humanity, especially where it meets us in one of the most prominent representatives of humanity at that time, in Pontius Pilate. He joins the two tragic figures revealed especially in the Scorpion's power of death in Mark's Gospel, Judas and Peter, as a third great and tragic personality inwardly bound to the being of this sign, that of the procurator Pontius Pilate. World-destiny determined that he should speak the death penalty ('*Condemno, ibis in crucem*') over Christ Jesus. He stands before us as a significant representative of humanity, that is, a representative of what humanity was then, what had become of it through the Fall of man. Thus he stands facing the Other, the true Representative of Humanity, Christ Jesus. It is the greatest and most harrowing drama of the entire happenings of the world. No dramatist has hitherto presented it.

Although it is seen only by very few, Pontius Pilate belongs to the most tragic personalities of the whole New Testament, of the whole Biblical history. His tragedy tops that of Peter, and in some aspects also that of Judas. The aspect of world-historical necessity, how it stands to the deed of Judas, not for that of Peter, also concerns what Pilate did. Also his deed was a great world-historic sacrifice, for without Pilate the Mystery of Golgotha would not have been possible. The judgement of Oswald Spengler in *Decline of the West* on [the question of] Pontius Pilate: *'das einzige Wort im Neuen Testament, das Rasse hat'*,

'the one word in the New Testament that shows quality, breeding', is spiritually incorrect, yet contains the presentiment of something significant.[41]

As Judas stands as the typical representative of Judaism within the group of disciples, Pilate stands as the representative of Romanism. Judaism and Romanism, which under Judas Maccabaeus, the spiritual forefather of the other Judas, made a pact (I Macc. 8), are the two governing powers in the time of Christ Jesus. These are the two powers in which the power of death, especially in its historical expression, stands over the whole section. There are pictures showing the Roman legionaries bearing the Scorpion on their uniform. If that is historically correct, it is at the same time inwardly meaningful.

On this pact made between the Romans and the Jews rests the compromise situation which Christ scrapped without any regard in the 'Cleansing of the Temple' (Mark 11:15-17) and answering the question of 'tribute tax to Caesar' (Mark 12:13-17). We have seen (p. 249) how in this lies the historical cause of His death.

We have discussed the connection of Judaism with the Scorpion's power of death. How is this relationship with Romanism? The great historical impulse, the actual greatness of Romanism, lay in the development of personality, of the 'I'—but the lower personal 'I', or self—and resting on it the concepts of the state and concepts of legal rights. We find that personal element, the 'I'-impulse in its lower, personal form, expressed in a concentrated form in Roman law, which has determined all modern law, as the Roman concept of the state has determined the modern concepts of the state. As in Judaism, the Scorpion's power of death governs in this whole Roman concepts of rights and of the state and in the manner the personal human alienates the truly human, the higher 'I'. It is not by chance but the inner harmony of world-history, that the earthly appearance of Christ Jesus, as the Representative of the higher 'I', or Self, of humanity, coincides in time with this personal revelation of humanity's 'I' in Romanism. In Jesus and Pilate the representatives

of both sides of the 'I' stand facing each other in a significant world-historical manner.

The tragedy of Romanism, that which constitutes its greatness, through the highest intensification of the will to personal power in the lower self, was the surrender of that humanity and the original divine spark in humanity. Christ clearly shows in his answer to the question of paying taxes to Caesar (Mark 12:17), that a compromise between counter-divine and the divine is not possible. The Roman Caesar appears the highest representative of that counter-divine will to power. Rudolf Steiner (Lectures 5-7, Berlin, 14, 17 & 19 April 1917, of his lecture-cycle *Building-Stones for an Understanding of the Mystery of Golgotha* [GA 175. Berlin, 27 March–8 May 1917]) has shown how the Roman Caesars with their will to power did not remain in the sphere of earthly politics, but moved over into the spiritual sphere by forcing a kind of initiation. This, however, was a 'dark' initiation comparable to that of Herod and Herodias. Here too lay the tragedy of Pilate's fate. Through the hopeless disappointment he experienced with Christ, he was finally brought together with Herod, with whom he was hitherto at enmity (Luke 23:12).

The will of the world had decreed that he who in the hour deciding world-destiny stood as judge facing the Representatives of Humanity, Christ Jesus, then has Him flogged and nailed to a cross, is none of the simple ignorant and 'harmless' people who then cry 'crucify!' who 'do not know what they do', but a high, or yet not insignificant, initiate. As such he stands facing Christ Jesus full of expectation. In one of his early lectures, Steiner once pointed out how already the name Pontius Pilatus = *Πόντος πυλητός* (*Pontos Pyletós*), contains an indication of initiation Mysteries, of the 'door of initiation'. Such endeavours played a great role in Rome of that time, which was 'tolerant' towards all possible foreign cults and Mysteries. Pilate was certainly one of the most splendid representatives of this endeavour. The passage in Matt. 27:19 best shows how in his personal sphere he was in touch with occult, atavistic, clairvoyant forces. It lay completely

far from him personally to hold Christ Jesus to account for something or other that set Him and the Jews at variance, or even to crucify Christ Jesus—behind Whom he sensed something spiritually above the normal, something super-humanly significant. The Romans had no interest at all to prepare some sort of 'unpleasantness' for this, to them, indifferent Galilean. Much rather they would have brought the Jews to account for what had happened (it had to do especially with what is recorded in Mark 11:15-18, or the events intended there), which then would have cost them their holy of holies (see above, p. 248). To hinder this, from their standpoint, they had no other means than the process against Christ Jesus.

It is the shocking tragedy of the situation, that Pontius Pilate, the prominent representative of Romanism, himself a Roman from head to toe, who had only disrespect for the Jews and everything Jewish, stood there before the Jews completely unfree. The Jews cleverly played out precisely his Romanism against him (John 19:12). He had to do what the Jews wanted, and could not do what he wanted. And what the Jews did, again in another way, was unfree in so far as they stood completely in thrall to what was past, handed down and finished. They were captives of their fear. They wanted to stop an event of the future that yet is not stoppable. Pilate is unfree, because precisely in his Romanism there lies that which makes him unfree in the face of the despised Jews. It is the greatest and most serious of all the tragedies of human unfreedom that have been, of that unfreedom closely connected with the causes of the Fall of man and the Scorpion's power of death at work in it.

And in the midst of this shocking tragedy of human unfreedom there stands as the only One who is free, Christ Jesus acting out of free decision (see above, p. 249), going into death out of unconditional love, scorned and spat upon by the people, scourged and crowned with thorns, and finally nailed to the cross. *Freedom in the 'I'*, stood facing the unfreedom of those who have lost their 'I' through the Fall of man to the adversary of humanity.

With all this the tragedy of Pilate is still not exhausted. As an initiate, at least to a certain degree, of spiritual knowledge, as a knower of all possible Mysteries and hidden strivings, he carries a high opinion as a feeling in his soul of the Galilean who has landed in conflict with the Jews. He divines something, feels something of the spiritual greatness of Christ Jesus. At the same time he sees how the Jews do *not* recognize the greatness of Christ, how they revolt against this spiritual greatness with a motive that seems to him, the Roman, most insignificant. For this he despises them even more.

However—and in this lies precisely the tragedy, the tragedy of humanity, of Pilate's drama—as an initiate of those Mysteries, with their view and outlooks that were then common, he can only see in the greatness of Christ Jesus some kind of initiate greatness. As an initiate, as he thought of himself, he hoped to receive from a greater initiate on deep questions of life some teachings on world-secrets. He had heard of the deeds of Christ Jesus, which had made a stir to the highest degree and, as it seemed, strongly touched on magic, and wants now to satisfy his occult inquisitiveness, as similarly Herod did (Luke 23:8-12)—with him, Pilate, it probably was a more noble striving for knowledge. Especially here, he experiences—as Herod did before him, who had hoped for the performance of all possible occult phenomena—the greatest of all disappointments. The most impressive here is the narration of John's Gospel. Questioned about His ostensibly claimed kingdom, Jesus answers that His Kingdom—if we take the words here freely, according to their meaning—lies not in the sphere of the Roman Caesar, not in the realm of Ahriman, over whose means of power the Roman Caesar rules, but in the realm of truth.

Especially this word of Christ, truth, releases in Pilate's soul the most terrible shock, the most horrifying of all disappointments. For his concepts from the Mysteries, all talk of truth in a human sense is a long-overcome viewpoint, a long-overcome illusion. We also know of Buddha, how he regarded all philosophizing, dogmatizing and theorizing on questions of knowledge as something lying deeply below

his sphere. He regarded it as something removed from reality (see H. Beckh. *Buddha's Life and Teaching*, 108-12, esp. 111). And in the Mysteries in which Pilate felt spiritually at home, there may have existed a kind of 'occult theory of relativity'. For the divine meaning anchored and carrying the reality of the world, in which Christ speaks of truth—the Greek *ἀλήθεια* expresses at the same time something like the completely clear, bright consciousness governed by the 'I', anchored in cosmic reality—he, Pilate, had no organ. In his consciousness Pilate now experienced the deep disappointment; he sees, or believes he sees, He whom he took for an initiate or even a higher initiate, is nothing of all that. He possesses no 'higher knowledge' at all, he has not even started on the lowest rung of what he, the Roman, imagines of a higher culture of the spirit. In his subconscious he experiences something different; there he experiences something like a deep shock, a deep horror of something to him completely unknown, ungraspable, not somehow reachable or fathomable through any of the normal Mystery-concepts. Both the deep disappointment and the deep shock are present in the tone of his question, 'What is truth?' It is the tone of this question in no way a mere contemptuous cynicism, but the question is asked out of certain Mystery depths and human depths, out of the complete distress of soul, with which he, the initiate, enters, placed before the boundaries of all human knowledge. Was the disappointment, was the terror of Pilate justified? What was unfathomable that so shocked him in the depths of his subconscious?

He thought to find an initiate in Christ, a high initiate who knew still more than he himself, and what he found was *no initiate*—thus the disappointment—but He was *the human being*. Rudolf Steiner always showed how the actual concept of the initiate cannot be applied to Christ Jesus, that he was not only an initiate, like another, perhaps a somewhat higher one. It was an initiate—Rudolf Steiner tells us—who earlier was immersed in the waves of the Jordan, a personality who carried the being of the greatest of all the initiates of humanity. What then arose after the Baptism out of the waves of the River Jordan, was in this sense no longer an 'initiate'. He had sacrificed his human 'I', made himself into a pure vessel of the divine, which now out of cosmic heights entered into him, that Divine Being Who had hitherto never inhabited a human body, the Christ. The unique thing of the Baptism in the Jordan was not that a human being had been raised to the rank of initiate or to a higher degree of initiation, but that therein a God became a human being, took on Himself the condition of humanity. Thereby He placed again into humanity the human 'I' and blueprint of the human being lost through the Fall of man. If the Christ were an initiate like the others, only of a special eminence, Pilate would have been able to grasp the fact with his own initiation and Mystery concepts. But all the concepts of the initiates of that time no longer sufficed to grasp that the *human being*, the human Mystery revealed in Christ, was standing before him.

All pre-Christian initiations, as they had become in the time of Pilate, fell apart at the *secret of the human being*, at the Mystery of Golgotha. According to its archetypal decree and in the times of its archetypal blossoming, all pre-Christian initiation was aligned towards this Fact of humanity, prophesied in particular in the Mysteries of Zarathustra. When this Fact became a real Deed, it produced the effect of annulling everything still living as Mystery knowledge. Everything could be grasped there, but not *the human being*. Humanity of those days had sunk deep under the niveau of what is human, unbelievably deep according to our ideas today, all-too-deep one would like to say; the sting of the Scorpion was anchored into the flesh of humanity. And particularly the greatness of Romanism lies on this estrangement from what is actually human.

In the behaviour of Pilate, too, one thinks of Luke 23:16, this Roman unfamiliarity with actual humanity is strongly expressed. He would have given every possible respect to the initiate. He would have tried and really did try to remove Him from the tribunal of Jerusalem (Luke 23:6, 7), and pass Him on to Herod, who also hoped for much from Jesus. The disappointment he experienced with Christ changed the expectant respect into immeasurable contempt. He expects no more out of the 'Galilean', sees in Him, at least in his consciousness, only a Jew like all the others. And as a Roman he deeply despised the Jews. He would probably have tried to protect the Jews from the 'initiate' and super-man he initially presumed He was. The Jew whom he now thought he saw before himself, he surrenders with cold disdain to the Jews. In his consciousness at least he was coldly disdainful; nevertheless, in subconscious depths, out of the Mystery depths of his being—especially Matthew reports on this (Matt. 27:19-24)—a puzzling, almost superstitious fearful conscience arises that seeks protection in a ceremony recalling something cultic (v. 24). In every soul, the hidden discord from the Fall of man, [brought out] by Christ, appeared in Pilate in harrowing dimensions.

And the greatest of all and most harrowing thing is this. To that knowledge which he could not grasp in his consciousness—the Fact standing before him, upon which he inwardly fell apart—something came out of the most hidden depths of his unconscious. Intentionally mocking, in reality it was prophetic as a great world-historic revelation, a fulfilment of all the Mysteries. Over the scourged Christ Jesus, crowned with thorns the spikes of which dig deep into His head, he utters the words: 'Behold the man' *Ἰδοὺ ὁ ἄνθρωπος / ecce homo* (John 19:5).

The Revelation of Death in the Archer: Golgotha (Mark 15:20ff.)

The Goat, Waterman, Fishes: The Turning Point of the World, the Grave and Resurrection (Mark 15:38-41, 42-47, Mark 16)

In looking at the three tragic figures of Judas, Peter and Pilate, we already stood in the midst of the Mystery of Golgotha. We saw this Mystery basically already beginning in the *Transfiguration of Christ on the Mount*, which like the cross on Golgotha stands in the zodiacal sign of the Archer, or rather begins in this sign, for like Golgotha it encompasses more than *one* heavenly sign. The death of Christ, as we saw, His dying into the Earth, had already begun at that time. The sign of the Archer in the Transfiguration expresses more what this process means for Christ and for the Earth; the Elijah-John-sign of the Goat and the Waterman expresses more what it means for John and his initiation. In the sign of the Fishes, in which the Transfiguration ends ('This is my Son, whom I love ...' NIV Mark 9:7), the Mystery of John touches the Mystery of the Sun of Christ.

In that which takes place from the Ram to the Crab and the Lion, we then saw how the initiation of John ends, but so that very strongly the earthly, historical side of the Mystery of Golgotha, the whole context of its earthly causes came to our notice. All this was assimilated by John as he was treading the path towards completing his initiation consciousness.

In the sign of the Virgin—the anointing of Christ through Mary Magdalene and the Last Supper—we then experienced the actual 'entry into the Mystery', the direct sacramental preparation for Golgotha. In the pictures of the gospels is expressed how, in going through his initiation, the disciple John takes active part in soul in the events of the Mystery of Golgotha. At the Last Supper he receives Communion differently from the others. In the alarming and critical hour of

Gethsemane, through his angelic powers he influences the outcome of the world-balance, so that the Mystery of Golgotha becomes possible. At the moment when Judas with the squad enter, the victory of Christ in Gethsemane is decided.

With Christ's victory in Gethsemane, this urge of Judas with the squad beginning the events that present in a still stricter sense the event of death on Golgotha; the events begin that lead directly to the earthly death of Christ Jesus. The zodiac sign of the Scorpion standing over this section helps us to see into the reasons for these events, especially the three figures of Judas, Peter and Pilate. Judas and Pilate are directly decisive for the accomplishing the Mystery of Golgotha, whereas Peter at the last minute wants to lay hindrances in the way of the effectiveness of this Mystery. The crisis of humanity connected with the death-sign of the Scorpion, a harrowing tragedy, is revealed in the figure of Pilate, whereas the betrayal of Judas, Peter's denial, and the 'flight of the disciples' in Gethsemane show how—always standing in the death-sign of the Scorpion—the 'crisis of the disciples' also ends in this sign, and how the saying of the 'flight in winter' points to the spiritual nature of this sign.

In this sense, especially in looking at Pilate, the whole section Mark 15:1-19 with the scourging and crowning with thorns, with the tremendous picture of the 'ecce homo' (John 19:5), still stands in the sign of the Scorpion.

The transition into the Archer, into the sign of consummating death, takes place in Mark 15:20: 'And when they had mocked him, they took off the purple robe and put his own clothes on him. Then they led him out to crucify him.' Here begins in the strictest sense the event of death on Golgotha, the crucifixion itself.

Only the initiate-consciousness of John is able to a certain degree to penetrate into that which are no longer human experiences and human suffering, but experiences, suffering and deeds of a God, into this revelation of the most exalted love for the world. This, as Rudolf Steiner often says, can only be understood through human love. To us,

the guide to this love is John, the 'disciple of love', whose becoming and development to an initiated disciple of Christ stands in the focus of Mark's Gospel.

An important point, that already leads us into John's Gospel, should be mentioned. It has to do here, not only with throwing light on world-backgrounds and contexts of the picture of Christ Jesus hanging on the cross, not only on Christ's sufferings and His deed. It has also to do with *how these sufferings* and this deed—which otherwise could somehow be assimilated into the consciousness and be grasped by none of the people of that time, even of the disciples, and least of all by Peter, the 'rock of the Church'—*is carried and witnessed by the disciple John.* Through this it is saved for the consciousness of later humanity. This carrying and witnessing of the Mystery of Golgotha through the disciple of Christ spiritually flows into John's Gospel, the most significant of all the documents of humanity.

In John's Gospel itself this fact is expressed through the *picture of the disciple standing under the cross.* Under the cross of Christ, John is united with Mary the mother—though no doubt it also corresponds to the physical reality. A new Mystery takes place here with John, even leading beyond the 'initiation', a Mystery we can sense when we recall especially Mark 10 (see the exposition p. 214f.). Here took place the Mystery of Spirit-man, which the primordial polarity of creation, that of male and female, was overcome in his own soul and spirit. The archetypal picture meant in Genesis 1:27 of the spiritual human being, with whom female and male were still bound together in the divine, is spiritually re-acquired (John 19:26, 27 is the counter-pole to Genesis 2:22). Among the great painters, Leonardo da Vinci sensed something of this Johannine secret and expressed it in the human countenance.

Only because he previously had already gone through the initiation, did John have the strength to stand under the cross to assimilate into himself, into his own soul, the whole world-encompassing suffering, the whole world-encompassing love of a God. This is why he had to penetrate through this entire experience of initiation, leading to

such heights and abysses, through such suffering, crises, tests and trials; this is why this Johannine spiritual path plays such a decisive role in Mark's Gospel. Of the others, who had not gone through the initiation, none had the strength 'to stand under the cross'. They already broke up at the great Communion of Christ's Last Supper; they were then really shattered at witnessing the cross. Initially it was only the weakness of their souls that was revealed through everything that Christ accomplished near them. Through the great experience of the Last Supper this weakness of their souls became an acute crisis. The cross that already as an Intuition was present in this experience of the Last Supper, they were not able to bear. At the deepest level, it was also what caused their flight in Gethsemane (Mark 14:50).

The events could not go otherwise than they did. Every human consciousness that was not strengthened through initiation has to be broken by them. No human consciousness today is in the position to approach grasping what the cross on Golgotha, what the accomplishing of the Mystery of Golgotha through Christ Jesus actually signifies, what depths of suffering for the world and love of the world it includes. But just as little is human consciousness today equally unable to grasp what this carrying of the great Mystery of the world through the disciple John and the Johannine consciousness was, what was involved in *standing under the cross*. A deed was brought into effect that led still unimaginably far beyond what was already lived through and suffered in the initiation. Dark forces are evoked by a compassionless witnessing of the suffering of any creature. This 'standing under the cross' carried by deepest love and deepest compassion, this witnessing and suffering of the entire suffering of the world and the suffering of humanity created a divine strength of the highest white magic. This is that earthly transforming power of a higher alchemy which gives meaning and content to *Johannine Christianity* today and further on, today first to be imagined, here and there preparing the future of the Earth and the future of humanity.

***

From the Archer, the sign of 'deep midnight' and of death, in which the events of *carrying the cross* and the *crucifixion* till the death of Christ on the cross (Mark 15:20-37) are to be thought, let us look to the counter-sign of the Twins, to the sign of the 'great midday' and of the Sacred Mount. The connection is revealed of the events of Golgotha with those of the 'Mount of Transfiguration'. We look from the 'Mount of Transfiguration' down to the other, most Sacred Mount, on which the 'three crosses of Golgotha' stand. These three crosses themselves shine spiritually, as in the event of the Transfiguration and in the heavenly sign to which it is allocated, so also they shine in the event of Golgotha and in the heavenly script expressing this event.

The Last-Supper constellation Virgin–Fishes (p. 66f.) together with the constellation Twins–Archer form the *great Christ-cross of the middle*, the cross of the etheric (see Introduction, p. 34f.). Here is revealed the connection of the events of Golgotha with the *secret of the Last Supper*—all this not only in a cultic meaning, but understood in the context of the great cosmic sacrifice of love of the Godhead in the development of Earth and humanity. This connection is then also received in the offering of the Mass of the [Western] Church, [the Liturgy of the Easter Church], and in The Act of Consecration of Man in The Christian Community, a Movement for Religious Renewal. In Christ's words of the Last Supper: 'Take, eat, this is my Body ... this is my Blood of the New Testament', this meaning of the Mystery of Golgotha is revealed.

What is decisive to understand the meaning of the Mystery of Golgotha is not what at that time already was taken up into the consciousness of people, but what passes over as the real substance of Christ and the seed of the future of the Earth. This is the event of the Holy Grail taking place on Golgotha, most intimately united with the events of the Last Supper and the Feedings (Mark 6 & 8, p. 142ff.). Those events stand under the constellation of the Fishes–Virgin; this, the event of Golgotha, stands in the constellation of the Twins–Archer, which primarily emphasizes the Archer, the sign of death. Both constellations

form the cross of Christ in the middle, at the same time the 'cross of the etheric' (Introduction p. 33f.). The Grail event is initially an etheric event, which, however, passes over into the physical, earthly element in order that, at the same time, a new, higher physical existence, the resurrection body and a resurrection Earth can come into being.

***

This passing over into the physical element takes place in the cosmic rhythm of the gospel with the death of the One who is crucified, in that the Goat follows the sign of the Archer, belonging to the 'cross of the physical'. We already know this sign from the beginning of Mark's Gospel as one of the two 'Elijah-John signs', in which the Baptist John points to the imminent Turning Point of the World and demands a change of thinking. In Christ's dying on the cross, the Mystery of Golgotha, the consecrating deed on Golgotha, is accomplished—the word *Τετέλεσται* 'It is finished, accomplished' (John 19:30) expresses in the language of the Mysteries the consecrated fulfilment. Now the Turning Point of the World, announced by John the Baptist, appears; now it has become present. It is fulfilled in the sign of turning—the mountain Goat. The rending of the veil of the Temple (Mark 15:38), with all the physical reality of the events (earthquake), is at the same time the picture of this Turning Point of the World. The Mystery of Death, otherwise concealed behind the veil in the 'holy of holies' of the Temple (see p. 84), is now, in the event of Golgotha, open. It is the 'open secret', placed before all the world, but in a completely new, life-carrying and future-carrying meaning, which [hitherto] the Jewish high priest still concealed. In death the secret of life was revealed. (See also Matt. 27:52, 53 and Sophie's words in Klingsohr's *Märchen* [in *Heinrich von Ofterdingen*] by Novalis:

> *Das große Geheimnis ist allen offenbart, und bleibt ewig unergründlich. Aus Schmerzen wird die neue Welt geboren, und in Tränen wird die Asche zum Trank des ewigen Lebens aufgelöst.*

(The great secret is revealed to all, and remains forever unfathomable. Out of pain is the new world born, and the ashes are dissolved into tears for a draught of eternal life.)

The mood of the sign of the Goat and its murkiness (see Introduction, p. 42) is expressed in the eclipse darkening the outer Sun, in the darkness which around the hour of the death on the cross lay over the whole land (Mark 15:33). And in the way the Elijah-secret is gently indicated in connection with that of Golgotha (Mark 15:34-46). The revelation of death of the angel of Elijah (see p. 197, also Luke 9:31) has now become the most sublime revelation of the world. The Elijah-sign of the Goat in Mark's Gospel never appears without Elijah also somehow being named (Mark 1:2, 6:15, 9:4, 12, 13; 16:34-37). Nothing reduces the passage (Mark 16:34-37), that here involves direct speech coming from the mouths of the unknowing and those who mock. Precisely the deepest secrets are not infrequently revealed in the gospel out of the mouths of the 'unknowing', not based on the Mystery-knowledge of the times. Thus Pilate too reveals what for himself and his Mystery-knowledge are ungraspable things, for that time the most hidden secrets of Christ: 'Behold the man' (John 19:5).

All the beings of the higher hierarchies that form the 'heavenly ladder of Christ' (John 1:51) now leave the fading body of Jesus of Nazareth on the cross, also, taking the lowest, the 'angel rung' of this heavenly ladder, the angel of Elijah leaves (Mark 15:34), who inclining for a long time towards the disciple John, was on the point of becoming the angel of John. Now he moves completely to John—this secret also lies at the basis of John 19:26. The suggested visionary event of Mark 14:51, 52—the flight of the 'young man with the linen wrap'—lies completely in this direction. (From here, too, from the seemingly divergent aspect expressed here, the scene in Mark 14:51, 52 becomes understandable, illuminated by Rudolf Steiner in the lecture-courses *The Gospel of Mark* and *Building Stones*.) In all these passages, as also Mark 16:5—with this scene, too, Steiner points in the same context—the secret of the Johannine angel is in the background.

The sign of the Waterman is always linked with the Elijah-John sign of the Goat. In the first octave of the Sun-rhythm, it was related to John's baptism by water, where at the same time we catch sight of the 'water of the etheric' world. As Jesus of Nazareth plunged into the waves of the Jordan, the sacrifice of John was at its first stage. In the second octave it appeared on a higher stage in the death of John the Baptist, which was also a sacrificial death. Here the sign of the Waterman no longer relates to the watery deeps and the etheric, but to the depths of the Earth, to which were entrusted the body of John the Baptist at his burial. Then the sign appeared in the third round, in the Transfiguration, and signified there again a stage of the sacrifice of Elijah-John. The Transfiguration has a specific alignment to the event in the Jordan (Mark 9:7 with 1:11); the burial of Christ to that of the Baptist John. Both stand in the sign of the Waterman (Mark 6:29 and 15:42-47). Here too we see the intensification of the meaning of the individual signs in the different rounds, spirals or octaves (see Introduction, p. 45f.). John the Baptist was only little bound to the physical Earth (Mark 1:6), he was the human being who lived more in the divine world; in Christ God united himself completely with the depths of humanity. Now in the Mystery of Golgotha He unites completely with the depths of the Earth. The earthly depths become planted with the heavenly, individual grain of wheat, the grain of wheat of the resurrection (John 12:24). In the entombment of Christ we touch on the most inner secret of Christ and the Earth.

***

In the sign of the Goat, with the death of the Crucified, the threefold progression of the Christ-Sun through the twelve holy heavenly signs is completed. The sign of the Goat and the Waterman (Turning-point of the World and the Entombment) already lead over beyond the 'three rounds'. At the beginning of Mark's Gospel these two signs form a kind of 'prelude', the 'Elijah-John Prelude' to the

Christ-Event—Mark 1. Here they appear, after the end of the third round, once again as the prelude to an event leading beyond the 'three years' of Christ's earthly ministry, lying in a higher sphere—to the *Resurrection* and to the Kingdom of the Resurrection. In it begins the realm of the angels—of whose preparation or foundation-stone laying, *Ἀρχὴ*, the beginning of Mark's Gospel speaks. It is the kingdom of 'Elijah who was to come' (*ὁ μέλλων ἔρχεσθαι*, Matt. 11:14), the Johannine Kingdom of Christ of the future of the Earth. Further details would lead us into the depths of John's Gospel. So we reserve it for the exposition of that gospel.

The final chapter on the Resurrection (John 16) is fragmentary and has to be taken with John 20 and 21. The rhythm of John's Gospel, at the beginning and in the middle is another, as presented in Part 2 of the sequel. The final chapter with the Mystery of Golgotha is congruous with that of Mark's Gospel. With the Resurrection the transition from Waterman to the sign of the Fishes occurs. The gentle mood of the Resurrection morning, as especially expressed in John 20, completely corresponds to the etheric sign of the Fishes. The counter-sign of the Virgin is emphasized in the appearance of Mary Magdalene. The constellation Fishes–Virgin is revealed here on a new level. We met it first as the constellation of the Jordan Baptism, the Feeding at night, and the revelation of Christ in the Transfiguration. Apart from its purely earthly reality, in the appearance of Mary Magdalene on the Resurrection morning there is expressed once again the part that the Johannine soul had in the Christ-event. In this is revealed how through his witness of Golgotha he can also experience the Resurrection at first hand—even though he appears from now on as the one accompanying and helping Peter.

John, too, tells of the 'appearances of the Risen One' only fragmentarily (John 20:30, 21:25). We can only sense that also in the heights of the sphere of the Resurrection once again the 'seven bright' heavenly signs of the zodiac are passed through, whereas the 'five dark' signs would then lead into the sphere of the 'ascension' (Mark 16:19).

Into this sphere Christ, by disappearing from the consciousness of His surroundings into the spiritual higher regions, at the same time links Himself completely with the physical Earth. The rhythm of the zodiac leads here increasingly out of the earthly-temporal into an event above the Earth and beyond time. Only the three rounds of Christ's earthly life lay in the earthly-temporal sphere. In these 'five dark signs' the Resurrection-event also disappears, as it were, from the sight of a felt 'cosmic rhythm'. We are only able to follow it through the 'seven upper' signs, at least where the two points of the horizon and the zenith shine to mark this arch. We experience the Resurrection morning in the sign of the Fishes, followed by the Resurrection-experience of Thomas (John 20:24-29) in the elevated sign of the Twins (the name Thomas means 'the Twin', John 11:16). (This experience of 'doubting Thomas' is in reality a great initiation-experience of the disciple who could not find initiation during the earthly life of Christ, but yet in his heart's yearning sought to unite with this initiation (John 11:16). The actual Johannine experience is related to the future of the Earth, that of Thomas relates to the present-day.)

The Resurrection event, as much as it is narrated in John's Gospel, finds its ending in this experience with the Risen One, which seems like a reminiscence of the experience of the Feeding and of the experience of the Last Supper (John 21). The 'Last-Supper constellation', always linked with the motif of Feeding of 'bread and fishes' of the signs of the Virgin and the Fishes, shines one more time. In this constellation forming in a certain way the middle point of the gospel, we see the gospel also finds its ending. All the details of this chapter rich in content and pointing to the future, in which ultimately also the relationship of Peter and John, that in the stories of Mark's Gospel play such an earnest and significant role shone over by the light of the future (John 21:20-23), belong to the exposition of John's Gospel.

***

From here we look back once more to Golgotha. From that climax of the gospel events, when on the cross of Golgotha the consecrated fulfilment of the great Mystery of the world is realized, where as we have seen in the 'heavenly starry script' the 'three crosses on Golgotha' shine, we look up to the starry heavens. Here too we find in the 'heavenly script' the picture of that greatest of all earthly events, in which the heavenly nature of the stellar spaces united with the earthly. We look on a midsummer night to the southern horizon. Already approaching its setting, the Virgin's star Spica still shines with its mild, loving, consoling light. Alongside it the constellation of the Scales is visible towards the south, dividing the Virgin from the threatening, sparkling, constellation of death of the Scorpion with its dragon-like tail. (The actual 'Scorpion sting' is not yet visible in our latitudes, but only visible in countries further south.) Human and world contexts, which have led to the Mystery of Golgotha and to the great crisis of mankind, appear here before the soul.

Then there follows at the horizon, fairly exactly in the south (the zodiac lies during the summer nights much flatter over the horizon than in winter) the point where the great heavenly stream of the Milky Way touches the horizon. There we see around the hour we are describing, with its many bright stars as though swimming in the mist of the Milky Way, towards the east a characteristic group of stars rearing over it, the *death constellation of the Archer* that reigned during the hour of Golgotha. Here the whole impression of this constellation is bound with that of the heavenly stream of the Milky Way—the early Indians called it the 'heavenly Ganga'—here we see, as it were, written in the heavenly starry script as out of the deed of death on Golgotha there springs a new stream of life bearing the future, a stream of cosmic life. We think of the 'sacred river of Paradise', of the 'four sacred rivers in Paradise' (Gen. 2:10-14), in whose secret everything of what is alive on Earth today is still closed as in a supersensory-etheric existence. [See H. Beckh, *Genesis* in *From the Mysteries.* TL 2020, 27ff., esp. p. 32.]

Here we can experience: in the spiritual etheric world, in the Paradise of mankind, the stream began which carries all later earthly life in itself, that earthly life that would have had to die, shrivel and dry up within itself, if a new living impetus had not come. In the same way there sprang out of the death on Golgotha the new life, the new river of Paradise, which changes and renews all the life of the Earth, containing and carrying in itself all the becoming of the future.

(This knowledge is found in a pictorial, liturgical form in an expressive ritual of the Roman church (consecration of the water of baptism on Easter Saturday), where in the *Das Messbuch der heiligen Kirche* by Anselm Schott (Herder, Freiburg i. B.), p. 362, we read: 'The priest divides the water on four sides in the form of the cross, in order to indicate that from the four-armed cross the flow of grace of the precious Blood streams in the four heavenly directions of the new Paradise.' Cf. also Rev. 22:1, 2.)

APPENDICES

Appendix 1

The Three Crosses on Golgotha and the Triangles of the Four Evangelists in the Zodiac

Christ, Lucifer, Ahriman and the 'Three Crosses on Golgotha'

At the end of our contemplations we arrived at the 'three crosses on Golgotha'. Let us look once more at the 'three crosses' from the aspect of the 'starry script' of the heavenly zodiac revealed in the 'cosmic rhythm' of Mark's Gospel. For the purposes of our whole contemplation, the twelve signs of the zodiac are arranged in these crosses. Already in the Introduction (p. 34f.) and repeatedly in the previous contemplations, we touched on this viewpoint. The three crosses were always referred to as the physical, etheric and astral crosses, or in more religious terms, *the cross of the Father, the Son and the Spirit*.

It could be asked, how can these three crosses tally with the 'three crosses on Golgotha'? Were not two thieves crucified to the right and left of Christ (Mark 15:27)? If we imagine the cross on which Christ hangs as the 'cross of the Son', from which springs the etheric stream of life (see the end of the previous chapter), how does it stand with the crosses of the Father and of the Spirit? What has the counter-divine to do with the divine?

Here, however, anthroposophy in particular shows how through the 'fall into matter', which results from the 'Fall of man', the original divine element, the divine primordial substance of the 'Fatherly Ground of the World', has become pulled down with the fall into matter. It has been drawn down into the world that bears in itself evil and death through the obscuring power of the dark adversary—that is, not in its objective reality, but for human consciousness today.

The Father has become to human beings a power of death; He has become obscure through the power of darkness, Ahriman. This is revealed in the gospel narrative so clearly through the way the Jews treat Christ. And the Spirit, too, is initially revealed in this era of humanity not in its true, but in a false form of light. It is revealed in that being, the 'bringer of light' that awoke in Peter the one-sided and premature insight, followed then by a so much deeper obscurity and darkening of consciousness. Between this 'light-bearer' (Lucifer) and this power of darkness (Ahriman), Christ holds the balance in the middle. The sequel on John's Gospel explores a specific section that expressively portrays this picture of the middle held by the Representative of Humanity between Lucifer and Ahriman.

Christ helps human beings to place themselves in the right, creative balance by overcoming the one-sided influence of these powers, between which all human life is arranged and placed. By helping to wrest human souls from the power of matter, the 'death of matter', Christ leads human beings from Ahriman back to the divine Father. The Spirit is revealed again in its true being—by helping to overcome the temptation also of the other seducer, Christ leads the human soul to the *Holy Spirit*. In the 'Holy Spirit' lies the overcoming of Lucifer, in the 'divine Father' that of Ahriman.

In Mark, this relationship of Christ to Lucifer and Ahriman forming the spiritual background is only briefly indicated (Mark 1:13); in Matthew 4 and Luke 4 the more detailed story is narrated of the 'Temptation of Christ'. Coming out of cosmic heights and diving into earthly corporeality and matter in the event at the River Jordan, He there has to meet first both 'adversaries' governing in that earthly region. Out of spiritual research, Rudolf Steiner has shown how the last of the three temptations of Christ told in Matthew's Gospel contains the overcoming of Lucifer, the first the coming to terms with Ahriman, and the middle temptation with the dismissal of Lucifer and Ahriman—who appear together. Luke's order is different.

Apart from a brief mention in the *Annals* of Tacitus (15, 44), there are no historical documents to prove the physical, historical reality of the scenes in the gospels. If we may take any picture of the gospels in that full sense of physical, historical reality, we may take the picture of Christ crucified between the two thieves (Mark 15:27). But at the same time it is also in a spiritual sense a tremendous picture for the relationship of the three powers governing earthly life. The picture shows how the world has become since the 'Fall of man', the divine is crucified between Lucifer and Ahriman. But it also shows how it is the redemptive power of Christ that leads the counter-divine again to the divine.

We also see this tremendous picture in the starry script, in the three times four signs of the heavenly zodiac. In this heavenly script the three crosses shine again in the light of their divine origin. They shine there as they do in the spiritual world, not as they are seen on Earth. The 'three crosses on Golgotha' reveal themselves as the cross of the Father, of the Son and of the Spirit.

***

The Cross of the Father

Out of the contemplations that simply followed the course of the gospel narrative, of the rhythm of the narrative leading three times through the twelve heavenly signs, let us now turn to a contemplation that looks less for the earthly and temporal, than for the inner lawfulness of this rhythm. For this inner lawfulness, the relationship of these 'three crosses' appears as something more real, in a much deeper sense the spiritual contexts of what is revealed in the gospel, than the presentation following the earthly and temporal events. In a certain pictorial and spiritual sense—from which we initially keep distinct from all mathematical concepts—we can see the 'three crosses' as the 'spiritual quadrature' of the heavenly zodiac. If the linking lines are not taken through the middle but outside the circle, one can also imagine it as three squares.

Ram–Scales

Let us look initially at the 'cross of the Father' (see the Fig. on p. 364 for this and what follows); it has as the cross beam the constellation Ram–Scales. Of all the constellations, it is the one—easily seen in the Figure—that lies in the bright, upper part of the zodiac, even if the Scales already forms the transition to the darkness. This already expresses the relationship of that questionable sign to the earthly forces, to the world of day-consciousness.

Here on the first level, round or octave of the Sun-rhythm, we see how Christ places Himself into earthly activities in the sign of the Ram (Mark 1:21f.), after passing through the Baptism in the Jordan, descending out of cosmic heights. This correcting, standing upright, placing oneself correctly into the earthly forces of the Ram, is revealed especially in the 'healing of the demoniac'. Where in the third round, again in the Ram, the possessed [epileptic] boy, whom the disciples could no longer heal, was healed through Christ, there appears in the gospel the saying of getting up and standing upright (Mark 9:27), so rightly revealing the essence of the Ram. On the first level, in the first round, all this is *picture*.

The second round concerns the disciples having to receive certain forces into the understanding of the heart in spiritual pictures, and to bring these securely into the physical realm, from the experiences at night to the shore of the day-consciousness (Mark 6:54). Here it moves up from the stage of Imagination to that of Inspiration. On the third stage it is to become Intuition, embraced in the depths of being, and does so for John in the Transfiguration.

Nine disciples are excluded; as picture for the failing forces of the others, the possessed boy appears. Out of the forces of Intuition, they should now heal him themselves, unite him soundly with the forces of the Earth, but they cannot do so. With all this, what the disciples have to wrestle through in soul is revealed especially in the Scales, the counter-sign of the Ram. In the Scales we initially find the struggle for inner balance, the Storm on the Lake (Mark 4:35ff.)—the story of the demoniac ['Legion'] in Mark 5 also points in this direction. Then, after a similar situation in the same constellation Ram–Scales (but this time the Ram is emphasized) another Storm on the Lake is undergone (Mark 6:47ff.). The peaceful voyage on the lake (Mark 8:10ff.) is found in the Scales, in the successful advance of the disciples from Imagination to Inspiration, from receiving to giving—expressed in the 'Feeding of the Four Thousand'. And the Healing of the Blind Man, which is a picture for how Christ wakens spiritual seeing in the disciples, takes place in this sign. Here Christ trains the consciousness of the disciples when the Scales appear in the second stage.

The meaning of the Scales in its highest intensification is revealed in the third stage. Here we see Christ Himself in the most intense anxiety for the world struggling for inner balance, involving the possibility to maintain Himself in His earthly body until the hour of Golgotha. We see Him wrestle from fiendish adverse powers the victory of inner balance, which then makes possible the fulfilment of the Mystery of Golgotha. The balance of the whole Earth was at stake; He, abandoned by His own, struggled alone in Gethsemane, only strengthened by angelic forces. Christ brings the shuddering and reeling equilibrium of the world back into balance. Here is revealed in utmost clarity why it has to do with the constellation Ram–Scales, the cross of the Earth, the cross of the physical element, the forces of the Earth.

Crab–Goat

No less clearly this 'cross of the physical element'—when we move from the cross beam to the longitudinal beam—is shown in the sign of the *Crab* that forms the top of this cross. Here initially everything negative of the physical, material existence is revealed, everything coagulating, causing illness in the blood, all human illness and human blindness. On the first stage, in the first octave, all this meets Christ and the disciples as in an outer picture (Mark 3:21ff.). On the highest stage, at the end of Mark 10, the disciple becoming John beholds it in Intuition, the motif of the 'blind who see in the midst of blind sighted people' there is revealed to him the whole blindness and darkness of humanity. In the first octave the expression of 'entering a house' (Mark 3:20, Luther [1534]: *sie kamen zuhause*, 'they came home') appears; here at the highest stage the depression of Jericho (Mark 10:46) as picture for the element contained in the sign of the Crab, of the descent and downward path. John does not stay with these negative elements in the sign of the Crab; with him the Crab in the meaning of Christian initiation becomes the sign of the metamorphosis, the transformation of matter (Mark, Chapters 11–13). From the descent He wrenches the ascent, from death the new life, the resurrection. In the Johannine initiation, the weight of the Earth is overcome, the new Earth is revealed, the Earth of Light, the resurrection-temple of the future of the Earth (Mark 13). The 'materialism' belonging to the Crab appears even there in an enhanced, alchemical form.

Thus the initiation of John ends precisely in the Crab, which is closely united with the Lion. The Christian initiation ends in the bright light of consciousness—this is indicated by this sign standing closest to the high-point of the zodiac. The pre-Christian initiation still stands in the dark counter-sign of the mountain Goat, that is, here the light of day-consciousness has to be extinguished, if the higher consciousness is to be found. In this sign Buddha finds his enlightenment; in this we find in the gospel the last great pre-Christian initiate, John the Baptist; here he holds his sermon 'change your thinking' that is repeated in the gospel linked with the motif of the Goat. Each new appearance of this sign signifies a new stage of the sacrifice of John the Baptist.

[i] On the first stage, at the Jordan, we see the man himself and this sacrifice still as in a picture;

[ii] later, in Mark 6, where the sign re-appears, we see John—the Elijah-John being—through the sacrifice of his death offering himself for the whole being and working of the group of disciples around Christ; here he works from the spirit realm into Inspiration, giving the disciples a new impetus.

[iii] Where this sign re-appears, in the Transfiguration, it is completely united with the disciple John; it is completely embraced

> by him in the innermost depths of his being. The whole Mystery of the 'two Johns' is expressed here in the constellation Goat–Crab. With the Goat stands the pre-Christian initiation; with the Crab stands the Christian Johannine initiation. The whole contrast of the pre-Christian and the Christian is revealed precisely with reference to the initiation of these two signs.

The mountain Goat is the only sign of the physical cross that belongs to the dark side of the zodiac. On that account the physical element of the Earth is least emphasized therein. John the Baptist, who is but loosely, not firmly bound to the forces of the Earth, has precisely here in truth his bodily needs; he 'ate locusts and wild honey', his earthly nourishment has something quite unearthly about it.

In the Mystery of Golgotha, after the death of the Crucified, in the transition from the third to an even higher octave, of the Resurrection-octave, the Goat then appears once more. Here the Turning-Point of the World that John the Baptist at one time announced becomes immediate earthly reality in the death of Christ. Here in the sign of the Goat it reveals its highest physical meaning for the Earth, in the rending of the curtain in the holy of holies.

All the Mysteries of the Earth are revealed in the sign of the Ram, the Crab, the Scales and the Goat. Here they light up in the cross of the divine Father.

***

The Cross of the Son

Virgin–Fishes

At the horizontal beam of this cross we found that constellation which really stands before all the others as the 'constellation of the middle' going right through the whole narrative of the gospel, the great Last-Supper constellation of the Virgin and the Fishes, which is so clearly revealed where the gospel speaks of 'bread and fishes'.

The *Virgin* is indeed the real bearer of the bread of life, the cosmic star-forces of the life-ether, the Holy Grail. In the heavens, the constellation of the 'Virgin with the sheaf (Spica)' corresponds.

In the sign of the *Fishes*, in the primordial beginning and then again in the Turning Point of Time, Sun-life and Earth-life are always united. In that sign, initially still completely revealing the etheric, this etheric is united with the Sun-'I'-power of Christ.

This is really the 'Last-Supper constellation', the constellation of divine Love sacrificing Itself into earthly becoming. This cosmic sacrifice of the divine to the Earth beginning in the Jordan Baptism reaches its climax in the 'holy Last Supper' that is inwardly woven with the Mystery of Golgotha, with the event on the cross. This event on the cross stands in the death-sign of the *Archer*, or rather the constellation '*Twins–Archer*'. In the *Twins*, the 'sacred Mount' is experienced as the point of departure of the initiation events, on which stands the world's altar of sacrifice. This constellation builds the longitudinal beam of this cross.

The unity of the horizontal beam and the longitudinal beam is most clearly revealed in this cross. The whole sacrifice of the Mass, the whole Act of Consecration of Man [of The Christian Community, the Western Rite reborn], is founded on this. They are the liturgical expression of the great cosmic Last-Supper event, the sacrifice of cosmic Love offering Itself in the Last Supper and on the cross into earthly events. It really needs no further explanation, in how far this 'cross of the middle' is the cross of the Son, the actual cross of Christ. That it is the 'cross of the etheric' is also quite clear.

- The *Virgin* is above all the sign of the etheric. In the arrangement of the zodiacal circle of fifths (Introduction, p. 33f.) it corresponds to the ether-body, as the Ram belonging to the 'physical cross' corresponds to the physical body.
- The *Fishes* is the sign of the etheric transformed by the 'I'—of the 'Life-spirit', in the sense of that arrangement [of the human supersensory members].

Likewise,

- the exalted experience of the *Twins* lies in the etheric, and
- the mystery of life is revealed on Golgotha in the death-sign of the *Archer*, which belongs even more to the sphere of the etheric.

With this cross the stages of the events through the three rounds, or octaves, of the Sun-rhythm are also especially evident.

We recall how the *Virgin* appears for the first time (Mark 4) in the picture of the individual seed of wheat, initially the seed of the great cosmic Last-Supper event, in which the Mystery of all 'development' lies enclosed, that is planted into the hearts of the disciples. Here everything is 'Imagination'; it then grows further and develops in the disciples, especially in the nocturnal experience of the first meal (Mark 6), which is pure spirit-vision; it is carried through inner crises (Storm on the Lake) and tests, until in Mark 8 the sign of the Virgin appears again and can gradually be raised to Inspiration. Here it becomes a force working from within, through which the disciples, progressing from taking to giving in the 'Feeding of the Four Thousand', are themselves able to give the living bread to starving humanity (Mark 8:6).

The disciples are not able to retain this climax of their initiation. They fail on the third level in the *Scales*, challenged on the physical level; they abandon Christ in His most difficult struggle. They also fail in the face of the Last-Supper event; here in the great Last Supper directly before Golgotha, they were to support this climax into the physical element. Only the one, John, consciously experiences the great Communion; the others collapse inwardly from the power of the experience. The climax of the sign, the level of Intuition, is in the Last-Supper event as well as the abandonment only experienced by the *one* as positive, by the others experienced as negative.

The path from the world of the stars, of the forces of the head (Imagination) through the rhythmic world of the inner soul (Inspiration) into the earthly world of the physical element (Intuition) is especially clearly trodden with this constellation in Mark's Gospel. (In his book *Der Künstler und die Erfüllung der Mysterien* ['The artist and the fulfilling of the Mysteries'], Dornach 1928, 50ff., Albert Steffen in his simple and expressive, poetical and graceful language has presented the levels of these experiences, also taking into account the results of recent gospel research.) In John's Gospel the experience of the Last Supper, the feeding with 'bread and fishes', then again in the resurrection-octave at the end of the gospel, appear again in the sign of the Virgin.

The Christ-Sun-sign of the Fishes initially appears at the Jordan-Baptism.

- As in a picture, in Imagination, the whole Sun-Mysteries of Christ are here revealed—the Baptist and the figure of Jesus of Nazareth, the waters of the Jordan and the Dove descending in the heavenly light. Imaginations of the Grail appear before the soul.
- On the second level, of Inspiration, the Grail pictures appear again in the nocturnal experience of the Feeding [of the 5000], which is indeed a heavenly Grail-experience, contrasting so effectively with the 'dark Grail', the bloody head on the platter appearing in the same chapter. Here in this nightly vision the Grail pictures become Inspiration for the disciples.

- On the highest level, of Intuition, the pictures appear in the 'Transfiguration of Christ on the Mount', which begins in the death-sign of the Archer but ascends to the Sun-sign of the Fishes. Therein is revealed the 'Sun-glory of Christ', and, pointing to the meaning of the sign, the same words clearly appear as at the Baptism, sounding from the heights of the cosmos: 'You are my beloved Son ...'

Twins–Archer

With the vertical signs Twins–Archer, forming the longitudinal beam of the cross of the middle, the stages of the experiences are also clear. In the sign of the Twins, on the Sacred Mount of Initiation and Inspiration, Christ initially calls the Twelve, to begin with them the work of initiation (Mark 3:13f.). Between Mark 7 and 8 on the stage of Inspiration where the sign should appear again, we do not find the words belonging to it in Mark, but we do in the whole connection with the exactly corresponding passage in Matthew's Gospel (Matt. 15:29). Here the experience of the Twelve has spiritually to be supplemented.

As the whole content of Mark 8 clearly shows, the initiation-experience of the disciples progresses from the stage of Imagination to that of Inspiration. The end of Mark 7 already clearly points in the same direction.

On the third stage, of Intuition—Mark 10:35ff.—the event on the Sacred Mount in the sign of the Twins forms an intimate experience of Johannine initiation. Only the two 'heavenly Twins' themselves, the sons of Zebedee, James and John (who somehow always appear in this sign) are involved. In the sense of being fully conscious, only John experiences this vision in his initiation (see p. 233f.). The whole experience on the Mount of Transfiguration in its cosmic significance for the future of the world appears once more before his soul, becoming for him Intuition. Here he assimilates the great Mysteries of Christ into the depths of his being.

In the death-sign of the Archer we initially experience the death of John the Baptist (Mark 6). Then, after the next higher stage, we experience the beginning of Christ's dying in the Transfiguration, and finally the fulfilment of Christ's dying on Golgotha. Here the meaning of this etheric sign becomes highest reality for the Earth.

***

The Cross of the Spirit

The Cross

Only with one of the three crosses, with the 'Cross of the Earth', do we find the constellation of signs and counter-signs, those of the cross beam, completely in the bright upper part of the zodiac; here both signs, the Ram and the Scales, are 'bright' signs, although the Scales also provides the transition into the darkness. With the cross of the middle, only the one comes into consideration here, the Virgin, belonging to the 'day' side of the zodiac. The Fishes belong to the 'night'-signs, even if it already leads to the day-side of the zodiac. Consequently, the 'night experience' of the 'Feeding of the Five Thousand' is primarily aligned to the Fishes.

With the third of the three crosses, that of the Spirit—which through the Fall of man has become the luciferic-cross—the 'cross of the astral element', the contrast of the day-side with the night-side of the zodiac is much more pronounced in the two constellations. With this cross we cannot really speak of a cross beam and a longitudinal beam as with the other two crosses. The cross we are discussing (red in the Fig.) is felt more as the slanting, diagonal cross.

Alongside the Figure—see p. 364—where the Christ-cross of the etheric forms the middle (in green), one could also imagine a figure where the earthly cross (in blue) would be pictured as the middle. With a presentation of the musical keys (see H. Beckh, *The Essence of Tonality*, or the later fuller account, *The Language of Tonality*), one would prefer this version. It allows most clearly a recognition of the bright and dark parts of the zodiac as 'above' and 'below'; the 'Johannine triangle' (see further in this Appendix) appears vertically in the middle of the circle.

For the presentation of the events in Mark's Gospel, though, the chosen figure is preferable, with the Christ-Sun cross as the middle carrying the Last-Supper constellation. One can imagine yet another, a third form in the middle of the other two. In this version both crosses would stand to each other in such a way that the zenith would be neither in the Twins nor in the Crab, but would fall in the middle between these signs.

Music

In music, the transitional keys expressing more the feeling element (G-, E-, D♭- and B-majors) are to be found here. Further details are to be found in the above-mentioned publications. If we look from the aspect of these musical studies once again at the two crosses of the physical and of the etheric levels, we find the constellation Ram–Scales of the physical cross completely on the day-side of the zodiac, connected to the keys of C-major and F#-major. C-major, of 'Let there be light' [in Haydn's *Creation*], is the breakthrough upwards to the light (already announced in F-major); F#-major, bound enharmonically to G♭-major, presenting here the transition to the lower, darker keys with flats, is, corresponding to the Scales, the key of the great experience of the threshold, the crossing of the 'threshold of the spiritual world', in many different ways clearly present in Wagner. A-major, the key of the Grail [*Lohengrin*], stands in the 'highest light', in the sign of the Johannine initiation. E♭-major, the opposite key, likewise clearly corresponds to the 'lowest depths' (cf. *The Rhinegold*) and carries in itself, as the Goat does in the gospel, the element of struggling to ascend. In the gospel, it has to do here with the 'change of thinking' and the Turning Point of the World.

To the etheric cross, the cross of Christ in the middle, the corresponding keys are F-major–B-major (cross beam) and D-major–A♭-major (longitudinal beam). These keys are especially expressive in presenting the religious, sacred element, the Christ-experience. Cf. Bruckner's F-major of his *Sixth Symphony*, middle movement; Bach's sunny D-major (especially the great resurrection movements); and Wagner's B-major, particularly expressive of the transformation (transubstantiation) in the *Liebestod*, the 'death in love' in *Tristan and Isolde*, and the *Karfreitagszauber*, the 'Good Friday magic' in *Parsifal*—the nocturnal, dark A♭-major of both *Tristan and Isolde* and the Grail-experience in *Parsifal*. The 'day-side' of the zodiac in D-major and the 'night-side' in A♭-major are especially clearly revealed.

Mark's Gospel: Bull–Scorpion

The constellation Bull–Scorpion, so very much linked with all the crises and drama of the events in Mark's Gospel, leads deeply into the secrets of the divine Word. As already in human physiology the connection with the forces of speech and the sexual forces, so here in the gospel the relationship of the divine creative Word, of the Sun-Logos, to that other Power, which in the primordial beginning of creation was the source of all life, but through the Fall of man became the power of death. Here the sign was changed, which in the language of Imagination was expressed as the change from Sun-Eagle to the Scorpion. It is the sign that John, stepping through the Christ-initiation, changed into the Sun-Eagle.

In this sign, in the gospel the 'dead leaven' or 'yeast' of the scribes and Pharisees is placed against the living word of Christ. This is revealed in all three stages of the Sun-rhythm.

[i] On the first stage (Imagination) it is still presented as a picture. Here (Mark 1:40 onwards) we see Christ performing His deeds of healing, revealing in the Bull the living, healing power of the divine Word, seeking the cause of illness in the Scorpion, in the astral, soul-element. We see the scribes and Pharisees opposing these healings when they take place on the Sabbath, the 'day of Saturn'.

[ii] On the second stage, in Mark 7—already the end of Mark 6, where the impeded healings of the sick again succeed everywhere, lying in the Bull—all this becomes an Inspiration for the disciples, becoming a power in themselves. Everything in this chapter, including the episode with the Syro-Phoenician woman (Mark 7:25ff., see p. 160ff.) stands in the sign of the Word, the Mystery of the revelation of the Word. Finally, the scene of the 'Healing of the Deaf and Mute Man', where Christ 'releases the spiritual bonds on the tongues of the disciples' (E. Bock), awakening in themselves the power of the Word, which in the 'Feeding of the Four Thousand' they then utilize for the healing of needy humanity.

[iii] On the third, the highest stage, that of Intuition, all this appears in the initiation of John, at the end of Mark 9 and beginning of Mark 10. Here John, who has been silent for a long time, becomes the spokesman (Mark 9:38). He finds the lost Word of Creation again—into this Mystery the beginning of Chapter 10 allows us to see so deeply. Here it prepares in him the experience out of which he even finds the Creative Word of the primordial beginning, placed so mightily and powerfully at the beginning of his gospel [John 1, Prologue]. All this was for him inner soul-experience, Intuition, in the 'third octave' of the Sun-rhythm. He completely unites himself with the divine Creative Word.

Through the victory over the might of death of the Scorpion, which for the others becomes the 'crisis', he could succeed although with difficulty. Already in Mark 5, where the Scorpion first appears, this overcoming by John is prepared; the crisis of the others is prepared. Already at the beginning of the chapter, in the story of the demoniac—still to be thought of in the Scales—the Scorpion can be felt; the two cases of illness at the end of the chapter especially indicate this sign. The scene for John's first victory of overcoming is here that of the raising of Jairus' daughter. When the Scorpion appears again in Mark 8 with Peter's failure at Caesarea Philippi, the 'crisis' already reaches a decisive climax. It ends in the same sign in the third round of the Sun-rhythm (Mark 13:43ff.) in Judas' betrayal, in the flight of the disciples in Gethsemane (Mark 13:50), and in Peter's denial. Even the tragedy of Pilate, and the crisis of mankind revealed in and behind it, of the 'Crucify!' (Mark 15:13, 14), lies completely in the sphere of the deadly sting of the Scorpion.

Mark's Gospel: Waterman–Lion

A brief look at the other constellation of this cross, Waterman–Lion, especially shows the relationship of the Waterman sign to the astral world, and the inwardly closely associated etheric relationship. In this sign, the baptism by water of John releases in people the knowledge of sin and the confession of sin (Mark 1:5). With this sign, it is especially the arranging of the order of the experiences in the individual octaves that is especially impressive:

- Firstly, it is shown with John's baptism by water; everything is still in pictures, in Imagination.
- On the second stage, the depths of water and the depths of the etheric have already become the depths of the Earth. The Waterman appears again in the burial of John the Baptist (Mark 6:29). For the disciples this experience becomes a deep Inspiration; through the sacrificial death of the Baptist John their forces are re-enlivened from within, so that their initiation can achieve once again a climax.
- Then, the same sign—always the 'Elijah-John sign'—is linked with the Elijah-John revelation in the Transfiguration.
- Finally, already in the transition from the third round of the Sun-rhythm to that of the Resurrection-events, it stands for the burial of Christ Himself. Here the meaning of this sign is married to the most inner depths of the Earth. The Johannine future of the Earth is prepared in seed-form.

The relationship of Waterman and Lion becomes in Mark's Gospel very clear in the words of John, 'I baptize you with water, but he will baptize you with the Holy Spirit' (Mark 1:8). Above all, in the Lion is revealed the being of the 'Holy Spirit' governing the character of the whole cross. The saying appears even more expressively in Matthew (3:11) and Luke (3:16): 'I baptize you with water ... He will baptize you with the Holy Spirit and with fire.'

Thus the motif of the Lion is certainly indicated, but, unlike the other signs, not outwardly developed. The Lion stands everywhere in the background as the 'esoteric sign' of the Sun, with Mark, the Lion evangelist; he is the heart, beating within, that from within determines the whole Sun-rhythm. Regarding the Crab, which it precedes, the Lion appears in relation to it as the one who overcomes; he changes the earthly-material of that sign towards the spirit. In this sense, the Lion appears where in the third round the Johannine initiation ends; the Lion is everywhere in the background of the Crab; the beings of both signs are closely connected.

(The saying of Walter Johannes Stein, in his book *The Ninth Century and the Holy Grail* [London: Temple Lodge 1991] (Germ. ed. p. 168): 'Out of the constellation of the Lion comes the power rightly to lay hold of the sensory world', is also absolutely to be applied to the initiation of John in the sense of Mark's Gospel; to this sign it lends its decisive voice. Stein's book appeared as the present work was already with the printer.)

In the arrangement of the zodiac to the human supersensory members (see p. 38f.), the human 'astral body' is aligned to the Waterman. 'Spirit-man' (*atman*) is aligned to the Lion, right into the rhythm of breathing and the pulsing of the blood. The 'I' changes the physical basis of man, which then carries in it the resurrection forces, the forces of the resurrection body. Here is revealed at its deepest, the contrast between the pre-Christian baptism with water and that other baptism of Christ which is a baptism with the Holy Spirit and with fire. This is what changes the 'water of the etheric' into the personal, 'I'-penetrated wine, what animates the blood, what cleanses in the sense of the Holy Grail, that which expresses the Christ-'I' and the strength of Christ in human beings (as the Crab expresses that which coagulates, brings illness into the blood). All this is only gently indicated in Mark's Gospel; it leads over into the world of John's Gospel, where especially in the great Mystery-scene of the 'Marriage in Cana' the mutual relationship of both signs of Waterman and Lion are expressively presented.

***

The Triangles of the Four Evangelists in the Zodiac

Ever new aspects and depths of the gospel and its context with the cosmic rhythm of the zodiac are revealed when we recognize how the twelve signs of the zodiac are not only arranged into three crosses, but also into four triangles. These things are not to be taken as 'dogma' but to be checked through one's own inner work. These triangles are inwardly related to what is revealed in the well-known differentiation of four temperaments and four elements. (These 'four elements' have nothing to do with the elements of today's chemistry. The word is used in a completely different sense, which, if one wanted to translate it into the material, would lead to the concept of 'aggregate condition of matter'. It is better to understand all these things lying more in the spiritual sphere, and to think of the solid (element of earth), fluid (water, not only in the sense of H_2O), airy and fiery in different stages of the world's revelation of its being. A valuable and important use of the four triangles to the 'four kinds of ether' is indicated in Vol. 2 of Dr. Günter Wachsmuth's book, *Die Äetherischen Bildekräfte in Kosmos, Erde und Mensch*, p. 15.)

We proceed from the beings of the four evangelists, connected—the signs also belong to the 'cross of the Spirit'—to the signs, as discussed in the Introduction (p. 22): Bull (Luke), Lion (Mark), Scorpion-Eagle (John), Waterman (Matthew).

- To the Bull the 'sanguine temperament' is assigned and the element of air,
- to the Lion the 'choleric temperament' and the element of fire,
- to the Scorpion the 'melancholic temperament' and the element of earth,
- to the Waterman the 'phlegmatic temperament' and the fluid element.[42]

According to the figure of Dr. Wachsmuth:

- the *Lion* triangle (Mark) is aligned to the warmth-ether,
- the *Waterman* triangle (Matthew) to the light-ether,
- the *Bull* triangle (Luke) to the life-ether, and
- the *Scorpion-Eagle/ Fishes/ Crab* (John) to the chemical [and sound-] ether.

In this way we can easily recognize how each of the four crosses shares its vertices with different triangles. Likewise, each of the four triangles shares its vertices with different crosses. For example, the 'cross of the physical' (or of 'the Father') belonging in the Scales shares this vertex, or point, with the 'triangle of the watery element', and we can from here understand from quite a new aspect why in the gospel it is precisely in the sign of the Scales that the stories of the Storm on the Lake and the voyage are told.

The meaning and aim of the present work is not somehow to exhaust the questions, but only to show a direction for individuals to research further. Yet this 'research' will only lead to the goal when it really is carried by meditation on the essentials, proceeding out of an inner peace.

***

Mark's Triangle

If we briefly look from this viewpoint to the triangle which can initially stand here in the foreground of interest, to that of Mark, we find how it touches with the 'physical cross' (that is, in a certain sense its 'physical vertex') in the *Ram*, its etheric vertex in the *Archer*, its astral vertex where it meets with the 'cross of the Spirit', in the *Lion*. This last vertex is that which above all determines the essence of Mark and his triangle. Here he appears as the Lion-evangelist. The Lion is the heart of the great cosmic Sun-Rhythm. Consequently, Mark is that evangelist who especially expresses this Sun-rhythm in his gospel. This was already recognized as a fact by the theologian Arthur Drews.

Mark himself, the Johannine initiate Mark, bore the heart of the great Sun-rhythm in himself. Consequently, he is called 'the Lion'. Furthermore, he is the evangelist who most expressively has the motif of the demoniac ['Legion'] allocated to the Ram. Straightaway in the first chapter (Mark 1:23ff.), he uniquely leads us into the demonic world revealing the Ram, portraying in such a unique way this revelation of the power of Christ in the world of the demons.

Moreover, Mark (Introduction p. 22) in particular portrays the cosmic revelation of the etheric sphere, as Matthew is allocated to the physical, Luke to the astral and John to the spiritual, to the '*I*'. In this sense, the third sign of the Mark triangle, the sign of the Archer, contains the deepest revelations of the etheric, the secrets of life, as they are revealed through the death on Golgotha. Precisely Mark is the one who with the greatest earnestness points precisely to this secret of life and death. With the event of Caesarea Philippi, Matthew emphasizes more Peter's shining confession of Christ—there he is declared the 'rock of the Church'—whereas with Mark, as the 'cosmic rhythm' clearly submits, the decisive point is precisely the *failure of Peter* in the face of the earnestness of the secret of death, of understanding the sacrifice of death.

The initiation of the disciples, ultimately that of the *one* John, stands at the centre of Mark's narration. The earnestness of the sacrifice of death on Golgotha stands in the background of the whole Christian, Johannine initiation. After the fulfilment of the initiation, John's further path of development is completely bound with the Christ-event in the Mystery of Golgotha. Even the Mystery of Golgotha, in all four gospels narrated in detail, shows very different sides and aspects. This helps us recognize—from everything that has already been said—how precisely it is the secret of life and death of this Mystery which Mark's Gospel decidedly emphasizes. This viewpoint, however, is that of the 'etheric' sign of the Archer.

***

The Triangles of the Gospels of Luke and Matthew

A few things should be said on the triangles of these two gospels, initially lying far from the theme of the present work, which has shown how they also—especially Luke's Gospel—have to be brought in to explain the deeper questions of Mark's Gospel, even those of the cosmic rhythm—one thinks of Matt. 15:29. In particular the harmony of the four gospels, with all the differences of their individual spiritual viewpoints, results from a spiritual contemplation which is the aim here. That which is timeless within the four gospels—not the incidental, temporal things—appears spiritually here as written in the starry script, into the heavenly zodiac itself.

In our figure, the triangle of Matthew's Gospel has as apex the Twins, the sign of the 'Sacred Mount'. This is illuminating, when we consider how an especially decisive characteristic of Matthew's Gospel is the 'Sermon on the Mount' (Matt. 5–7). With individual reminiscences, which we find in other gospels (Luke 6:20-49, Mark 9:40-50), precisely the 'Mount' is missing. Matthew's Gospel otherwise aligned more than the other gospels to the physical sphere, emphasizes the motif of the 'Sacred Mount', raising it to the heights of the etheric; the elevated sign of the Twins occupies the etheric vertex of Matthew's Gospel. The physical vertex would then be with the Scales, the astral with the Waterman. The sign of the Twins, however, for the essence of Matthew's Gospel appears supremely significant.

For Matthew's Gospel the sign of the Mount of the Twins is significant. For Luke's Gospel the etheric sign of the Virgin is especially significant. The physical vertex of this triangle is shared with the Goat, its astral vertex with the Bull.

The Mystery of the Virgin, the 'Eternal Feminine' and divine-virginal quality forms a basic motif of Luke's Gospel. In his *Studies in the Gospels*, Emil Bock has already emphasized this. It has to do here not only with the stories of Mary and the stories of the Birth at the beginning of the gospel, but that which as an intimate esotericism runs right through the whole gospel of Luke, strongly linked to this 'Mystery of the Eternal Feminine', which is to be found in the Egyptian Isis-Mysteries (see above p. 215f.) as also in the Indian yoga teachings. The Indian element in Luke's Gospel, which Rudolf Steiner has pointed out in his lecture-cycle on Luke's Gospel [*The Gospel of St Luke*, GA 144, Basel, 15-26 Sept. 1909], here is nevertheless positively pre-Christian. Several things in Luke's Gospel said about the 'light of the body' (Luke 11:34-36) point in this direction. The role which the element of the Virgin plays in the Johannine Mysteries and in the Johannine initiation meets us in these considerations, namely in Luke 7 (together with Mark 14 and John 12). Out of all this we can understand why Luke's Gospel has its 'etheric vertex' with the sign of the Virgin, why in the main this sign is decisive for the character of Luke's Gospel.

In connection with this aspect of the cosmic Virgin, of the 'Eternal Feminine' (Isis-Mary) in Luke's Gospel, the fact is also correct, that the Luke triangle (Wachsmuth) aligns the Isis-element to the life-ether. Likewise, corresponding to its intimate character, the triangle of Luke's Gospel is precisely the counter-triangle of John's Gospel, the most spiritual of the four gospels, just as Mark's triangle is the counter-triangle to that of Matthew's Gospel. All this can offer practical and important aspects to understand the individual gospels and their mutual relationships.

(In Wachsmuth, the aspects which are presented are absolutely full of suggestion. Already in the first chapter emphasizing the *mother*, Luke's Gospel is aligned with its viewpoint to the life-ether of the Eternal-Feminine; Matthew's Gospel emphasizing at the beginning the *Father*, aligns the 'Eternal Father' to the light-ether. Cf. *Gäa-Sophia*. Jahrbuch der Naturwissenschaftl. Sektion, Goetheanum, CH-Dornach. Jg. 1926, 388; Jg. 1927, 292.)

Another viewpoint should be mentioned. From the twelve signs of the zodiac we can recognize three above all as 'Christ-signs': the Scales, the Fishes, and the Lion. These three, when we relate the zodiac to the 'supersensory human members', align to the three upper human members, that is, to the already 'Christened' human nature:

- the *Scales* correspond to 'Spirit-self' (*manas*),
- the Christ-Sun sign of the *Fishes* to 'Life-spirit' (*buddhi*)
- the *Lion* to 'Spirit-man' (*atman*).

We find:

- the *Scales* in the triangle of Matthew's Gospel,
- the *Fishes* in that of John's Gospel,
- the *Lion* in that of Mark's Gospel.

The triangle of Luke's Gospel that emphasizes the character of the 'Jesus-gospel' most of all, has—in this strict sense—no 'Christ sign' (while in a more extended meaning *all* the signs of the zodiac are 'Christ signs'); but instead of this it emphasizes the Mary-sign of the Virgin. And this which results above all in its relationship of the Christ-Sun sign to the Fishes (in the 'Last-Supper constellation'), stands to the Mysteries of Christ in close esoteric relationship—as also to the Egyptian name of Isis: 'H-S-T, I-S-T, taken purely as sounds, is contained in the name Christ. [Further details in the essay 'On the name Isis', in *From the Mysteries*, Temple Lodge, 2020, 170-75; see Appendix 3, p. 376.]

***

The Johannine Triangle

After following everything resulting from Mark's Gospel regarding the secret of John and the initiation of John, we shall bestow particular attention to the 'Johannine triangle' with these contemplations on the zodiac. We shall say to ourselves, that in the three signs of this triangle somehow that has to be expressed which above all is characteristic precisely of the Johannine initiation and thereby also forms an essential content of Mark's Gospel.

Immediately a special characteristic of the Johannine triangle meets us. Each of the three other gospel-triangles has two vertices in the upper, bright part, on the day-side of the zodiac. The Johannine triangle, however, has only one vertex, the *Crab*, in the light. The other two, the *Scorpion* and the *Fishes* are in the dark, on the night-side of the zodiac—even if the Fishes already carry a moment of lighting within.

It is absolutely characteristic for John and the Christian-Johannine initiation that precisely its own triangle has two vertices in the dark and only one in the light, though this is in the highest light, where in music the bright 'Grail's key' A-major stands [cf. Wagner's *Lohengrin*]. John is aligned to the element of earth and the earthly temperament—the melancholic. How often, when we attempted to portray the 'becoming of John', the picture appeared before our eyes of the lonely, silent, 'melancholic' disciple, the picture of the 'invalid', of Lazarus.

His chronic illness ultimately reached the threshold of death, until the word of Christ to him woke him out of the slumber of the grave in Bethany. Still as a dead person who arises from the grave, we see him in John 12 (where still, and for the last time, the name 'Lazarus' is used), but who then, as if out of the power of the 'Holy Grail', freshly blossoming in youthful beauty and grace, bears on his countenance the secret of Leonardo's portraits, that 'something' that can only be where in the light of the divine, the Mystery of the Eternal Feminine is united once again with that of the ego-like, 'I'-filled Masculine.

The melancholic temperament, which is the most obstinate, the one most difficult to 'transform', that opposes with 'earthly resistance' all attempts to change it, appears precisely in the Johannine initiation transformed. It is that temperament in which the most difficult of all resistances, the resistance of earth, is overcome. The element of earth itself is changed, 'transubstantiated'. This metamorphosis or transubstantiation takes place in the sign of the *Crab* in such a way that the Lion spiritually participates. United with the Lion, the Crab appears as the sign of change, of transubstantiation, the highest alchemy. It is consequently profoundly meaningful when on the figure given by Dr. Wachsmuth (Vol. 2, p. 15) the triangle ♓–♋–♏, drawn in blue, which from the viewpoint of the gospel is the Johannine triangle, is aligned to the chemical-ether, or sound-ether.

Some people see the Crab altogether as the sign of the disciple John. This, however, is the *Virgin*—not contained in the Johannine triangle. In this there is expressed especially what John has as the characteristic trait of his being. The sign of the Virgin appears then as the transformation of that other sign so profoundly united to the Johannine Mystery, which as such does belong to the 'Johannine triangle'.

In the 'Johannine triangle' the *Scorpion* truly belongs as that power of death, whose overcoming is the decisive moment of all genuine Christian-Johannine initiation. This most earnest, critical of all the twelve signs of the zodiac, in which all the disciples fail, with the exception of John, this sign not only of the group of disciples but of the crisis of humanity and with it the effects of the Mystery of Golgotha, can in a certain sense be seen as the 'esoteric vertex' of the Johannine triangle.

Likewise important for the Johannine triangle is the third sign, which is the actual 'Christ-sign' of this triangle, the Sun-sign of the *Fishes*. In this sign John the Baptist and Jesus of Nazareth meet, Jesus who then at the Jordan becomes the Christ, receiving into himself the cosmic Christ, the 'Christ-Sun-being'. And in the 'Transfiguration' the

Sun-secret of Christ meets with the Mystery of John in the sign of the Fishes.

- With its *Crab* vertex, the Johannine triangle belongs to the 'cross of the physical' (or 'the Father');
- with its *Scorpion* vertex to the 'cross of the astral' (or 'of the Spirit');
- with its third vertex lying in the Christ-Sun-sign of the *Fishes,* it belongs to the 'cross of the etheric' (or of 'the Son'), the Christ-cross of the middle.
- In the *Scorpion* the overcoming of the might of Death is revealed,
- in the *Crab* the metamorphosis of the Earth,
- in the *Fishes,* as in the sign where Earth and Heaven find each other in Christ, as a third viewpoint the essence determined by the Johannine experience of the Sun-'I' of Christ is revealed.

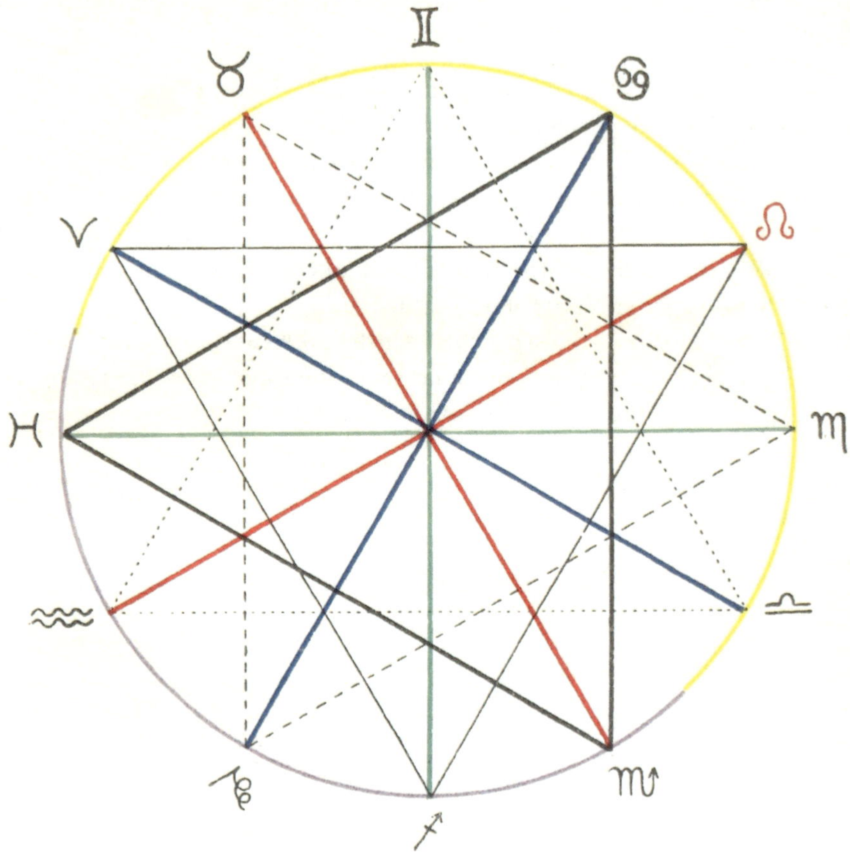

FIGURE I: The three crosses in the zodiac are shown through the different colours: the physical cross ('Cross of the Father') in blue, the ether-cross ('Christ-Cross of the Son') green, and the astral cross ('Cross of the Spirit') in red.

The 'triangles of the four evangelists' are emphasized in this figure through stronger and weaker lines (John and Mark), and through stronger and weaker dotted lines (Luke and Matthew).

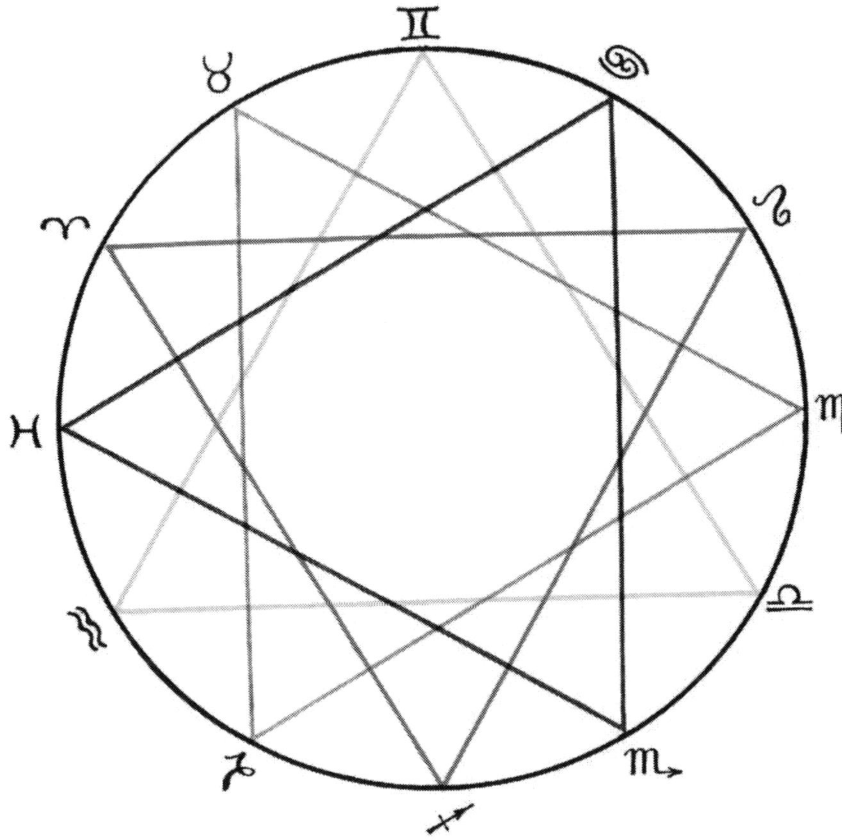

FIGURE II: taken from the book by Dr Günther Wachsmuth, The Etheric Formative Forces in the Cosmos, Earth and Man, *Bk 2, p. 15. The position of the axes is reversed (with Wachsmuth ♈ ♎ is the traverse axis, ♋ ♑ the longitudinal axis) for a certain point of view, initially only decisive for the Christ-cross (traverse axis ♓ ♍, longitudinal axis ♊ ♐) to allow it to appear as the 'cross of the middle'. For the position of the axes as chosen by Wachsmuth the Johannine triangle (sound-ether, bold) the apex would stand with the point above, which is likewise significant.*

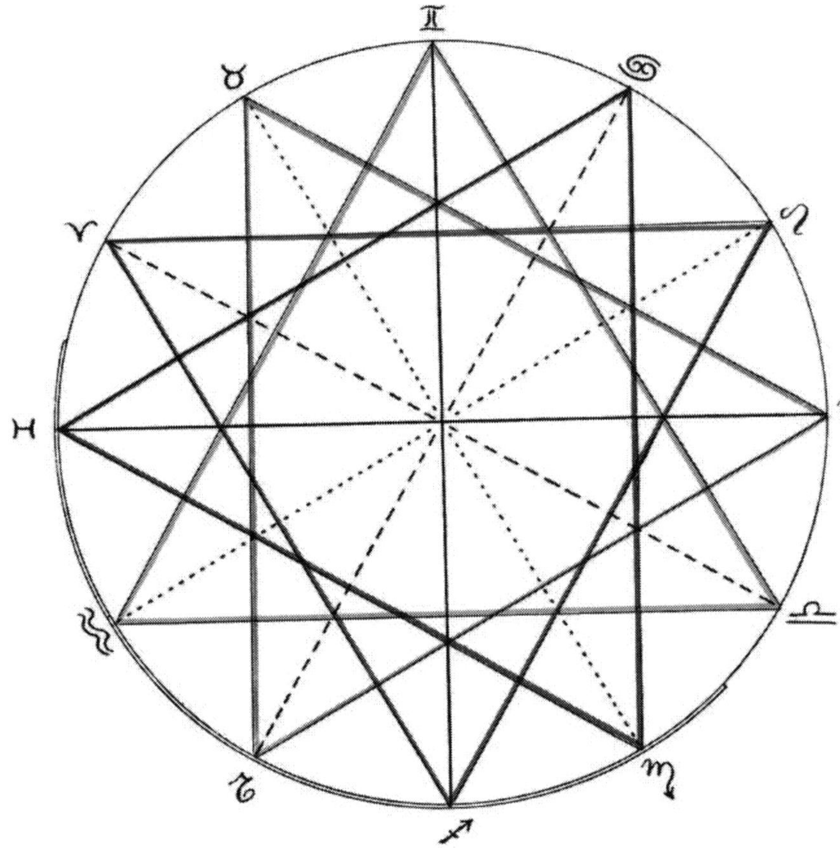

FIGURE III is to be thought as the summary of the first two figures.

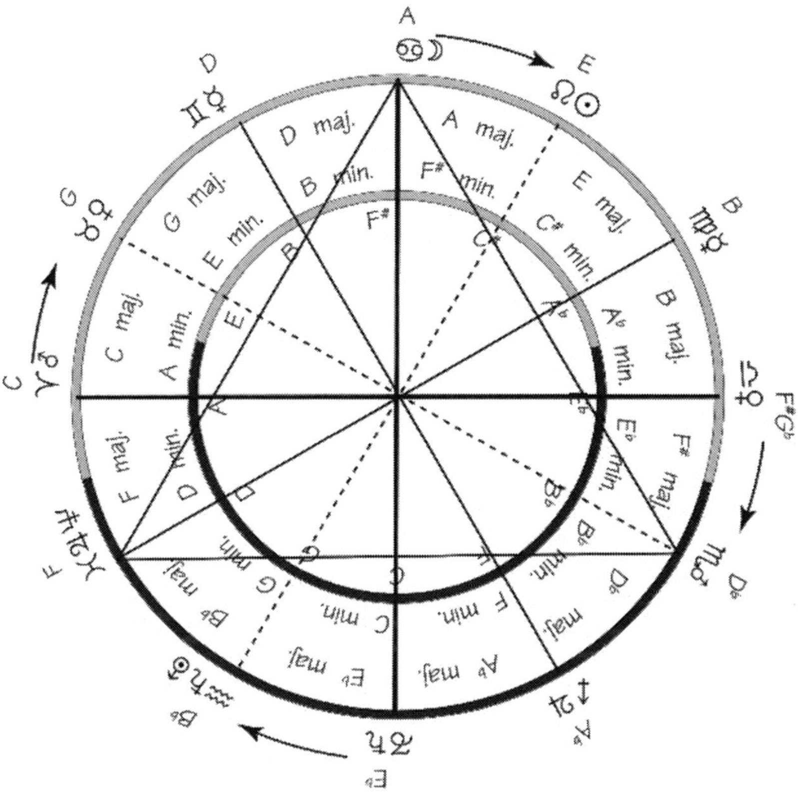

*FIGURE IV. This tone-zodiac appears in the author's publications on the musical keys (*The Essence of Tonality, *and* The Language of Tonality, *Anastasi Ltd). It serves to show musical and tonal phenomena, as they correspond to the character of John's Gospel, mentioned at various places in the book.*

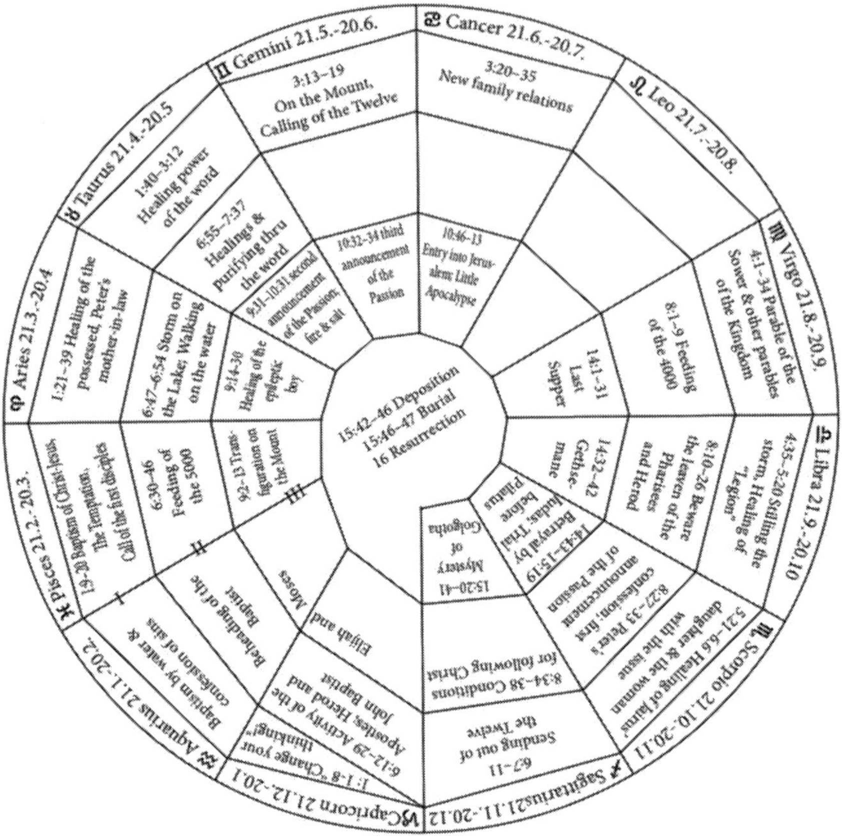

FIGURE V The Cosmic Rhythm in Mark's Gospel, after Hermann Beckh, shown as three circuits of a zodiacal spiral.

Each circuit begins in the Goat. The life of Christ itself, however, only begins in the sign of the Fishes. The individual zodiacal gestures are only given by keywords.

Immanuel Klotz, Die Europäer, *Nr. 12/Nr. 2/3 Dec./Jan. 2007/2008*

Appendix 2: Rhythmical Events in the Gospel

Hermann Beckh

(*Die Christengemeinschaft* 6. Jg. Nr. 11. Feb. 1930. 334-38)

The old Indian word *ṛta* (pronounced 'rita'), for which, amongst other translations 'law, order, custom, sacred cosmic order, truth', we find especially a threefold meaning: firstly, the course of the year, then that of the stars that regulate that course, moving their eternal ordering on preordained paths, and finally the religious ritual of sacrifice in harmony with the annual events of the permanent order of the stars in their courses.

Recalling the Latin *ritus*, this Indian word *ṛta* comes from a root from which also the Greek word *rhythmós* derives. According to its innermost meaning, it means a *rhythmical event*, expressing the thought that the eternal divine being, where it reveals itself in earthly time, is expressed in *rhythmical events*. Not only the events of the year like the stars in their courses, but also the sacred order of the cultic rites of sacrifice are based on such a rhythm, *ṛta*, and everything rhythmical appears as a revelation of a higher lawfulness. The inner being of everything cultic is here stated; the inner nerve of the cultic events is shown. And what concerns the early Indian ritual of sacrifice is shown to be true in this sense also for the Christian rite. The sacrifice of the Mass of the Catholic Church and the Act of Consecration of Man of The Christian Community are based again on the course of the stars, constructed on the rhythm of the stars measured according to the rhythmical events of the course of the year.

In pre-Christian Mysteries, too, in the Eleusian, likewise the Adonis and Attis Mysteries, this regard for the rhythmical events in the course of the year plays a significant role—the eternal change and rotation of growing and withering, ripening and fruiting, becoming and passing away, death and resurrection. What is meant, however, is initially always but a natural event reflected in the human soul, a revelation of the course of nature falling to the human soul. The significantly new, innovative and unique thing about the Christian event lies in the fact that what in blossoming and decaying and in the fresh growth of the plant-world is merely a revelation of nature. What—in the Mysteries of Eleusis—the soul could dimly divine as the secret of its destiny, becoming manifest throughout long periods of human history, was placed on the plane of earthly history as an *historical event* in the death and Resurrection of Christ. Thereby, the secret is gently indicated why in the Christian ritual, the Mass of the Catholic Church as in The Act of Consecration of Man of The Christian Community, initially the concern is not to celebrate some mere natural event, a mere revelation of nature. An historical fact, the sacrifice of Christ Jesus for humanity, is celebrated. Nevertheless, in this sacrificial celebration that appears woven so significantly with the rhythmic events of the course of the year, the externals also of this Christian ritual always change, fashioned according to the different times of the year.

The Gospels

At the same time, a new and remarkable light falls on the Christian gospel, especially on the gospel according to Mark. In this narration of the Christian gospel of the earthly life and earthly death, of the death and Resurrection of Christ Jesus, regardless of the historical character of the narrated events, nevertheless it can be understood why a rhythmical element can be found that recalls the rhythmical events in the course of the year, on the eternally regular change of blossoming and withering, growth and ripening, becoming and decaying, sleeping and waking, summer and winter, day and night. All these are meanings also contained in the Indian word *ṛta*. In the book, *Mark's Gospel: The Cosmic Rhythm*, the attempt was made to point to the connection of the gospel narration with the rhythmic events of the year. Thereby the following came into consideration.

In the early Mysteries, in which the soul was led through specific experiences, initially revealed out of natural events, the concern was for a specific inner path of becoming, a specific path of stages of spiritual development that was always called *Initiation*. The human soul was brought into a certain rhythmic accord and harmony with higher Mysteries of nature and Mysteries of existence. In this connection, what was experienced in the early Mysteries and was protected as a deep, inviolable secret—to betray this was punishable with death—also this *initiation event* was placed on the plane of world-history in the suffering, death and Resurrection of Christ Jesus. But it was done so that what was experienced in the earlier Mysteries as a divining parable was now published abroad. What in pre-Christian times was long before divined and prophesied stood there in the Mystery of Golgotha as the fulfilment of all the Mysteries.

That is why the entire appearance of Christ Jesus, especially in the 'raising of Lazarus', to the Jewish Pharisees and high-priests appeared as a betrayal of the Mysteries, worthy of death. This placing of the Mysteries openly on the plane of world-history in the Mystery of Golgotha did not mean that everyone had to experience the Mystery. Much rather, as Novalis [Sophie, in *Heinrich von Ofterdingen*] expresses it: 'the great secret is revealed to all, and remains forever unfathomable. Out of pain is the new world born, and the ashes are dissolved into tears for a draught of eternal life.' Only *one disciple stood under the cross* (John 1:25), after the others in Gethsemane had abandoned their Master in a confusion of consciousness, that is, only one consciously participated in the great Mystery. In this experience, as the gospel indicates, the 'Mother' and Mary Magdalene take a certain part. For actual humanity it remained, and to a considerable extent still remains, a Mystery. This fact sufficiently shows what significance the Initiation of the one disciple—fulfilled under the cross—has for the future of humanity, as the secret of the new, the Christian initiation presented in the disciple John. The initiation of the earlier pre-Christian Mysteries is discharged at the cross on Golgotha—which, again, stands in mysterious connection with the Mystery-events of Bethany, the 'raising of Lazarus'—through the new Christian-Johannine initiation.

Understanding what was said of the historical revelation of Christ connected to the revelation of nature in the early Mysteries, illuminates without more ado all the variety of pre-Christian, yet also the Christian initiation-events. These initially must have to do with how an understanding and living with the Mystery of Golgotha is connected with the revelation of nature, with the rhythmical events of nature. No initiation exists that does not concern the soul brought into accord and harmony with this eternal rhythm of blossoming and withering, growth and ripening, becoming and decaying, birth and death. And for all recent training of the soul, in such a significant book for all 'modern initiation' as *Knowledge of the Higher Worlds: How is it Attained?* Rudolf Steiner points to the importance of this beholding of the eternal facts of blossoming and decaying, becoming and dying away for the development of higher organs of perception of the soul.

The narrations of the life of Christ in the gospels are something other than only external, historical reports. That they otherwise have the character of 'initiation writings' is emphasized by Rudolf Steiner.

In the future this will become increasingly known and understood. One can certainly read such a document as Mark's Gospel, simply interested in what is told of the deeds and experiences of Christ Jesus and the group of disciples. But one can also read the account as a very significant portrayal of the Christian-Johannine path of initiation, of the initiation of the disciples. One can especially recognize the experiences of John leading to his initiation by Christ. This point of view nobody can forcefully open up; it cannot be proved in the normal sense through some kind of 'convincing' arguments—for it concerns precisely those areas that leave the soul free, not to be compelled. It can only be said that, for those who have opened to the point of view, Mark's Gospel becomes something more important than it was before. In John's Gospel one can find the way to Christ; in Mark's Gospel such a person can find the way to John in a completely special sense. And it will dawn on him when precisely in Mark's Gospel this rhythm, essential for all initiation, becomes more obvious in a completely special way, so obvious that also someone so completely distant from representatives of all mysticism, all occultism, and all anthroposophy as the [historian and philosopher] Arthur Drews [1865–1935] became aware of the fact of this rhythm.

Such persons—especially Arthur Drews in a here and there spirited, though often plainly in a fantastically strange manner—however, introduce into the fact of this 'cosmic rhythm' that cannot be denied, all kinds of possible 'astral mythology' and astronomical connections. The fact of this rhythm becomes at first only mutilated and obliterated. What for itself is to be taken seriously is changed into a mystical frivolity, which Drews, who consequently also denies the historical reality, naturally does not personally advocate but merely finds an interesting superstition. Thereby the accounts by Drews and others have failed to lead readers, introduced to such great cosmic views, to approach the significant and honourable Christian gospel with its wonderful and sublime questions of the gospel-rhythm. In many respects they have rather deterred people.

The Cosmic Rhythm

For comprehending the governing rhythm of Mark's Gospel, what has to be seen is that the stars in the abstract are not at all necessary. This rhythm can be understood purely from observing the events of the year. The events of Mark's Gospel—all one, whether we take the events of Christ of the three years (which as such in Mark's Gospel are not at all obvious), or whether we take the Johannine initiation-event that inwardly follows the events of the three years—lie basically in the same sphere in which we stand in experiencing the year and, what is especially important, likewise in experiencing the Christian Eucharist, the Act of Consecration of Man. For this reason the objection is invalid, for example, that for those initially searching only for the Christian experience in the Eucharist, taking the cosmic view of the gospel should be something completely distant and 'far-fetched'.

Precisely being present at the Eucharist creates favourable circumstances to experience the rhythmical element. A premature introduction of extensive astronomical aspects in a justified and understandable manner can appear detrimental here. The eternal rhythm of blooming and withering, becoming and decaying, of death and resurrection rules both in the course of the year and in the Service, as it does in the Christ-events and the initiation process of the gospel. This rhythm can be recognized as something for itself, as understandable and illuminating on its own terms. When we see how at the corresponding place of the rhythm—this concerns the threefold return [over the three years] of the same section or '[zodiac] sign'—a similar or meaningfully-related event always returns. For example, the voyage on the Lake of Galilee and the Storm on the Lake are found always at a quite specific place, clearly given through the gospel-rhythm. At a specific point the descent always follows the ascent and the new ascent always follows the descent—the details have to be viewed out of the whole presentation. Thus, without all the 'astral mythology', the 'cosmic rhythm' meant here can become clear on its own terms, and from all that has been said we can well understand precisely in the gospel what such a rhythm signifies.

But when 'zodiac signs' are discussed, won't there be an incessant reference to the stars? Here too it is not as many people imagine. Recall much rather what was given at the beginning—the three meanings of the word *ṛta*. To the revelation in the events of the year specific movements of the stars proceed in parallel, specific events in the starry heavens, in the Sun, Moon and stars. The word *ṛta* ('rhythm') also relates to this eternal ordering of the course of the stars. What since olden times have these movements of the stars in connection with the events of the year—as with the events of the day—always been for humanity? Initially simply the great *cosmic clock* given simply through the nature of the thing, according to which ultimately all our earthly clocks join and are attuned. If one wanted to establish in the heavens the section of the Sun's heavenly arc corresponding to the annual events, one looks up to the starry heavens. The 'zodiac pictures' came about, whose unity of twelve once again is connected with the course of the Moon, with the unity of the twelve months. (The question whether and how far an earlier consciousness of humanity really experienced the starry heavens in pictures can for the moment rest on one side.)

Sign and Constellation

This aspect of the *cosmic clock* is not the last but the first, initially more important point, for considering the whole question. During the time when Christ walked the Earth, one looked up to the starry heavens, and found how the Sun:

- with the spring equinox entered the constellation of the Ram,
- in the summer solstice into the constellation of the Crab,
- in the autumn equinox into the constellation of the Scales, and
- in the winter solstice into the Goat.

This connection no longer exists today, because of the retrograde motion of the spring equinox. Orientating to the [current] starry heavens:

- the spring equinox today lies in the Fishes,
- the summer solstice in the Twins,
- the autumn equinox in the Virgin, and
- the winter solstice in the Archer.

Yet we stand from the point of view of the course of the year even today in the Crab, when the Sun in the summer solstice goes backwards again, commencing its 'crab's walk', when the increasing shortening of the day ensues. Even today, seen from the Earth, in the Scales, when in the autumn day and night are provisionally equal in duration, we 'enter into the Scales'. In astronomy, by dividing the whole heavenly arc into twelve equal sections, one is actually calculating with these sections as 'signs' and differentiating them from the constellations. The sign, even when it retains its name from the constellation (which it no longer indicates today) in the abstract, nevertheless regarded purely from the earthly side, is a specific section of the rhythm of the year having nothing directly to do with the fixed stars.

And so we can understand the rhythms of Mark's Gospel without concerning ourselves with the stars, simply out of these 'signs', these rhythmic sections of the course of the year. It remains a fact that precisely in the age of Christ's earthly life, sign and constellation coincided, that is, the place of the rhythmic 'sign' was really decided by the constellation by which it carries the name. This agreement was at its most complete in the hour of the Mystery of Golgotha. For this reason it can appear meaningful to point—as happens in the book on Mark's Gospel—from the sign to the constellation, to the actual heavenly picture. For in the time of Christ's earthly life this heavenly picture, like a great 'cosmic script' stood there for the earthly event. Later the relationship was displaced and in the future will be displaced ever further. This should here initially be stated as a purely astronomical fact, about whose spiritual background much can be said, much conjectured. Yet this would have to form the subject of a further special article. In such an article one can pursue the question of sign and constellation further, and some other star-Mysteries and questions.

Appendix 3: Search for the New Isis, the Divine Sophia: The Quest for the Isis-Sophia

A Lecture by Rudolf Steiner

Dornach, 24 December 1920 (in GA 202)

IN THE FESTIVAL of Christmas something is given to Christendom that directs the thoughts of all circles of Christian people straight to the very deepest questions presented by the evolution of humanity upon earth. Regard the evolution of history from whatever point of view you will, take into consideration historical events in order to understand human evolution, to penetrate the meaning of human evolution on earth—in all history you will find no thought as widely understandable or having as much power to lift the soul to this mystery of human evolution as the thought of the Mystery of Golgotha, as the thought that is contained in the festival of Christmas.

When we look back upon the beginning of human evolution on earth, and follow it through the thousands of years that preceded the Mystery of Golgotha, we find that, although the achievements of the peoples in all the various nations were so great, nevertheless, in reality all these achievements constituted only a kind of preparation—they were a preparatory step toward what took place for the sake of humanity at the Mystery of Golgotha. Furthermore, we find we can only understand what has happened since the Mystery of Golgotha when we remember that the Christ who went through the Mystery of Golgotha has played an active role in the evolution of humanity ever since. Many things in human evolution may at first appear incomprehensible. However, if we investigate them without narrow-minded superstition, for example the kind of superstition that believes that unknown gods should come to the aid of human beings without their active involvement, and that such aid should come just where human beings consider it necessary—if we leave aside such views, we find that even the most painful events in the course of world history can show us the significance and meaning that the evolution of the earth has acquired through the fact that Christ went through the Mystery of Golgotha. It is appropriate for us to study this Mystery of

Golgotha—and the Mystery of Christmas belongs to it—from a point of view which can reveal, as it were, the meaning of the entire evolution of humanity. We know how intimate the connection is between what takes place in the moral-spiritual sphere of human evolution and what takes place in nature. And with a certain understanding of this link between nature and the world's moral order we can approach also another relationship with which we have been concerned for many years—namely, the relationship of Christ Jesus to that being whose outer reflection appears in the Sun. The followers and representatives of the Christian impulse were not always so hostile toward the recognition of this connection between the Mystery of the Sun and the Mystery of Christ as the decadent present-day representatives of Christianity so often are. Dionysius the Areopagite, whom we have often mentioned, calls the Sun, God's monument, and in Augustine we continually find such allusions. Even in Scholasticism we find such references to the fact that the outwardly visible stars and their movements are images of the divine-spiritual existence of the world.

However, we must understand the Mystery of Christmas in a far wider context, if we wish to understand what should concern us most of all in view of the important tasks of the present age. I would like to remind you of something which I have repeatedly brought forward in various ways in the course of many years. I have told you: We look back into the first post-Atlantean age, which was filled with the deeds and experiences of the ancient Indian people; we look back into the ancient Persian epoch of post-Atlantean humanity, into the Egypto-Chaldean, and into the Greco-Latin. We come then to the fifth epoch of the post-Atlantean humanity, our own. Our epoch will be followed by the sixth and by the seventh. And I have drawn your attention to the fact that the Greco-Latin, the fourth epoch of post-Atlantean humanity, stands, as it were, in the middle, and that there are certain connections (you can read of this in my litttle book *The Spiritual Guidance of the Individual and Humanity*) between the third and the fifth epochs, that is, between the Egypto-Chaldean epoch and our own. Furthermore there is also a certain connection between the ancient Persian epoch and the sixth, and between the ancient Indian and the seventh epoch of post-Atlantean humanity. Specific things repeat themselves in a certain way in each of these epochs of life.

I once pointed out that the great Kepler, the successor of Copernicus, had a feeling that his solar and planetary system was repeating, of course in a way appropriate to the fifth post-Atlantean age, what had lived as the world-picture behind the Mysteries of the Egyptian priests. Kepler himself expressed this in a certain sense very radically when he said that he had borrowed the vessels of the ancient Egyptian teachers of wisdom in order to carry them over into the new age.

Today, however, we will consider something which stood, in a sense, at the centre of the view found in the cultic rituals performed by the priests in the Egyptian Mystery religion; we will consider the Mysteries of Isis. In order to call up before our minds the spiritual connection between the Mystery of Isis and that which also lives in Christianity, we need only look with the eyes of the soul upon Raphael's famous picture of the Sistine Madonna. The Virgin is holding the child Jesus, and behind her are the clouds, representing a multitude of children. We can imagine the Virgin receiving the child Jesus descending through the clouds, through a condensation, as it were, of the thin cloud substance. Created out of an entirely Christian spirit, this picture is, after all, nothing more than a kind of repetition of what the Egyptian Mysteries of Isis revered when they portrayed Isis holding the child Horus. The motif of that earlier picture is in complete harmony with that of Raphael's picture. Of course, this fact must not tempt us to a superficial interpretation, common among many people since the eighteenth century and throughout the nineteenth century right up to our own day— namely, to see the story of Christ Jesus and all that belongs to it as a mere metamorphosis, a transformation, of early pagan Mysteries. From my book *Christianity As Mystical Fact* you already know how these things are to be understood. However, in the sense explained in that book we are permitted to point out a spiritual congruence between what appears in Christianity and the early pagan Mysteries.

The main content of the Mystery of Isis is the death of Osiris and Isis's search for the dead Osiris. We know that Osiris, the representative of the being of the Sun, the representative of the spiritual Sun, is killed by Typhon, who, expressed in Egyptian terms, is none other than Ahriman. Ahriman kills Osiris, throws him into the Nile, and the Nile carries the body away. Isis, the spouse of Osiris, sets out on her search and finds him over in Asia. She brings him back to Egypt, where Ahriman, the enemy, cuts the body into fourteen parts. Isis buries these fourteen parts in various locations, so that they belong to the Earth for ever after.

We can see from this story how Egyptian wisdom conceived of the connection between the powers of heaven and the powers of Earth in a deeply meaningful way. On the one hand, Osiris is the representative of the powers of the Sun. After having passed through death he is, in various places and simultaneously, the force that ripens everything that grows out of the Earth. The ancient Egyptian sage imagines in a spirit-filled way how the powers which shine down from the Sun, enter the Earth and then become part of the Earth, and how, as powers of the Sun buried in the Earth, they then hand over to the human being what matures out of the Earth. The Egyptian myth is founded upon the story of Osiris—how he was killed, how his spouse Isis had to set out on her search for him, how she first brought him back to Egypt and how he then became active in another form, namely, from out of the Earth.

One of the Egyptian pyramids depicts the whole event in a particularly meaningful way. The Egyptians not only recorded what they knew as the solution to the great secrets of the universe in their own particular writing, they also expressed it in their architectural constructions. They built one of these pyramids with such mathematical precision that the shadow of the Sun disappeared into the base of the pyramid at the spring equinox and only reappeared at the autumn equinox. The Egyptians wanted to express in this pyramid that the forces which shine down from the Sun are buried from spring to fall in the Earth where they develop the forces of the Earth, so that the Earth may produce the fruit which humanity needs.

This, then, is the idea we find present in the minds and hearts of the ancient Egyptians. On the one hand, they look up to the Sun, they look up to the lofty being of the Sun and they worship him. At the same time, however, they relate how this being of the Sun was lost in Osiris, and was sought by Isis, and how he was found again so that he is able to continue working in a changed way.

Many things which appeared in the Egyptian wisdom must be repeated in a different form during our fifth post-Atlantean age. Humanity must increasingly come to understand from a spiritual-scientific point of view the Mysteries of the Egyptian priests in a form appropriate to our own age, in a Christian sense. For the Egyptians, Osiris was a kind of representative of the Christ who had not yet arrived on Earth. In their own way they looked upon Osiris as the being of the Sun, but they imagined this Sun being had been lost in a sense, and must be found again. We cannot imagine that our Being of the Sun, the Christ, Who has passed through the Mystery of Golgotha could be lost to humanity, for He came down from spiritual heights, united himself with the man Jesus of Nazareth, and from then onwards remains with the Earth. He is present, he exists, as the Christmas carol proclaims each year anew: 'Unto us a Saviour is born.' It thereby expresses the eternal, not the transitory nature of this event. Jesus was not only born once at Bethlehem, but is born continuously; in other words, He remains with the life of the Earth. What Christ is, and what He means for us, cannot be lost.

But the Isis legend must show itself as being fulfilled in another way in our time. We cannot lose the Christ and what he, in a higher form than Osiris, gives us; but we can lose, and we have lost, what is portrayed for our Christian understanding standing at the side of Osiris—Isis—the mother of the saviour, the divine wisdom, Sophia. If the Isis legend is to be renewed, then it must not simply follow the old form—Osiris, killed by Typhon-Ahriman and carried away by the waters of the Nile, must be found again by Isis in order that his body, cut into pieces by Typhon-Ahriman, may be sunk into the Earth. No, in a sense, we must find the Isis legend again, the content of the Mystery of Isis, but we must create it out of imagination, suited to our own times. An understanding must arise again of the eternal cosmic truths, and it will when we learn to think and compose imaginatively, as the Egyptians did. But we must find the right Isis legend.

The Egyptian was permeated by luciferic powers, as were all human beings who lived before the Mystery of Golgotha. If luciferic powers are within the human being and stir the inner life, moving and weaving through it, the result will then be that ahrimanic powers will appear as an active force outside the human being. Thus the Egyptians, who were themselves permeated by Lucifer, rightly see a picture of the world in which Ahriman-Typhon is active.

Now, we must realize that modern humanity is permeated by Ahriman. Ahriman moves and surges within human beings, just as Lucifer moved and surged within the Egyptian world. However, when Ahriman works through Lucifer, then human beings see their picture of the world in a luciferic form. How does the human being see this picture of the world? This luciferic picture of the world has been created, it is here. It has become increasingly popular for modern times and has taken hold of all groups of people who want to consider themselves progressive and enlightened.

If the Mystery of Christmas is to be understood, we must bear in mind that Lucifer is the power wanting to retain the world-picture of an earlier stage. Lucifer is the power trying to bring into the modern world-conception that which existed in earlier stages of human development. He wants to give permanence to what existed in earlier periods. All that was moral in earlier stages also exists of course today. (The significance of morality always lies in the present, where, like seeds for the future, it provides the basis for the creation of worlds yet to come.) But Lucifer strives to separate morality as such, all moral forces, from our world-picture. He allows the laws of natural necessity alone to appear in our picture of the external world. Thus the impoverished human being of modern times is presented with a wisdom of the world in which the stars move according to purely mechanical necessity, in which the stars are devoid of morality, so that the moral meaning of the world's order cannot be found in their movements. This, my dear friends, is a purely luciferic world-picture.

Just as the Egyptians looked out into the world and saw Ahriman-Typhon as the one who takes Osiris away from them, so too, we must look at our luciferic world-picture, at the mathematical-mechanical world-picture of modern-day astronomy and other branches of natural science, and realize that the luciferic element holds sway in this worldview, just as the typhonic-ahrimanic element held sway in the Egyptian worldview. Just as the ancient Egyptians saw their outer world-picture in an ahrimanic-typhonic light, so modern human beings, because they are ahrimanic, see it with luciferic characteristics. Lucifer is present, he is working there. Just as the Egyptians imagined ahriman-typhon working in wind and weather, in the storms of winter, so modern human beings, if they wish to truly understand the world, must imagine that Lucifer appears to them in the sunshine and in the light of the stars, in the movements of the planets and of the Moon. The world-picture of Copernicus, Galileo, and Kepler is a luciferic construction. Precisely because it arose from and corresponds to our ahrimanic forces of knowledge, its content—please distinguish here between method and content—is a luciferic one.

When the Mystery of Golgotha took place, the divine Sophia, the wisdom that enables us to see into the world with understanding, worked in a twofold way. Divine wisdom, heavenly wisdom, worked in the revelation to the poor shepherds in the fields, and in the revelation to the Wise Men from the East. This wisdom was still present in its later form among the Gnostics, from whom the early Christian fathers and teachers of the Church took this wisdom and used it to understand the Mystery of Golgotha. This wisdom could not be continued into our times. It was overwhelmed and killed by Lucifer, just as Osiris was killed by Ahriman-Typhon. We have not lost Osiris, that is, the Christ, we have lost that being who for us takes the place of Isis. Lucifer has killed her. But the Isis-being killed by Lucifer was not sunk into the earth, as Typhon sunk Osiris into the Nile. Lucifer carried the Isis-being, the divine wisdom whom he had killed, out into the cosmic spaces; he sunk her into the ocean of space. When we look out into this ocean and see the stars moving according to mathematical lines, then we see the grave of what spiritually permeated this world, for the divine Sophia, the successor of Isis, is dead.

We must create this legend, for it presents the truth of our times. We must speak of the dead and lost Isis, the divine Sophia, in the same way the early Egyptians spoke of the dead and lost Osiris. With the power we do not understand but which nevertheless is in us, with the power of Christ, the power of the new Osiris, we must set out in search of the dead body of the modern Isis, the dead body of the divine Sophia. We must approach luciferic natural science and seek there the coffin of Isis; in other words, in what natural science gives us we must find something that stimulates us towards Imagination, Inspiration and Intuition. In this way we acquire the help of Christ within—Christ, Who remans hidden for us in darkness if we do not illuminate Him with divine wisdom. Armed with this power of Christ, with the new Osiris, we must set out in search of Isis, the new Isis. Lucifer will not cut Isis in pieces, as Ahriman-Typhon did with Osiris; on the contrary, this Isis is spread out in her true form in the beauty of the whole universe. This Isis shines out of the cosmos in an aura of many luminous colours. We have to learn to understand Isis when we look out into the cosmos, to see this cosmos in its aura of luminous colours.

But just as Ahriman-Typhon once cut Osiris into pieces, so Lucifer comes to blur and wash out the colours in all their clear distinctness; he blends and merges into one single whole the parts which are so beautifully distributed over the heavens, the limbs of the new Isis which go to make the great firmament of the heavens. Just as Typhon cut Osiris into pieces, so Lucifer blends the abundant colours that stream down to us from the aura of the universe into a uniform white light that radiates through the universe. This is the light that Goethe fought against in his treatise on colours, opposing the statement that white light contains all the colours, which in truth extend over the mysterious, abundant and secret deeds of the whole universe.

But we must persevere in our search until we again find Isis. And when we have found her, we must find a way to place into the universe what we are then able to discover and to know. What we acquire through the newly found Isis, we place before our souls in a living way, so that the whole universe, the cosmos, becomes spiritual for us again. We must understand Saturn, Sun, Moon, Earth, Jupiter, Venus and Vulcan from within. What Lucifer has made of Isis, we must transfer into the heavenly spaces just as Isis buried in the earth parts of the body of Osiris, cut into pieces by Typhon-Ahriman. We must realize that through the power of Christ we can find an inner astronomy that will show us the universe proceeding from and working out of the power of the spirit. Then the rediscovered power of Isis, which is now the power of the divine Sophia, will allow Christ, who has united with the Earth since the Mystery of Golgotha, to become active in the new insight into the universe, to become active within us because of our new knowledge. We do not lack Christ; but the knowledge of Christ, the Sophia of Christ, the Isis of Christ is lacking.

This is what we should engrave in our souls as a content of the Mystery of Christmas. We must realize that since the nineteenth century even theology has come to look upon Christ merely as the man from Nazareth. That means that theology is completely permeated by Lucifer. It no longer sees into the spiritual background of existence. External natural science is luciferic; theology is luciferic. Of course if we are speaking of the inner aspect of the human being as you can see from my previous words we could just as well say that in this theology the human being is ahrimanic. Then in the same way we must say of the Egyptians that they were luciferic, just as we say of them that their perception of the external world was ahrimanic. Modern human beings must understand the Mystery of Christmas in a new way. They must realize that they must first of all seek Isis, in order that Christ may appear to them. The cause of our misfortunes and the problems of modern civilization is not that we have lost Christ, who stands before us in a far greater glory than Osiris did in the eyes of the Egyptians. It is not that we have lost him and need to set out in search of him, armed with the force of Isis. No, what we have lost is the knowledge of Christ Jesus, insight into his being. This is what we must find again with the power of the Jesus Christ Who is in us.

This is how we must look upon the content of the Christmas Festival. For many modern people Christmas is nothing more than a festival for giving and receiving presents, something which they celebrate every year through habit. Like so many other things in modern life the Christmas festival has become an empty phrase. And it is just because so many things have become nothing more than a phrase that modern life is so full of calamities and chaos. This is in truth the deeper reason for the chaos in our modern life.

If in this our community, we could acquire the right feelings for everything which has become mere phrases in the present age, and if these feelings could enable us to find the impulses needed for the renewals that are so necessary, then this community, which calls itself the anthroposophical community, would be worthy of its existence. This community should understand the terrible significance for our age that such things as the Christmas festival are carried forward as a mere phrase. We should be able to understand that in the future this must not be allowed, and that these things must be given a new content. Old habits must be left behind and new insights must take their place. If we cannot find the inner courage needed to do this, then we share in the lie which keeps up the yearly Christmas festival merely as a phrase, celebrating it without our souls feeling and sensing the true significance of the event. Are we really lifted up to the highest concerns of humanity when we give and receive presents every year out of habit at this festival of Christ? Do we lift ourselves up to the highest concerns of humanity when we listen to the words—which have also become a phrase—spoken by the representatives of the various religious communities? We should forbid ourselves to continue in this inner hollowness of our Christmas celebrations. We should make the inner decision to give such a festival a content which allows the highest, worthiest feelings to pass through our souls. Such a festival celebration would raise humanity to the comprehension of the meaning of its existence.

Ask yourselves whether the feelings in your hearts and souls when you stand before the Christmas tree and open the presents which are given out of habit, and the Christmas cards containing the usual phrases—ask yourselves whether feelings are living in you that can raise humanity to an understanding of the meaning of its evolution on Earth! All the problems and misfortune of our time are due to this—we cannot find the courage to lift ourselves above the empty phrases of our age. But it must happen, a new content must [be]come the content which can give us entirely new feelings that stir us powerfully, just as those people were stirred who were true Christians in the first Christian centuries, and who felt the Mystery of Golgotha and the appearance of Christ as the highest which humanity could experience upon the Earth. Our souls must again acquire something of this spirit.

Oh, the soul will attain to altogether new feelings if it feels committed to experience the new Isis legend within modern humanity. Lucifer kills Isis and then places her body into the infinity of space, which has become the grave of Isis, a mathematical abstraction. Then comes the search for Isis, and her discovery, made possible through the inner force of spiritual knowledge. In place of the heavens that have become dead, this knowledge places what stars and planets reveal through an inner life, so that they then appear as monuments to the spiritual powers that weave with power through space. We are able to look at the manger today in the right way only if we experience in a unique way what is weaving with spiritual power through space, and then look at that Being Who came into the world through the child. We know that we bear this Being within us, but we must also understand Him. Just as the Egyptians looked from Osiris to Isis, so we must learn to look again to the new Isis, the holy Sophia. Christ will appear again in His spiritual form during the course of the twentieth century, not through the arrival of external events alone, but because human beings find the power represented by the holy Sophia. The modern age has had the tendency to lose this power of Isis, this power of Mary. It has been killed by all that arose with the modern consciousness of humanity. And the confessions have in part exterminated just this view of Mary.

This is the Mystery of modern humanity: fundamentally speaking, Mary-Isis has been killed, and she must be sought, just as Osiris was sought by Isis in Asia. But she must be sought in the infinite spaces of the universe with the power that Christ can awaken in us, if we devote ourselves to Him in the right way.

Let us picture this rightly, let us immerse ourselves in this new Isis legend which must be experienced, and let us fill our souls with it. Then we will experience in a true sense what humanity in many of its representatives believes, that this new legend fills the holy eve of Christmas, in order to bring us into Christmas day, the day of Christ. This anthroposophical community could become a community of human beings united in love because they feel the need, common to them all, to search. Let us become conscious of this most intimate task! Let us go in spirit to the manger and bring to the Child our sacrifice and our gift, which lie in the knowledge that something altogether new must fill our souls, in order that we may fulfil the tasks which can lead humanity out of barbarism into a truly new civilization.

To achieve this, of course, it is absolutely necessary that in our circles we are prepared to help one another in love, so that a real community of souls arises in which all forms of envy and the like disappear, and in which we do not look merely each at the other, but together face the great goal we have in common. The Mystery brought into the world by the Christmas child also contains this—that we can look at a common goal without discord because the common goal signifies union in harmony. The light of Christmas should actually shine as a light of peace, as a light that brings external peace, only because first of all it brings an inner peace into the hearts of human beings. We should learn to say to ourselves: If we can manage to work together in love on the great tasks, then, and only then, do we understand Christmas. If we cannot manage this, we do not understand Christmas.

Let us remember that when we do sow discord, this discord hinders us in understanding the one who appeared among human beings on the first Christmas on Earth. Can we not pour this Mystery of Christmas into our souls, as something which unites our hearts in love and harmony? If we do not properly understand what spiritual science is, then we will not be able to do this. Nothing will come of this community if we merely bring into it ideas and impulses we have picked up here and there from all corners of the world, where clichés and routine hold sway. Let us remember that our community is facing a difficult year, that all our forces must be gathered together, and let us celebrate Christmas in this spirit. Oh, I would like to find words that could speak deeply into the heart of each one of you on this evening. Then each one of you would feel that my words contain a greeting, which at the same time is an appeal to kindle spiritual science within your hearts, so that it may become a power that can help humanity which is living under such terrible oppression.

Beginning with such points of view, I have gathered the thoughts which I wished to speak to you. Be assured that they are intended as a warm Christmas greeting for each one of you, as something that can lead you into the new year in the very best way. In this spirit, accept my words today as they were intended, as an affectionate Christmas greeting.

Isis-Sophia
Des Gottes Weisheit
Sie hat Luzifer getötet
Und auf der Weltenkräfte Schwingen
In Raumesweiten fortgetragen.

Christus-Wollen
In Menschen werkend,—
Es wird Luzifer entreißen
Und auf des Geisteswissens Boten
In Menschenseelen auferwecken
Isis-Sophia
Des Gottes Weisheit.

Isis-Sophia,
Wisdom of God,
she has been slain by Lucifer,
and on the wings of the powers of the world
carried her hence into the infinite space of the universe.
The willing of Christ
Working in man
Shall wrest from Lucifer
And on the boats of Spirit-knowledge
Awaken in human souls
Isis-Sophia
Wisdom of God.

[Tr. James Hindes. This translation is slightly edited for clarity—A. S.]

Appendix 4: Rudolf Steiner's Last Address

Dornach, Michaelmas Eve, 28 Sept. 1924 [GA 238]

Translated by George Adams

My dear friends,

It has not been possible for me to speak to you on the last two days. But today—the day when the Michael mood of dedication must pour its light into all our hearts, I did not want to let pass without speaking to you at least a few words. That I am able to do so is due entirely to the loving and devoted care of our friend Dr. Ita Wegman. And so I hope that I will still be able to say today what I desire particularly to say to you on the occasion of this festival.

In recent months we have frequently spoken, my dear friends, of the in-streaming of the Michael-Power into the spiritual events of man's life on earth. And it will be one of the more beautiful results that can follow from our anthroposophical understanding of times and seasons, if we are really able to add to the other festivals of the year a rightly ordered Michael Festival. That however will only be possible when the might and power of the Michael-Thoughts, of which today men have no more than a dim feeling, have taken hold in a number of human souls who will then be able to create the right human starting-point for such a festival.

What we can do at present is to awaken, in this Michael-time, the Michael-mood in our souls by giving ourselves up to thoughts that will prepare the way for a future Michael Festival. And such thoughts are especially stirred to activity within us when we turn our gaze upon all that we have seen taking place—partly on Earth, partly in super-sensible worlds—through long periods of time, in preparation for all that can now be accomplished for human evolution in the course of this present century by souls who in full sincerity feel themselves drawn to the Michael-stream.

That you yourselves, my dear friends, in so far as you truly and honestly incline to the Anthroposophical Movement, belong to these souls—this I have endeavoured to make clear to you in the lectures of the last weeks and especially also in the lectures where I spoke to you directly of the karma of the Anthroposophical Society. We can however carry these considerations a little further, and that is what I want to do today.

Let us now bring before our souls beings who are intimately connected, and will always be intimately connected, with the Michael stream, in the sense in which we have described it here. Let us direct our gaze to beings who in at least two successive incarnations made a powerful impression on great numbers of their fellow-men, beings who, however, only show themselves in their true unity when we recognize them as successive incarnations of one and the same being.

When we look back into olden times, we see rise up before us within the traditions of Judaism the prophetic figure of Elijah. We know what significance the prophet Elijah had for the people of the Old Testament, and therewith for all mankind; we know how he set before them the goal and destiny of their existence. And we have shown how in the course of time the being who was present in Elijah appeared again at the very most important moment of human evolution, appeared again so that Christ Jesus Himself could give him the Initiation he was to receive for the evolution of mankind. For the being of Elijah appeared again in Lazarus-John—who are in truth one and the same figure, as you will have understood from my book *Christianity as Mystical Fact*.

Furthermore, we saw that this being appears once more in that world painter who let his artistic power unfold in marvellous depths of tenderness, as it moved hovering over the Mystery of Golgotha. And we saw how the deeply Christian impulse that lives in Raphael, as it were impelling into colour and form the very nature and being of Christianity itself—we saw how this impulse rose again in the poet Novalis. In the poet Novalis stands revealed in wondrously beautiful words what Raphael had placed before mankind in colours and forms of rarest loveliness. We see, thus following one another in time, beings who are brought together into a unity when incarnation is understood.

We know (for I have often spoken with you of these things) how, when man has gone through the gate of death, he enters the world of the stars. What we are accustomed to call 'stars' in the external, physical sense are no more than the outer sign and symbol of spiritual worlds which look down upon us and take their share and part in all the deeds of the evolution of mankind.

We know that man passes through the Moon-sphere and through the spheres of Mercury and Venus, through the spheres of the Sun and of Mars, and of Jupiter and Saturn. And we know that when, together with the beings of these spheres and together too with other human souls who have also departed from the life on Earth, he has elaborated his karma, he then turns back again to earthly existence.

Bearing this in mind, let us look for a moment at Raphael and see how he passes through the gate of death, and how he enters the realm of the starry worlds, the realm of spiritual evolution, taking with him the power of his art, which already on earth shone with the bright light of the stars. We behold, my dear friends, how Raphael enters the Moon-sphere, and we see how he comes into association here with the Spirits who live in the Moon-sphere and who are the spiritual Individualities of the great original Leaders of mankind, with whose wisdom Raphael, as Elijah, had been deeply inspired. He meets these Moon Beings, and he meets too all the souls with whom he has lived in earlier stages of Earth-evolution. We see how he unites himself spiritually with the spiritual origin of the Earth, with that World of Being which first made it possible for man to be, and for the Earthly to be impregnated with the Divine. We behold Raphael, as it were, completely 'at home', united with those with whom he had most loved to be in the Elijah-existence, inasmuch as it was they who at the beginning of Earth existence set the goal for the life on this Earth.

Then we behold him wander through the Mercury-sphere where, in association with the great Cosmic Healers, he transforms for his spirituality the power that had been his to create what is so infinitely whole and healthy in colour and line. All that he has painted, whether on canvas or as a fresco on the wall, for the help and comfort as well as for the unending inspiration of such as can understand—all his work that was so radiant with light, showed itself now to him in the great cosmic connection in which it is able to stand when it passes through the Beings of the Mercury-sphere.

And thus was he, who on Earth had unfolded so great a love for art, whose soul had been aflame with love for colour and for line, transplanted now into the sphere of Venus, which in turn lovingly bore him across to the Sun, to that Sun existence which lived in all his incarnations so far as they are yet known to us. For it was from the Sun that he, as the prophet Elijah, brought to mankind through the medium of his own people the truths that belong to the goals of existence.

We see how in the Sun-sphere he is able to live through over again in a deep and intimate sense—in another way now than when he was on Earth as a companion of Christ Jesus—he is able to live over again what he underwent when, through the Initiation of Christ Jesus, he, Lazarus, became John. And all that he has painted in shining light for the followers of Christ Jesus—he now beholds all this pour its rays into the cosmic transformation of the human heart.

We see further how what he thus had at the foundation of his life penetrates, wisdom-filled, the sphere of Jupiter. In this sphere he is able in wisdom to enter into a relation of understanding with such spirits as Goethe—the spirit, that is, that afterwards became Goethe—as well as also with spirits who had gone astray on other paths, but who nevertheless led over World-Being and World-Thought into the magical realm. The foundation is laid for his magic idealism in the experience he had of the evolution of the later Éliphas Lévi. And we behold, too, how he partakes in all that was living there in Swedenborg.

Now I must draw your attention to something in the life of Raphael that is of very great significance. A person who was most deeply devoted to Raphael—Hermann Grimm [1828-1901]—set to work four times to write a life of Raphael. His *Life of Michelangelo* he brought to a beautiful completeness, but he never succeeded in drawing any picture of Raphael's earthly life that gave him satisfaction. In his own view all he wrote was unfinished and incomplete. The first book he undertook was intended to be a biography. What is it? Nothing but a reproduction of old anecdotes told by Vasari! No biography of Raphael at all, but something altogether different—a description of what Raphael became on Earth after his death, in the respect and recognition of his fellow men. Hermann Grimm relates what people have thought of Raphael—what the Italians, the French, the Germans have thought of Raphael in the course of history through the centuries. What he gives us is a biography of the Raphael-thought as it has lived here on Earth since his death. He finds the way to tell what remains of Raphael in the hearts and minds of men, what lives of him still in their reverence and understanding. But he does not find the possibility to give a picture of the earthly life of Raphael.

After Hermann Grimm has made the attempt four times over, he says: all that one can really do for Raphael as a personality is to write of how one picture passes over into the next, as though it had been painted by a super-sensible being who had simply not touched the Earth at all with his earthly life. The pictures are there, but one can look right away from Raphael who painted the pictures and reproduce the sequence of what is expressed in their inner content.

And so, shortly before his death, Hermann Grimm began to speak once again about Raphael; yet once more he made the attempt to put pen to paper and write about him. This time however he spoke only of his pictures and not about the earthly personality of Raphael at all.

The truth is, my dear friends, this earthly personality of Raphael was completely yielded up and was only present through what Lazarus-John gave to this soul to be poured out into colour and line for all mankind. Such was the life of this being. And it was so, that this Raphael life could only be, as it were, absolved in another life of 30 years—in Novalis. And so we see Raphael die young, Novalis die young—one being, who came forth from Elijah-John, appearing before mankind in two different forms, preparing through art and through poetry the true Michael-mood of soul, sent down by the Michael-stream as messenger to men on Earth.

And now we behold the wonderful artistic power of Raphael come to life again in Novalis in poetry that stirs and enraptures the hearts of men. All that through Raphael was given to human eyes to see—of this could human hearts drink deep, when it came again in Novalis.

When we consider the life of Novalis, what an echo we find there of the Raphael life for which Hermann Grimm had so fine an understanding! His beloved dies in her youth. He is himself still young. What is he going to do with his life now that she has died? He tells us himself. He says that his life on Earth will be henceforth to 'die after her', to follow her on the way of death. He wants to pass over already now into the super-sensible, to lead again the Raphael-life, not touching the Earth, but living out in poetry his magic idealism. He would fain not let himself be touched by Earth-life.

When we read the *Fragments* of Novalis, and give ourselves up to the life that flows so abundantly in them, we can discover the secret of the deep impression they make on us. Whatever we have before us in immediate sense-reality, whatever the eye can see and recognize as beautiful—all this, through the magic idealism that lives in the soul of Novalis, appears in his poetry with a well-nigh heavenly splendour. The meanest and simplest material thing—with the magic idealism of his poetry he can make it live again in all its spiritual light and glory.

And so we see in Novalis a radiant and splendid forerunner of that Michael-stream which is now to lead you all, my dear friends, while you live; and then, after you have gone through the gate of death, you will find in the spiritual super-sensible worlds all those others—among them also the being of whom I have been speaking to you today—all those with whom you are to prepare the work that shall be accomplished at the end of the century, and that shall lead mankind past the great crisis in which it is involved.

This work is: to let the Michael-power and the Michael-will penetrate the whole of life. The Michael-power and the Michael-will are none other than the Christ-will and the Christ-power, going before in order to implant in the right way into the Earth the power of the Christ. If this Michael-power is able verily to overcome all that is of the demon and the dragon (and you will know what that is), if you all, who have in this way received in the light of anthroposphical wisdom the Michael-Thought, have indeed received it with true and faithful heart and with tender love, and will endeavour to go forward from the Michael-mood of this year, until not only is the Michael-thought revealed in your soul, but you are able also to make the Michael-thought live in your deeds in all its strength and all its power—if this is so, then will you be true servants of the Michael-thought, worthy helpers of what has now to enter Earth-evolution through Anthroposophy, and take its place there in the meaning of Michael.

If, in the near future, in four times twelve human beings, the Michael-thought becomes fully alive—four times twelve human beings, that is, who are recognized not by themselves but by the Leadership of the Goetheanum in Dornach—if in four times twelve such human beings, leaders arise having the mood of soul that belongs to the Michael Festival, then we can look up to the light that through the Michael-stream and the Michael-activity will be shed abroad in the future among mankind.

Because this is so, my dear friends, I have made the effort today to rise up and speak to you, if only in these few short words. My strength is not sufficient for more today. May the words so speak to your soul that you receive the Michael-thought in the sense of what a faithful follower of Michael may feel when, clothed in the light rays of the Sun, Michael appears and points us to that which must now take place. For it must even be so that this Michael-garment, this garment of Light, shall become the Words of the Worlds, which can transform the Logos of the Worlds into the Logos of Mankind. Consequently, let my words to you today be these:

Springing from Powers of the Sun,
Radiant Spirit-powers, blessing all Worlds!
For Michael's garment of rays
Ye are predestined by Thought Divine.

He, the Christ-messenger, revealeth in you—
Bearing mankind aloft—the sacred Will of Worlds.

Ye, the radiant Beings of Aether-Worlds,
Bear the Christ-Word to Man.

Thus shall the Heralds of Christ appear
To the thirstily waiting souls,
To whom your Word of Light shines forth
In cosmic age of Spirit-man.

Ye, the disciples of Spirit-Knowledge,
Take Michael's Wisdom beckoning,
Take the Word of Love of the Will of Worlds
Into your soul's aspiring, a c t i v e l y !

*

Hermann Beckh himself humbly and briefly acknowledges the experience of the 'Last Address' by Rudolf Steiner inspired his exposition of Mark's Gospel, and again in the Foreword to his study on John's Gospel. 'Without the inner work on what was then received, the whole present work would not have been possible' (*Mark's Gospel: The Cosmic Rhythm*, p. 48). The spiritual research came to fruition in the writing of that book, when the *occasion* was offered by the appearance of the 'astral mythology' of Arthur Drews and others.

The 25-year-old Ralph Kux, the first male eurythmist, recollects:

> This last address was like a tremendous ritual. It was also received as such by the listeners. As Rudolf Steiner entered the hall and as he left after he had spoken the tremendous words of the Michael verse, everyone present in deeply stirred concentration rose to their feet, something that did not usually happen. He looked very pale and we had the impression that he summoned his last strength in order to be able to manage this. He spoke unusually fast and urgently.
>
> [Ralph Kux, Willi Kux. *Erinnerungen an Rudolf Steiner*. Ralph Kux. *Eurythmie und Musik* (in one volume). Stuttgart: Melinger Verlag. 1976. 24. Eng. tr. in MS. A. S.]

Beckh's biographer writes:

> The year 1924 brought an abundance of lectures and courses by Rudolf Steiner up to then unequalled. His activities intensified to a hitherto undreamt extent. The climax took place in September, in which Steiner

frequently gave five lectures daily: for the craftsmen working on the Goetheanum, for the actors, the priests, the priests with the doctors, and for the members [of the Anthroposophical Society]—that is, for all those present in Dornach. After the end of the course given on the Apocalypse of John, the last lecture of which took place on 22 September, the priests had to return to their communities. By this time Hermann Beckh also belonged to those few of the group of priests who were able to remain a few days longer in Dornach. Rudolf von Koschützki and Gottfried Husemann were also in this fortunate position. They heard the last karma-lecture [in GA 238] on 23 September. On the following day, Rudolf Steiner spoke in the morning to the workers. The lecture announced for the evening for the members had to be cancelled, something that had never happened during all those long years. People were shocked and full of concern. Rudolf von Koschützki describes how, with Hermann Beckh, he was on his way to the lecture:

> It was already dark and it was raining. A car came towards us down the hill. The driver stopped and said, 'The lecture is cancelled; Dr. Steiner is taken ill.' Professor Beckh then stepped closer to learn more. When the car moved on, Beckh was very concerned and said, 'Now it starts with him just as with Buddha.' The latter's organism apparently refused to take any further earthly nourishment. Nobody could recall a single announced lecture by Steiner ever having to be cancelled. But he wanted to speak to his friends one more time. We waited from day to day for his recovery sufficient to hold the lecture. As he ascended the speakers' desk we saw he looked terribly wretched and struggled for breath. Then he became increasingly animated, until after twenty minutes he stopped and left the room (Rudolf von Koschützki. *Fahrt ins Erdenland*. 1952. 332).

The people present were deeply moved. At first absolute silence ruled; the people did not dare to move. 'Then Professor Beckh got up with the words, "*Das war erschütternd!*—That was most astonishing!" More or less silent, we left the room.' So it was reported by someone who was present (Chlothilde Votteler. 'Letzte Ansprache Rudolf Steiners' in *Mitteilungen aus der anthroposophischen Arbeit in Deutschland*. 1978. 258).

That was the farewell. After this day, Michaelmas Eve 1924, Rudolf Steiner spoke no longer to the Members [of the Anthroposophical Society, though he continued to write, for example the *Anthroposophical Leading Thoughts* for the weekly newspaper *Das Goetheanum*]. He could no longer leave his sickbed, and died 30 March 1925. Those who had experienced this farewell have kept the memory their whole life long, feeling it an inner duty through it to have felt more strongly and closely united with Rudolf Steiner and his task for humanity.

> In this 'Last Address' that remains a fragment, Rudolf Steiner spoke again of Elijah and his mission as a forerunner of Christ, as already in that first lecture that Hermann Beckh heard thirteen years previously, on 14 December 1913 in Berlin. For him a circle closed on this Michaelmas Eve 1914.
>
> (Gundhild Kačer-Bock. *Hermann Beckh: Life and Work,* Temple Lodge 2021. 99.)

Perhaps Dr. Rudolf Steiner was even speaking in particular to Professor Hermann Beckh?—A. S.

Meeting Rudolf Steiner

Hermann Beckh

Whoever through life's destiny has been led to meet Rudolf Steiner will consciously or unconsciously have met an experience that could be expressed in the following words: *To meet Rudolf Steiner is to become acquainted with the essence of the living word.* Such a person would learn to recognize not only a word that is not merely word, but destiny. It bears in itself the power of world-fashioning, fashioning one's being and one's humanity, because it is taken from those depths of the world governed by the destiny-fashioning will itself. In order to counteract misunderstandings here that so easily arise facing the greatest, something has to be added. The destiny-effect of this word did not lie in the fact that it would have overcome the soul like a higher compulsion, but that it was like a tremendous 'knocking at the door' of sleep, of the sleeping soul.

Wherever it is at work, this word cannot do other than waken. To awaken through this word means to find the forces that hitherto slumbered in depths of the soul, and then through one's own will to use these forces consciously.

The destiny-carrying quality of this person and his words lead to an understanding that whoever today speaks or writes to another in memory of Rudolf Steiner will feel compelled to connect to personal elements in his recollection. It was in Berlin in 1911, in a public lecture on Elijah [14 Dec. 1911, in GA 61] held in the hall of the

'Architects' House' that the writer of these lines saw and heard Rudolf Steiner for the first time. Amongst the many tremendous lectures, which were then held in public by the founder of the later Anthroposophical Society, this was one of the strongest. More than what usually occurred in public lectures, results of meditative research were directly presented to the audience. He began by carefully mentioning that nothing would be conveyed for a mere believing acceptance, but with this a key was offered, a kind of working method through which everyone using it in their own work may attempt to approach the secret of the biblical word and the biblical manner of presentation. With such a work he finds the possibility to make true for himself what has been said in increasing measure.

The more the lecture developed the more one was carried into a true Elijah-experience, the more one felt a fire from heaven, a force living and working in the words. One suddenly recognized the spiritual reality working behind the pictures of the Bible—which hitherto had remained hidden in those pictures—because the one speaking himself lived in that reality of the spirit. One could feel, here somebody is speaking on the Bible not with abstract thoughts but out of that element out of which the Bible word itself had received its imprint. The letters became alive. It was as if scales fell from one's eyes; everything fell off that hitherto in the traditional notions lay like a veil over the Bible.

At that time the writer of these lines came out of completely different areas of study; he represented Indology at the University of Berlin. The pictorial world of the Old Testament, as though of forgotten archetypal memories of humanity, had once shone into the dreams of his early childhood. Then for decades almost hardly valued, they were put *ad acta* [were 'shelved']. Through that lecture they were returned to him anew, only what then was beheld as in a dream was now present in an awake consciousness.

Through the course of the years what was taken up in that lecture—for it worked further in the soul—became a key for the secrets of the biblical language in general. It was for him as for others who since then have worked within this realm in the Movement for Religious Renewal. A sense could awaken there for a way of narration, so characteristic for the Bible and especially for the Old Testament, that after it has initially related events of the sensory world, it then almost unnoticed goes over into that way of narration where what has been described, seemingly a continuation of the events in the sensory world, becomes a picture for a spiritual event, for experiences of soul and spirit ...

The first lecture I experienced of Dr. Steiner was a lecture on Elijah. The very last address he gave, that Michaelmas lecture in Dornach that a benign destiny had allowed me to hear, led deep into the mysteries of Elijah's being. Steiner was ill, more ill than we knew then; through the power of spiritual will he once more held at bay the weakness and pain of the illness in order for a last time to speak to us. His words were like a moving last testimony for understanding Christ and to understand the gospels in future; almost unlimited vistas opened up here. It was like a sacrificial outpouring and communicating of that living power of the word to all who, from then on, had decided to make themselves pure serving vessels for it. As a sacrament, like a sacred 'Receive ...', this Last Address was able to work on the soul.

[From: *Die Christengemeinschaft*. 1924. 44-9. Tr. A. S. 2015]

Appendix 5

The Name Isis

Hermann Beckh

[Prof. Dr. Hermann Beckh. *From the World of the Mysteries*. Temple Lodge 2020. 170-77. Eng. tr. A. S. 2014]

***

Amongst the many expressive names the early Egyptians gave to the goddess Isis—a collection can be found in Heinrich Karl Brugsch, *Religion und Mythologie der alten Ägypter* [Nabu Press 2010/ Rarebooksclub.com 2012] in his chapter on Isis—we can find the main ones characterizing most immediately the being of Isis as the *lady* or *goddess of love*. The secret of Isis is none other than the *secret of love*. Love, seen more externally, is that power which *creatively fashions*, which magically fashions the substance of the world. More internally, it is the power that *awakens* the 'I' in human consciousness—in the highest sense that the word 'I' possesses. The Egyptian Isis is also the Mother of substance and the Awakener of the higher 'I' of Osiris.

As the *one giving birth to the 'I'* and *the fashioner of substance* she stands before us already in the sounds of her name. If we look at the sounds and the writing of the name, initially in its Egyptian form, already the Isis hieroglyph, the *seat (throne)* 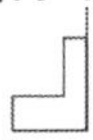 points towards that sublime region of that divine-spiritual world in which all those spiritual forces are active, revealed in all later fashioning of substance. We also find the throne-seat in the hieroglyph of *Osiris* (Egyptian: *wsjr*, Usiri), there still connected to the *eye (iri)* of the seeing consciousness, so that for *Usiri, Osiris*, in sound and pictorial image, the meaning arises: 'Eye of power, the Sun's power of seeing' (cf. Brugsch. 81).

With the throne-seat, built up out of squares and rectangles (for itself alone can mean Isis), we find from the sounds of the various words with the name Isis (Egyptian: *Isit*), connected to the t-hieroglyph, the half-moon , or the half-circle standing on the diameter as its basis and underneath an egg-shaped form indicating the feminine within Isis 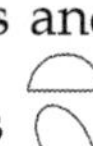. According to Dr. Wachsmuth (*The Etheric Formative Forces in Cosmos,*

Earth and Man) on the forming tendencies of the four kinds of ether (square with the life-ether, half-moonlike with the sound-ether) these Egyptian pictograms of the name of Isis are to remind us of the connection of the *life-ether* with the sound-ether that carries the force which fashions substance (cf. Wachsmuth, Germ. ed. p. 164). With these two higher kinds of ether there lies the secret of the Tree of Life that has been lost to human beings in Paradise, and with it also the secret of the *Eternal Feminine* in its (today forgotten) higher spiritual meaning, that secret of the *Primordial Feminine of the world*, which the early Egyptians expressed with the name of Isis.

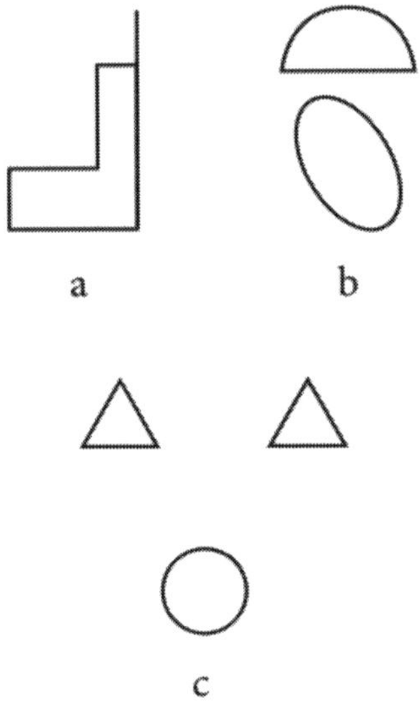

The sounds of the name Isis have to be found out of the Egyptian writing that does not picture the vowels. There we initially find 'H-S-T (with 'h the *Spiritus lenis*, the 'silent breath', the sound standing at the border of the inaudible is indicated, corresponding to the Hebrew Aleph). The still undifferentiated archetypal spiritual element (h) connects with the *principle fashioning matter* S-T. This connection of sounds works archetypally and expressively from the primordial language right into modern languages, indicating the firm and rigid quality of the physical, mineral element [see the monograph, H. Beckh, *Etymologie und Lautbedeutung*, 24ff., pub. separately Edition Geheimes Wissen 2013, also in *Neue Wege zur Ursprache.* Stuttgart: Urachhaus 1954; Eng. tr. *The Source of Speech*, Temple Lodge 2020]. The star-radiant (*St*erne-*St*rahlende) element working *above* in the etheric element, *below* in the physical, mineral element becomes the firm, rigid, *st*ony cry*st*al (zum Fes*t*en und *St*arren des *St*eins, zum Kris*t*al). To connect in the right way this *above* and *below* in the spirit, is to lead towards a veiled secret in Isis and the sounds in her name. The names of the gods are indeed above all others those in which there still communicates to us in each individual sound something of its divine archetypal meaning. Only out of this eurythmical, primordial interpretation of the sounds, a name such as the Egyptian name Isis can be meaningfully read.

It is no mere whim that the vowels in the Egyptian as well as the Semitic languages in their writing remain initially un-notated, but there are many reasons and spiritual contexts. The *pure spiritual* element uncoloured by the psychological, or soul-aspects of the being is presented in this writing without vowels. One may try slowly to speak the Egyptian name Isis 'H-S-T in this way purely consonantally and yet expressively; one will perceive something of the *sacred, primordial keeping silence* of the *'voice of [thin] silence'* [cf. LXX 1 Kings 19:12 *Tr. note*] of that *divine, archetypal stillness* which the gnostic called *Sige* and revered as the female part, the archetypal consort of the World-Father. This uncertain 'H-S-T' (which in the trinity of its sounds keeps veiled the *secret of Christ*), the divine-spiritual, in which works the primordial female force-fashioning substance, then becomes vocalized (though this involves much interpretation). The Egyptologists interpret *I-s-t, Iset Isit,* also as U-s-t (see Brugsch. 83). The archetypal sound *U* would still point towards the pure archetypal being, the archetypal darkness—Isis is truly also the Queen of the cosmic night. In the *I* there already lies the light shining in the darkness; the Egyptians thought of the star Sirius. In this light (*Licht*) lies the German *Ich* ('I'), the vowel of light I, which at the same time is the vowel of the *Ich*.

This is no mere 'feeling of sounds', regarded with horror by our academic etymologists, but for the Egyptian language (as well as for the Assyrian and Hebrew languages, and then significantly for the Teutonic languages) a real fact of language that is expressed in the word *Ich*, or at least certain pronoun derivatives, for example, '*mein*, mine', etc. are expressed through the vowel I, or the I-suffix is grammatically expressed, also the meaningful *J* (*Jod* in German) while in Hebrew the name of *Jahve* (Y-H-V-H) is to be recalled in this connection. [The Hebrew letter yod is used to represent both the consonantal Y and at times the vowel I.]

In this way the Egyptian name Isis *I–S–T, Iset, Isis* can appear to us truly like the archetypal word-connection of that which also in our language speaks to us out of the inscription to the goddess of Sais: '*Ich* bin alles das ... *ist*—*I* am everything that ... *is* ....'

***

In ancient languages as spoken, S and T frequently lie together, and so the name for the goddess became for the Greeks *Isis*. For academic etymologists, who only research the historical origins, this Greek form of the name as such has no significance. They take it as an aid to unlock the Egyptian form, especially the Egyptian vowels. But apart from this, that to all exploration of Egyptian word-forms something problematic and hypothetical always adheres, we can feel towards the Greek work Isis, as if in it a certain nuance of the archetypal word-content of the name of the Egyptian goddess is only then fully expressed therein. (The actual archetypal word lies indeed in eternity, outside time, not at all always in what historically went before.) There lives in the two equal syllables—only to be distinguished through the long and short vowels—a *rhythmic element* of repetition, corresponding to the nature of the *etheric*, and with it at the same time a secret of the *archetypal feminine*, ordered to the rhythm and the form-principle of the number two. In his book *Das Land der Inca in seiner Bedeutung für die Urgeschichte der Sprache und Schrift* ['The land of the Incas in its significance for the prehistory of language and writing' (Fourier 1989; Nabu Press 2010)], Rudolf Falb shows with insight how in the various languages words relate on the one hand to the *rhythm of time*, and on the other hand to the rhythmic movements of the *maternal breast*. They connect amongst themselves and also with the Egyptian-Greek Isis.

Purely factually, Isis means in the most primeval sense, the *feminine aspect of the world*. This meaning already lies in the sounds, in the S as the sound of the earthly, feminine, material and sensory element. The ancient symbol for this was the snake. In this sense, in many of the old written signs (also in Egypt) the snake can be recognized in S and Z signs. In many primeval words, this S—and even more the sound combination ST—we recall the *snake of knowledge* that winds itself around the *Tree of Life*. And the double S of the Egyptian-Greek Isis causes us think of the *two snakes* that wind around the staff of Hermes-Mercury. This Staff of Hermes with the two snakes is again a picture of the Egyptian Mystery-wisdom and star-wisdom. This, seen as a being, is Isis. Words, too, which mean the number six and the lily (the secret of the water-lily is connected to the secret of Isis and the number six), possess in Hebrew and in Egyptian characteristically the double S (Hebrew *shushan* 'lily', Egyptian s-sh-n, Coptic *shoshen* 'water-lily, lotus').

In the name Isis we do not experience the physical content of matter, but the *etheric formative forces* that effect the fashioning of matter, and its connection with the 'I'. But where we behold the formative forces of the fashioning of matter in the *etheric element*, they are still shown as *related to the stars* (the Assyrian goddess *Istar*, who in her name is related to Isis, Isit, still clearly carries the *star* in her name, cf. in Avestan the primeval word for *star*). All this is pictured and parabolic in outer nature, when we do not look at the fashioning of the physical, mineral element, where it takes its course here below on the earth, but in the higher regions of the atmosphere. Up there, where starry, cosmic activity still governs, there are formed out of the activity of the light-ether in the element of water in the atmosphere (see Wachsmuth, Germ. ed. 182) the ice-crystal forms of snowflakes with their expressive star-forms. And with the covering of snow formed by these ice-crystal snowflakes earthly matter still appears in its purest, *virginal* form, which is closest to the cosmos. In the *ice-crystal of the snowflake* we experience the *etheric-virginal quality of the cosmos*, which the Egyptians called *Isis*. As explained elsewhere (H. Beckh, *The New Jerusalem* [a poetic work] the relationship to the '*I*' is indicated), the *force weaving in the etheric light of the snow-crystal enchants starry forms* (ibid. p. 110: 'As in the snow-crystals ether-fluff a shining cosmic starry light condenses to a tender veil of earthly matter.') And if we have arrived at the stage of deeply contemplating these spiritual contexts, it can be raised into meditation—for it is not only a superficial playing with speech sounds—then we gain an inner right to point out how in the German word *Eis* (ice) the same *etheric formative forces* out of the stellar element of the cosmos forming earthly matter are expressed right into the sounds themselves. We are allowed, when we also call up before our souls the fairy-tale figure of the *ice-virgin* with the ice and ice-crystal, to think of that which is revealed in the sounds of the name *Isis*.[43]

That all this is truly more than a phonetic fairy-tale imagination becomes clear from Rudolf Falb's interesting book, mentioned above. The author points (57, 66, 69, 362, etc.) to the veil, or the 'weave' of Isis, the veil of matter which in Egyptian would be called, as a reversal of Is-is, *si-si*. *Si-si-ra* would then be the 'Sun-veil, veil of glory'. This word *sisira* is meaningful for Falb, because he finds it again with a similar meaning in the primordial language and monuments of Peru, researched by him, pointing to primordial Atlantean times. The same word in the American primordial language we find in Sanskrit in the form *shishira* (emphasis on the first syllable); here it expresses the 'frozen tears of the Sun', the hoarfrost, the ice, the coldness, and in this Indian word we can find a true linguistic connection (based on metathesis) with the German word *Eis* (in the older form *is*). The veil of maya of Isis has here become the veil of the ice-virgin, which then especially conjures up the shining red colour. One recalls the snowy mountains glowing rosy pink in the crimson of the setting Sun. (According to Falb, this also relates to the Peruvian word—which has many other meanings.) This meaning of 'the colour red' can also be found in the Hebrew word based on the same consonants. We seem to be standing here before one of the oldest and most universal, primordial words.

Something quite meaningful arises when, to conclude, we direct our gaze to the Peruvian hieroglyph of the word *sisira,* which can be found in temples there as a sacred symbol (often mentioned by Falb). It consists of *two equal triangles,* and underneath in the middle a *circle* in italics 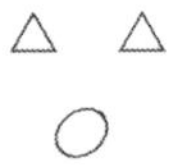 . From Wachsmuth's book we know the *triangle* and the *circle* as the forming tendencies of the two lower kinds of ether: *light-ether* and *warmth-ether*. If we place this facing what the *Egyptian* hieroglyph of the name Isis has shown us, with its connections of the form-principles of the *life-ether* and *sound-ether* (forms of square and half-moon), then in the mystery of the two higher kinds of ether (life-ether and sound-ether), there appears to us the being of *Isis,* in the two kinds of ether (light-ether and warmth-ether), the *veil of Isis* (si-si-ra). Through the Fall of man, human consciousness has lost the immediate connection with the *Tree of Life,* with the two higher kinds of ether; the human being today only lives in that which reveals the lower kinds of ether. This revelation of light and warmth veil to man today the secret of the higher revelations of cosmic life and cosmic harmony (life-ether and sound-ether): the earthly and feminine veils to him the secret of the *higher,* the *Eternal Feminine*. Thus for him Isis is still the veiled goddess. One day human beings will lift her veil again when the power of the Risen Christ has become strong in them.

Rudolf Steiner movingly describes the decline and fall of the Egyptian Mysteries.[44]

He describes when the soul of the initiate, having penetrated to the shores of cosmic existence, when it had become one with *Isis,* during the time of the glory of the ancient Mysteries, he perceived the revelation of cosmic Music (music of the spheres) and the cosmic Word. In this the soul experienced how *Osiris* was born or spoken (*ausgesprochen*) out of *Isis,* how the soul then in later times, after the crisis of the year 1322 BCE, stood before the silent, the mute, muffled goddess of the 'mourning widow'. 'No Osiris could be born in the later time, no cosmic harmony could sound, no cosmic word explained that which fearfully showed itself now as cosmic-warmth and cosmic-light.' In *cosmic-warmth* and *cosmic-light* the higher revelation of *cosmic life* and *cosmic harmony* is veiled! In this way, we are impressively led by the spiritual researcher towards the same conclusion, from quite a different angle, arising from the sounds and hieroglyphic contemplation of the name Isis.

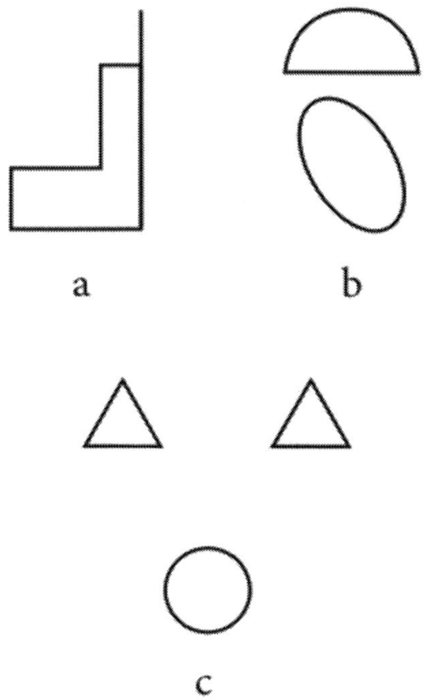

Appendix 6: *Pniel und Gethsemane*

('Peniel and Gethsemane')
Kurt Piper

[from Kurt Piper, *Zwischen Welt und Gott*. Dornach: Goetheanum Verlag 1925. 66f. Original poem in German, with English prose rendering, and in square brackets [ ] some explanatory notes by A.S. 2014.]

Mit sich und seinen Makeln tief zerfallen,
Ward hier ein Mensch im Gotteskampf vollkommen;
Die Furie ward zum Engel-Eumeniden.
Dort rang ein menschgewordner Gott in allen,
Von denen er die Kainslast übernommen,
Im Blutschweiß sich zum Gott- und Menschheitsfrieden

With himself [Jesus] and his deeply disintegrated imperfections [from taking on the human condition], a man was here made complete [divine] in the struggle as a God [in the garden of Gethsemane, Jerusalem; Mark 14:32-42]: the Furies became the angel-Eumenides [Greek deities of vengeance become blessing angels]. There a God who has become Man wrestled in everything of Cain's burden [or curse] which He had taken on [Cain committed the first fratricide], in a bloody sweat (Luke 22:44) preparing Himself for the peace of God and humanity [the atonement].

Moija, Pniel sind vorausgegangen
Dem Geist Gethsemanes, die Schicksalsstätte
Bereitend für die Gottesopfers Größe,
Durch das die Kainserde erst empfangen
Den Einschlag, der sie noch zum Geiste rette
Inmitten Kains schwerster Gegenstöße,

Moriah [Gen. 22:2, the land, southern part of the Holy Land, in which the sacrifice of Isaac took place, traditionally on the Temple Mount in Jerusalem] and Peniel [the place so named after Jacob struggled through a whole night with the 'angel', was himself re-named 'Israel', and had demanded a blessing of the angel; Peniel means 'the face of God', Gen. 32:30] happened [long] before the spirit of Gethsemane, the place of fate [karmic retribution that also decided the future of the earth and humanity] preparing for the greatness of the divine sacrifice through which Cain's earth [he spilt Abel's blood] had first received the impetus [Christ's blood] which [is the only means to redeem the past and] saves it, the Earth, for the Spirit [spiritualization] in the midst of Cain's heaviest counter-blows [i.e. since the first murder, much blood has flowed into the earth from many another murder, struggle and war—fratricide in the family of mankind].

Inmitten seiner größten Pyrrhussiege
Und Scheintriumphe, die durch Blutepochen
Die Schöpfungsseele in sich selbst gespalten,
Doch heut an einer neuen Menschheitswiege
Hat schon der Geist Gethsemanes durchbrochen
Die Phalanx widergeister Gewalten

In the midst of its greatest Pyrrus-victories [= victories with heavy losses] and apparent triumphs, which through epochs of blood [= strife and wars] splitting in itself the creative soul [human beings, divided in themselves, feel 'two souls within my breast', as Goethe's Faust expressed it, one spiritually aspiring ('Israel'—traditional meaning 'the one who has seen God'), one pulling down ('Jacob')], but today at a new cradle of humanity the [victorious] spirit of Gethsemane has broken through the phalanx of counter-spiritual forces [the ordered military forces of the adversary breached through integrated human beings who practice spiritual, moral deeds, making 'positive', or Christian, karma, following Christ's example, and in the sense Beckh emphasizes, following the one disciple who did attain initiation].

Und gab schon seine großen Segensproben
Vom Dasein Christi in der Erdensphäre,
Da wie durch zwei Jahrtausende vergraben
Sich still wie unterirdisch vorgeschoben,
Bis seinem Innendruck der Geist der Schwere
Nachgab in eines Menschen Sternengaben,

And already gave its great foretastes of blessing from the presence of Christ in the earthly sphere which, as if buried through two millennia, quietly moves as if underground [the Christ impulse works in universal human depths of soul more profoundly than the level of held beliefs/un-beliefs], until to its [the Christ impulse's] inner pressure, the Spirit of Weight/Gravity gave in, in a human being's starry gifts [= rises to the light of day, above ground, in Christ's deed, implying others who follow, certainly the disciple John, and, bearing in mind one of Kurt Piper's respectful intentions with his book of poems, also implying the effect of Rudolf Steiner's cognitive victories and further influence through his revelations of the Spirit],

> *In welchem Pniels Siegergeist zum Geiste*
> *Gethsemanes ein Brückenwerk geschlagen,*
> *Das seine Strahlungen im Licht entfaltet*
> *Und schon in tausend Seelen weiterkreiste,*
> *In eine Werdewelt hineinzuragen,*
> *Die aus dem Geiste neu sich umgestaltet ...*

to which Peniel's victorious spirit has build a bridge to the [victorious] spirit of Gethsemane from which rays unfold in light and productively move around this centre between and in a thousand [= many] souls in order to reach into a future world that will be formed anew out of the Spirit [reconstituted = re-acquired innocence that works against the results of the Fall of man, from which ultimately the Earth is re-born, since such reconstitution is a shared virtue both amongst humanity and the earthly kingdoms of nature; cf. Rom 8:22].

[NB Rudolf Steiner comments on Jacob's wrestling: R. Steiner, *Metamorphoses of the Soul,* Vol. 2 [GA 59]. Lecture 4, 'The Nature of Prayer', Berlin, 17 Feb. 1910. London: Rudolf Steiner Pres. 47ff. Owen Barfield suggests the 'blessing' of the Angel is the giving of the alphabet in order for human beings to be able to 'name' God, come to self-knowledge and offer back something humanized that makes for the cosmic future. Owen Barfield. 'Israel and the Michael Impulse'. *Anthroposophical Quarterly.* Vol. 1, No. 1, Spring 1956. London. 2-9.]

Appendix 7: Book Reviews

Mark's Gospel: The Cosmic Rhythm

by Prof. Dr. Hermann Beckh

'This work of the well-known many-sided scholar and expert of Oriental languages, music, theology and law, introduces something totally new and unique in the realm of biblical research. In a thoroughly spiritual as well as deeply founded and artistic manner, Prof. Beckh unfolds the cosmic and mystical connections between the event in Mark's Gospel and the starry pictures of the zodiac. Moreover, he notes how they mirror in the human organism and the 12 musical keys. In a special illumination stimulated by Rudolf Steiner's lectures on Mark's Gospel, the writer follows the pictures of the gospel. Like a fascinating journey through many levels, the heights and depths of Christian initiation appear before the reader's eye. This gospel may have already inspired abundant research and exposition, but it is mostly taken as a simple and devotional chapter. For the layman as well as the theologian, this work by Prof. Beckh will be a source of spiritual joy and elevation. The book's dignified and tasteful format contributes. A further work on similar lines on John's Gospel is in preparation.'

Bremer Nachrichten, May 1929.

'... these "influences of the stellar facts and solar-rhythms in the gospel narratives" are based—according to the "anthroposophical spiritual manner of contemplation"—on Christ, a heavenly being, uniting with the earthly vessel of Jesus of Nazareth; the spiritual Sun-being united with the Earth! Prof. Dr. Hermann Beckh pursues this thesis throughout his abundantly rich and beautifully presented book, producing a continuous exposition of the gospel. With great acuteness all these mysterious connections are uncovered with the zodiac.'

Neue Zürcher Zeitung, April 1929.

'The Orientalist and Buddha-researcher Prof. Beckh has put into this book an abundance of new and novel thoughts. Earlier Drews, Stucken, Erbt and others spoke of connections between the gospel narratives and the events in the starry sky; not one of them however had found the key recognizing that the gospels as books of Christian initiation.

Written from higher levels of consciousness, they allow the so-called contradictions to disappear. Beckh shows us the cosmic Christ in the earthly life. Rudolf Steiner first recognized in full clarity and taught this reflection of heavenly events. It can be deeply moving how far Beckh's manner of contemplation opens the door to the secrets of the gospel, to what depths we can accompany the path of initiation of the disciples. Such a commentary as this on a gospel has hitherto not been written. Whoever impartially occupies himself enough with it, is offered the possibility of a religious deepening opening up unimagined worlds.'

Hamburg Fremdenblatt, December 1929.

'... brilliantly accomplished, we find here the fruit and penetrating power of the anthroposophical method of observation in a book of life of humanity. Only through this method can we recognize Judas, Peter and Pilate in their human limitations as tragic personalities, as Hermann Beckh is able to do. Having read the book, you await with intense interest the appearance of the sequel on John's Gospel...'

Anthroposophie, January 1929.

***

Beckh's most recent publication deserves special attention for several reasons. He attempts in his own way to show in detail the influence of the stars in the details of Mark's Gospel. In the figure of Christ Jesus they are revealed in every moment from the baptism in the Jordan to the Mystery of Golgotha. Beckh follows a path indicated by Rudolf Steiner in his book, *The Spiritual Guidance of Man* (GA 15). The special interest of the present book is to observe how the anthroposophical way of spiritual-scientific knowledge inspired a personality such as Beckh's to these anthroposophical and astrosophical studies. They initially don't appear to belong to his professional task in the strict sense of the word. And yet if, with understanding, you inwardly sympathetically follow Beckh's development, from his professorial seat in Indology to this book, you can see the logical line of destiny allowing him in this life, especially tangibly to experience the cosmic-earthly stream of development from ancient India up to the present.

In this book—which will be followed with a sequel on John's Gospel—Beckh summarizes all his knowledge and insights in order with them to illuminate the cosmic-starry revelations brought through Christ. He accomplishes this right into the style, not only researching scientifically but experiencing with a religious and artistic sensibility.

In the midpoint of the exposition stands the Apostles' drama of Christian initiation, the greatest drama of world-history. With a strong, sacred seriousness Beckh has worked out how Christ with and in the souls of the disciples struggles for the balance between cosmos and earth, between God and man, spirit-world and sensory world. With great love he immerses himself into Christ's work of initiating the souls of the twelve apostles. With this seriousness and with this love, Beckh dares to approach the Mystery surrounding the two great figures, John the Baptist and John the Apostle and Apocalyptist. To a high degree Beckh has enriched the thoughts of each true pupil of Dr. Steiner's anthroposophy, concerning in intimate consecrated hours with this great triad—John the Baptist, Christ, and John, the disciple whom the Lord loved—in order to experience these thoughts in the centre of their concern as a seed of a new cosmic rhythm of the Christened Earth.

Mark's Gospel is written in the sign of the Lion. It is the sign in which the great cosmic Christ-Sun reigns. In the human organism it is revealed essentially at work in the heart-forces. Both Johns are impulsed by the virtue of courage, where they are pure, by the courage of 'great love'. Beckh rightly calls John the 'Disciple of Love', for his 'I' in the truest sense of the word is a child of Christ's love, engendered and brought to birth in the act of initiation, in 'the awakening of Lazarus'.

Something of this courage of the sign of the Lion flows through Beckh's thoughts when he shows right into the details of the apostolic, Christian movements from the individual disciples to the present day. Much becomes clear as though present, experienced by each individual human soul in their way, as the *'drama of Christianity'*, as far as the quarrels of the confessions and the sects. This is shown as especially significant with the spiritual impulses of Judas and Peter. The betrayal by Judas and the threefold denial by Peter are part of the whole 'flight before the cross' by the whole group of disciples. They consequently cannot experience the Mystery of Golgotha with full consciousness. Only John is able to do so, out of the strength of the love of Christ. Thus Beckh finally leads the reader with John, the disciple and Apostle of Love, before the three crosses on Golgotha.

This book, however, is not intended only as a religious and artistic treatment, but at the same time a special reminder to self-knowledge. This reminder is not expressly made, but certainly as the inner result of such thoughts as Beckh expresses, climaxes in the question of readers to themselves: 'Am I able with John to stand before the three crosses on Golgotha?'

Dr Bruno Krüger in *Das Goetheanum*, 9. Jahrgang, Nr. 3. 19 Januar 1930. 22f.

John's Gospel: The Cosmic Rhythm – Stars and Stones

by Prof. Dr. Hermann Beckh

Hardly two years after the appearance of the book on 'Mark's Gospel: The Cosmic Rhythm', there appears as a kind of sequel, though also understandable on its own—once again a significant book. After that first beginning, to present and appreciate Mark's Gospel with its narration of Christ's mission pre-eminently in the light of the cosmic rhythm, one can meet the announced appearance of the sequel of such a manner of exposition with a certain expectancy. How will Prof. Dr. Beckh be able to achieve this task in relation to the 'I'-Mystery of Christ? With this new title he succeeds surprisingly in making a significant advance in the soul-aspect of the stellar-earthly influence and its characterizing the 'I'-activity in the human being and the world.

The first thing to be emphasized is the beautiful perfecting of the style, which corresponds to the manner of exposition in rhythmic repetition, and at the same time reveals with constant inner development the path of initiation of John's Gospel in its mutual significance for the human being and the world. Although he deals with the most difficult regions of knowledge, Beckh knows how to unlock these in a manner that with a really serious study and familiarity can be available to *everyone*. The abundance of material, which Beckh offers us, is kept together through the great inner thread; the whole thing harmonizes to a tremendous composition. The attentive reader is called to co-operate in soul, able to transmit to him/her at the present time the urgently necessary deeper understanding of the gospels.

In a pleasant contrast to many astrological utterances, Prof. Dr. Beckh avoids outer sensationalism in order to evoke something popular; and he also avoids one-sided and specialist technical terms. The whole work is traversed and glows through with an elevated enthusiasm for the sublime, world-encompassing mission of Christ in the cosmos, in the stream of time, in the world of the stars and in the earthly world. With the anthroposophical manner of knowledge gained from

Dr. Steiner, the work is presented as a completely free, autonomous and self-creative achievement. As such it is a beautiful testament to the creative strengths of the human individuality through the awakening force of anthroposophy, without which this work would not have been presented to human beings to attain self-knowledge.

Out of the rich abundance of the content the great rhythm of initiation may be taken as especially important, which coming out of the pre-Christian ages of the Earth, is crystallized in John the Baptist. From him it is led through the Jordan-Baptism to the initiation of Lazarus-John, which was the first Christian initiation. The motif of the 'Johannine triangle' in the stellar realm of Waterman, Crab and Scorpion, shone over by Uranus, sounds like a basic chord through everything. And what sounds into earthly manifestation, through the great discord of the crisis of humanity through the 'Scorpion', is harmonically resolved through the initiation of John to the 'Eagle'. To recognize, to experience this as the greatest of all transubstantiations, all metamorphoses, becomes the leading-thought of the whole book. The expositions relating to this, already contributing many valuable things in the 'cosmic rhythm of Mark's Gospel', are deepened through John's Gospel. Something of the Johannine eagle's vision and eagle's flight of thought striving for the light pulses through the author's bold flight of thoughts, directed towards and working aloft to the cosmic-'I', in which he seeks with great love to place himself into the soul of John.

In the beautiful chapter on 'giving the name', Beckh has valuable things to say on the great rhythm of breathing, the starry constellation and the earthly zodiac, constellation and zodiacal signs, on human destiny and the Christ-'I' in mutual interpenetration. 'For everything which is really the opportunity of the "I" as the future supersensory member of the human being, today in a seed stage, belongs to a higher world as that of the earthly zodiac and the planetary contexts of destiny; it point us to the real worlds of the stars' (Germ. ed. p. 155).

The various etymological word-studies of the author with a comparison of the relationships of the languages contribute to a further enlivening of the whole and lead in the same way to yet other paths to understand the 'cosmic word'. Expositions like those on 'body' as Sun-dress, 'life' as Moon-dress, on 'light' as Star-dress, and 'love' as Cosmic-'I' (Cosmic Word) in connection with the changes of the incarnation of the Earth illuminate the tremendous Primordial Word in the beginning of John's Gospel, concerning the metamorphosing creative power of the Cosmic Word, that with eagle's pinions circles the universe.

With his manner of exposition, Beckh deeply illumines the connections of the Mystery of Golgotha with the Ancient Egyptian, Persian and Indian Mysteries of the past, and with the 'I'-Mystery of the future. It is very interesting to follow the development of the author of his studies in language out of the soul of the ancient epochs of the peoples to the stellar script of the cosmos. The intimate connection of both languages—the language of the divine stellar script and the human stellar language of words—as it is also shown in Wolfram's *Parzifal,* becomes especially clear through Beckh's explanations.

Right into the tangible details he points with this stellar script and the cosmic language of Christ to the possibility of cosmic-earthly prophecy, as lies before us in the Apocalypse of John in grandiose pictures, signs and symbols.

The nature of the three crosses, the physical (of the Father), the etheric (of the Son), the astral (of the Holy Spirit) in their relationships and influence to the will, the feelings and the thinking of the human soul, as well as their metamorphosis through the reception of Christ become clear in many mutual constellations of the stellar clock in the cosmos. The 'Word in the primordial beginning' in the sign of the Bull and the Ram, the 'Jordan Baptism' in the sign of the Fishes, the 'Marriage in Cana' in the sign of the Waterman, the 'Conversation by night with Nicodemus' in the sign of the Goat, the 'Samaritan woman at the well' and the 'Healing of the Centurion's son' in the sign of the Archer, that of the 'invalid in Bethesda' in the sign of the Scorpion, etc., then the great crisis of humanity, 'and the darkness comprehended it not', in the further events in the signs of the oscillating Scales, which between the Virgin and the Scorpion seeking the balance, furthermore, the raising of Lazarus-John and the great Mystery of the cross with the resurrection of Christ Himself become for us in reading the cosmic starry clock revealed as *the* rhythm, in which the inner human being walks initially unconsciously, as he awakes during the day, in the rhythm of clock-time experiences his everyday destiny.

Thus the cosmic extent becomes humanly accessible. We experience the core of the Mystery-drama of all time, how through all the pictures and events right through John's Gospel the seed is laid and nurtured, in order in the human 'I' to un-bind the will to join Christ and therewith again to go to the Father: 'I go to the Father'; 'No one comes to the Father, but through me' (through the 'I') …

The book is raised to the highest seriousness in the presentation of the crisis of humanity in the sign of the Scorpion, which *alone* John overcomes; it is changed to the sign of the Eagle. For this reason the Eagle is also the occult sign of John's Gospel. This crisis, before which humanity stands anew today, becomes at the same time the 'verdict' for human beings, whether they want to entrust themselves to the adversary of the depths or the divine in the height. At the division of the ways Christ stands as the 'love in the primordial beginning'. Therewith Christ becomes the 'Lord of destiny'. Cf. John 3:19: 'This is the separation and the decision: Light has come into the world, but men loved darkness more than the light, because their deeds weighed on their destiny.' Beckh impressively works out the motif of 'changing destiny' through Jesus Christ in the scene with the woman taken in adultery, as the motif of the *Richtens*, judging out of the '*I*', in the sense of *Aufrichten*, getting up, straightening up.

We receive strong stimuli out of the cosmic-earthly stellar constellation with the initiation of Lazarus-John which, in itself and in its relationship to the Mystery of Golgotha forms the actual culmination of John's Gospel, as the one-off, unique example of initiation of *those* human beings who decide out of free-will of love of the I-AM to become 'imitators of Christ'.

For a time there came through Frau Dr. Steiner's worthy decision to publish Dr. Steiner's lecture-cycle on John's Gospel in book form, somewhat earlier the Apocalypse of John in duplicated form. Whoever seriously works through this with the seriousness with which Beckh studied them and inwardly re-experienced them, will through both of Beckh's works with quite special deepening of the soul gain much that will contribute a deeper understanding of the lecture-cycles of Dr. Steiner.

Dr. Bruno Krüger in *Das Goetheanum*, 9. Jahrgang. Nr. 42. Oktober 19, 1930. 333f.

Bibliography

by Hermann Beckh, updated by A. S., 2020

In none of the following 'sources' for the cosmic rhythm of the zodiac signs in the gospel is the subject followed up in detail. Rudolf Steiner, who always pointed out the existence of this rhythm, did not go into the details. In the Introduction it was emphasized that the viewpoints of a book such as Arthur Drews differ completely from those of the current presentation. The individual works listed below should help the reader, not familiar with the way of contemplating questions on the gospels advocated here, to appreciate the spirit of such a manner of contemplation. Clearly, a limited selection from the Collected Works of the comprehensive life's work of Rudolf Steiner is given, suitable in the first instance to give such an introduction, and which are directly significant.

A main basis for the content of the book—taken as granted but not everywhere known—is the gospel itself. In the first place, of course, the text of Mark's Gospel to hand (for those not familiar with the Greek, in translation the AV/KJV or more modern versions, for example, NIV, JB, or RSV; and the reconstructed Aramaic made by C.C. TORREY, *The Four Gospels,* NY/London 1933; Nabu Press 2010/11), and especially John's Gospel is important. From the Old Testament the following passages are relevant: Genesis 1–4, I Kings 5–8 (the building of Solomon's Temple, also 2 Chron. 2–7); I Kings 16ff. (the story of Elijah).

From the work of Rudolf STEINER (for the whole relationship of the present work to his spiritual work, see note above), first a purely human introduction is valuable, the study of contemporary worldviews in his autobiography *The Course of my Life* [GA 28]. For the second-hand market www.bookfinder.com is useful. [The Collected Works are numbered 'GA xx' from the German '*Gesamtausgabe*'; the early numbers (1–28) refer to the written works. The many subsequent numbers refer in the main to reports on the many lecture-courses, which follow a line of development over the years.]

Further biographies of Steiner:

Günther WACHSMUTH, *Life and Work of Rudolf Steiner,* New York: Whittier Books 1955; Garber Communications 1988.

Emil BOCK, *The Life and Times of Rudolf Steiner*, 2 Vols, tr. Lynda Hepburn. Edinburgh: Floris Books 2008, 2009.

Christoph LINDENBERG, *Rudolf Steiner A Biography*, tr. by John McAlice. Steiner Books Inc. 2013; tr. of: *Rudolf Steiner eine Chronik*, Stuttgart: Freies Geistesleben 1988.

Helmut ZANDER, *Rudolf Steiner, die Biografie*, Piper, München 2011.

For the basic study of questions of the world, the Earth and the human being and occult [= 'hidden'] cosmogony, *Occult Science* [GA 13] is fundamental (tr. Monges is closest to the original German; Adams a little freer; Creeger [title: *Esoteric Science*] in more modern English is sometimes even more free, also available for downloading);

for questions on the gospels and the ancient Mysteries:

Christianity as Mystical Fact [GA 8] and:

The Spiritual Guidance of Man [GA 15] both mention the cosmic rhythm of the stars connected with Mark's Gospel.

Of the various lecture-cycles on the gospels, important, in particular for the Lazarus-John question for Mark's Gospel and its cosmic rhythm, both lecture-cycles on:

The Gospel of St John, Hamburg 1908 [GA 103] and Cassel 1909 [GA 112]. Furthermore, the lecture-cycles on:

The Gospel of St Mark, Basel 1912 [GA 139] and

Excursus on the Gospel According to St Mark, Berlin 1909/10 [GA 124]; also

Building-Stones for an Understanding of the Mystery of Golgotha, Berlin 1917 [GA 175].

For insights into Christianity and the pre-Christian Mysteries, above all:

Mysteries of the East and of Christianity, Berlin 1913 [GA 144].

Questions on the zodiac:

Man in the Light of Occultism, Theosophy and Philosophy, Christiania, Oslo 1912 [GA 137] and

Human and Cosmic Thought, Berlin [GA 151].

Cosmic Being and Egohood, Berlin 1916 [GA 169], especially lecture 3.

The question of 'spiritual hierarchies', alongside the earlier lecture-course:

The Spiritual Hierarchies, Düsseldorf 1909 [GA 110], especially the cycle:

The Spiritual Beings in the Heavenly Bodies and in the Kingdoms of Nature, Helsinki 1912 [GA 136].

The theme of the 'starry script' and its new revelation through Christ is touched on especially in the lecture-course:

Christ and the Spiritual World, Leipzig 1913 [GA 149]; the single lecture on the 'New Isis', Dornach 6 Jan. 1918, in:

Ancient Myths and the New Isis Mystery, Anthroposophic Press 1994. 57-75. The new revelation of the spiritual star-wisdom through Christ with the spiritual understanding of the gospel goes hand in hand with the Mystery of Golgotha and the 'Johannine meaning of the Logos'; researching the future through an understanding of the gospels linked with such a star-wisdom gives new tasks and aims; specific phenomena still burdened with the materialism of the age are overcome through such research.

For the way to spiritual self-knowledge and to understand everything said in the present book on initiation:

Knowledge of the Higher Worlds – How is it Attained? (current editions, disregarding Steiner's intentioned question-form, are entitled 'How to attain ...') [GA 10],

The Evolution of Consciousness, Penmaenmawr 1923 [GA 227] and
True and False Paths in Spiritual Investigation, Torquay 1924 [GA 243].

Of Albert STEFFEN's work, above all we should mention:

Der Künstler und die Erfüllung der Mysterien, Dornach 1928/64; and the drama:

Hiram und Salomo 1925/33/60, etc.; *Hiram and Solomon*, Eng. tr. Virginia Brett (Dornach 1970).

Important to understand the gospel and the way of contemplation followed here, equally instructive and most serviceable for understanding of the gospels as known, and here often mentioned:

Emil BOCK, *Studies in the Gospels*, Vol. 1, Edinburgh: Floris Books 2009; Vol. 2, Floris Books 2011.

Of my own writings touching on the present book:

Hermann BECKH, *From the Mysteries*, seven essays, Temple Lodge 2020.

For understanding the 'cosmic rhythm' and the question of the zodiac, the important monograph:

The Essence of Tonality, Anastasi 2008; much expanded as:
The Language of Tonality, Anastasi 2014; TL forthcoming.

Buddha's Life and Teaching, TL 2019, mentioned three times in the present book. The objectively present question of the zodiac has not yet [written 1928] been followed up.

From Buddha to Christus, TL 2019 (complete & with new material).

Der Hingang des Vollendeten, the account of Buddha's farewell to the Earth and of *nirvāṇa* (*Mahāparinibbānasutta* of the Pali canon) in Germ. tr.; Eng. tr. forthcoming.

Genesis, chapters on scenes from Genesis, and *Zarathustra*, chapters on Nietzsche, the Avesta and spiritual-scientific research; both titles in *From the Mysteries*, TL 2020.

'Das neue Jerusalem', a poetic treatment, a chapter in *Gegenwartsrätsel im Offenbarungslicht* (along with chapters by R. Meyer, E. Kurras, J.W. Klein, R. Frieling, E. Bock, and Fr. Doldinger), Stuttgart 1925. 105-121. Eng. tr. 'The New Jerusalem', incl. in *John's Gospel: The Cosmic Rhythm*, Anastasi 2015. 459-77, TL 2021; also in *Alchymy*, TL 2019, 100-13.

The Language of the Stars, TL 2020, contributions to a new star-wisdom. The author was present at Leipzig 1913 [GA 149], and was the first to establish a new astrosophy based on spiritual science.

Collected Articles of Rev. Prof. Hermann Beckh, 1922-1937, contains 73 items, including articles on Johannine themes and the first draft of the present book: 'The Starry Life of Christ: The Path of the Christ-Sun through the 12 Zodiac Signs in Mark's Gospel' (1926), TL 2021.

Beckh's biography:

Gundhild Kačer-Bock, *Hermann Beckh. Leben und Werk*. Stuttgart: Urachhaus 1997. Eng. tr. *Hermann Beckh: Life and Work*, Anastasi, 2016; new edition, Temple Lodge, 2021.

After Beckh's death, valuable appreciations on his life and work by Friedrich Rittelmeyer, Emil Bock, Rudolf von Koschützki, Erwin Schüle, Rudolf Frieling, Gottfried Husemann, etc., with a poem by Kurt Piper, appeared in *Die Christengemeinschaft*, 14. Jahrgang 1, April 1937. 19-27. Eng. tr. in *Hermann Beckh and the Spirit-word*, Anastasi 2015.

Also mentioned:

Rudolf STEINER, *The Last Address* (Dornach, Michaelmas Eve 1924), tr. George Adams with a preface by Alfred Heidenreich, London: Rudolf Steiner Press 1967 [the Germ. text of the address is included in GA 202]; it is a fragment, the 'second half' was never given. Beckh was present at this last address, and was the first to stand up during the stunned silence that followed, exclaiming, '*Das war erschüttend!*', 'That was totally amazing!'—reported by his biographer, who claims Beckh said this Address together with the Christmas Foundation Meeting was the climax of his own life. The experience of the address, Beckh mentions, fuelled him to write the present book on Mark's Gospel (see p. 48 above).

Günther WACHSMUTH, *Etheric Formative Forces in Cosmos, Earth & Man* (1932). Sacred Science Institute 2006 (deluxe hardbound ed.); Borderland Sciences Research (simplified facsimile edition). Download availabe from <www.scribd.com>.

Alan STOTT, *Meditations on the Epistles of The Act of Consecration of Man*, Anastasi 2013, TL 2022. German version in MS: *Jahreszeitliche Gebete: Meditationen über die Episteln der Menschenweihehandlung*.

Further research on Mark and particularly the 'two Johns' (actually four: John the Baptist, John the evangelist, John the apostle and John Mark), include:

Adolf Arenson, *On the Christ-Mystery* (2), lecture 30 Mar. 1931 (pamphlet, tr. H. Collison) emphasizes the part of Elijah-John;

Emil Bock, *Einiges über das Geheimnis der beiden Johannes* (available from Archiv der Christengemeinschaft, Berlin), Eng. tr. in MS; discusses esoteric revelations (including a report of an Esoteric Lesson, possibly 21 or 23 Jan. 1911, by Rudolf Steiner, now published in GA 264, AP 1998, pp. 215-27);

Johannes Hemleben, *Evangelist Johannes*, Rowohalt, Hamburg 1972, summarizes much; intent to distinguish the apostle from the evangelist;

Kurt von Wistinghausen, *Der verborgene Evangelist*, Stuttgart 1983, follows on Hemleben; a basic presentation with original insights; supplemented by seven articles in *Die Christengemeinschaft*, on 'Thirteen disciples' and related Johannine themes in fine art of the Middle Ages; 1984, pp. 106-12, 224-27, 365-71; 1985, pp. 62-6, 102-07, 147-53, 188-94. The author was a younger colleague of Beckh's in Stuttgart;

Chr. Rau, *Die Vier um den Einen*, Bochum 2008 (Eng. tr. 'The Four around the One', TL forthcoming): details on the literary form of all four gospels;

Chr. Rau, *Mit dem Feuergeist des Löwen*, Stuttgart 2004 (Eng. tr. forthcoming), in-depth research on Mark, the gospel and the evangelist; suggests Lazarus-John in Ephesus could have edited all four gospels and argues he was responsible for the present ending to Mark;

Chr. Rau, *Struktur und Rhythmus im Johannes-Evangelium*, Stuttgart 1972 (Eng. tr. forthcoming); insights on the structural rhythms of the text.

The Works of Prof. Dr. Hermann Beckh

'An abundance of books came into existence whose significance perhaps will only be properly appreciated in the future.'

Lic. Emil Bock,
'Hermann Beckh' in *Zeitgenossen Weggenossen Wegbereiter*,
Stuttgart: Urachhaus 1959. p. 132.

*

Die Beweislast nach dem Bürgerlichen Gesetzbuch
'The burden of proof according to the Code of Civil Law'
Prize essay, awarded distinction from the Law Faculty the University of Munich, München und Berlin 1899. Download: http://dlib-pr.mpier.mpg.de/m/kleioc/0010/exec/books/%22103926%22/

Ein Beitrag zur Textkritik an Kālidāsas Meghadūta
'A contribution for the text criticism of Kālidāsa's Meghadūta'
Doctorate dissertation approved by the Department of Philosophy of the University of Berlin 1907.

Die tibetische Übersetzung von Kālidāsas Meghadūta
'The Tibetan translation of Kālidāsa's Meghadūta'
Edited and with a German translation, Berlin 1907/2011.

Beiträge zur tibetischen Grammatik, Lexikogaphie, Stilistik und Metrik
Habilitationsschrift. Berlin 1908.
'Contributions to Tibetan grammar, lexicography, style and prosody'
Inaugural dissertation.

Udānavarga
A collection of Buddhist sayings in the Tibetan language
Berlin 1911 (also reprinted by Walter de Gruyter 2013).

Verzeichnis der tibetischen Handschriften
'Catalogue of Tibetan MSS in the Royal Library in Berlin' (Vol. 24 of the Manuscript Catalogue)

First division: Kanjur (Bhak-Khgur)
Berlin 1914/2011/14.

Buddha und seine Lehre
Vol. 1: *Das Leben*. Vol. 2: *Die Lehre.*
Sammlung Göschen. Berlin & Leipzig 1916. Third edition 1928.
Later one-volume editions, Stuttgart: Urachhaus 1958/98/2012. Tr. into Dutch and Japanese.
Eng. tr. *Buddha's Life and Teaching,* TL 2019.

'Rudolf Steiner und das Morgenland'
in *Vom Lebenswerk Rudolf Steiners*
Ed. Friedrich Rittelmeyer, München: Chr. Kaiser 1921
Reprint by HP, Univ. of Michigan (www.lib.umich.edu) (download: www.archive.org).
Eng. tr. 'Rudolf Steiner and the East' in *Hermann Beckh and the Spirit-Word,* Anastasi 2015. 33-65; also in *The Source of Speech,* 16-71.

Der physische und der geistige Ursprung der Sprache
'The physical and the spiritual origin of language'. Stuttgart 1921.
'Es werde Licht!'
'Let there be light!'
The primordial biblical words of creation and the primordial significance of the sounds in the light of spiritual science. Stuttgart 1921.
Etymologie und Lautbedeutung
Etymology and the significance of speech sounds in the light of spiritual science
Stuttgart 1922/2013.

All three essays on language (above) reprinted in
Neue Wege zur Ursprache, Stuttgart 1954
Eng. tr. *The Source of Speech,* with all relevant essays and articles. TL 2019.

Anthroposophie und Universitätswissenschaft
'Anthroposophy and University Knowledge'
Breslau 1922. Eng. tr. in *Hermann Beckh and the Spirit-Word,* Anastasi 2015. 71-101; also in *The Source of Speech.* TL 2019, 181-207.

Vom geistigen Wesen der Tonarten
The Essence of Tonality: An Attempt to view musical Problems in the Light of

Spiritual Science. With diagrams. Breslau 1922. Third edition 1932. Eng. tr. Anastasi 2008.

Der Ursprung im Lichte. Bilder der Genesis
Our Origin in the Light: Pictures from Genesis. Stuttgart 1924. Eng. tr. *Genesis* with *Zarathustra*, in *From the Mysteries*. TL 2020.

Von Buddha zu Christus
From Buddha to Christ
Stuttgart 1925 (tr. in Norwegian, Oslo 1926); Eng. tr. of short digest Floris Books 1978. New Eng. tr. of full text, with additions, TL 2019.

Das neue Jerusalem
'The New Jerusalem'
A poetic work, in the collaborative work *Gegenwartsrätsel im Offenbarungslicht* ('Riddles of the present in the light of revelation'), Stuttgart 1925. Eng. tr. incl. in *John's Gospel: The Cosmic Rhythm—Stars and Stones*. Anastasi 2015. 459-77; also in *Alchymy*. 100-13.

Der Hingang des Vollendeten
'The Passing of the Accomplished One and his Nirvāṇa (Mahāparinibbāna Sutta of the Pali canon)'.
Translated and with an Introduction. Stuttgart 1925/60.
Eng. tr. 'Buddha's Passing', TL forthcoming.

Zarathustra
Stuttgart 1927
Eng. tr. in *From the Mysteries* with *Genesis*, TL 2020.

Aus der Welt der Mysterien
From the Mysteries
Seven articles (reprinted). Basel 1927.
Eng. tr. as triple book with *Genesis* and *Zarathustra*, TL 2020.

Der kosmische Rhythmus im Markus-Evangelium
Mark's Gospel: The Cosmic Rhythm
Basel 1928/60/97. Eng. tr. Anastasi 2015. TL 2021.

Der kosmische Rhythmus, das Sternengeheimnis und Erdengeheimnis im Johannes-Evangelium
John's Gospel: The Cosmic Rhythm—Stars and Stones
Basel 1930. Eng. tr. Anastasi 2015; corrected ed. TL 2021.

Das Christus-Erlebnis in Dramatisch-Musikalischen von Richard Wagners 'Parsifal'
The Parsifal Christ-Experience in Wagner's Music Drama
Stuttgart 1930. Eng. tr. with 'Richard Wagner and Christianity' (1933) and essays by Emil Bock (1928) and Rudolf Frieling (1956), Anastasi 2015; TL forthcoming.

Vom Geheimnis der Stoffeswelt (Alchymie)
Alchymy: The Mystery of the Material World
Basel 1931/37/42/2007/13. Eng. tr. with appendices, TL 2019.

Der Hymnus an die Erde
The Hymn to the Earth: From the Old Indian Atharvaveda: A memorial to the oldest poem and to the early Aryans. Stuttgart 1934/60. Eng. tr. TL, forthcoming.

Psalm 23 aus der Heiligen Schrift
Psalm 23: Newly translated from the original text and set to music, op. 7. Stuttgart 1935.

Die Rosen von Damaskus
The Roses of Damascus. 'Thibaut von Champagne'. The ballad by Conrad Ferdinand Meyer. For solo high voice with piano accompaniment set to music, op. 8. Stuttgart 1937.

Die Sprache der Tonart
The Language of Tonality in the Music from Bach to Bruckner with special reference to Wagner's Music Dramas
Stuttgart 1937/87/99. Eng. tr. Anastasi 2015, TL forthcoming.

Richard Wagner und das Christentum
'Richard Wagner and Christianity'
Stuttgart 1933. Eng. tr. incl. in *The Parsifal Christ-Experience in Wagner's Music Drama.* Anastasi 2015.
Indische Weisheit und Christentum

'Indian Wisdom and Christianity'
Articles: 10 reprinted and 9 from the literary estate
Stuttgart 1938. Eng. tr. in *Collected Articles*, TL 2021.

The Mystery of Musical Creativity: The Human Being and Music
A recently discovered history of music in Ms (1936):
Five chapters pub. in three articles in *Der Europäer*, Basel 09.2005/09.2006/02.2007-08.
http://www.perseus.ch/archive/category/europaer/europaer-archiv
Full restored text translated into English, TL 2019.

The Language of the Stars: Zodiac and Planets in Relation to the Human Being with a chapter on the Anthroposophical Soul-Calendar (1911-12) (1930-33)
by Prof. Dr. Hermann Beckh
and *The Cosmic Rhythm in the Creed: for readers of Beckh's books* (1930-31)
by Dr. Rudolf Frieling
with an Introduction and Reviews by Rudolf Frieling and others
translated from the German by Maren & Alan Stott
edited by Neil Franklin, Ph.D.
Temple Lodge Publishing 2020.

Collected Articles of Rev. Prof. Hermann Beckh (1922-1937). Over 70 items translated into English, ed. Neil Franklin, Ph.D., TL 2021.

Three further publications:

Hermann Beckh: Leben und Werk
Hermann Beckh: Life and Work
by Gundhild Kačer-Bock (d. 2008)
Stuttgart 1997. Eng. tr. Anastasi 2016. TL forthcoming 2021.

Hermann Beckh and the Spirit-Word:
Orientalist, Christian Priest and Independent Scholar
Anastasi 2015. Contents includes:
Alan Stott, 'Hermann Beckh and the Twenty-First Century'
H. B., 'Rudolf Steiner and the East'
H. B., 'Anthroposophy and University Knowledge'
H. B., 'Meeting Rudolf Steiner'

Numerous appreciations by Beckh's colleagues and his biographer; introducing the 'Collected Works of Prof. Hermann Beckh'.

Festschrift in Honour of Hermann Beckh
Published on the centenary of *Buddha und seine Lehre* and the publication of the English translation *Buddha's Life and Teaching* also the first publication of Beckh's *The Mystery of Human Creativity: The Human Being and Music* and the English translation of Gundhild Kačer-Bock's biography *Hermann Beckh: Life and Work.*
Anastasi 2016.

Contents includes:
Prof. Hermann Beckh: 'Steiner und Buddha' (1931; previously unpublished)
Prof. Hermann Beckh: 'Buddhism and its Significance for Humanity' (1928)
Prof. Hermann Beckh, 'The Little Squirrel, the Moonlight Princess and the Little Rose', illustrated by Tatjana Schellhase
'Prof. Hermann Beckh' by Johannes Lenz (Berlin)
'Daniel Simeon and Asita the Sage' by Manfred Krüger (Nuremberg)
Oliver Heinl: 'Prof. Dr. Hermann Beckh—Pioneer linguistic work in the light of Christ'
Susana Ulrich-Alvarez Ulloa (Öschelbronn): 'The Search for the Lost Word'
Katrin Binder (Nottingham): 'Buddha's Life and Work one hundred years on'
Alan Stott (Stourbridge): 'Hermann Beckh: Musician' (a lecture, Dornach, April 2016)
Rosemaria Bock (Stuttgart): 'Recollections' (with photos)
Gundhild Kačer-Bock (1924-2008) Memories & Appreciations.

Note: Useful sources for texts by Beckh:
www.rudolf-steiner-bibliothek.de/
bibliothek@goetheanum.ch/
archiv@christengemeinschaft.org/

Endnotes

1 Christoph Rau, *Die Vier um den Einen*, Bochum 2008, FN 20, p. 18; Eng. title (TL forthcoming): *The Four around the One*, endnote 21.

2 See Chr. Rau, 'Fire, Water, Air and Earth as heavenly powers (1)', in *Die Christengemeinschaft*, 8/1969, pp. 229-31, Eng. tr. in 'Collected Articles …', TL, forthcoming.

3 Rudolf Steiner, *From the History & Contents of the First Section of the Esoteric School 1904-1914*, GA 264, tr. John Wood, Hudson: Anthroposophic Press 1996, p. 226. See also, Emil Bock, 'Einiges über das Geheimnis der beiden Johannes' in *Studienmaterial für die Priester Heft 1*, Archiv der Christengemeinschaft 1995, 27-47. Eng. tr. in MS.

4 Wistinghausen submits evidence of 'thirteen disciples' present at the Last Supper, as seen in works of fine art (in *Der verborgene Evangelist*, Stuttgart 1983 and extended in 7 articles, some illustrated, in *Die Christengemeinschaft*, 1984 pp. 108-12, 224-27, 365-71 and 1985: pp. 62-6, 147-53, 188-94). Leonardo most likely knew of the tradition, but according to his commission had to paint his famous picture with twelve disciples. Lazarus-John (Wistinghausen suggests) is portrayed in the seat of honour as a guest, while the disciple John is portrayed next to his brother James, as was customary. (Philip would thus appear to be absent from the commissioned painting, where twelve disciples were expected to be portrayed.) With the departure of Judas, it was necessary that the cosmic twelve should be retained at the Mystery of Golgotha. In the event, however, the other disciples were soon scattered leaving only Lazarus-John and the women as witnesses at the cross.

5 Neil Franklin, Boehme and Blake scholar, traces Beckh's development in 'Farther Up! Hermann Beckh: Passing through four levels of consciousness, 1916-1931' in *The Language of the Stars*, TL 2020, 503-20.

6 Further discussion could include the remarkable lecture of Adolf Arenson (original: Studienergebnisse aus der Vortragstätigkeit Rudolf Steiners III. Über das Christus-Mysterium. (Elias—Johannes—Lazarus). Copies from: rsb@anthroposophische-gesellschaft.org/ www.rudolf-steiner-bibliothek.de), Eng. tr. 'On the Christ-Mystery' (2) (Elijah—John—Lazarus), lecture held Stuttgart, 30 March 1931, and again Dornach, 15 April 1931, pub. H. Collison, London.

7 The Western rite, for example, celebrates the Christian Mysteries in the unfolding context of the Christian year: the Mass and its derivative, also its rebirth in The Act of Consecration of Man of the 'Movement for Religious Renewal'. Cf. A.S. *Meditations on the Epistles*. See Bibliography—*Tr. note.*

8 Rudolf Steiner's terms for the human members, as described in his *Theosophy* [GA 9] and *Occult/ Esoteric Science* [GA 13]—*Tr. note.*

9 The author clearly states his choice of zodiac is the traditional Tropical Zodiac, the 'signs'. To counter any misunderstandings, he emphasizes this even more in the sequel on John's Gospel—*Tr. note.*

10 Beckh clearly points to inwardness. However, the Greek word for 'belly' is regarded as 'one of the most perfect examples [of] the fact [of] mistranslation [of the Greek version of the gospels], its cause, and the reason for the precise word chosen being alike obvious' (Charles Cutler Torrey. *The Four Gospels*. London 1933/2018, 200f., a version in English from the reconstructed Aramaic originals; and *Our Translated Gospels: Some of the Evidence*. 1936. 108-11. <*www.archive.org*>). The quotation is a paraphrase of Ps 46:4f.; the river flows 'out of the midst of her [Jerusalem]'. The source of the living water is the temple. Note, too:

(a) *koilia* also—'womb'

(b) in the N.T. *koilia* renders O.T. Hebrew בטן *beten* = the innermost part of a man, soul, or heart—*Tr. note.*

11 See R. Steiner. *The Mysteries of the East and of Christianity*. Berlin. Lecture 3, 5 Feb. 1913 [GA 114].

12 See Emil Bock. *Studies in the Gospels*. 2 vols. Edinburgh: Floris Books 2009 and 2011.

13 The whole question of the relationships of John the Baptist, John the disciple and Lazarus-John the evangelist is of primal significance. It is suggested (J. Hemleben, K. von Wistinghausen) that both Beckh and Bock somewhat confuse the disciple John, son of Zebedee, with the 'one becoming John', that is, Lazarus, who is only called 'John' after his initiation and is not 'one of the Twelve'. If Beckh lapses here, he compensates by fully acknowledging the Baptist's role as a group-soul of the disciples who inspired the first half of the Fourth Gospel and who united with Lazarus at his initiation, or raising. To repeat, the riddle of the 'two Johns' involves the Baptist and the Evangelist, Lazarus-John. One imagines that as an initiate Lazarus-John, if not 'one of the Twelve', is spiritually 'present' at the Transfiguration, as is the evangelist Mark who writes from inner vision. One might consider: are not all who read or who hear the story also 'present', inasmuch as Johannine initiation is callng?—*Tr. note.*

14 A revealing vista opens up here. 'Already during the copying of the Aramaic original text of Matthew's Gospel, the word *chagobim* (= locust) has appeared in place of the word *charubim* (= carob) ... [T]he tiny stone or kernel in the beans (because of their hardness not suitable for consumption) presented the first reliable weights for balances, known as "carats". For—wonder of nature!—whether the fruit is small or big, whether it stems from a wild or cultivated carob tree, each stone or kernel for millennia

retains its weight of 0.2 grams. Thanks to these unassuming stones goldsmiths and pharmacists since ancient times were able to weigh accurately ... Only those who produce their own fruit, those who out of insight and moral imagination, find their own life's path, become active from within, are on the right path. They will not only find themselves, not only discover leadership in their own inner being, but also recognize that Lord who gives the whole of humanity the meaning of its existence, because He is the "I" of humanity itself. This power to decide, this faculty of the "I", lives hidden within human beings like the kernel in the pod in the fruit of the carob tree. At the same time, this kernel places the individual on the same level as all other people; here no one is higher than another; here everyone is equal before the higher judgment.' Chr. Rau, 'Die Nahrung Johannes des Täufers als Ausdruck seiner Sendung (The Food of John the Baptist as Expression of his Mission), *Die Christengemeinschaft*, 1997 p. 324-27—*Tr. A. S.*

15 Knowledge that the two different accounts of the births and childhoods in Matthew and Luke refer to two Jesus boys was known in the School of Chartres; numerous artistic depictions can be seen in cathedrals, churches and paintings of Middle-Age and Renaissance Europe. Steiner goes into the details, including the merging of the families. See also the first theological study, Chr. Rau, *The Two Jesus-Boys and the Messianic Expectations of the Essenes*, Temple Lodge 2019—*Tr. note.*

16 The time of Christ's earthly life is always meant. Through the precession of the equinoxes, the already characterized shift has taken effect (see p. 27). Yet one speaks today of the 'sign of the Ram' for a part of that time when the Sun still stands in the Fishes. [Permanent] *sign* and [present day] *constellation* are distinguished.

17 On the 'higher ethers' in the context of the Tree of Life, see the lecture-cycle R. Steiner, *Christ and the Human Soul* [GA 155] Norrköping, 12-16 July 1914; and Günter Wachsmuth, *The Etheric Forces in Cosmos Earth and Man* (see Bibliography).

18 Cf. Heb. 4:12—*Tr.*

19 As examples out of the gospel for what is meant here: the 'dreamy, playful' pictures with the Feedings or the Storm on the Lake are still lower astral visions; the experience of the Transfiguration (Mark 9) is highest spiritual beholding of spiritual reality.

20 Apart from the two parallel passages of the Caesarea-Philippi story (Matthew 16:16 and Luke 9:20), we should cite especially the significant entrance to Mark's Gospel (1:1), which immediately announces this gospel as the 'Christ gospel' (see Introduction p. 51); Mark 12:35 (paralleled in Matt. 22:42); the question of Pilate Mark 14:61; some passages in Luke (2:11, 23:35, and especially the interesting passage, Luke 4:41, where the demons call out the name of Christ). The name 'Christ' appears in John's Gospel,

though only in individual places, such as John 1:17, 1:25, 3:29. 4:25; 7:26, 27, 41, 11:27 and especially John 17:3, 20:31.

21 See the author's essay 'The Name Isis' in *From the Mysteries*, Basel: Rudolf Geering Verlag, 66-74. In Egyptian, Isis was called 'H–S–T, I–S–T, and these sounds are again contained in the name 'Christ'. This observation is purely about the sounds, not from the justified grammatical point of view of its derivation from *χριω*.

22 Cf. R. Steiner, lecture, London 27 Aug. 1924 [*Karmic Relationships*, vol. 8, GA 240].

23 Further details in R. Steiner, *The Mysteries of the East and of Christianity* [GA 144], lecture 2, Berlin, 4 Feb. 1913; and in the author's monograph *Zarathustra* [in *From the Mysteries*, TL 2020, 74-7].

24 Exact research into the ethers, based on Rudolf Steiner's indications (see especially, R. Steiner, *Christ and the Human Soul* [GA 155], lectures 3 & 4, Norrköping, July 14 & 15, 1914; also R. Steiner, *Genesis* [GA 122], lectures, Munich 17-26 Aug. 1910), by Günther Wachsmuth, *Etheric Formative Forces in Cosmos, Earth and Man*. New York: Anthroposophic Press 1932, presents the 'Tree of Life' with the two 'upper kinds of ether' (life-ether and sound-ether); with the 'tree of knowledge' the two lower kinds of ether (light-ether and warmth ether). The two latter are subject to the influence of the Fall of man that depresses the human being below his original niveau. For example, the light-ether to the earthly eye that only sees the sensory-physical phenomena, in Steiner's word, 'is killed', whereas the two upper kinds of ether are removed from this action.

25 In this sentence, appearing in the discussion in the widest contexts, the Professor sums up the tremendous Mystery of the two Johns (without the need to mention a third John): Elijah-John in the spiritual world and Lazarus, way ahead of the other disciples and who alone concludes his initiation, meet 'over the "grave of Lazarus"' and become 'the Christian John'—*Tr.*

26 For example; John 3:19 NIV, 'This is the verdict: Light has come into the world…'; *αὕτη δέ ἐστιν ἡ κρίσις ὅτι τὸ φῶς ἐλήλυθεν εἰς τὸν κόσμον …*
John 9:39: *Εἰς κρίμα ἐγὼ εἰς τὸν κόσμον τοῦτον ἦλθον,*
AV/KJV: For *judgement* I am come into this world.
John 5:22: *οὐδὲ γὰρ ὁ πατὴρ κρίνει οὐδένα, ἀλλὰ τὴν κρίσιν πᾶσαν δέδωκεν τῷ υἱῷ …*; NIV 5:22: Moreover, the Father judges no one, but has entrusted all judgement to the Son, …—*Tr. addition.*

27 With 'echoes of the Sermon on the Mount', it is not claimed that the 'cosmic rhythm' of Mark's Gospel as a whole is valid for Matthew's Gospel. In *John's Gospel*, where the rhythm can likewise be found, it is different from Mark's Gospel. Much of the substance of Mark's Gospel has flowed into the gospels of *Matthew* and *Luke*; at least for some sections of these gospels the rhythm of Mark's Gospel is heard. For example, Matt. 3 [the Jordan-Baptism]

would stand in the constellation of Mark 1 [♓]; Matt. 4 very clearly in the Ram, the sign of the Incarnation and of placing oneself in the forces of the Earth—only the episode with the disciples Matt. 4:18-22 is misplaced in the rhythm; Matt. 5ff.—the Sermon on the Mount—would then be thought of in the Bull, the sign of the word; perhaps in the 'mountain' the motif of the Twins sounds as well.

28 Because of certain legendary traditions, Albert Steffen in his play *Hiram and Solomon* has dramatically worked on some of the questions and connections mentioned here.

29 More on these things is to be found in Rudolf Steiner's book *Knowledge of the Higher Worlds: How is it Attained?* in the final chapters on the splitting of the personality and the Guardian of the Threshold. Whoever experiences difficulties in this exposition of the gospel, of what has been said on the 'splitting of the personality', may be reminded how already normal dream-life knows this 'splitting of the personality' when we dream that we are another, or at the same time are somebody else. In his *Parerga und Paralipomena,* Schopenhauer has devoted an interesting section to this phenomenon. But it has to be clear that the initiation-experience in the gospel is not about a normal dreaming, but with phenomena of consciousness of a higher kind. The indication of dreaming is only to serve as a bridge to understand the phenomena. Psychiatry also uses the expression 'splitting of the personality', or the expression from the Greek, 'schizophrenia', meaning the same thing only sounding more learned. An illness is meant. This again is a viewpoint that has to be kept completely at a distance from the 'experience of initiation' as meant in an exposition of the gospel.

30 See. R. Steiner, *At the Gates of Spiritual Science,* GA 95, lecture Stuttgart, 4 Sept. 1906, on the interior of the Earth: the eighth layer is 'the divisive layer'—*Tr.*

31 Note also that in everyday Jewish knowledge the letter gimel ג (= camel) is primarily understood to represent a rich man who is striving to reach the next letter in the alphabet daleth ד (= door) a poor man to bring alms and charity. Christ Himself is now the door. *Ed. note.*

32 *sich selbst.* This initially refers to the son of Zebedee. Yet the Prof. has repeatedly emphasized that the gospel—and particularly the chapters under discussion—are to be taken as spiritual events, particularly involving recollection. 'What the one, who actually became the bearer of the initiation process, works through, he gains for the others', he writes. And, to avoid a posible confusion, this 'one', 'far in advance of the others', is Lazarus, soon to become Lazarus-John—*Tr.*

33 The inserted story is there assigned to the Ram, at whose ascent the donkey star in the Crab stands in the lower meridian.

34 Nietzsche's critique in *Thus Spake Zarathustra* directed against 'brotherly love' does meet certain limited and socially-narrow interpretations that Christianity has made of it, or imagined it to mean. However, the apocalyptic meaning of love, wide and deep in the universe, revealed to John in his initiation contains, as the Apocalypse itself shows most clearly, the furthest reaching love that Nietzsche meant—and much more besides. The phrase 'brotherly love', which still contains many Mysteries that Nietzsche has not thought of, points out where the love reached by John, precisely because it is the 'furthest love', also has the power to become practically active in ways demanded by the prevailing world-situation.

35 Goethe. *Faust* II, V; 12093.

36 In one of the coloured glass windows of the Geotheanum, CH-Dornach, a remarkable arrangement of the twelve signs of the zodiac can be seen. It begins below left with the Fishes and ends below right with the Waterman. Above in the heights in a line (so that the Crab alone stands in the middle) it shows the signs Twins, Crab and Lion, those which could appear over the present section as the respective signs of the Christian Johannine initiation.

37 We cannot enter here the philological issue. What is relevant has already been expressed by Hans Blüher, *Die Aristie des Jesus von Nazareth* (1921), pp. 34-8 [BiblioLife 2008]. [The view that John's Gospel was written late is challenged; see John A.T. Robinson. *Redating the NT*. London: SCM 1976; for this author's final views on John, see John A.T. Robinson. *The Priority of John*. London: SCM 1985. On the authorship issue, J.N. Sanders. *Commentary on the Gospel According to St John*. Peabody, Mass.: Hendrickson 1988, interestingly suggests the 'memoirs of Lazarus' are featured. *Tr. addition.*]

38 The Indian (Pali) title is Mahāparinibbānsutta 'The Story of the great Nirvāṇa', translated by the present writer as *Der Hingang des Vollendeten*. Stuttgart 1925. See the article 'Buddha's Passing' in H. Beckh, *From the Mysteries*. Temple Lodge. 185ff., especially 191ff.

39 Prof. Plumtre ('Lazarus', William Smith [ed.]. *Bible Dict*. 1863. II, 80), suggests for external reasons that he was Lazarus—*Tr. note*.

40 On this passage, Rudolf Steiner speaks in this sense in his lecture-course on *The Gospel of St Mark* (GA 139), lecture 9, Basel, 23 Sept. 1912, and *Building-Stones to an Understanding of the Mystery of Golgotha* (GA 175), Lecture 3, on the '*jungen Christuskraft*—the youthful power of Christ', the 'youthful Christ-impulse' and the 'youthful cosmic impulse'. What falls into the hands of the captors in Gethsemane is a physical body progressing towards dissolution. The forces bearing the seed of resurrection link themselves increasingly with John.

41 The published translation of the quoted passage seems inaccurate. Oswald Spengler. *Der Untergang des Abendlandes: Umrisse einer Morphologie der Weltgeschichte. II. Band, Welthistorische Perspektiven*. München: Oskar Beck

1922. 262: 'In der berühmten Frage des römischen Prokurators: Was ist Wahrheit?—das einzige Wort im Neuen Testament, das Rasse hat—*liegt der ganze Sinn der Geschichte*, die Alleingeltung der Tat, der Rang des Staates, des Krieges, des Blutes, die ganze Allmacht des Erfolges und der Stolz auf ein großes Geschick. Darauf hat nicht der Mund, aber das schweigende Gefühl Jesu mit der andern, über alles Religiöse entscheidenden Frage geantwortet: *Was ist Wirklichkeit*? Für Pilatus war sie alles, für ihn selbst nichts...'

Oswald Spengler. *The Decline of the West: Form and Actuality*. Tr. Charles Francis Atkinson. New York: Alfred A. Knopf 1926. 216: 'In the famous question of the Roman Procurator: 'What is truth?'—the one word that is race-pure in the whole Greek Testament—lies *the entire meaning of history*, the exclusive validity of the deed, the prestige of the State and war and blood, the all-powerfulness of success and the pride of eminent fitness. Not indeed the mouth, but the silent feeling of Jesus answers this question by that other which is decisive in all things of religion—*What is actuality*? For Pilate actuality was all; for him nothing....'

42 This designation of the Waterman the author withdrew, both in his book on *John's Gospel* and in RB 102, 10 March 1933. The Waterman belongs to the light-ether, an air-element—*Tr. note*.

43 If we turn from Egypt and its Mysteries to the group of legends of Old French and Middle High German which is inspired by the Christianized echoes of the Celtic Mysteries, to which also belong the Grail legend and the Parsifal saga, then we find there the cosmic-virginal element of the ice in the likewise significant *secrets of the higher Eternal Feminine* veiled in the name *Isolde*, if the exploration of this name with the Nordic *Ishild* (= Eis-Hilde, Eis-Holde) given by linguistic research is correct. The Old French form of the name *Isôt* (also used in the Middle High German poetry) appears quite close to the Egyptian *Iset, Isit*. The more we penetrate into the esoteric connections of these names, the more *this* echo [to Isis] is lifted out of the realm of the mere arbitrary into an inwardly meaningful realm.

44 *The Mysteries of the East and of Christianity*. GA 144. Berlin, 4 lectures, 3-7 Feb. 1913. London: Rudolf Steiner Press 1972. Lecture 3: http://wn.rsarchive.org/GA/GA0144/19130205p01.html.

[Synopsis: *Lecture 3*: Ascent into the spiritual worlds is accompanied by certain unavoidable experiences. Possibility of a retrospect into the far past, a reading of the Akashic Record. In the higher worlds a seer is able to discern the activities of beings associated with the Sun and the Moon in engendering the physical and etheric bodies of men. How the astral body and ego are brought into being is veiled in secrecy. The Zarathustrean Initiation. The Hermes Initiation. Two phases of the Isis Initiation, separated by the point of time when Moses lived. When Moses led his people out of

Egypt he took with him the part of the Egyptian Initiation which added the Osiris Initiation to that of the mourning Isis. 'Sons of the Widow'. In the later Egyptian Initiation the candidate experienced the dying of a God in the Heavens in order that he may descend into another world. *5th February 1913.*]

A note from the publisher

For more than a quarter of a century, **Temple Lodge Publishing** has made available new thought, ideas and research in the field of spiritual science.

Anthroposophy, as founded by Rudolf Steiner (1861-1925), is commonly known today through its practical applications, principally in education (Steiner-Waldorf schools) and agriculture (biodynamic food and wine). But behind this outer activity stands the core discipline of spiritual science, which continues to be developed and updated. True science can never be static and anthroposophy is living knowledge.

Our list features some of the best contemporary spiritual-scientific work available today, as well as introductory titles. So, visit us online at **www.templelodge.com** and join our emailing list for news on new titles.

If you feel like supporting our work, you can do so by buying our books or making a direct donation (we are a non-profit/ charitable organisation).